Finding Your Jewish Roots in Galicia

A Resource Guide

Austria was a land of the free in the eyes of most Russian Jews, and their cousins just across the border—the Galitzianer, with their strange Yiddish accent and irksome quality of seeming coarseness combined with Germanic airs of cultural superiority—were inclined to agree.

—Ronald Sanders, *Shores of Refuge*

Finding Your Jewish Roots in Galicia:

A Resource Guide

BY SUZAN F. WYNNE

AVOTAYNU, INC.
Teaneck, NJ 07666 • USA

Requests for permission to make copies of any part of this publication should be addressed to:

Avotaynu, Inc.
P.O. Box 900
Teaneck, NJ 07666

Printed in the United States of America

First Printing

Photo credits: Przemyśl marketplace, courtesy Blossom W. Glasser; Łancut synagogue, courtesy Leon Gold; Drohobych, Kraków, Lwów, Stanisławów, Stryyj, Tarnopol and Tarnów, courtesy Boris Feldblyum.

Library of Congress Cataloging-in-Publication Data

Wynne, Suzan F.
    Finding your Jewish roots in Galicia : a resource guide / by Suzan F. Wynne
        p. cm.
    Includes bibliographical references and index.
    ISBN 1-886223-08-4
    1. Jews—Galicia (Poland and Ukraine)—Genealogy—Archival resources—Directories. 2. Galicia (Poland and Ukraine)—Genealogy—Archival resources—Directories. I. Title
CS878.G35W96 1998
929'.1'08992404386—dc21   98-7531
                                                                CIP

To Rabbi Malcolm H. Stern (1915–1994)
whose high ethical standards and strong
sense of mission touched so many of us

Contents

❁ Preface ❁

This guide is the result of more than 20 years of collective effort to document and develop information and processes for researching Jewish family history in the old Austro-Hungarian province of Galicia.

The Jewish genealogical movement began in the late 1970s. The first Jewish genealogical society was organized in New York City. Today, there are more than 60 functioning societies around the world affiliated with the Association for Jewish Genealogical Societies. Many of these organizations publish newsletters and conduct regular meetings of their members.

In the late 1980s, researchers began to organize specialized groups to address the particular characteristics of geographical regions or countries. Gesher Galicia, which means bridge to Galicia, is one such Special Interest Group (SIG). It was founded in Toronto in 1993 at the annual gathering of Jewish genealogists.

With no initial formal structure or governing body, but a mailing list of about 100 people with roots in Galicia, the group came together to exchange information through a newsletter and the publication of a directory listing the towns and surnames being researched by members. Members were asked to name both the SIG and the newsletter. George Bodner contributed the name, Gesher Galicia; many members suggested *The Galitzianer* as an appropriate name for the newsletter. Bea Cohen agreed to maintain the membership list and generate labels for mailings.

In 1995, at a SIG meeting at the annual conference of Jewish genealogists in Washington, D.C., volunteers were solicited to serve as a governing body and assume some of the tasks of running the growing organization. Eight people volunteered to help and, over lunch one day during the seminar, tasks were assigned and Gesher Galicia was launched to a new era.

Since then, membership has grown steadily. Today, almost 700 people have become involved with Gesher Galicia. In addition to the quarterly newsletter, which facilitates teaching and information exchange among members, Gesher Galicia publishes a directory listing the towns and surnames being researched by members. It also has a presence on the Web at http://www.jewishgen.org/galicia/.

The current direction of the SIG is to create projects to develop new information and to translate materials that will benefit as many of our members as possible. You may join the SIG by contacting Shelly Pollero, 549 Cypress Lane, Severna Park, MD 21146; e-mail: <rpollero@umd5.und.edu>. Alternatively you can download the Gesher Galicia InfoFile located at the JewishGen website <http://www.jewishgen.org>. Follow the link to the InfoFiles.

❀ Acknowledgments ❀

So many people contributed to the information base in this guide over the years that it is impossible to acknowledge all who added their ideas and knowledge. However, some people deserve special mention. David Einsiedler, a native of Drohobycz (now Drogobych), has helped in many ways since I first met him in 1982. He has translated material, extended my knowledge about written resources, and provided generous assistance with respect to rabbinic genealogy.

Fay and Julian Bussgang were instrumental in developing information about Eastern Galician records now housed in a Warsaw archive. Their work has enabled a much fuller understanding of Jewish vital records in present-day Poland and Ukraine. Their exhaustive review of a draft of this book contributed much needed improvements to the text.

Rabbi Meir Wunder of Jerusalem spent many years crafting a multi-volume effort that documents the lives and the religious and literary contributions of Galician rabbis and scholars. His seminal work, *Encyclopedia of Galician Rabbis and Scholars*, has benefitted many thousands of descendants of the individuals his work addresses. On a personal level, despite his busy schedule, he always has been available to provide information and guidance.

Jeffrey Cymbler reviewed a portion of an early draft and permitted me to incorporate articles that he had written for *The Galitzianer*. The efforts of Alex Dunai from Lviv, the Bussgangs and Alexander Kronick have resulted in a definitive listing of vital records in the Lviv and Ivano-Frankovsk archives. Dunai continues to research those archives.

Gesher Galicia is the Special Interest Group for persons researching their Galician-Jewish family history. Members of the 1995–98 Gesher Galicia Steering Committee helped make this book possible in many ways: Nat Abramowitz, Bea Cohen, William Fern, Milton Goldsamt, Lawrence Kahaner, Laurance Krupnak, Paul Lieberman, Sheiala Moskow, Shelley Pollero, Miriam Rubin and Peter Zavon. Specific contributors to the information in this guide include Susan Gelber Cannon, Judith Langer Caplan, William Feuerstein, Judith Frazin, Leon Gold, Michael Honey, the late Pauline Horwitz, Peter Lande, Gershon Lauer, Gayle Schlissel Riley, Georges Rosenfeld, Alan Roth, Marian Rubin, Richard Schwartzstein, Phyllis Simon, Philip Steinberg, Andrew Tanenbaum and Barbara Urbanska-Yeager. The contributions of other individuals are noted throughout the book.

Lorin Weisenfeld led us to material that added to our understanding of economic life in Poland. Arye Barkai, Florence Marmor and the late Ely Maurer were pioneers in traveling to Poland in the early 1980s to investigate surviving records, cemeteries and other traces of Jewish life. Estelle Guzik and I followed in their footsteps in 1986, and together, we gathered information that laid the groundwork for others. Arthur Kurzweil's writings have inspired thousands of Jews to explore their roots, but to those of us with Galician roots, Arthur offered hope that there was some information that had survived. Miriam Weiner was the first to mark the trail in Ukraine, and her bold efforts there and in Poland have assisted many individuals to connect with their ancestry. Neil Rosenstein's work has greatly enhanced the field's understanding and knowledge of rabbinic families throughout Europe. Dov Rubin recently returned from a whirlwind trip through many towns in southern Poland, and the results of his efforts to determine the availability of records and the condition of cemeteries are published in this guide.

All Jewish genealogists owe a debt of gratitude to the volunteer members of the Jewish Genealogy Society of Greater Washington (JGSGW) who compiled the indexes to U.S. resources presented in Appendix E. Don Melman provided technical assistance with the reproduction of the revised version of *The Galician Gazetteer* that appears in Appendix G. David M. Fox and Roberta

Solit contributed their advice and knowledge of database programs. Other JGSGW members who contributed information to this book are acknowledged in the text.

I am deeply grateful to Gary Mokotoff for his guidance in recommending valuable additions to this book, as well as Irene Saunders Goldstein and Ruth Mokotoff for their fine editorial work that has contributed to the clarity and uniformity of the material. Henrietta Butor was of assistance in checking the spelling of Polish words and towns.

Lastly, my thanks go to my husband, Ronald David Wynne, and my children, Michael Simon Wynne and Melanie Lisabeth Wynne, who have tolerated my passion for family history for the last 20 years.

Suzan F. Wynne
Kensington, Maryland

❈ Introduction ❈

Organization of This Book

This book presents the most up-to-date information about researching Jewish-Galician family history.

Chapter 1 focuses on various aspects of the Austrian Crownland named Galicia. Presented are the geography, history, cultural, educational, religious and socioeconomic context of the Galician places where our ancestors lived and worked, as well as the laws that generated the surviving documentation about our ancestors' lives. Chapters 2 and 3 focus on vital records (birth, marriage and death) and the present location and accessibility of these records. Because the Holocaust (or Shoah) effectively ended Jewish history in most of the towns where Jews had lived for centuries, materials that document the fate of the family members who had not emigrated to safety before World War II are discussed in Chapter 4.

Chapter 5 presents written and visual references to guide the reader to informative and stimulating reference and other materials. Chapter 6 is an introduction to other types of resources available to readers, including researchers and translators who can provide specific services, Internet resources, and organizations. Chapter 7 is designed as an aid to people who might wish to travel to Poland or Ukraine. Chapter 8 presents information about United States resources and offers indexes to a number of other resources, some in Hebrew. Chapter 9 offers a window into the value of belonging to Gesher Galicia. The chapter reprints articles about specific towns that originally appeared in the SIG's newsletter. The reader will find tips for doing effective research and reports about findings from both onsite and mail searches for information.

The appendixes in this book are varied and rich. They offer language aids, guidance on map resources, sources for information and reports about Galician synagogues and cemeteries, examples of vital records, indexes to collections at the U.S. National Archives and Records Administration, a listing of Galician towns and their administrative districts, an article on 18th- and 19th-century Kraków, a list of towns for which there are *yizkor* books, and a finding aid to a specific group of microfilmed records at the archives of the U.S. Holocaust Memorial Museum.

The geopolitics of what once was Galicia is complex, and you will be called on to know a great deal about history as well as geography. Because Poland and Ukraine are now the governing bodies of the territory, we must learn something about the characteristics of the Polish and Ukrainian languages and be attuned to the nuances of pronounciation in order to move ahead. But because Galicia was once part of the Austro-Hungarian Empire, we also must factor in the influences of the German language on our ancestral names and town names. Some records were in German or, at least, some forms were printed in German.

You are likely to be stretched in a number of important ways as you navigate through learning new terms, new ways of looking at your family history, and, indeed, much about Jewish history in Eastern Europe. Together, we have progressed, and together we will share with others what we know.

Special Note about Geographical References

The use of town names in this guide requires two general approaches: There was the old name, as it was between 1772–1945, and there is the current name, the name used by Poland and Ukraine. For the most part, Poland changed few town names; those with roots in Western Galicia, now within Polish borders, will have little difficulty with this issue. However, the Ukrainian language is written in the Cyrillic alphabet which may result in linguistic difficulties when transliterating words into English and other languages that use the Roman alphabet. Moreover, when some Galician territory reverted to Soviet-controlled Ukraine after World War II, nationalistic political considerations resulted in the renaming of many towns. Additionally, the current, accepted transliteration alters the spelling of town names. Whenever practical, this guide uses the spellings found in *Where Once We Walked*, by Gary Mokotoff and Sallyann Amdur Sack, because the authors use the spellings of the U.S. Board on Geographic Names. This government organization defines the recognized international standard for place names.

To add to the complexities of the geopolitical situation, many towns had Yiddish-language nicknames—our ancestors gave towns a different name than the official one. In some cases the official town name translated into a term that was religiously offensive to Jews. But the reasons are less important than the fact that you may have to cope with translating the Yiddish name for the town, which your family knows, to a town name you can find on a map. Chester Cohen's *The Shtetl Finder* is useful to guide a researcher from the Yiddish name to the official name(s). Cohen's book does not list every town, but an amazing number of places are included in this small paperback volume. He also includes a few facts about and a location guide to the towns as well.

So, having plowed your way through the initial obstacles posed by geographical issues, get ready for the adventure of your life: learning about your Jewish-Galician family history.

Tarnopol, Poland (now Ternipol, Ukraine) in the 1920s.

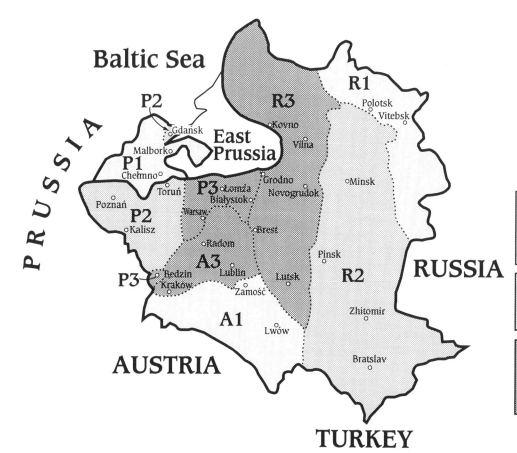

Partitions of Poland

Annexed areas:

First Partition of Poland
R1 By Russia in 1772
P1 By Prussia in 1772
A1 By Austria in 1772

Second Partition of Poland
R2 By Russia in 1793
P2 By Prussia in 1793

Third Partition of Poland
R3 By Russia in 1795
P3 By Prussia in 1795
A3 By Austria in 1795

Baltic Sea

PRUSSIA

East Prussia

AUSTRIA

RUSSIA

TURKEY

P2
Gdańsk
Malborko
P1
Chełmno
Toruń
Poznań
P2
Kalisz
P3
Będzin
Kraków

R3
Kovno
Vilna
P3
Łomża
Grodno
Białystok
Novogrudok
Warsaw
Brest
Radom
A3
Lublin
Zamość
Lutsk
A1
Lwów

R1
Polotsk
Vitebsk
Minsk
Pinsk
R2
Zhitomir
Bratslav

❀ Chapter 1 ❀

Galicia: Its History and Jewish Life

Brief Geopolitical History of Galicia and Its Territory

1768–1795

In 1772, the vast territory that was then Poland was carved up by the rulers of the Prussian, Russian and Austrian Empires in the first of three partitions that would take place before the end of the century. Only Prussia and Russia participated in the second partition in 1775. In the third partition in 1795, Austria absorbed more of Poland's territory; the country that had been known as the Commonwealth of Poland was wiped off the map. Austria dubbed its newest acquisition to her growing empire "Galicia and Lodomeria," but the province was commonly known as "Galicia."

The roots of the three partitions go back several centuries, as Russia and Poland vied for power and land. By 1768, Poland ruled over Lithuania and a large area of what historically had been, and is again today, western Ukraine. The region was still mired in feudalism, and Polish society was stratified into a highly rigid class structure. At the top were the gentry, comprised of 150,000 ethnically Polish nobles. Of this number, real power was held by about 300 magnate families, owners of most of the land, who dominated social, political and economic life. The Parliament, which was composed of the gentry, elected the kings who served for life. Chorzempa (1993) and Subtelny (1988) discuss in detail the friction that existed between the Poles and Ukrainians as a result of this class structure.

In the seventeenth century, about 15 percent of the population were members of the middle class, primarily town and city dwellers who were merchants, traders and craftsmen. Most members of the middle class, including Jews and Germans, were legally considered foreigners (Chorzempa 1993).

By the middle of the eighteenth century, a small professional or intelligentsia class had emerged from the middle and noble classes. The members of this class were physicians, lawyers, teachers, clergy and writers, and served in other roles requiring education (Chorzempa 1993).

The peasant class constituted about half of the population. At the top of this class were a small number of landowning peasants; at the bottom were those with no resources except those that their daily labor produced. The rest lived on and farmed land owned by the nobility and were obligated to work a fixed number of days each week to pay their rent. Serfs could be sold and needed the landlord's permission to marry or to work in an occupation other than farming (Subtelny 1988).

Against this background, Poland began to unravel when the peasants revolted in 1768. Russian troops occupied Poland as part of Russia's efforts to the government to grant religious freedom to members of the Orthodox Church. The peasant revolt failed, but Empress Catherine of Russia took advantage of the chaos to force the Polish parliament to elect her former lover, Stanisław Antoni Poniatowski (1732–98), to be the new Polish king. Despite his election, he enjoyed only weak support among the nobles. Conditions throughout Poland continued to deteriorate until, in 1772, Catherine joined Frederick of Prussia and Maria Theresa of Austria in dividing Poland in the first of the partitions.

Stanisław Augustus, as Poniatowski was known, fought bitterly against this partition. He attempted, unsuccessfully, to gain support from other European powers, but lacked organized support among the nobles and the peasants over whom he ruled. In 1775, Prussia and Russia reorganized their Polish territorial agreement, and Austria added Bukowina to its share of Poland. In 1795, Austria joined Prussia and Russia to complete the partition of Poland and Stanisław Augustus finally admitted defeat and abdicated. (Poland did not regain independent status again until 1918.) In this third partition, Russia absorbed 62 percent of the land and 45 percent of the population; Prussia took 20 percent of the land and 23 percent of the population; and Austria acquired 18 percent of the land and 32 percent of the population (Subtelny 1993).

In the final partition, Austria retained its hold on southern Poland, which had been known officially as Lesser Poland (Małopolska), and the territory historically known as western Ukraine or Red Russia. In 1772, Empress Maria Theresa named her new province the Kingdom of Galicia and Lodomeria. The name Galicia is derived from the ancient Ukrainian name for the region and for Galych, the ancient capital city. Ronald Sanders, in his *Shores of Refuge: A Hundred Years of Jewish Emigration*, described Galicia:

> This geographically ill-defined province formed a right-angled triangle whose base and side, to the east and to the north, backed onto the Russian Empire, and whose hypotenuse was a northwest-to-southwest line of some five hundred miles running from Cracow to Bukovina along the foothills of the Carpathian Mountains. Beyond the Carpathians, to the south and west, was all the rest of the Habsburg Empire, to which this forlorn province, its largest and poorest, remained a kind of stepchild.

To the south, Bukowina remained part of Galicia until 1849, when it became an independent Austrian province or *Kronland*. With the annexation of Galicia, Austria's Jewish population increased by more than 800,000 (Henisch 1967).

Empress Maria Theresa failed to consider that the various ethnic groups that came under Austrian rule so hated their Polish landlords that they would never lose their desire for independence. Moreover, the area was desperately poor, and most of the population was uneducated and economically mired in feudalism. As a result, there were relatively few urban centers.

Maria Theresa, who shared power with her son Joseph II, designated the city of Lwów as the capital of Galicia. She changed the name of the city to Lemberg and installed a governor and a bureaucracy. Lemberg was a sophisticated city, boasting both a university and a healthy economy. The bureaucracy was composed largely of German-speaking Austrians and Germans who set about to attract German colonists to settle and farm in the territory not owned by the Polish nobility. Galicia was subject to Austrian laws and taxes, but certain local matters were under the jurisdiction of locally elected governments. The Jewish community, discussed in some detail below, also played a role in governing itself.

Joseph II naively believed that because he was an absolute ruler, he would be able merely to command and changes would be made. When he came into full power in 1780 after his mother's death, he attempted to establish a number of reforms to promote improvements to the social and economic conditions of his subjects. Joseph was attracted to Western forms and philosophy of government and tried to use his empire as a laboratory for those ideas. For instance, he created an educational structure in 1774 and instituted major reforms in 1781 to reduce the burden of feudalism. Among his significant "reforms" was a measure ensuring that Jews could be conscripted. In his view, this would offer Jews an opportunity to participate more fully in the general society and, thereby, weaken the hold of Judaism (Brook-Shepherd 1996). But unfortunately for Joseph II, he underestimated the importance of gaining popular support for his reforms. Even before his death in 1790, much of what he had tried to accomplish already had fallen apart.

1795–1918

Joseph's brother Leopold II ruled only briefly, from 1790 to 1792. At his death, Leopold's son, Francis Ferdinand I, became emperor of a seemingly ever-increasing empire. The third partition of Poland came in the early years of his reign.

Francis Ferdinand opposed most of his uncle Joseph's reform efforts and moved quickly to reverse his remaining initiatives. The Jews fared poorly under his rule, which lasted until 1835. He encouraged harsh measures concerning Jewish occupations, taxes, marriage and military service. During his reign, Napoleon seized much of the territory that once had been Poland. After Napoleon's defeat in 1815, Poland was restructured again by the Congress of Vienna. A small part of what had been Galicia was split between Russia and Prussia (Pogonowski 1987). Francis Ferdinand was followed on the throne by the extremely weak Emperor Ferdinand, who abdicated in 1848 in favor of his nephew, 18-year-old Franz Josef (Schevill 1930).

Franz Josef ruled from 1848 until his death in 1916. During his 68-year reign, the world changed dramatically. The structure of the Austrian Empire, never well organized, deteriorated under increasing demands from the many nationalities and ethnic groups within the empire. In 1848, tensions erupted in several quarters of the empire, as well as in other countries in Europe. Hungarians rose up and demanded independence from Austria. Austria retained its weak hold on Hungary, while at the same time staving off other groups seeking national identity. The issue was not resolved completely until 1867, when the Austrian Empire reorganized into a dual monarchy, and the Hapsburg Empire became known as the Austro-Hungarian Empire.

Franz Josef was a considered a benevolent ruler by his Jewish subjects. Many Jewish families with roots in Galicia relate stories about Franz Josef hunting in nearby woods and visiting their towns and even homes. He had moved quickly to reform the restrictive and harsh policies of his father. He sought to make the Jews his allies in his efforts to retain his foothold in Galicia. And, as Henisch (1967) notes, he sought to "make them useful to the State" since, in his view, the Jews' adherence to their traditional customs and practice kept them from being productive citizens.

1918–Present

Upon Austria's defeat in World War I, the Austro-Hungarian Empire was dismantled as a condition of the Treaty of Versailles. Emperor Charles, who had assumed the Austrian throne two years earlier upon Franz Josef's death, was stripped of his title. Polish deputies to the Austrian parliament declared their independence from Austria. Austria transferred political control to the Ukrainian Committee in Lemberg/Lwów on November 3, 1918. Within days, armed conflict broke out between Poles and Ukrainians over rival claims to the territory that had been Eastern Galicia. (Fighting between ethnic Ukrainians and Poles again erupted after World War II and raged until 1947.)

After World War I, Poland's territory consisted of virtually all the land that had been Galicia. Only a small portion of southeastern Galicia went to Russia. After the war, Lemberg was again called Lwów.

Following World War II, the borders were once again redrawn, giving Eastern Galicia to the Ukrainian Soviet Socialist Republic, then a part of the Soviet Union. Western Galicia remained within Polish territory. The name of the city of Lwów was Russianized to Lvov. Today, Ukraine is an independent country, and Lvov is called Lviv. Many other town names were also changed back to their ancient names or simply modified to conform to the Ukrainian language.

Kraków: Special Status

Although never the capital of Galicia, Kraków (also spelled Cracow) played an important role in Galicia's history. Kraków became a sub-provincial center of government for Western Galicia in the late 19th century. In the 1795 partition, the city was granted status as an independent city-state. As part of the Treaty of Vienna in 1809, Napoleon absorbed the city into his then growing empire. In 1814–15, the Congress of Vienna made Kraków an independent ward of Austria, Germany and Russia. This tripartite arrangement lasted until 1831, when Russia invaded the city. When the dust had settled, Austria was the sole overseer of the city which returned to a semi-independent status. In 1846 the Polish nobility attempted to mobilize an army to oust Galicia's Austrian government. Austria countered by arming the Polish peasants who were angry with the nobles' feudal control over them. Before the nobles' revolt broke down, peasants had massacred a number of them in the region of Tarnów. Austria capitalized on this revolt, using it as their justification for fully annexing the city to Galicia and renaming it Krakau, in the German style.

Jews were expelled from Kraków in 1495 by King Jan Olbracht. Most moved outside the city walls to nearby Kazimierz, where a small number of Jews had already established a community. Though separate from the main city by geography, the Jews of Kazimierz were permitted to trade in Kraków's main market and, from that time until the Holocaust, they prospered. See Appendix F for more about 18th- and 19th-century Kraków.

Jewish Life in Galicia

Socioeconomic Framework

During the years of Austrian rule, depending on the whims of those who governed the province, the Jews of Galicia were subject to greater or fewer restrictions on the occupations in which they could engage. The agrarian society in which the Poles and Ukrainians lived had been feudal, and even after feudalism was abolished officially, remnants of that system crippled efforts to build a modern, industrialized society. Trades and crafts were generally learned through apprenticeships; guilds were tightly controlled organizations that were difficult to break into. Today, it is difficult to imagine that our ancestors lived in places where everyone had an assigned societal role that was resistant to change. Jews, a generally non-agrarian population, were more sophisticated in the ways of trade and commerce. But their sophistication placed them in a highly visible social role that enabled economic competitors to target the Jewish people as "dangerous" to the economic welfare of Poles and Ukrainians.

Although the primary economic characteristics of Galicia were its poverty and lack of material resources, it did have good soil for farming. A very small number of Galician Jews were wealthy landowners. The vast majority of Jews were poor, even though they were classified as members of the burgher, or middle class. Jews typically engaged in certain occupations, such as peddling goods to non-Jews who lived in villages and rural areas and bringing back home agricultural products for resale and personal use. Jews were also merchants with established stores and stalls; craftsmen or artisans in various trades; traders of horses, cattle and other goods; and professionals.

Some Jews served as tax collectors for the landowning nobles. These Jews were able to negotiate leases with the nobles for agricultural land, using the trees for lumber or growing grain used to make liquor products. But the economic role of Jews as middlemen came at a price that was to prove high. The resentment that uneducated peasants felt toward the Jews was generously fanned by the Catholic clergy (Brook-Shepherd 1996; Subtelny 1988).

According to the *Encyclopedia Judaica*, in 1827, of the 115,000 Jewish males in Galicia, 50,000 of whom were of working age, fewer than 60 percent were gainfully employed. Some men devoted much of their time to religious matters: daily prayer meetings, Torah study and, of course, the celebration and observance of the Sabbath and the Jewish holiday cycle. Women provided for their families by doing or overseeing all of the household chores. In addition, many engaged in a variety of occupations to increase the family income. In fact, the wives of religious scholars were often the main source of income so that their husbands would be free to study, visit with other scholars in distant towns and, sometimes, to teach children and/or adults.

In the late 19th century, the Jewish occupational profile was: 15 percent leaseholders and tavern-keepers, 35 percent merchants, 30 percent artisans and 20 percent miscellaneous occupations. Most Jewish traders were petty merchants, but a tiny minority was exceedingly wealthy and influential and carried on much of the large-scale trade in Galicia. (Subtelny 1988)

Subtelny (1988) maintains that Jewish involvement in trade and small, capital-producing enterprises was key to Ukraine's emerging, if primitive, prewar economy. Jews dominated trade between the towns and villages. Jewish peddlers brought modern products to isolated villages, and Jewish merchants bought up peasant crops for sale in the towns. In the towns themselves, almost all the shops and stalls in which a peasant could buy finished products, such as cloth, boots or iron pots (which were produced by Jewish artisans), were owned by Jews. If the peasant lacked cash to buy these products, the Jewish merchant would offer credit. In short, it was the Jews who pulled the peasantry into the money economy centered in the towns.

Jews and the Liquor Trade

Many Jews engaged in some aspect of the liquor trade: growing the grain, making barrels for distilling it, distilling and refining it into drinkable alcohol, or running a tavern where mostly Poles and Ukrainians consumed it. In 1900, however, the Poles and Ukrainians pushed through laws that excluded Jews from selling their agricultural products, and in 1910, Jews were forbidden to sell alcoholic beverages. Overnight, 15,000 Jews lost their source of income.

Lorin Weisenfeld, a Galician SIG member, brought attention to a book by Hillel Levine, a professor of sociology and religion at Boston University's Center for Judaic Studies. *Economic Origins of Antisemitism: Poland and Its Jews in the Early Modern Period* (New Haven, CT.: Yale University Press, 1991) extensively describes and analyzes Jewish economic participation in Poland. Levine earlier had written a *New York Times* op-ed piece in which he mentioned the occupation of *propinator*, and Weisenfeld, knowing that his ancestor had been a *propinator*, wrote to Levine. Much of Levine's scholarly book discusses the essential role of this occupation.

Market scene outside the Old Synagogue in Przemyśl

Quoting Levine (1991, 9), the term *propinacja* refers to the "site and the institution of the trade in alcohol . . . after the small hovel that generally served as drinking room, hostel, barn, and storage room for this enterprise." Thus, the *propinator* was the proprietor of this establishment. According to Levine, "The Jewish tavern, the *kretchme* or 'shenk,' was found in even the smallest village in . . . Poland." He goes on to explore the economic and sociological role of this complex institution.

In a letter to Weisenfeld, Levine states that his basic argument is that " . . . the manufacture of vodka saved the Polish economy, at least for the Polish gentry who were calling the shots." Because Jews could not own land, they could gain access to grain only by a complex system that was something like sharecropping in the United States. Once harvested, "Jews were then heavily engaged in distilling the grain, making the barrels that held the grain (*kupfer*) and selling the liquor at the consumer level."

According to Levine (1991, 9), "in mid-eighteenth century Poland, as much as 85 percent of rural Jewry . . . was involved in some aspect of the manufacturing, wholesaling, or retailing of beer, mead, wine, and grain-based intoxicants like vodka."

Levine's book, which offers a fascinating, if controversial, view of the economic conditions and lives of some of our ancestors, documents the Polish system of feudalism and the role of Jews in managing the use of the nobles' land and in collecting taxes.

Georges Rosenfield, a SIG member from Neuchatel, Switzerland, investigated the occupations of family members. He wrote:

> As for the tavern the Lermer family held in Buszkowice (a suburb in Przemyśl), mother told me it had white-washed walls. The roof, after suffering from a fire, was covered by plated metal or tiles (mother wasn't sure which). The tavern stood directly at the end of a road. There a field path began that went to the River San. To cross the river to Przemyśl, one had to use a boat (a ferry?).

Education

Joseph II perceived Galicia's Jews as potential allies against the province's Poles and Ukrainians. Among his initiatives to Germanize and encourage the secularization of the Jewish population of Galicia was his plan for education. Among his innovations was introducing liberal religious agents and organizations and encouraging use of the German language (Henisch 1967; Metzler 1997). Although Joseph's plan was implemented before his death, subsequent rulers radically altered his educational system. It was during Franz Josef's long reign that a universal education system began to result in some of what Joseph II had hoped to achieve among the Jews.

Until Austria instituted universal education, peasants, for the most part, were illiterate. Most Jews, on the other hand, could read and had some level of education, if only in the *cheder* (religious school) that boys started attending at the age of three. The Austrian system of education included parochial schools in which Jewish children focused on religious subjects, such as Bible studies, the *Talmud* and preparation for rabbinic duties. However, judging from the memoirs of people who grew up in the World War I–II era, as depicted in *yizkor* (memorial) books and books about individual experiences during the Holocaust, many Jewish children went to school in secular schools with non-Jews. After elementary school, students attended four-year schools that prepared them for the gymnasium (roughly equivalent to high schools in the United States though more rigorous). Jewish attendance in high schools, universities and the professions was far in excess of their proportion to the population. In 1890, Jewish scholars in the gymnasiums represented 18 percent, and in the universities 21 percent. As a reflection of their educational status, Jews composed 25 percent of the physicians and 48 percent of the lawyers (*Jewish Encyclopedia*, V 549–53, 1925).

In *The Boys* (Gilbert 1997), several Galitzianers confirmed that children typically began their knowledge of Hebrew and prayers at a *cheder* at the age of three or four. Austria mandated that all children attend secular school between the ages of 7–14. Some of these secular schools were actually run by Jewish organizations. Others were run by the Catholic church. It seems that a typical school day for boys involved attending secular school from about 8 a.m. to 1 p.m. After lunch, boys would go on to *cheder* until 6 or 7 p.m. Some boys from very observant homes would go to *cheder* before as well as after secular school!

One of the men stated that, as a boy, he attended a secular school with non-Jews and was frequently taunted by his non-Jewish school mates about killing God, "something which I could never understand, but since it was told to me, it must have been true. I never actually learned Jewish history as such. I learned first of all to pray, then *chumash* and Rashi and from then on I went to *gemara*. . . . but I never actually went through the *Tanach*."

Another described his *cheder* classroom as the rabbi's kitchen. At the age of seven, he entered the local school, while continuing his Jewish studies after secular school, where he, too, encountered hostile schoolmates. The family of a third boy, who was more orthodox, preferred that he attend the Catholic junior school so that he would not be exposed to learning "a distorted view of the Bible." His account of the vicious treatment there appears to be fairly typical of how Jewish children fared in such a setting.

Finally, a fourth man was fortunate in that a Hebrew-language Tarbut school opened for secular purposes in Opatów when he was seven. He remembered starting *cheder* at an early age and would be brought, along with other youngsters, to the *malamud* (teacher) by "the Belfer, a type of Pied Piper figure."

Language

Because Galicia's territory spanned regions that had been historically both Polish and Ukrainian, the issue of what was to be the official language of Galicia had to be dealt with, and documents at different periods reflect the internal struggles on this issue. Early in Austria's rule of Galicia, no apparent effort was made to impose on Galicia the German language as the official language of the government. In fact, there was a high degree of autonomy in such matters. In 1869, however, German was designated the official language of all governmental offices in Galicia. In 1872, this order was revoked and Polish and Ukrainian again were restored as official languages, in addition to German. Polish was the official language used in universities in Kraków and Lemberg. After 1877, official documents were printed in both German and Polish. The Ukrainian language had lost out. Following WWI, independent Poland permitted some forms to include Ukrainian instructions.

Population and Emigration

The table below shows what percentage of the population Jews comprised in Galicia at various times in history.

Table 1.1. Population of the Jews of Galicia

Year	Jewish Population	Pct	Total Population
1772	224,980	9.6	2,159,808
1773	171,851	6.5	1,117,031
1785	212,002	N/A	N/A
1789	178,072	6.0	3,039,391
1827	246,146	6.0	4,382,383
1850	317,227	7.0	4,734,427
1869	575,433	10.6	N/A
1880	686,596	11.5	N/A
1890	768,845	11.6	N/A
1910	811,103	11.0	8,025,675

(Sources: *Encyclopedia Judaica*, "Migration," Vol. 16 (1520) and *Jewish Encyclopedia*, "Galicia," Vol. 5 (549–53), 1925 Edition); Krochmal, 1993.

At the time of the first partition of Poland in 1772, 224,980 Jews comprised 9.6 percent of the population of Galicia. Jews lived in 187 cities, 93 small towns and 5,467 smaller jurisdictions. It appears that either a large number of Jews left the province over the next year, or there were errors in the data collection, because in 1773, that number had declined to 171,851, just 6.5 percent of the population. In fact, Empress Maria Theresa's tax policies with respect to the Jews were severe, and it is likely that many Jews were expelled from the province because they were unable to pay the taxes. With Joseph II's assumption of the Austrian throne in 1780, the Jewish population of Galicia began to increase. By 1785, the Jewish population had crept up to 212,002.

In 1869, of the 820,000 Jews residing in Austria, 575,433 lived in Galicia, about 10.6 percent of the total population of Galicia. Jews then comprised the third largest religious group after Roman Catholics and Greek Catholics. By 1880, the Jewish population of Austria had grown to 1 million, a majority of whom lived in Galicia. Subsequent censuses in 1880, 1890 and 1900 showed that the percentage of Jews grew slightly, from 11 to 11.5 percent.

Population estimates for the early period of Austrian rule are controversial among historians. Censuses were conducted under new and more reliable rules beginning with the census of 1869 (Krochmal 1993). In 1874, 3 percent of the Galician population was then Austrian, 45 percent Polish, 41 percent Ruthenian (Ukrainian), and 11 percent Jewish. According to Pogonowski (1987)

> There were 200,000 public officials ruling over 180,000 Jewish merchants and 220,000 Jewish innkeepers and a mass of undersized Jewish businesses and equally undersized Polish and Ukrainian farms supporting 81 percent of the population. Only 400 families had enough land to be considered wealthy.

Subsequent censuses followed every ten years between 1880–1910. Though sources differ about the exact number of people counted in the 1910 census, Galicia had seven to eight million people, at least 10 percent of whom were Jewish. (In that census, families were designated by language spoken and 10 percent of the population was Yiddish speaking.)

Citing 1931 census data, Metzler (1997) said that though "one out of every ten persons in the Galician provinces was Jewish, in cities, nine out of every ten households or businesses were owned by Jews. . . . In the province of Stanisławów, 94 percent of the stores, 96 percent of the distributors, and 82 percent of the cafes and restaurants belonged to Jews."

Galicia had the highest birth and death rates in Europe and was the most backward area in its industrial and agricultural technologies. Heavy floods in 1836 and famines in 1846–55 and 1907, along with typhus and cholera outbreaks in 1847–48, 1854, 1866, 1873, 1884 and 1892 were heavy burdens on the Galician population. Tuberculosis was a major killer. Between 1830 and 1850, the death rate in Galicia exceeded the birth rate. (Subtelny 1988; Chorzempa 1993)

With this background of poverty, disease and disaster, it is no wonder that between 1881 and 1910, 236,000 Jews left Galicia. But Jews were not alone in leaving this region. Austrian emigration figures show that about two million Galicians emigrated from the area by 1914, most to the United States (*Encyclopedia Judaica*). Galician Jews began coming to the United States in the mid-1880s. Most settled for at least some period of time on the Lower East Side of New York City, where they established synagogues and many social, cultural and welfare organizations known as *landsmanschaftn*. As word spread that the community had synagogues and burial space, young people began to join those who had emigrated before. This stream become a flood that would not end until World War I effectively ended large scale emigration from Galicia.

Some Galician Jews emigrated to Austrian and German cities (most Jews spoke German in addition to Yiddish) as well as to other European capitals. After 1924, when the United States severely limited immigration, Galician Jews began moving in larger numbers to Canada, South America and the Caribbean countries. Those who were reluctant to leave Galicia included older people, the most observant Jews, and those who were doing well financially. Most who stayed in Europe ultimately were among the victims of the Holocaust.

Jews as Town and City Dwellers

Although there were some differences in the proportion of urban Jews in the eastern and western halves of Galicia, in general Jews were overrepresented in the towns and cities of the province. This tendency was undoubtedly due to economic factors. Some of the differences in Jewish urbanization of the two halves stemmed from the fact that western Galicia had fewer large communities.

In the years 1880–90, more than 70 percent of Galician Jews lived in towns, 20 percent in villages and 8 percent on royal (rural) grounds. In 1880, in 19 of 102 cities and towns in Western Galicia, Jews comprised more than 50 percent of the total population, with the highest proportions in Dukla and Tarnobrzeg (80 percent). In Eastern Galicia in the same year, Jews were a majority in 65 of the 205 cities and towns, with the highest proportions in Lubycza Królewska (83 percent), Borysław and Zaleszczyki (79 percent) (Krochmal 1993).

In Przemyśl district, the Jewish population residing in urban areas held steady at about 76–77 percent from 1880 to 1900. In the city itself, the numbers of Jews increased but the proportion declined, as the city increasingly became an economic magnet for non-Jewish people from surrounding areas. In 1880, the percentage of Jews in the city was 34.7 percent, but, by 1900, it had declined to 30.4 percent because of the influx of Poles to that city (Krochmal 1993).

In 1900 only 10 percent of Galicia's population lived in towns and cities, yet Jews comprised 40 to 45 percent of the urban population. In some towns such as Brody, 70 percent of the population was Jewish (Subtelny 1988).

Jews visiting what had been Galicia today are surprised to find towns that resemble those in Austria and Germany. The typical town had a market square in its center. On market days, when the peasants came to sell their wares and Jews had booths in which to sell or trade theirs, the market square was a central meeting place. Market days also attracted ancillary activities, such as political and community meetings.

It was common for Jews living in towns to raise chickens and to tend vegetable gardens. Indeed, this was an economic necessity for people whose incomes were uncertain. But Jews were not major players in producing food in either Eastern or Western Galicia. Their economic base was in small crafts, trade, precious metals, leather goods, clothing, printing, all aspects of the production and sale of alcoholic beverages, specialty foods and the provision of goods and services needed or desired by Jews and non-Jews alike, such as innkeeping. A small number of Jews were engaged in the production of goods and services that served only the Jewish population. Jewish involvement in the professions was slow to develop and became more common only in the last quarter of the nineteenth century. Metzler (1997) notes that Galician Jews were forbidden to practice law until 1890.

Organization of the Jewish Community

Julian and Fay Bussgang, who have spent a great deal of time studying documents in Polish archives, provided the following history of the Jewish community after World War I. Ronald Kleinman assisted with translating and summarizing some of the information that they retrieved.

In May 1789, Austrian Emperor Joseph II divided the Jewish population in Galicia into 141 religious communities, however the number of communities varied over time. By the end of the 19th century, there were about 160 communities. At the head of each community was a *kahal*, consisting of three members (in Lemberg and Brody, there were seven members) who had been selected by the community.

In discussing the 1789 changes in the structure, role and purpose of the *kahal*, Krochmal (1993) stated: "This change had significant impact on the *Kehillot*, since they had carried on their social, educational and religious activities with considerable financial support from the Polish treasury."

In political matters, the communities were ruled by the state authorities; in legal matters, they were governed by the secular courts. In every community, a Chief Rabbi maintained the list of vital records and supervised education. The activity of each religious community was regulated by statutes approved by the state authorities. The *kahal*'s role consisted of representation of the community's interests to the authorities, defense of the legal rights of Jews, taking care of the homeless, satisfying the religious needs of the community, supporting institutions for religious needs, making reports to the state, preparing a budget for the community's needs, and collecting taxes. This organizational structure existed without major change during the entire era of Austrian rule.

The Austrian legislation was intended to give the Jews the same rights as the rest of the population, to encourage assimilation and Germanization of them. Synagogues, the focus of the new system of organization, were to reinforce the idea that Judaism was a religion, like other religions that existed in the country. At the same time, limitations on Jewish trade were eliminated and Jewish real estate purchases simplified. Joseph II made a number of efforts to encourage Jews to become farmers. Also, as part of his plan to Germanize the Jews, he insisted on legislation that required them to adopt German surnames. By his mandate, Jewish children were required to attend public schools and to learn secular subjects.

March 1890 legislation revamped the Jewish community structure into 257 Jewish communities with no central governing body. Each community was mandated to organize its own governing body along standard lines. This structure remained in place until 1927.

In the 1890 legislation, each community was governed based on its statutes, including its own bylaws. The statutes of each community were enacted to set forth such matters as the means of electing a rabbi and other officials of the communities, methods of obtaining funds, methods of resolving controversies, religious education, and regulations regarding private and public religious practices.

Two years later, in 1892, national legislation required the rabbis leading the 20 largest communities to have earned at least a diploma from the gymnasium. The rabbis in the rest of the communities were required to have had four years of elementary school education. In Przemyśl district, the Jewish community was organized based on the statute approved in Lemberg on December 31, 1874. According to the 1890 census, the district consisted of 110 towns. The obligations of the Jewish religious community were outlined in paragraph 2 of that 1874 statute:

> The Przemyśl Jewish [community] is to maintain and conduct all rituals, serve God, teaching and charitable organizations that are completely or partially supported by it and exist under its supervision and approval. It is satisfy the religious needs of members, help with burial, help the poor and sick within allowable funds.

The Przemyśl Jewish community owned three synagogues and several houses of prayer. Various Jewish institutions and associations existed in the city, such as Jewish Hospital and the *Bikur Cholim* Society, which supported poor and ill Jews. (Krochmal 1993)

On August 6, 1894, the Austrian government published a sample of the statutes for reorganized Jewish communities, particularly those governing eligibility of voters for the governing board that had the power to appoint or dismiss the rabbi. Over the next 15 years, statute changes increasingly emphasized the importance of financial status of voters, which effectively reduced the number of eligible voters (Krochmal 1993).

After Poland gained independence, the Jewish communities were incorporated into the Jewish Religious Union created on November 1, 1916, and legalized on February 7, 1919. The March Constitution that guaranteed Jewish communities the right of self-government had been largely based on the 19th-century statutes. The laws governing the Jewish community of Galicia remained in effect until their repeal in 1927. But the Jewish community could not agree on the actual role and structure of the community. Zionist groups wanted religious institutions to be self-governing; orthodox representatives opposed this format. Finally on March 6, 1928, the Polish president decreed that all of Poland's Jewish community would be governed by regulations that restricted religious institutions to religious and commercial activities that would be managed by county boards responsible for selecting rabbis and other religious officials and for overseeing the budget of the community. In the 1930s government interference in internal conflicts reduced the authority of these district boards. Post World War II legislation established Jewish congregations that reassumed the role of providing religious and charitable functions for the survivors of the Holocaust.

Taxes on Jews

The people of Galicia, the largest province of the Austrian Empire and the poorest, paid the highest rate of income taxes in Europe; taxes paid by Jews were disproportionately higher than they were for non-Jews (Pogonowski 1987). Empress Maria Theresa instituted special taxes on the Jews, including the infamous "candle tax" that directly impacted the religious custom of lighting candles to celebrate the coming of the Sabbath on Friday evening. Her son, Joseph II, revoked her taxation policies, but Joseph's successors reinstituted some of them. Alice Solovy (1991) discussed European tax lists:

> A Jewish marriage tax in Galicia in the late 1700s was so heavy that it was meant to discourage legal marriages of Jewish couples. It did not, however, discourage Jewish marriages because Jewish couples simply had ritual marriages and bypassed the tax regulations.

Citing Isaac Lewin's book, *The Jewish Community of Poland*, Solovy noted that Empress Maria Theresa doubled the "head tax" and renamed it *Toleranzgebuehr* (payment for tolerance). She also increased the Jewish marriage tax, and those who could not pay it were expelled. This provision offered Jewish communities a means to counteract the Draconian regulation. Since the number of resident Jews was known to the authorities, and that number did not correspond to the number of taxpayers, the Jewish communities presented lists that included fictitious names. It was later explained that the fictitious Jews had been expelled from their respective communities. Authorities soon became suspicious and ordered that all lists be carefully checked by the local officials.

Jewish Religious Observance

For the most part, Jews in Galicia were expected to conform to community standards of religious practice and ritual. Deviance was rare, and community pressures operated to enforce compliance with Jewish law. In general, when there was controversy, it usually related to the "other group's" failure to adhere sufficiently to Jewish law.

As in Jewish communities everywhere in the late 19th and early 20th centuries, there were various levels of observant Jews in Galicia. Particularly in the larger cities of Galicia, however, secularism gradually took hold, and, after World War I, increasing numbers of young people identified themselves with youth movements rooted more strongly in socialism than in Judaism. On the other hand, the influence of the Hasidic movement was extremely strong in Galicia; a number of important Hasidic communities were established throughout Western and Eastern Galicia. Small towns, such as Bukowsko, Bełż, Ropczyce, Rymanów, Dynów, Brzesko and Bóbrka were important centers of Jewish religious life because an influential Hasidic leader had established a center of learning in those towns. The influence of these leaders radiated into surrounding towns and villages and sometimes into distant towns.

Many Hasidic leaders extended their influence by assisting their sons and sons-in-law to settle in other towns, as extensions of their own religious communities. Thus, the

Interior of the synagogue in Łancut, Poland.

Belzer and Dynower rebbes' influence extended far and wide through whole regions. In much of Galicia, the "government" rabbi—the rabbi recognized by the government as the head of a Jewish community—was a representative of one of the Hasidic groups. Affiliation with Hasidic groups frequently provided candidates for marriages; affiliation alone was considered a factor in the candidate's favor.

Often more than one Hasidic community would take root in a town. While the groups would sometimes forge positive ties through marriage, all too often bitter, animosity grew between them. Seemingly minor ideological or observance differences were very real and, according to some *yizkor* books, sometimes generated violence between adherents.

Boys began their formal Jewish education at the age of three, generally just after their first haircut. They were usually taught by a poorly paid teacher in a group with other boys, where they were expected to sit attentively for long hours. Because children of that age are not developmentally ready for such a regime, it is not surprising that obedience was often enforced by harsh physical discipline. Girls were exempt from learning Torah. In fact, most girls did not formally learn any Hebrew other than basic prayers. Few girls were exposed to Jewish learning, except that which enabled them to manage a Jewish home and to teach their children fundamental ritual observances.

As part of Joseph II's efforts to secularize and Germanize the Jews of Galicia, he proposed a series of measures designed to encourage a Jewish religious reform movement. While never strong, these measures did produce Jewish secular schools, particularly in the larger urban areas. These schools educated generations of youths who were exposed to secular subjects and formed the basis of a small but influential group of men. Yizkor books and other Holocaust memoirs make reference to families and individuals who had been directly affected by these secularizing influences.

As a religious phenomenon, the reform efforts do not appear to have had deep roots in Galicia. By the end of the 19th century, apart from one synagogue in Kraków, there were few signs of this movement. Two Scottish missionaries who wrote about their travels through Galicia in 1839 made frequent mention of Jews attracted to this movement. For example, in describing Brody, they noted:

> There are many adherents of the New School, although they have only one synagogue. Most of the rising generation are giving up the study of the Talmud; and several have been baptized. There is some learning among them; for in one synagogue we met with several lads who understood and spoke Hebrew. many of the young men are beginning to attend the Government schools, in which they are taught Latin, and acquire general knowledge. The rabbi of the New School speaks Latin and French.

Marriage As the Cornerstone of Jewish Society

Under Emperor Joseph II, the 1782 Toleration Patent gave equal rights to all of Austria's religions. Among other provisions, this patent made marriage a civil contract (Brook-Shepherd 1996). Thereafter, marriage was a civil matter throughout the empire, an issue that became highly controversial among Jews who considered marriage to be a religious matter in which the state had no business meddling. There was great resistance among Jews in Galicia to the requirement that marriages be conducted and registered civilly. A law existed until the 1830s that permitted only one son from each family to marry legally. In order for other sons to marry, a stiff fine had to be paid, which led to widespread subterfuge and suspicion of Austrian law. (Subtelny 1988; Pogonowski 1987)

Jews typically married in their teens and early twenties in Galicia, and, in virtually all cases in the 19th and early 20th centuries, marriages were arranged by parents and a matchmaker. After World War I, marriages that were not arranged became more common, particularly among young adults involved in one of the 40 or so Zionist groups that arose in the 1920–40 period.

It was extremely rare for a Jew to marry a non-Jew in Galicia. Social norms simply did not support extensive social interaction between young unmarried Jewish girls and boys with any other religion in Galicia. Participation in the Zionist movement became a way for Jewish boys and girls to have legitimate interaction, although many older Jews saw such contact as shocking and immoral.

Virtually everyone married, but men and women generally led quite separate lives. Women managed their domains of the home and, often, the marketplace. Men were not expected to participate in housework or in child rearing apart from religious and moral instructions and guidance. Men who were drawn to a life of study were marginal participants in making a living. Some men would spend much of their married life away from their families, traveling for religious or economic reasons.

In the 19th century, though relatively rare, divorce seems not to have carried the level of social stigma that characterized divorced persons in other societies. Indeed, if a woman did not bear a child within a few years of marriage, religious law required that the husband divorce his wife so that he would be free to seek a new wife. (It was assumed to be the woman's fault when there were no children.) On the other hand, wives whose husbands were impotent or uninterested in fulfilling their sexual obligations were also within their rights to request a *get*, a Jewish divorce.

Surname Acquisition

Joseph II decreed on July 23, 1787, that before January 1, 1788, all Jews must adopt German-language forenames and family names. (*Jewish Encyclopedia*, V, 549–53, 1925). By a subsequent patent, however, the choice of forenames was relaxed in all regions of Austria except Bohemia and Moravia. Legislation mandating that surnames be adopted by the Jews was passed in 1789.

Prior to 1789, most Jews had no real surnames. They were known by patronymics, metronymics or by some personal, geographic or occupational characteristics that distinguished them from their neighbors. Thus, five men named Mottel in a given town might be identified uniquely by patronymic (Mottel, Aron's son), by metronymic (Mottel, Sarah's son), by some personal characteristic (Tiny Mottel), by geographic description (Mottel from Lublin) or occupation (Mottel the tailor). These early surnames helped to distinguish one person from another, but they were not hereditary surnames; that is, surnames passed down from father to son. An exception was well-known rabbinical families who often bore surnames that were hereditary.

Michael Honey (1994/5) described the development of surnames in Tarnobrzeg in an article in *The Galitizianer*. A record of names of the early Jews of Tarnobrzeg is found in the *yizkor* book *Kehilat Tarnobrzeg—Dzików sefer zicharon veedut* (Witness and memorial book Tarnobrzeg—Dzików). The names in the book illustrate the naming pattern of Jews in Poland before the requirement to adopt surnames. In 1718, the Jewish community of Tarnobrzeg/Dzików borrowed 100 Polish florins from the local Dominican friar Antoni Dembowski to build a synagogue. On behalf of the Jewish community, the responsible signatories used the patronymics Aronowicz, Abramowicz, Berkowicz and Zeinderowicz. A further loan of 2,000 Polish złotys was made in 1741 by the Dominican friar Stanisław Lipski to men with the patronymic Levkowicz.

The Central Archives for the History of the Jewish People at the Hebrew University in Givat Ram, Jerusalem, holds microfilmed records that list license fees paid by Jewish businessmen in Tarnobrzeg, *propinacja*—innkeepers and refiners of spirits.

The *propinacja* list of 1779 is as follows. Note the patronymics.

Wolf Tyma	Motko Bogaty (Rich) Itzkowicz
Jankiel Motkowicz	Josef Itzkowicz (from Musikowe)
Leyzor Izraelowicz	Icek Motzkowicz
David Dawidowicz	Leybush Nysynowicz
Jakob Skotricki Majorowic	Wolf Strzypek
Szmal (Shmuel) Leybowicz	Moisek Dawidowicz
Dawid Jakubowicz	Zeylik Leyzerowicz
Leybusz Chaimonowicz	Abraham Nutowicz
Chaim Bornchowicz	

An 1814 list of *konsynacja* (wholesale distributors) demonstrates the adoption of surnames among the Jews of Tarnobrzeg/Dzików. Note that most names are rooted in the German language, though some are spelled in the Polish style.

Leybusz Nusbaum	Chaimka wdowa (Chaim's widow)
Herszek Szalmonowicz	Simcha Handler
Leybusz Cwirn	Herszel Cynamon
Gimpel Gurfinkel	Klimanowa wdowa (Kliman's widow)
Susman Lorbaum	Szmul Galman
Wolf Ender	Lewi Morgenlender
Szmul Wahl	Eyzik Fegier
Wolf Pomeranz	Dawid Eched
Motka Klemer	Nuta Spicer
Moysesz Stainhard	Leyba and Bona Forgang

The following individuals were named in the 1822 *propinacja* list:

wdowa Esterka (the widow Ester)	Leybusz Hoffort
wdowa Ita Cwirn	Motka Klemer
wdowa Pepsia Wisenfeld	Dawid Kramer
Dom Pansky Morowany (The Manor Estate)	
Wolf Ber	Nisan and Nusen Nusbaum
Leybusz Cytrin	Israel Nusbaum
Wolf Ende	Wolf Pomerancz
Wolf Erlich	Josek Safir
Eyzyk Fegier	Judak Schnat
Liba Fortgang	Mila Spicer
Baruch, Samuel, and Isaak Garfünkel	Mosesz Staynard
Samuel Greher	Moysesz Stern
Szloma Goldmann	Leyzor Szekin
Simcha Handler	Dawid Umfang
Hersz Hartmann	Moyszesz Wahl
Israel Hauzer	Samuel Wahl
Dawid Hecht	Samuel Wisenfeld
Motka Henich	Herzek Wizenfeld
Lewi Morgenlender	Dawid Wisenfeld
Motka Wisenspil	

❀ Chapter 2 ❀

Jewish Vital Records

Historical Overview

The Austrian government began requiring civil registration of births, marriages and deaths in 1784. Civil registration of all Galicians appears to have been the responsibility of the Catholic Church in the early years, although no Jewish records have been found among the Catholic records. Duplicate records were required, according to the 1784 law, but no duplicates of Jewish records have been located thus far, from this period or any other.

In the years that followed, Jewish records were maintained separately by the Jewish community, but the forms they used to record the information and the procedures used to collect and maintain records varied widely. The collection of records was somewhat haphazard; some towns maintained records, while others did not.

Legislation in 1875 restructured and standardized the collection of Jewish records. An 1877 manual entitled *Führung Der Geburts-, Ehe- und Sterbe-matrikeln für die Israeliten in Galizien*, developed by the Austrian justice ministry, set forth official requirements for maintaining vital records in the Jewish communities of Galicia. The manual provided for the creation of 74 major administrative districts, most of which were divided into subdistricts. The administrative districts appear to have substantially overlapped with judicial districts, but the Jewish administrative districts were created with sensitivity to religious politics. Rabbis nominated by the Jewish community were employed by the Austrian government to oversee the collection of the records in these main districts and subdistricts. The job offered a salary and considerable responsibility and authority.

The vital records collection system worked well for recording information about births and deaths, but not as well for marriages. Jews resisted the government's insistence on civil marriages for a number of reasons. As described in Chapter 1, the Austrian government imposed a tax on Jews who wished to marry. Also, because Jews considered marriage to be a religious matter, they believed the Austrian government should not interfere with how their marriages were conducted. Official rabbis (and, presumably, their delegates) were empowered to perform civil marriages, but these individuals were not always representatives of the same congregation or Hasidic group as that of the individuals getting married. It is also important to keep in mind that until 1830, Austrian law forbade the civil marriage of more than one Jewish male per family. This law was largely ignored, as noted above, because Jews felt it necessary only to marry under Jewish law.

Regardless of why particular individuals chose not to comply with the government's mandates concerning marriage, their long-standing resistance began to ebb only when Jews began to emigrate to other countries in large numbers. The need to prove one's identity and to demonstrate one's good standing with the Austrian government led many couples finally to submit to a civil ceremony long after their children were grown. Civil marriages performed after the birth of a child were generally so noted in the comments section of the official birth record.

There were negative consequences of this resistance. One was that children sometimes had trouble proving inheritance claims. Another was that the births of children were registered with the surname of the mother; sometimes the father's name would be absent from the register. In these cases the mother's surname would frequently be carried by the individual for life. Sometimes the name would be hyphenated with the father's name or would be styled to include the word *false*, or *vel*, as in *Spira false Kahan* or *Spira vel Kahan*, meaning "Spira also known as Kahan." On some birth records, the father's surname is crossed out and the mother's name is inserted, with the comment *recte*, meaning "rectified." Often, after a civil marriage took place, *recte* also referred to the correction of the surname from the mother's to the father's.

The official rabbi in each administrative district collected and recorded information for all of the towns he oversaw. A few exceptions existed in Eastern Galicia, where records for a few towns were kept in town books. Births, marriages and deaths were recorded in separate volumes in chronological order. The volumes sometimes covered a number of years for a region with a small population. Birth information included the name of the child, names and birthplaces of the parents (including maiden name of mother), names and towns of the grandparents, date of birth, date and place of circumcision for boys and naming for girls, whether parents were married under civil law, names of the two witnesses, and the name of the midwife. The last column had space for comments; this space often included relevant genealogical data about the child or family.

Death records were recorded haphazardly, with missing information quite common. For the reasons explained above, relatively few marriages were recorded.

Regulations governing the collection and maintenance of records included the following:

- Registrars were to be males of Austrian citizenship residing in the places of registration. Selection was to be made by the governors in Lemberg and Krakau.
- Births or deaths were to be reported within eight days of the event. The father was primarily responsible for reporting births, but in his absence or if the birth were illegitimate, the midwife or mother was responsible. Stillbirths were required to be reported.
- Rabbis were to report all information about marriages in accordance with legal requirements.
- Circumcisers of boys and those who blessed girls, as well as the administrators of cemeteries, were required to report their activities to the registrar. Discrepancies in information were to be reported. The leader of each religious community was to provide the political authorities with the names of all religious supervisors, *mohels* (ritual circumcisers), and synagogue and cemetery administrators.
- Vital records were to be maintained in duplicate. Indexes were to be constructed and maintained in duplicate. Each registry book was to have headings in Polish or Ruthenian—and, in every case, in German—and was to be maintained in one of the three languages.
- The circumstances under which a child was considered legitimate—proof of the civil marriage was to be submitted. The nature of the proof was to be specifically cited. If no documentary proof of marriage was available and the marriage was simply attested to by witnesses, the entry was to read "reportedly married." If the mother had never married or married according to Jewish ritual without complying with legal requirements, the child was to be declared illegitimate.
- If the child was illegitimate, the name of the father could be registered only if the alleged father so declared personally to the registrar, in the presence of a witness, or two witnesses if the registrar did not know him, or if the father had appeared before a notary or court to so declare. If an illegitimate child were later made legitimate through the civil marriage of the parents, the date of the marriage was to be registered. This could occur only if the man acknowledged that he was the father.
- The registrar was to receive the registry books from the political authorities, with numbered pages and connected by a string. The last page was to list the number of pages, and the end of the string was to be sealed with an official seal.
- Annual compilation of a surname index was mandated.

Present-Day Organization and Location of Vital Records

Introduction

One of the most important facts to learn about your family, regardless of where they originated, is the name of your ancestral town. Armed with a town name or names, you can search effectively for several types of records that may have been kept regarding your Galician ancestors, including vital records (birth, marriage and death), notary, court, land, tax, military, school and residence (or census) records. In addition to dealing with personal and property rights, contracts, wills, and receipts for land and farm animals, courts also registered citizens for occupational purposes. This chapter presents all information currently known about these records and their current whereabouts.

To search for Galician records, you first must determine whether that town is in present-day Poland or Ukraine. If the town was in Eastern Galicia, you will seek records in Ukraine. If your town was in Western Galicia, you will seek records in Poland. Appendix G will help you determine the present-day country of your town and the name of the district and subdistrict in which records are kept. Appendix A offers a guide to pronouncing and recognizing Polish towns and family names.

Though the records were collected and stored in Galicia according to Austrian government regulations, today the original records are held in accordance with the governmental regulations of Poland and Ukraine. Therefore, if you wish to locate these records, it is important to know the present-day name and spelling of your town, and to understand how the records are stored today and the context for how to access them—assuming the records survived two world wars, fires and other catastrophes.

Because the records are in bound books collected under the Austrian system of government (see Chapter 2) from 1782 until 1919 and, following that, by Poland until 1942, it is essential that you know to which Galician administrative district your town was assigned. Poland seemed to have continued collecting vital information in the Austrian style except that the records were only in Polish after World War I.

Foreigners who wish to conduct research in the Polish National Archives system must receive permission to do so from the director of the Polish Archives in Warsaw (see p. 19). Some individuals have been required to substantiate in writing that they were related to the family they were researching to protect their personal and property rights. All directors of all National Archives are obliged to grant such authorization. Should permission be denied, the researcher may appeal to the director general of the National Archives for a final decision. Additionally, inventories, guides and directories are to be made available, and archivists are to assist researchers in accessing appropriate fonds. Procedures for conducting research in Ukraine are discussed later.

Background: Fate of Eastern Galician Vital Records

When Poland became an independent country in 1918, all but a very small western portion of what had been Galicia was absorbed into the newly created nation. Vital record keeping practices in the districts of Galicia appear to have continued with little change. Forms remained in the columnar style, and administrative districts remained much as they had been. The major change was that instructions were given in Polish instead of German and the entries were handwritten in Polish.

After World War I, with Ukraine under firm Soviet rule, Poland began negotiating an exchange of records with the Soviet government. In the 1960s, this negotiation resulted in Poland being given vital records from the districts that had once been Eastern Galicia. These records are known as the Zabużański Collection; *zabuzański* means "other side of the River Bug," which separates Poland from Ukraine. This collection was deposited in two archives in Warsaw. Regardless of the intent, not all records from Eastern Galicia were transferred in this exchange. Researchers have found that many records remain in Lviv. (See section below on Eastern Galician records.) In the mid-1990s, Fay and Julian Bussgang cataloged the Jewish records in the Zabużański Collection. They later assisted with organizing the contents for publication here.

In addition to vital records, the Zabużański Collection records include protocols before marriage, copies of birth certificates, banns, additional entries in the books, birth certificates from Israelite Rabbinical Offices kept in connection with establishing patrimony, correspondence with administrative offices and private persons, books of community dues, evidence of disbursements to the poor, documents of activities, communal statutes, documentation of community membership, and books documenting the income and expenses of deceased persons.

These records are now deposited in two archives in Warsaw whose addresses are given below. You must write to them to obtain information. The records have not been microfilmed by the LDS (Mormon) Family History Library. See Chapter 2 for a description of this repository's holdings.

For records less than 100 years old:
> Urząd Stanu Cywilnego-Warszawa Srodmiescie
> Archiwum Akt Zabużańskich
> ul. Jezuicka 1/3,
> 00-281 Warszawa, Poland

For records more than 100 years old:
> Archiwum Główne Akt Dawnych
> ul. Długa 7
> 00-263 Warszawa, Poland

Not all Eastern Galician vital records are in the Zabużański Collection. Many, particularly the older records, remain in the main archives in Lviv, along with some school and other types of community records.

To date, searches for census records in the Lviv archives has been disappointing. Alexander Dunai, a professional researcher who lives in Lviv, has examined extensively the Jewish records, and, though he continues to be hopeful that census records will eventually be found, to date, he has found nothing. Dunai has also researched the contents of the archives in Ivano-Frankovsk (formerly Stanisławów). The results of his research are given below.

To conduct research in Lviv, you can either do so in person or hire a private researcher to assist you. If you plan to go in person, you must notify the archives in advance. The name and address of the main Lviv Archives is:

> Tsentral'n yi Derzhavnyi Istoryehnyi Archiv u.m. L'vovi
> 290004 Lviv 4, Ukraine
> pl. Vozz'iednannia 3'a.

Fay and Julian Bussgang obtained and translated a general inventory of Fond 701, a collection of Jewish records in the Lviv archives. Alexander Kronick later obtained the inventory of Jewish records and translated the contents. The efforts of the Bussgangs, Kronick and Dunai are summarized in the list of vital and other records below.

Background: Fate of Western Galician Vital Records

Western Galician records have not fared as well as those from Eastern Galician districts. Western Galicia was on the front line of attack from German forces in World War II. In this region, many synagogues were deliberately burned (often along with the town's Jews and their vital records) or were destroyed in the course of the fierce fighting that raged throughout the area. Postwar fighting in this region, between the Poles and Ukrainians, further damaged towns and the records offices that were located there.

Just after the end of World War II, Polish archival officials grappled with the issue of what to do with surviving Jewish vital records. There is some evidence that between 1948 and 1968, vital records were gathered and moved a number of times. In 1968, Polish anti-Semitism again surfaced, and the few Jews who remained in Poland found themselves thrown out of jobs and subject to both official and unofficial persecution. Shortly thereafter, Jewish vital records were to be redistributed to the appropriate branch of the state archives system. In the course of these moves, except for records from about a small number of districts, it appears that most vital records for Western Galicia did not survive.

In Poland today, vital records are received and stored in two general locations under the jurisdiction of different ministries of the Polish government. Because of this bureaucratic arrangement, problems frequently arise in locating and obtaining records.

Poland has completed a survey of vital records held in all of its regional archives, the results of which have been published in Miriam Weiner's *Jewish Roots in Poland: Pages from the Past and Archival Inventories*. Unfortunately, it appears that Jewish records from Western Galicia are only sparsely represented in the regional archives.

Note: With the exception of the Jaworów District, records for Western Galicia are *not* in Warsaw, but they may be in a branch of the national archives or in a local records office.

Records less than 100 years old. The *Urząd Stanu Cywilnego* (USC), civil registration offices, are administered by the various administrative districts within Poland called *powiats*. To obtain information about a vital record that is less than 100 years old, use the letter-writing guide in Appendix B to write to the USC of the town.

Under current policy, the USC sends the results of its research via Warsaw to the Polish consulate closest to you. The consulate contacts you in your language and asks for money. This fee is imposed by the consulate for processing the request, not by the USC office. Consequently, even if the USC cannot find records of interest to you, a fee must be paid. When the consulate receives payment, they will mail you the information.

Records more than 100 years old. Polish statute requires that when records are about 100 years old, they must be transferred to the Polish archives, which is under a different ministry and administrative system from the USCs. (The archival system is under a national ministry not always in tune with the administrative structure that oversees the USCs.) The old records are stored in regional archives located throughout the country. The offices that have, or may have, records for Western Galicia are listed below.

When beginning a search for records more than 100 years old, start by sending a personal check for $30 (or equivalent) with your request for permission to request records to:

Naczelna Dyrekcja Archiwów Państwowych
00-950 Warszawa
ul. Długa 6
Poland

The structure of the Polish National Archives (*Archiwów Państwowych*) is similar to that in other countries. The main archives is located in the capital, Warsaw, and regional archives hold materials pertinent to the region. In Poland, however, all requests are processed through the main archives in Warsaw. If you send a letter to a regional archives, it will delay the process because they will merely forward the request to the main archives in Warsaw.

You may write to the Warsaw archives in English, but it is best to write in Polish. Compose a typewritten letter (see Appendix B) in Polish that provides specific names of people and, if possible, the approximate dates of the event(s). The main archives will forward your request to the proper regional archives. You will receive a letter in Polish telling you that (1) they have found nothing in the records, (2) they do not have Jewish records for the town, or (3) they have found records. Current charges for photocopies are $20. The hourly research fee seems to vary, but may be as much as $20 per hour.

If information is found, you will be notified by letter in Polish, with a bill for what you must pay to obtain photocopies. If they send a list of the records that were found, send back a copy of the letter identifying which items you want, together with a personal check or money order in Polish złotys for payment. By return mail, you will receive copies of your documents.

What Do the Records Look Like?

Early records, those created before 1877, may be on Latin-language forms, on forms written in old German script, or on any form that was made up by the local district. Following the 1877 publication of regulations for carrying out the 1875 law governing the collection of vital records, all forms were to be standardized. Even so, political changes over time resulted in some differences in the languages used on the forms. Sometimes the forms were only in German, sometimes in German and Polish; after World War I, the forms were printed in Polish. The columnar format remained in use until the collection of Jewish records ended.

The records themselves were handwritten in Polish. Sometimes signatures were written in Yiddish or Hebrew, but all other information was in Polish.

Except for Kraków records (which for some time followed the narrative style that Napoleon had introduced), all Galician records between 1790 and 1942 are in the columnar style. The format of the column headings changed very little over time. For instance, birth records were organized as follows:

Column 1. Number of the record in the book. Events were recorded in the order in which they were reported.
Column 2. Date of birth. This is often written out in the Polish words for the months and days.
Column 3. Date of *brit milah* (circumcision) or naming, in the case of a female child.
Column 4. Name of child.
Column 5. Whether married or not married (not married is *nieślubny*).
Column 6. Name of father, place of birth, occupation.
Column 7. Name of mother, place of birth, names of parents.
Column 8. Witness.
Column 9. Name of *mohel* (circumciser) for a male child.
Column 10. Name of midwife, nurse or doctor.
Column 11. Stillborn children.
Column 12. Remarks. Headed *Anmerkung* in German and *Uwaga* in Polish, this column was used for remarks and/or for signatures attesting to the fact that the father was, in fact, the father, when the parents were not married under civil law, or for noting when a civil marriage had taken place, thus legitimizing the child. The remarks also may offer the signatures of the witnesses, godparents and father. If the parents' civil marriage was performed after the birth, this fact was often noted here.

It is important to note the house number where the family lived, since this information may help build a record of who lived in a particular household. The placement of the house number on the forms changed from time to time. Seek the words *Ort u. haus N.* (German) or *miejsce i dom* (Polish). In small towns, houses were given numbers; in larger towns, there were street names. Sometimes the house number is in the far left column, and sometimes in the column after the year (*jahr* in German, *rok* in Polish) of the event.

Where to Find Vital Records for Eastern Galicia

Before describing the vital records for Eastern Galicia that have been found in various archives in Poland and Ukraine, a few words about transliteration problems are in order. The Ukrainian language is similar linguistically to that of Russian, and both are written in the Cyrillic alphabet. Thus, when translated into languages in the Roman alphabet, some adjustments must be made. For instance, the equivalent of *H* does not exist in the Cyrillic alphabet. Generally, the letter for *G* is substituted, but this is not always the case. The Roman letter *J* sometimes becomes the Cyrillic alphabet equivalents of *Y* or *O*.

After Eastern Galicia came under Soviet rule following World War II, many town names were changed. A few additional town names have changed since Ukraine declared its independence.

1	2 Der Geburt Urodzenia					3 Der Beschneidung oder Namens-Beilegung Obrzezania lub nadania imienia					4 des Kindes Dziecięcia		5 Eheliche, angeblich eheliche oder uneheliche Geburt	6 Vor- und Zuname des Vaters, sowie Stand, Beschäftigung und Wohnort
Fortlaufende Zahl Liczba porządkow.	Tag Dzień	Monat Miesiąc	Jahr Rok	Ort Miejsce	Haus-Nr. Nr. domu	Tag Dzień	Monat Miesiąc	Jahr Rok	Ort Miejsce	Haus-Nr. Nr. Domu	Name Imię	Geschlecht Płeć (männlich męzka / weiblich żeńska)	Urodzenie Ślubne, rzekomo ślubne lub nieslubne	Imię i nazwisko, stan, zatrudnienie i miejsce zamieszkania ojca
228	7 Juli 1880 № Kołacy					10 Juli 1880 № Kołacy					Jente Metzger	/	unehelich	

7 Vor und Zuname der Mutter, ihr Stand und Wohnort, dann Vor- und Zuname, Beschäftigung und Wohnort ihrer Eltern	8 Eigenhändige Unterschrift, Beschäftigung und Wohnort Własnoręczny podpis z wymienieniem zatrudnienia i miejsca zamieszkania	9	10	11	12
Imię i nazwisko, stan, miejsce zamieszkania matki i jej rodziców	der Pathen oder Zeugen des Sandeks oder Schemes kumów lub świadków Sandeká lub Szemes	des oder der Beschneider obrzeznjącego lub obrzezujących	der Hebamme oder des Geburtshelfers akuszera lub akuszerki	Todt geborene Kinder Dzieci nieżywo urodzone	Anmerkung UWAGA
Chane Metzger Tochter des Jidel u. der Chaje Sara Metzger	Abraham Lieb. hard	...	Strachaczka		

Typical Galician birth register showing columnar format. Additional examples of birth, marriage and death records are shown in Appendix D.

In the listing below, main districts are shown in capital letters. Within a main district grouping are the subdistricts shown in bold face. To know whether there are records for your town, you must know in which main and subdistrict it is located. This information is provided in Appendix G. In cases where the main district is today in Ukraine, the name is spelled (and alphabetized) as it was under Austrian rule, and then the current Ukrainian name is shown. Records in Warsaw are presented first; records in Lviv and elsewhere follow. Some districts were redrawn in 1890 and later. Therefore, some records were moved to new districts. It appears that some districts held their records for individual towns instead of including surrounding villages.

Key to abbreviations:

ai	Includes alphabetical index
B	Birth records
BD	Birth and death records
BDM	Birth, death and marriage records
BM	Birth and marriage records
D	Death records
M	Marriage records
MD	Marriage and death records
S	School records
USC	Urząd Stanu Ciwilnego (Civil registration office in a town)

BÓBRKA DISTRICT

Bóbrka. *In Warsaw:* (B) 1863–1915; (M) 1866–76; Unbound acts, 1863–1915. *In Lviv:* No records for main or subdistricts.

Brzozdowiec (now Berezdivtsi), **Chodorów** (now Khodoriv), **Mikołajów** (now Mykolaiv). No records have been found.

Strzeliska Nowe (now Strilychi Novi). *In Warsaw:* (B) 1877–79, 1880–94; (D) 1877–93.

BOHORODCZANY (now BOGORODCHANY) DISTRICT

Bohorodczany (now Bogorodchany). No records have been found.

Lysiec (now Lisets) and **Solotwina** (now Slotvina). No records have been found.

BORSZCZÓW (now BORSHCHEV) DISTRICT

Borszczów (now Borshchev). *In Warsaw:* (B) 1873–94; (M) 1846–76; (D)1877–94.

Mielnica (now Melnytsia). *In Warsaw:* Some records for the town of Mielnica are held with records of **Krzywcze** and **Kudryńce**. (B) 1823–91; (M) 1908–12; (D) 1851–90. Includes towns of **Germakówka, Olchowiec, Okopy**. There are separate books of records for **Krzywcze**: (B) 1830–76; (D) 1818–76; **Kudryńce**: (B) 1853–76; **Uście Biskupie**: (B) 1831–76; (D) 1831–76. There are records for Mielnica and surrounding communities. *In Lviv:* (D) 1820–51 [File 158]; (M) 1858–76 [File 159]. See Files 96 and 257 for: **Kudryńce** (D) 1854–76; **Kudryńce** and **Okopy**: (D) 1872–76; and **Okopy**: (D) 1823–76.

Skała (now Skala Podolskaya). *In Lviv:* (B) 1872–82, 1886–92; (D) 1839–92; marriage register, 1923–38, fragments of pages 19–118; includes town of **Zbrzyz**.

BRODY DISTRICT

Brody. *In Lviv:* (BDM) 1815–19; (BM) 1819–26, 1827–33, 1829–71, 1858–61, 1935; (BD) 1840–55; (B) 1831–40; 1855–58; (D) 1819–26, 1829–31, 1831–37, 1838–48, 1855–61.

Leszniów (now Leshnev), **Podkamien** (now Podkamen), **Stanisławczyk** (now Stanislavchyk), **Szczurowice** (now Shchurovichi), **Toporów** (now Toporov). No records have been found.

Sokolówka (now Sokolivka). *In Warsaw:* (B) 1897, 1900, 1902; (M) 1905–06, 1910, 1912–13, 1921–32; (D) 1906.

Założce (now Zalzitsi). *In Warsaw:* (B) 1877–90; (M) 1853; 1925–39; index 1877–1938; (D) 1823–61, 1877, 1914; index 1877–1938. Register of announcements, 1922–39; includes records from the towns of **Ratyszcze** and **Zagórze**.

BRZEŻANY (now BEREZHANY) DISTRICT

Brzeżany (now Berezhany). *In Warsaw:* (B) 1864–81; (M) 1875–76; (D) 1870–76, 1882–87. *In Lviv:* (B) 1846–55, 1855–64; (M) 1825–74; (D) 1820–50, 1850–70.

Kozłów. *In Warsaw:* (B) 1864–94, 1926–28, 1937; (M) 1937; (D) 1870–76, 1877–85, 1882–91, 1925–31, 1933–38. *In Lviv:* (M) 1877–1901 [File 78], 1902–27 [File 79], 1923–30 [File 80], 1926 [File 81], 1927 [File 82], 1928 [File 83], 1928–39 [File 84], 1929 [File 85], 1930 [File 86], 1933 [File 87], 1934 [File 88], 1935 [File 89], 1936 [File 90].

Kozowa (now Kosova). *In Warsaw:* (B) 1876–86, 1887–92.

Narajów (now Narayev). *In Warsaw:* (B) 1876–87. *In Lviv:* (BD) 1897–98 [File 230], 1900–02 [File 231]; (MD) 1913 [File 235], 1920–24 [Files 236–40]; (BDM) 1925–36 [Files 241–9]. (B) 1839–69 [File 222], 1877 [File 190], 1878 [File 223], 1879 [File 191], 1880 [File 193], 1881 [File 195], 1882 [File 197], 1883 [File 224], 1884–85 [File 225], 1897 [File 212], 1898–99 [Files 214–5], 1905 [File 232], 1911 [File 234]; (D) 1879 [File 192], 1880 [File 194], 1881 [File 196], 1882 [File 198], 1883 [File 199], 1884 [File 200], 1885 [File 201], 1886 [File 202], 1887 [File 203], 1889 [File 204], 1890 [File 226], 1891 [File 227], 1891–95 [Files 205–09], 1894 [File 228],

1896 [File 210], 1895 [File 229], 1896 [File 211], 1897 [File 213], 1899–1900 [Files 216–7], 1902 [File 218], 1906 [File 219], 1906–07 [File 233], 1907 [File 220].

BUCZACZ (now BUCHACH) DISTRICT

Barysz (now Barysh), **Jazłowice** (now Pomortsy), **Monasterzyska** (now Manastryska), **Potok** (now Potik Zoloty). No records have been found.

Buczacz (now Buchach). *In Warsaw:* (B) 1849–90.

CZORTKÓW (now CHORTKOV) DISTRICT

Budzanów (now Budanov). *In Warsaw:* (B) 1867–75, 1877–83, 1884–88; (D) 1877–89. *In Lviv:* (M) 1881–1908, 1910–39; (D) 1825–66.

Czortków (now Chortkov). *In Warsaw:* (B) 1874–94, 1900–01, 1921, 1926, 1934–35; (M) 1923, 1927, 1930–38; (D) 1884–91, 1893. *In Lviv:* (BM) 1874–76 [File 362], 1888 [File 362], 1925 [File 362]; (D) 1874–76; (S) 1894, 1913.

Jagielnica (now Yagelnitsa). *In Warsaw:* (B) 1860–80, 1881–89, 1890, 1892–97, 1902–06, 1913, 1926–32, index 1929; (M) 1874–6, 1899–1900, 1911–14, 1920, 1923–31, 1937–38; (D) 1862, 1892, 1894–95, 1900, 1905, 1907–11, 1913, 1920–23, 1926–29, 1931–32. *In Lviv:* (B) 1817–59 [File 363]; (D) 1817–61 [File 363].

Ulaszkowce (now Ulashkovtsy). *In Warsaw:* (B) 1875, 1884–85, 1889–90; (D) 1874, 1875, 1884, 1886, 1889–90.

DOLINA DISTRICT

Bolechów (now Bolekhov). *In Warsaw:* (B) 1877–81; 1881–88; (D) 1877–84, 1885–94. *In Lviv:* (B) 1844–56, 1857–76; (D) 1811–46, 1860–76.

Dolina, Rożniatów (now Rozhnyuv). No records have been found.

DROHOBYCZ (now DROGOBYCH) DISTRICT

Borysław (now Borislav). *In Warsaw:* (B) 1878–86, 1886–92, 1894; (D) 1877–90, index 1878, 1879–81, 1880. Includes towns of **Dołhe, Kropiwnik Stary, Mrażnica, Rybnik, Schodnica, Tustanowice, Wolanka**.

Drohobycz (now Drogobych). *In Warsaw:* (B) 1882–95; 1888; (M) 1877–81, 1884–91; (D) 1852–94, index 1880, 1892. *In Lviv:* (B) 1816–35 [File 36], 1852–57 [File 38], 1857–69 [File 39]; (D) 1816–35 [File 37].

GRÓDEK JAGIELLOŃSKI (now GORODOK) DISTRICT)

Gródek Jagielloński (now Gorodok). *In Warsaw:* (B) 1870–76, 1929, 1931; (M) 1931–32, 1935, 1938; (D) 1933–34, 1937. *In Lviv:* (B) 1847–69 [File 32].

Janów (now Janiv). No records have been found.

HORODENKA (now GORODENKA) DISTRICT

Horodenka (now Gorodenka). *In Warsaw:* (B) 1867–76, 1879–92, Index 1841–81; (M) 1856–76; (D) 1851–81. Prenuptial reports: 1928, 1935–36. Includes towns of **Czerniatyn, Potoczyska, Strzylcze**. *In Lviv:* For Horodenka, Fond 701 includes drafts of abstracts from metrical records for the second half of the 19th century and the early 20th century [Files 30–31].

Czernelica (now Chernilitsa). *In Lviv:* (S) 1919–36.

Obertyn (now Obertin). *In Warsaw:* (B) 1849–73, 1877–84; (M) 1861–75, 1877–89; (D) 1877–93. Includes towns of **Chocimierz, Czortowiec, Niezwiska, Piotrow**.

HUSIATYN (now GUSYATIN) DISTRICT

Chorostków (now Khorostkov). *In Warsaw:* (B) 1830–71; 1874–76; 1877–86. According to researcher Andy Tenenbaum, "The 1830–71 birth register has only one entry per line. The

1874–77 register is in terrible condition. It may have once been under water. Starting in 1877, the records are much more extensive and are in better shape than the older records."

Husiatyn (now Gusyatin). *In Warsaw:* (B) 1815–76; (M) 1820–76. *In Lviv:* (D) 1816–76 [File 35]; (S) 1934–39.

Kopyczyńce (now Kopychintsy). *In Warsaw:* (B) 1877–84; (M) 1850–71; (D) 1816–76, 1877–89. *In Lviv:* Records for **Suchostaw** (now Sukhostav). (M) 1814–75 [File 320]; (B) 1814–76 [File 321]; (D) 1814–76 [File 322].

Probużna (now Probezhna). *In Lviv:* (D) (D) 1817–76 [File 294].

JAWORÓW (now YAVOROV) DISTRICT

Jaworów. *In Warsaw:* (see Eastern Galicia below for more information) (B) 1848–92, 1905–07, 1909–11, 1913–36, 1938–39; (M) 1861–76, 1913–24 (including some crossed out), 1939; (D) 1842–81, 1939. Activity reports: bound books for 1881–84, 1890–94, 1890–95, 1899–1901, 1904. Comparison of birth and death records, 1886–87. Includes towns of **Czerczyk, Kurniki, Laszki, Ożmla, Rogozno, Starzyska, Troscianiec, Wierzbiani, Zaluze, among many others.**

Krakówiec. *In Warsaw:* (B) 1877–80.

Wielkie Oczy. *In Warsaw:* (B) 1843–74; (D) 1843–74. *In Lviv* (see Eastern Galicia for more information (BD) 1791–1853 in File 259.

KALUSZ/KALISH (now KALUSH) DISTRICT

Kalusz/Kalish (now Kalush). No records have been found in record repositories, but Alexander Dunai has located a register of births from Kalusz for 1830–50.

Wojnilów (now Voynilov). No records have been found.

KAMIONKA STRUMIŁOWA (now KAMENKA BUGSKAYA) DISTRICT

Busk, Chołojów (now Uzlovoye), **Dobrotwór** (now Dobrotvor), **Stojanów** (now Stoyaniv). No records have been found.

Kamionka Strumiłowa (now Kamenka Bugskaya). *In Warsaw:* (B) 1859–72, 1880–84, 1890–92; (M) 1866–76; (D) 1880–90. *In Lviv:* (M) 1789–1861 [File 75]. Records for Kamionka Strumiłowa cover 1789–1942, according to Fay Bussgang.

Radziechów (now Radekhov). *In Lviv:* (B) 1832–60 [File 295]; (S) 1925–35.

Witków Nowy (now Novyy Witkiv). *In Lviv:* (B) 1829–60 [File 29].

KOŁOMEA (now KOLOMYYA) DISTRICT

Gwoździec (now Hvizdets). *In Warsaw:* (B) 1858–76, 1936–37, 1939; (M) 1936–37; (D) 1937, 1939. Alexander Dunai has located a list of 137 Jewish taxpayers from this town.

Kołomea (now Kolomyya). *In Warsaw:* (B) 1865–81, 1884–94, 1916, 1922, 1932, 1934–39; (M) 1874–94, 1932, 1934–39; (D) 1865–82, 1883–94, 1932, 1934–39. *In Lviv:* (B) 1865 [File 91]. *In Ivano-Frankovsk:* 16 files of community records, 1931–39.

Jabłonów (now Yablonov). No records have been found.

Peczeniżyn (now Pechenezhin). No records have been found.

KOSSÓW (now KOSOV) DISTRICT

Kossów (now Kosov). *In Warsaw:* (B) 1868–92; (M) 1877–91; (D) 1877–92, 1909–13. Later entries—1909–13—in 1868–76 books. *In Lviv:* (B) 1842–46 [File 92]; (B) 1847–68 [File 93]; (M) 1852–76 [File 94].

Kuty and **Pistyn**. No records have been found.

Żabie (now Verkhovina). *In Warsaw:* (B) 1877–92, Index 1891–1914.

Lwów, Poland (now Lviv, Ukraine). Open air market circa 1938. Before World War I, it was part of the Austro-Hungarian Empire and was named Lemberg.

LEMBERG (also known as LVOV, LWÓW, now LVIV) DISTRICT

Jaryczów (now Novyy Yarychev). *In Warsaw:* (B) 1888–90, 1892–93, 1897; (M) 1879, 1892; (D) 1879–81, 1883, 1889–92. The Central Archives for the History of the Jewish People in Jerusalem has a *brit milah* (circumcision) register for 1790–1835 from this town.

Lemberg (also known as Lvov, Lwów; now Lviv). *In Warsaw:* (B) 1814–37, 1863–94, 1894, 1903, 1905–07, 1909, 1912, 1922–24, 1926, 1928, 1930–31, 1935, 1937; (M) 1870–94, 1908, 1920 (recorded in vol. 1, 1908), 1921–25, 1929–32, 1937; (D) 1864–81, 1882–94, Indexes 1880–82, 1887. *In Lviv:* (B) 1808–13 [File 101], 1809–13 [File 103], 1814–16 [File 104], 1823–28 [File 110], 1828–32 [File 112], 1832–34 [File 115], 1834–37 [File 119], 1852–1939 [File 156 ai, LVOV w], 1837–44 [File 122–23], 1844–48 [File 144], 1846–50 [File 145], 1849–58 [File 130], 1849–59 [File 131], 1844–49 [File 127–28], 1850 [File 146], 1851–58 [File 132], 1858–63 [File 136], 1863–72 [File 138], 1894 [File 142], 1896 [File 143]; (M) 1801–14 [Files 98,99], 1814–26 [File 106], 1814–26 [File 107], 1827–28 [File 111], 1828–32 [File 113], 1832–34 [Files 116–17], 1835–42 [File 120–21], 1842–54 [Files 125–26], 1854–60 [File 134], 1854–66 [File 135]; (D) 1809–13 [File 102], 1814–16 [File 105], 1816–22 [File 108], 1822–28 [File 109], 1828–33 [File 114], 1833–40 [File 118], 1841–48 [File 124], 1848–56 [File 129], 1851–59 [File 133], 1859–64 [File 137], 1863–89 [File 139], 1869–72 [File 140], 1891 [File 141], 1887–95 (found by Dunai but file not noted); (BD) 1805–08 [File 100]; (BM) 1902–12 [File 157 Lvov w], 1890 [File 157 Lvov w]. List of Electors, 1936; Jewish taxpayers, 1938.

Nawarya (now Naviriya). *In Warsaw:* (B) 1878, 1883–87, 1889–94; (M) 1878–81, 1892–94; (D) 1877. Includes towns of **Glinna, Kahajów, Lesniowice, Ludwikówka, Milatycze, Miloszowice, Mostki, Podciemne, Podsadki, Porszna, Sokolniki, Solonka, Tolszczów, Wolkiew**. *In Lviv:* Records for the subdistrict may be in Lviv Archives.

Szczerzec (now Shchyrets). *In Warsaw:* (B) 1875, 1878, 1880–82, 1885, 1888–89, 1893–94; (M) 1877–78, 1880–83, 1885, 1887–90, 1893–94; (D) 1878, 1881–82, 1884, 1886, 1889. Includes towns of **Chrusno, Ostrów, Piaski, Zagrodki**.

Winniki (now Vinniki). *In Warsaw:* (M) 1883, 1885, 1886, 1887–91; (D) 1881, 1883, 1886. Includes towns of **Czyszki, Czyżków, Dawidów, Gaje, Gliniany, Głuchowice, Lesienice,**

Miklaszów, Mikołajów, Swirz. *In Lviv:* (B) 1857 [File 147], 1922–26 [File 148]. For the town of Kozelniki: (B) 1859 [File 155].

Zniesienie. *In Warsaw:* (B) 1871–94; (M) 1870–81, 1882–84, 1886–1904, 1908, 1917, 1918–20, 1921–25, 1929–32, 1933–34; (D) 1877–94, 1928–32, 1935–38. *In Lviv:* (B) 1858–59 [Files 150–5 1]; (B) 1862 [File 152]; (B) 1867 [File 153]; (B) 1868–69 [File 154]. For town of Kulparków: (D) 1885–1906 [File 374]. For the town of Zimnowoda (now Zimna Voda): (B) 1854 [File 149].

MOŚCISKA (now MOSTISTKA) DISTRICT

Mościska (now Mostistka). *In Warsaw:* (B) 1882–89; (M) 1862–76. Includes towns of Buchowice, Czyżowice, Lacka Wola, Radenice, Starzawa: *In Lviv:* (B) 1827–62 [File 184], 1862–76 [File 186], 1877–82 [File 188]; (D) 1827–72 [File 185], 1872–76 [File 187], 1877–85 [File 189]; (S) 1925–35 for Buchowice.

Hussaków (now Gusakov) and Sadowa Wiśnia (now Sudovaya Vishnya). No records have been found.

NADWORNA (now NADVORNA) DISTRICT

Nadworna (now Nadvorna). *In Warsaw:* (B) 1866–92, 1903; (D) 1876–92. *In Lviv:* (B) 1850–65 [File 221].

Delatyn (now Delyatin) and Lanczyn (now Lanchyn). No records have been found.

PODHAJCE (now PODGAYTSY) DISTRICT

Podhajce (now Podgaytsy). *In Warsaw:* (B) indexes 1866–77, 1879, 1886, 1890–92, 1894; (M) 1847, 1877, 1879–80, 1882, 1887–89, 1891–94, 1898; (D) 1879–82, 1884, 1887, 1893–94, 1899. *In Lviv:* (B) 1854–76 [Files 273–74], 1877–78 [Files 275–76], 1879 [File 278], 1880–81 [Files 280–81], 1884 [File 284], 1886–89 [Files 286–89], 1916 [File 281]; (D) 1879–80 [File 279], 1878 [File 277], 1882–83 [Files 282–83], 1884 [File 285], 1891 [File 285], 1892–95 [Files 290–03], 1897 [File 292].

Zawalów (now Zavaliv) and Zlotniki (now Zolotnyky). No records have been found.

PRZEMYŚLANY (now PEREMYSHLYANY) DISTRICT

Przemyślany (now Peremyshlyany). No records have been found.

Dunajowce (now Dunaiv). No records have been found.

Gliniany (now Glinyany). *In Warsaw:* (B) 1860–83, 1888–93; (D) 1877–87. *In Lviv:* (D) 1852–76 [File 73]; (M) 1851–75 [File 95].

Swirż (now Svirzh). No records have been found.

RAWA RUSKA (also known as RAWA; now RAVA RUSSKAYA) DISTRICT

Rawa Ruska (also known as Rawa; now Rava Russkaya). *In Warsaw:* (B) 1816–65, 1845–92; (D) 1844–70, 1877–94.

Lubycza Krolewska (now Liubycha). *In Warsaw:* (D) 1844–76. *In Lviv:* (M) 1880–1931 [File 97].

Magierów (now Mageriv) and Niemirów (now Niemirov). No records have been found.

Uhnow (now Ugnev). *In Warsaw:* (M) 1876, 1877–89; (D) 1853–76.

ROHATYŃ (now ROGATIN) DISTRICT

Rohatyń (now Rogatin). *In Warsaw:* (B) 1859–81, index 1889, 1914 (Jan.–Aug.), 1922, 1934, 1938, 1939 (Jan.–July); (M) 1923, 1925, 1927 (Jan.–Nov.), 1935, 1938–39; (D) 1877–98, Index 1877–86, 1914 (Jan.–Aug.) 1938, 1939 (Jan.–Aug.); index 1887–98. *In Lviv:* (S) 1923–39. *In Ivano-Frankovsk:* Seven files of community records for Knihynicze, 1931–39.

Bursztyn (now Burshtyn). *In Warsaw:* (B) 1848–73, 1877–92, 1923, 1935; (M) 1849–76, 1923, 1935; (D) 1848–84, 1891–93, 1923, 1935. See also records for town of **Bolszowce** in Bursztyn subdistrict: (B) 1923, 1929, 1931, 1934, 1937; (M) 1937; (D) 1923, 1929, 1934. Town of **Bukaczowce** in **Bursztyn** subdistrict. *In Warsaw:* (B) 1848–73, 1877–89, 1923, 1935; (M) 1849–76, 1923, 1935; (D) 1848–84, 1923, 1935. *In Lviv:* (B) 1840–65 [File 28].

RUDKI DISTRICT

Rudki. *In Warsaw:* (B) 1828–50, 1863–84, 1885, 1889–90, 1898–99, 1901–02, 1904, 1910; (M) 1883–85, 1896, 1903; (D) 1867–76, 1878–82, 1888–90, 1892–97. *In Lviv:* (B) 1850–62 [File 297]; (D) 1850–66 [File 298].

Komarno. *In Warsaw:* (D) 1876, 1878–84, 1889–91, 1893, 1895–1900, 1908–12; duplicate of birth registers and additional records for 1888, 1903–04, 1906.

SAMBOR (also known as ALTSTADT) DISTRICT

Sambor (also known as Altstadt). *In Warsaw:* (B) 1862–83, 1885–94; (M) 1877–91; (D) 1868–83, 1887–94. Includes towns of **Biskowice, Dublany, Głęboka, Hordynia, Torczynowice, Wojcietycze, Wola Blazowska, Wolszcza, Wykoty** and many others. *In Lviv:* (B) 1829, 1833–52 [File 300]; (M) 1859–76 [File 301]; (D) 1835–52 according to Dunai.

SKAŁAT DISTRICT

Skałat (main and subdistrict). *In Warsaw:* (B) 1859–94; (M) 1877–1901; (D) 1859–94. Includes towns of **Chmieliska, Iwanówka, Józefówka, Kamionka, Kaczanówka, Kołodziejówka, Orzechowiec.** *In Lviv:* (B) 1897 [File 303]. (D) 1827–45 [File 302].

Podwołoczyska (now Pidvolochyska). *In Warsaw:* (B) 1877–89; (D) 1877–96. See also Tarnopol and Zbaraz. *In Lviv:* (B) 1877–93 [File 260 ai], 1900 [File 262 ai]; (D) 1877–96 [File 263], 1896–1939 [File 261 ai], 1896–1907 [File 264], 1908–10 [Files 265–67], 1911–13 [File 268], 1914–20 [File 269], 1923–28 [File 270], 1928–37 [File 271], 1937–39 [File 272], 1942 [File 263].

Grzymałów (now Grimaylov). *In Warsaw:* Only five marriages listed in Grzymałow marriage book. *In Lviv:* (M) 1890–1940 [File 33], 1934–39 [File 34].

Tarnoruda (now Ternoruda) and **Touste** (now Tovste). No records have been found.

ŚNIATYN (now ŚNYATYN) DISTRICT

Śniatyn (now Śnyatyn). *In Warsaw:* Register of marriage announcements, 1920–42.

Zabłotów (now Zabolotov). *In Warsaw:* (B) 1861–76, 1879–82, 1888–92; (D) 1884–93. *In Ivano-Frankovsk:* 8 files of community records, 1931–39.

SOKAL DISTRICT

Sokal. *In Warsaw:* (B) 1858–80, 1882–94; (M) 1863–94; (D) 1831–94. Includes towns of **Baranie Peretoki, Jósefówka, Steniatyn, Wojsławice, Zawisznia.** *In Lviv:* (B) 1831–58 [File 304].

Bełż (now Beltsy). No records have been found.

Krystynopol (now Krystonopil). *In Lviv:* (M) 1933 [File 361]; (S) 1868–1910, 1921–36; Franciskan metric 1820.

Tartaków (now Tartakiv). *In Warsaw:* (B) 1858–91, 1932, 1935; (M) 1845–75; (D) 1906, 1933–37. *In Lviv:* (B) 1815–58 [File 323].

Warcz/also known as Warez (now Variazh). No records have been found.

STANISŁAWÓW (ALSO KNOWN AS STANISLAV; NOW IVANO-FRANKOVSK) DISTRICT

Stanisławów (also known as Stanislav and Stanislau; now Ivano-Frankovsk). According to Bill Feuerstein who wrote to the USC, "Jewish books for the towns of Ivano-Frankovsk, Tysmenitsa and the townships of Otynya and Gostov in the district of Tlumach'skyi have not survived." This is only partially true in the case of Ivano-Frankovsk; some books for the town itself are in Warsaw as part of the Zabużański Collection. *In Warsaw:* (B) 1864–74, 1877–92, 1937–41; (M) 1872–76; (D) 1863–82, 1883–87, 1890–91. *In Lviv:* (B) 1817–45 [Files 306–07]; (M) 1789–1871 [File 305] (Dunai says records begin in 1782); (D) 1845–63 [File 308] (Dunai says records begin in 1840); (BDM) 1870–1911, 1894–1922 and 1934 in file 309 Stanisławów; *Other:* Pre–1960 printed inventories show that there may be 22 files for the Jewish community in either the Ivano-Frankovsk or Ternipol archives. *In Ivano-Frankovsk:* List of real estate owned by Jews; census of the Jews; list of lawyers, doctors and merchants; lists of Jews deported by the Nazis. There were also files for the Stanisławów Private (Jewish) Factory Women's School (1929–38), court records, magistrate records, school records (1925–35) and emigration records (1929–39). The civil record archives has vital records after 1924.

Halicz (now Galich), **Jezupol** (now Zhovten), **Maryampol** (now Mariampil Miasto). No records have been found.

STAREMIASTO (ALSO KNOWN AS ALT SAMBOR) DISTRICT

Staremiasto (also known as Alt Sambor). *In Warsaw:* (B) 1856–91; (M) 1856–76; (D) 1870–80. *In Lviv:* (D) 1856–76 [File 310].

Chyrów (now Khirov) and **Felsztyn** (now Skeliva). No records have been found.

Starasól/Stara Sól (now Staraya Sil). *In Warsaw:* (B) 1892–1903.

STRYJ (now STRYY) DISTRICT

Stryj (now Stryy). *In Warsaw:* (B) 1870–72, 1875–94, 1899; indexes 1877–81, 1899; (M) 1877–83, 1885–94; (D) 1869–94. *In Lviv:* (B) 1846–58 [File 313]; (M) 1827–55 [File 312], 1855–76 [File 315], 1864–76 [File 316]; (D) 1827–47 [File 311], 1847–63 [File 314].

Skole (now Skolie). *In Warsaw:* (B) 1878–80; 1883–94; (M) 1882, 1888–91, 1893; (D) 1877–82, 1884–87, 1889–94.

TARNOPOL (now TERNOPOL) DISTRICT

Tarnopol (now Ternopol). *In Warsaw:* (B) 1866–76, 1878–90, index 1861–81; (M) 1878–90, 1937, index 1878–81, 1936–43; (D) 1870–76, 1878–90. Public relief register, 1934; index to emergency relief payments, 1938–39; extracts from 1903 birth registers; marriage certificates, 1920–27; marriage announcements and extracts, 1921–39; extracts from death register and correspondence, 1915–38; card file index of Jewish residents, post-1931; correspondence regarding paternity, 1931; main accounts ledger of estate of Majera Byka, 1904–20, and account books, 1934–37; activity reports regarding vital records, 1927–36; religious taxes and appeals to Jewish community administration, 1905–30; applications for exemption from religious community taxes, 1934; documents from notaries. Includes towns of Hluboczek, Kuskowce, Podwołoczyska (see also Skałat district for some years), Zagrobela. *In Lviv:* Book listing Jews living in the Tarnopol district 1850–1900 with birth dates and occupations [File 356]. Fragmentary censuses of Jews, 1880–1940; (BDM) 1816–20 [File 326], 1820–34 [File 327]; (BDM certificates) 1833–1913 [File 357], 1886–89 and 1896–1937 [File 357]; (B) 1852–57 [File 329], 1858–65 [File 333], 1900 [File 336], 1927 [File 324 ai], 1927 [File 325 ai]; (M) 1853–58 [File 330], 1923 [File 337], 1931 [Files 342–43], 1932–42 [Files 345–55]; (D) 1845–54 [File 328], 1854–63 [Files 331–32], 1864–69 [File 334], 1877–1942 [File 335], 1926 [File 337], 1929 [File 338], 1930 [File 340–41], 1931 [File 344].

Mikulińce (now Mykulyntsi). *In Warsaw:* (B) 1847–71, 1873–94 (some with indexes); (M) 1877–81, 1883–86, 1888–89, 1891, 1893–94 (some with indexes); (D) 1877–84, 1886, 1891–92. *In Lviv:* (B) 1850 (according to Dunai), 1860 [File 161], 1901 (according to Dunai); (M) 1900 [File 174], 1901 [File 175], 1932 [File 178], 1934 [File 179], 1935 [File 180], 1936 [File 181]; (D) 1835–58 [File 160 ai], 1877 [File 162], 1885 [File 163], 1887 [File 164], 1888 [File 165], 1889 [File 166], 1890 [File 167], 1893 [File 168], 1894 [File 169], 1896 [File 170], 1897 [File 171], 1898 [File 172], 1899 [File 173], 1929 [File 177]; surname changes 1905–22 [File 176].

Stryj, Poland (now Stryy, Ukraine). View of the 3rd of May Street circa 1918.

TŁUMACZ (now TLUMACH) DISTRICT

Tłumacz (now Tlumach). *In Warsaw and Lviv:* No records have been found. *In Ivano-Frankovsk:* Six files of community records, 1931–39. See note for Stanisławów district for additional information about records.

Chocimirz (now Khotimir), **Niżniów** (now Nizhnev), **Ottynia** (now Otynya), **Tyśmienica** (now Tysmenytsia), **Uście Zielone** (now Ustia Zelene). No records have been found.

TREMBOWLA (now TEREBOVLYA) DISTRICT

Trembowla (now Terebovlya). *In Warsaw:* Charter and bylaws of Jewish community, pre-1919.

Janów (now Janiv). No records have been found.

Strusów (now Stusiv). *In Warsaw:* (B) 1877–90; (M) 1871, 1875; (D) 1871–76. *In Lviv:* (M) 1837–70 [File 317], 1853–70 [File 318]; (D) 1837–70 [File 318].

TURKA DISTRICT

Turka. *In Warsaw:* (B) 1914–22, 1938. *In Lviv:* There are records for Turka in the Lviv Archives. Whether records are included for surrounding communities is not known.

ZALESZCZYKI (now ZALESHCHIKI) DISTRICT

Zaleszczyki (now Zaleshchiki). No records have been found.

Gródek (now Horodek), **Tłuste** (now Tovste), **Uścieczko** (now Ustechko). No records have been found.

Korolówka (now Oleyevo Korolevka). *In Warsaw:* Register of residents circa 1938.

ZBARAZ (now ZBARAZH) DISTRICT

Zbaraz (now Zbarazh). *In Warsaw:* (B) 1877–89; (M) 1859–76; (D) 1859–90. Includes records for towns of **Czernichowice, Dobrowody, Klebanówka, Medyń, Obodówka, Romanówka, Terpilówka, Zaluze**. Records for **birczaoczyska** may also be included for some years. *In Lviv:* (B) 1816–30 [File 42], 1831–58 [File 43], 1859–76 [File 45] also 1886; (D) 1805–44 [File 41], 1844–58 [File 44], 1894–1907 [Files 46–59], 1912–13 [Files 60–61], 1914–1942 [Files 62–68]; (S) 1925–33.

ZŁOCZÓW (now ZOLOCHEV) DISTRICT

Złoczów (now Zolochev). *In Warsaw:* (B) 1865–71, 1876–88, 1891, 1893, 1899, 1904–05; (M) 1876, 1893, 1895, 1913, 1938; (D) 1855–75, 1877–86, 1894. *In Lviv:* (B) 1825–55; 1844–94 [File 72]; (D) 1825–55 [File 71].

Bialy Kamień (now Belyy Kamen). *In Warsaw:* (B) 1879, 1883–88, 1895–97; (D) 1862–76, 1892. *In Lviv:* (D) 1823–69, 1858–66.

Gołogóry (now Holohory). *In Warsaw:* (B) 1876–81, 1883–94, 1897–1900, 1903, 1909, 1911, 1927; (D) 1887–94, 1902, 1912, 1924–26.

Jezierna (now Ozernyany). *In Lviv:* (B) 1816–76 [File 254], 1876–1942 [Files 250–53]; (M) 1849–76 [File 257]; (D) 1816–76 [File 256].

Olesko (now Olesko). *In Warsaw:* (B) 1925–27; (M) 1859–75; (D) 1914, 1916. *In Lviv:* (B) 1852–76 [File 258].

Pomorzany (now Pomoryany). No records have been found.

Sassów (now Sasiv). *In Warsaw:* (D) 1859–76.

Zborów (now Zboriv). *In Warsaw:* (B) 1877–90; (M) 1921–31, (D)1877–86. Miscellaneous documents: birth and death certificates, correspondence, activity reports, 1925–35. *In Lviv:* (B) 1819–46 [File 70], 1838–64 [File 69]; (D) 1819–49 according to Dunai, 1875–76 [File 74].

ZOLKIEW (now ZHOVKA) DISTRICT

Zolkiew (now Zhovka). *In Warsaw:* (B) 1862–94, index 1853–70; (M) 1815–73, 1877–80, 1888–92, 1927, 1937; (D) 1870–94. *In Lviv:* (D) 1855–70 [File 40].

Kulików (now Kulikov). No records have been found.

Mosty Wielki (also called Gross Mosty) (now Velikiye Mosty). *In Warsaw:* (B) 1861–74, 1877–94; (M) 1918; (D) 1918. Includes towns of **Batiatysze, Kupiczwola, Rozanka**. *In Lviv:* (B) 1813–61 [File 182]; (D) 1813–76 [File 183].

ŻYDACZÓW (now ZYDACHOV) DISTRICT

Żydaczów (now Zydachov). *In Warsaw:* (B) 1877–80, 1882, 1885, 1887–89, 1891–92, 1894–95, 1897–98, 1900–01, 1903–10, 1912, 1928–29, 1931–33; (M) 1878, 1881, 1888–91, 1899–1901, 1907–09, 1913, 1928–34; (D) 1877–82, 1883, 1887–88, 1890–95, 1897–1900, 1903, 1905–06, 1908–13, 1928–33, 1935, 1938.

Rozdol (now Rozdil). *In Warsaw:* (B) 1869–91; (D) 1877–84. *In Lviv:* (B) 1832–68 [File 296].

Żurawno (now Zhuravno). *In Warsaw:* (B) 1877–85.

Where to Find Vital Records for Western Galicia

The following is a list of the administrative districts as they were constituted in Western Galicia in 1877. There were minor changes in the composition of districts after 1877, but those changes are not reflected here. Main districts appear in bold, uppercase letters. Subdistricts are in lower case and bolded.

The main and subdistrict town names are spelled in this list as they were under Austrian rule. Poland has made few changes to the spellings of the names of the towns that were in Western Galicia.

BIAŁA DISTRICT

Biała, Kęty, Lipnik, Oświęcim. No records have been found.

BIRCZA DISTRICT

Bircza, Dobromil, Nowemiasto, Rybotycze. No records have been found.

BOCHNIA DISTRICT

Bochnia. Records exist for this district at the USC and the Kraków archives.

Wiśnicz Nowy. Records exist in the USC and the branch archives in Bochnia. In addition the LDS (Mormon) Family History Library holds: (B) 1814–59 and (M) 1827–70.

BRZESKO DISTRICT

Brzesko. The USC has (BDM) 1894–1992. The LDS (Mormon) Family History Library holds: (B) 1849–86; (D) 1863–76.

Czchów. The USC has (B) 1894–1942; (D) 1894–1942; (M) 1904–1939. Tarnów archives: (b) 1877–93; (D) 1877-93; (M) 1877–93.

Radłów. USC has birth and death records from 1882.

Szczurowa. USC has birth, marriage and death records after 1902.

Wojnicz. No records have been found.

BRZOZÓW DISTRICT

Brzozów. The main district records in Brzozsów are confined to three volumes of marriage records, 1902–06, according to Dov Rubin, who was there in August 1997.

Dynów. No records have been found. Both synagogues in Dynow were burned by the Germans (with Jewish townspeople inside), and the records were presumed to be in one of the buildings.

Jasienica. USC has (BDM) 1939–41.

CHRZANÓW DISTRICT

Chrzanów. USC has very limited vital records.

Trzebinia. USC appears to have some birth and marriage records.

CIESZANÓW DISTRICT

Cieszanów. No records have been found.

Lipsko. No records have been found.

Lubaczów. USC has records from interwar period.

Oleszyce. The branch of the National Archives in Przemyśl holds the following records: (B) 1814–76; (M) 1860–76; (D) 1814–69. USC has later records.

Narol. Researcher Georges Rosenfeld wrote to this town and was informed that the records were destroyed during World War II. A local history teacher is willing to provide information; he has an old civil registration list. Contact Henryk Wolanczyk, 3710 Narol, ul. Lwówska 10.

DABROWA DISTRICT

Dąbrowa (now Dąbrowa Tarnowska). USC, Tarnów and Kraków regional archives have limited BDM records.

Szczucin. USC has fairly complete BDM records.

GORLICE DISTRICT

Gorlice. Reported in 1987: (B) alphabetical index of births 1904–21, but no book; (M) index to marriages giving the names of bride and groom and year of marriage 1928–37; (D) 1928–42. According to the head of the USC in Gorlice (letter dated May 1977), other books of records were destroyed by the Germans after the liquidation of the Gorlice ghetto. If you write to the USC, you will be referred to other resources, including a recent book on the Jews in Galicia and a person living in Israel.

Rzepiennik Strżyzowski. USC has some post 1922 BDM records only.

Biecz. USC has the following records: (B) vol. I, 1850–76; vol. II, 1877–90; vol. III, 1891–1907; vol. IV, 1907–25 is missing; (M) vol. I, 1918–42; (D) vol. I, 1851–74; vol. II, 1874–1915. Additionally, the LDS (Mormon) Family History Library holds microfilms for: (B) 1850–67 and

(D) 1851–68. The branch of the Polish National Archives in Przemyśl: (B) 1850–1937 and (D) 1851–74.

GRYBÓW DISTRICT

Grybów. Researcher Georges Rosenfeld, who wrote to the mayor of this town, was informed that the USC holds some pre-1900 birth, marriage and death registers: 1878–81; 1883–85; 1888–89. Rosenfeld also received a book, *Studia z dziejów miasta i regionu* (Studies in the history of the town and region), an interesting historical study written by Danuta Quirini-Poplawka and published by Universitas in Kraków in 1992. A yet-to-be-published second volume will discuss the Jews of Grybow. The late Pauline Horwitz wrote to the civil registry office in Grybow and was informed that Jewish birth and marriage registers for 1820–30 and 1860–70 were destroyed in World War II.

Bobowa. Researcher Georges Rosenfeld was told that the records were destroyed during World War II, but Miriam Weiner's book shows that the USC has good records after 1882.

JAROSLAU/JAROSŁAW DISTRICT

Jaroslau/Jarosław. The regional archive in Przemyśl has some records for 1877. The USC holds: (B) 1883–87, 1889–91, 1893–1926, 1928–34, 1936–38; (M) 1889–1906, 1908–09, 1911–22, 1925–27, 1929–38; (D) 1882–1909, 1911–13, 1918–20, 1922–23, 1926, 1928, 1930–38.

Radymno. (B) 1877, (M) 1920, 1925; (D) 1877. These records are in the branch of the National Archives in Przemyśl; the USC has additional records.

Sieniawa. The USC has post-1882 BMD records.

Pruchnik. Researcher Leon Gold during a 1997 visit found that birth records for 1834–76 are in the Przemyśl branch of the National Archives. The USC holds: (B) 1882–1942; (M) 1898–1939; (D) 1882–1920, 1922–34, 1938. The LDS (Mormon) Family History Library holds: (B) 1834–70.

JASŁO DISTRICT

Jasło. USC and the Przemyśl regional archive have good collections of BDM records.

Frysztak. No records have been found.

Olpiny. USC has (B)1889–1941; (D)1918–1942; (M)1918–41 records.

KOLBUSZOWA DISTRICT

Kolbuszowa. No records have been found.

Majdan and **Raniżów**. No records have been found.

Sokolów (now called Sokolow Małopolski) Lorin Weisenfeld, who visited in 1990, states that the USC has: (B) 1826–68, 1867–77, 1877–86, 1887–90 and 1891–99 (no indexes); (M) small folder of papers containing Jewish marriage records for 1882–1929. (D) The clerk could not find the pre-1877 volume; Lorin saw only the register for 1877–93, later volumes may exist. There was no index for 1877–93. Some records have been transferred to the Rzeszów archives.

KRAKAU (now spelled KRAKÓW or CRACÓW)

Both the USC and the regional archives in Kraków hold Jewish records. The LDS (Mormon) Family History Library has a large holding of Jewish records in its microfilm collection (see p. 35).

Julian and Fay Bussgang report that, in addition to metrical books, they saw "lists of residents that give wonderful information—a whole family on one page. Records as late as 1920 are in the archives. Newer ones are in the USC, but staff must search the records."

KROSNO DISTRICT

Krosno. The USC has BDM records for 1900–41, but with no indexes. A regional branch of the National Archives in Krosno houses old records for the region. Records in Warsaw may have been found for Krosno, but it is possible that the records are from Krosna near Limanowa in Eastern Galicia. Miscellaneous documents, certificates and correspondence in Polish, Yiddish and Hebrew, 1930.

Dukla. Leon Gold obtained records from the USC in 1995. The USC holds: (B) 1916–17, 1920, 1923–26, 1930–33, 1939–41; (M) 1914–16, 1939–40; (D) 1914–33, 1939–41.

Żmigrod. USC has Jewish vital records for Nowy Żmigrod.

Korczyna. USC has a good collection of birth and marriage records and a limited collection of post-1905 death records.

ŁANCUT DISTRICT

Łancut. Vital records were destroyed in a fire.

Przeworsk. Leon Gold visited the USC and reported they have no Jewish records. The branch of the National Archives in Przemyśl has population registers from 1787 and registers of births, marriages and deaths for 1815–51. The 1996 catalog *Akta Miasta Przeworska w zasobie Archiwum Panstwowego w Przemyślu* (Documents of the town of Przeworsk in the inventory of the National Archives in Przemyśl) by Michal Proska lists four pages of mostly pre-1860 Jewish community records, including acts imposing kosher meat and candle taxes, discussion of Jewish community expenses, compensation of rabbis and housing issues concerning other members of the community, Jewish burial and cemetery issues, and other matters relating to buildings owned by the Jewish community. There are 1,613 items in this collection. The period covered is from the 18th century to 1950. The archives also has uncatalogued material from 1944 to 1950.

Żolynia. The branch of the National Archives in Przemyśl holds: (M) 1916–22.

Leżajsk. The LDS (Mormon) Family History Library holds: (D) 1826–66. These records are also in the branch of the Polish National Archives in Przemyśl. The USC may have Jewish vital records: (B) 1902–06; (MD) 1898–1901.

Kańczuga. The Kańczuga USC has vital records, according to Lorin Weisenfeld: (B) indexes and records for 1851–76, 1877–1905, 1905–30; (M) no indexes; records only for 1859–76, 1877–1918, 1919–38; (D) index in two volumes (1851–76, 1877–1941), with some overlapping between the two, and four registers of records: 1851–86, 1887–1918, 1919–22, 1923–34.

LIMANOWA DISTRICT

Limanowa, Mszana Dolna. No records have been found.

LISKO/LESKO DISTRICT

Lisko/Lesko. Dov Rubin reports that he saw only one volume of Jewish births 1927–42 at the USC. Their records show they have marriage and death records as well. The archives in Przemyśl has birth records 1882–84.

Baligród. The USC has no Jewish records. The town was repeatedly ravaged by wars, and only records after 1951 survive.

Ustrzyki Dolne. No records have been found.

Wola Michowa. No Jewish records are in this town today. The USC for the district has been moved to Komancza, but there are no Jewish records there.

Lutowiska. There may be some vital records for this subdistrict among those for Sambor or Staremiasto in Lviv. See above for Eastern Galicia. There are Jewish Religious School documents for 1925–27 in Lviv.

MIELEC DISTRICT

Mielec. The USC office has BD records for 1920–35.

Radomyśl Wielkie. Records for the subdistrict are reported to have been destroyed.

MYŚLENICE DISTRICT
Myślenice, **Maków** and **Jordanów**. No records have been found.

NISKO DISTRICT
Nisko, **Ulanów**, **Rudnik**. No records have been found.

NOWY SĄCZ/NEU SANDEZ DISTRICT
Nowy Sącz/Neu Sandec. The USC has extensive records.
Stary Sącz/Alt Sandec, **Piwniczna**, **Łabowa**, **Lacko**, **Szczawnica**. No records have been found.
Krynica. Moishe Miller reports that the USC in Muszyna has records from 1885 forward.
Muszyna. Moishe Miller reports that the USC has records from 1885 forward.

NOWY TARG DISTRICT
Nowy Targ. No vital records have been located for this district. The Kraków Archives has census records for 1870 and 1880.
Krościenko. No records have been found.

PILZNO DISTRICT
Pilzno. No records have been found.
Dębica. Dov Rubin visited the USC which has only 10 birth records, reconstructed after World War II.
Brzostek. No records have been found.
Jadlowa. The USC has BDM records.

PRZEMYŚL DISTRICT
Przemyśl. Both the USC and the regional branch of the National Archives have Jewish records. Old records for the Przemyśl district are housed at the regional branch archives in Przemyśl: (B) 1853–90; (M) 1790–1893; (D) 1790–1893. Later records for Przemśyl and surrounding towns are in the USC, but some years are missing. Leon Gold visited the USC in 1997 and was informed that all existing pre-1894 records had been turned over to the archives. The USC does not have 1894–99 birth records, presumed to be missing. Records that exist for 1894–1942 are now at the USC.
Sosnica and **Niżankowice**. No records have been found. They are not in the Przemyśl Archives.
Krzywcza. Records for this subdistrict are in the Lviv Archives.
Dubiecko. Pre-1939 records are missing and are presumed lost. Miriam Weiner shows some post-1939 death records in the Przemyśl archives.

ROPCZYCE DISTRICT
Ropczyce, **Sędziszów** and **Wielopole**. No records have been found.

RZESZÓW DISTRICT
Rzeszów. The regional archives in the city has tax records and records of other types of legal transactions, but there are no vital records. Records that are less than 100 years old are in the USC as follows: (B) October 1866–November 1942, with some gaps, in 23 volumes, indexes cover 1844–1940; (M) Index and records for 1882–86, 1888–1943; (D) 1875–April 1943 in 14 volumes; one researcher saw death records from 1842 to 1847, but the records do not appear in the catalog; there are no indexes to the death records. Neither the USC nor the regional archives has Jewish records for other communities in its region. *In Lviv* (see below for more information on the records here): (B) 1841–66 [File 299 in Fond 701].

Błazowa. No records have been found.

Czudec. According to Miriam Weiner, limited post-1940 BDM records are in the Rzeszów archives.

Głogów. No records have been found.

Niebylec. Rzezsów archives has some BD records.

Strzyżów. No records have been found.

Tyczyn. The USC has: (B) 1881–1902, 1913–42; (M) 1877–74, July 1942; (D) 1877–1902. The regional archives in Rzeszów also, reportedly, has birth records for Tyczyn, 1877–80. *In Lviv:* (D) 1792–1876 [File 358 in Fond 701].

SANOK DISTRICT

Sanok. The branch archives in Sanok and the USC have fairly complete BDM records dating from 1874 to 1940.

Rymanów. Dov Rubin determined that the USC has birth and death records amounting to about 100 entries, for 1939–41.

Bukowsko. Records for this town existed after World War II but are now missing.

Nowotaniec. No records have been found.

Tyrawa Woloska. The branch of the National Archives in Przemyśl has a 1937 inventory of the Jewish religious community for personal property and real estate. The USC reports that no other Jewish records have been found.

TARNOBRZEG DISTRICT

Tarnobrzeg. Fred Wexler received records from the USC (ul. Mickelwicze 4, Tarnobrzeg 0526895). Gayle Riley reports that the branch archives in Sandomierz has the following records for Tarnobrzeg: 1880 census; books of inhabitants 1901–05, 1925; books of inhabitants who left Tarnobrzeg 1929–39, books of noninhabitant Jews 1843–1948. The USC holds: (B) 1889–1901, 1903–32, 1935, 1937; (D 1862–1948; (M) 1889–1945. Riley says that the Przemyśl archives has additional birth records for 1786 and 1888. She has a list of school and employment records for early 1898–1905. Riley's e–mail: < key2pst@pacbell.net >. Her home address is: 612 East Live Oak, #A, San Gabriel, CA 91776. The Lauder Project at the Jewish Historical Institute in Warsaw has some records from the 1930s. There is an 1815 tax list for Tarnobrzeg on microfilm in Israel at the Central Archives for the History of the Jewish People at Hebrew University in Jerusalem.

Radomyśl. Sometimes called Radomysl nad Sanem. The USC has post-1882 birth records and extremely limited death records.

Rozwadów and **Baranów**. No records have been found.

TARNÓW DISTRICT

Tarnów. The archives in Kraków has records for Tarnów, 1849–1900. Reported in 1987, the USC has: (B) 1902–44; (D) 1909–44. There are also marriage records, but the reports on dates have been variable. The LDS (Mormon) Family History Library holds: (B) 1808–10, 1815–49, 1849–63, 1863–70; (M) 1849–70; (D) 1808–55, index only 1863–70, 1855–70. See Chapter 3 for more information. Additionally, the Central Archives for the History of the Jewish People in Jerusalem (see Chapter 3 for additional information about this archives) has civil records for Tarnow—types and dates unknown.

Ryglice, Tuchów. No records have been found.

Zabno. The USC and Tarnów archives have good collections of BDM records.

WIELICZKA DISTRICT

Wieliczka. The USC in Kraków has BDM records for this subdistrict.

Podgórze. The Kraków archives has extensive BDM records.

Tarnów, Poland. Cathedral Street circa 1922. Store signs on the left read Jewelry, Watch Repair, Goldsmith, Furs. On the right are W. Brach's Perfume Store; Maczin's Rubber, Household Goods; Factory outlet: Paints, Lacquers, Household Goods.

Klasno. The town of Dobczyce reportedly has some vital records, but it is not known if they are for the town or the subdistrict.

WADOWICE DISTRICT

Wadowice. The LDS (Mormon) Family History Library holds marriage records for 1879–1929.
Andrychów, **Kalwarya**, **Zator**. No records have been found.

ŻYWIEC DISTRICT

Żywiec. No records have been found.
Zabłocie. No records have been found.

Holdings of the LDS (Mormon) Family History Library

The Family History Library (FHL) of the Church of Jesus Christ of Latter-day Saints (LDS or Mormons) has never been permitted to conduct its own microfilming in Poland, but has relied on the Polish National Archives to supply films. Although the Mormons have a standing request for all Jewish birth, marriage and death records (among others), the Polish National Archives has provided films for very few Jewish districts from the region that was Western Galicia.

To order the microfilms listed below, go to your nearest Family History Center, usually housed within a parish church or stake of the Church of Jesus Christ of Latter-day Saints. Complete an order card for each film. Pay the small fee and fill out a postcard so that you can be notified when the films arrive. In the U.S., it takes four to six weeks for films to arrive, and then you have two weeks to review them at the facility. If you need more time, you can pay an additional small fee to extend the rental time.

The FHL holds a substantial number of microfilms for districts in Western Galicia, but the records do not include Jews. Some of these records go back into the 18th century. While non-Jewish clergy were authorized to register Jewish births, marriages and deaths until 1873, none of the FHL-held records of these areas contain Jewish entries.

Most of the records in the small collection of Galician-Jewish records held by the Family History Library were filmed in the Warsaw City Archives in the 1960s. Tarnów records were in the *Archiwum Panstwowe* (National Archives) in both Kraków and Warsaw. Wadowice marriage records were found in Berlin-Dahlem (which suggests that perhaps other records might be found there in time).

FHL microfilms containing Jewish records for Galicia are almost all within the modern Polish provinces of Kraków and Rzeszów, shown in the list below as KR and RZ, respectively. The exception is the film for 1814–37 births from Lwów (LW) in Ukraine.

The list below shows the record type, followed by the year(s) covered, followed by the microfilm number. B=births; M=marriages; D=deaths. Where a microfilm number is followed by a numbers in parentheses, the numbers refer to the item number on the film (some microfilms include more than one set of data). For example, the first entry in the list shows that for the town of Biecz, the FHL has records of births 1850–67 and deaths 1851–68, both on microfilm number 718,912, Items 1 and 2, respectively.

Biecz (RZ)
 B: 1850–67; D: 1851–68, #718,912 (items 1–2)
Brzesko (KR)
 B: 1849–86; D: 1863–76, #948,419
Krakau (listed as Kraków) (KR)
 B: 1798–1819; D: 1816–19, #718,912
 B: 1820–29, #718,913
 B: 1830–36; D: 1848–54, #718,914
 B: 1837–43, #718,915
 B: 1844–50, #718,916
 B: 1851–55, #718,917
 M: 1798–1816, #718,918
 M: 1817–38, #718,919
 M: 1830–39, #718,920
 M: 1840–52, #718,921
 D: 1811/28, #718,922
 D: 1829–38, #718,923
 D: 1839–47, #718,924

 B: 1874–76, #1,201,162
 BDM: 1876–77, #1,201,163
 BDM: 1877 index, #1,201,164
Leżajsk (RZ)
 D: 1826–66, #766,021 (item 8)
Lemberg is listed as Lwów (LW)
 B: 1814–37, #905,274
Pruchnik (RZ)
 B: 1834–70, #766,039 (item 13)
Tarnów (KR)
 B: 1808–10; 1815–49; D: 1808–55, #742,702
 B: 1849–63; D: index, 1863–70, #948,420
 B: 1863–70, #948,421
 M: 1849–70; D: 1855–70, #948,422
Wadowice (KR)
 M: 1877–1929, #127,748
Wisnicz (KR)
 B: 1814–59; M: 1827–70, #936,648 (items 4–6)

❀ Chapter 3 ❀

Information in Sources Other Than Vital Records

Strategies for Finding Information in Sources Other Than Vital Records

Some researchers have found information by writing to the town's mayor or local history museum, which most towns of any size seem to have. Many towns have 20th-century school records, tax records, residence information (described in the Census Documents section) and court records. These rich sources of information are often overlooked. Writing to the mayor in Polish or Ukrainian also might assist you in locating a researcher or someone well versed in local history who can become your onsite aide in obtaining information—or even someone who will photograph cemeteries and buildings of significance to you.

Census Documents

An Austrian official has stated that no Austrian law required authorities to keep original census documents after the statistics were compiled. For that reason, some of the original census documents were destroyed.

The late director of the Polish National Archives, Prof. Dr. Jerzy Skowronek, confirmed that none of the national archives branches that serve the area of former Galicia were able to find a comprehensive set of [census] records. The National Archives in Kraków, however, has records that show the location and people who lived in the following places in the following years:

> Kraków: 1850, 1857, 1870, 1881, 1890, 1900 and 1910
> Nowy Targ: 1870 and 1880
> Podgórze: 1870, 1880, 1890, 1900 and 1910.

Gayle Riley reports that some census records for the town of Tarnobrzeg are in its town hall.

Geoffrey Weisgard viewed the 1795 German-language census of Kazimierz (the ancient Jewish suburb of Kraków), at the Central Archives for the History of the Jewish People in Jerusalem, as well as the regional archives in Kraków. The less-detailed 1790 census of Kazimierz is also at the Kraków regional archives. Weisgard believes that the 1787 census of Kazimierz, conducted by the Catholic Church, is held at the archives of the Bishop of Kraków.

The Central Archives for the History of the Jewish People also has lists of male members of the Kraków Jewish community who were eligible to vote in *kehillah* (Jewish community) elections in 1883 and 1929. Though birth dates are not included, these lists resemble a census for males over age 13. Also at the Central Archives are lists compiled for tax purposes. According to Hanna Volovici, the Central Archives has 1856 and 1895 lists of Jews who lived in small towns near Kraków, such as Balice, Czulice, Górka, Grebalowa, Krzeszowice, Liszki, and Mogila among others. The archives also has school lists that, while they do not include birth dates, indicate the grade a pupil was in for the year, which permits the year of birth to be estimated. The Central Archives has 20th-century lists of members of five synagogues in Kraków.

Fay Bussgang wrote an excellent article for *Avotaynu* (Vol. XII, No. 2, Summer 1996) that sheds light on related records in the Kraków regional archive. She described finding records called *spis mieszkancow* (list of residents), kept by many Polish municipalities, that show the members of a household, date and place of birth, names of parents, religion and occupation, among other information. She wrote that the list seems to have included notations of arrivals, departures, deaths, marriages and other information. Fay saw *spis mieszkancow* records from 1921.

To research these *spis mieszkancow* records by mail, you need permission from the Polish National Archives (write to Naczelna Dyreckcja Archiwow Państwowych; ul. Długa 6; skr. pocz. 1005; 00-950 Warszawa). However, according to Fay Bussgang, in Kraków one can check the indexes without such permission at the regional archive located at ul. Sienna 16, Monday–Thursday, 9 a.m.–2 p.m. and 4–7 p.m.; Friday 9 a.m.–1 p.m. Bussgang's *Avotaynu* article offers tips on using the index.

In the Winter 1993 issue of *Avotaynu*, George Bolotenko and Lawrence Tapper reported on their visit to five archival institutions in Lviv. Orest Matsiuk, director of the Ukrainian Central State Historical Archives, showed them through the vault in which Jewish records are preserved. Boletenko and Tapper saw hundreds of records, including Jewish town records of Lwów from the 1700s that appear to be census-like records, according to their description:

> Additionally, there are censuses of Galicia from the 18th and 19th centuries. In the basement storage areas . . . a number of Torahs are kept on top of a tall bookcase, under cover. There are no rollers, just fragments of old Torahs. We also saw record books dating back hundreds of years. Many of these books are so bulky and heavy that they require several people to handle them. We were allowed to photograph everything.

Boletenko and Tapper reported that Matsiuk emphasized that the archive is ill equipped to handle foreign mail inquiries. That remains the case to the present. For that reason, Gesher Galicia has recommended hiring one of the researchers listed in Chapter 6.

Louis Goldman found a German reprint of a book that summarizes the 1869 census of Galicia, *Orts-Reportorium des Konigreiches Galizien und Lodomerien mit dem Grossherzogthume Krakau* (1874). The census listing included the number of houses, the number of males, the number of females and the total inhabitants. The census figures were taken from the *k.k. statistischen Central-Commission*. The reprint was published in 1989 by Helmut Scherer Verlag GmbH Berlin, 1000 Berlin, Boothstr. 21a (ISBN 3-89433-015-3). The phone number listed on the title page was 030/773 80 12. Georgetown University Library in Washington, D.C. has a copy of the original book.

Pinkas Hakehillot: Poland, vol. 3 (Jerusalem: Yad Vashem, 1984) provides, among other information, census data for Galician towns. Although there is some inconsistency with respect to dates, population data are provided for 1563, 1678, 1765, 1808, 1865, 1880, 1890, 1900, 1910 and 1921.

The Blackbook of Localities Whose Jewish Population Was Exterminated by the Nazis (Jerusalem: Yad Vashem, 1965) offers 1931 summary census data about Jews. However, this source appears to be of questionable accuracy, since population figures are sometimes much lower than those indicated in certain *yizkor* books.

Notary Records

Notary records can be a useful source of genealogical information. Today, in the era of photocopy machines, computers and other easy methods of duplicating original documents, notaries are not thought of as sources for copies. However, our ancestors and their governments once relied on notaries to make exact copies. Thus, when someone wanted a passport to travel outside the country or needed to prove one's identity for marriage, school or another official purpose, hiring a notary was the most common method of having copies made. Notary records, including real estate documents, for Western and Eastern Galicia appear to be housed in large numbers at the branch or regional archives in Przemyśl. To research this material, obtain permission from Main Archives in Warsaw; otherwise, there is a risk that you may be charged more than the official government rates for research and copying.

Because notaries were licensed by the Polish government, their records were technically the property of the government. While not all records were collected and stored in archival repositories, some 19th- and 20th-century notary records survived. However, notary records are covered under privacy laws, and you must provide proof that you are descended from the person discussed in the record. If there is a possibility that the person could still be alive, you will also be asked for proof that the person has died.

Richard Schwarzstein succeeded in obtaining notary records from Przemyśl for residents of Nisko and Ulanów. After following their instructions exactly, he received word from the archivists that they had spent five hours in research at $15 per hour and had located several documents. Upon payment, he received good reproductions of the documents. One document related to the transfer of title to the family home, while another related to his great-grandmother's family business.

An excellent new source of specific information about notary records is *Jewish Roots in Poland: Pages from the Past and Archival Inventories* by Miriam Weiner (Secaucus, N.J.: Routes to Roots Foundation, 1998).

School Records

School records, also good sources of information, can be found in town archives, as well as national archives, in Poland and Ukraine. Alexander Dunai, a professional researcher who lives in Lviv, discovered the following school records in the Lviv archives:

School year certificates of primary school pupils, Galicia, 1874–1920
School year certificates of teacher college students, Galicia, 1894–1920
School year certificates, state secondary schools, Lviv, 1894–1920
School year certificates, state secondary schools, Galicia, 1871–1920 (only letters B-K and L-Z)
Documents from Jewish primary school, Lviv, 1881 and 1903 school year certificates, lists of pupils, etc.; some documents have photos.

From Rzeszów:

Documents of Jewish private primary school, lists of teachers, 1832–39
Documents of secondary school, list of pupils, 1879
Documents of secondary school, list of teachers, 1919–20
Documents of state secondary school, list of teachers, 1918
Documents of secondary school, list of pupils, 1836
Documents of secondary school, 1891–1904

Military Records

[David Fox, Ellen Sadove Renck, Ada Greenblatt and Barbara Urbanska-Yeager contributed to this section.]

In 1789 Austrian legislation mandated universal male military service. In practice, however, Jews did not serve in the military in any great numbers until the 20th century because most Austrian military officers opposed having Jews under their command.

The best source for Austrian military records is the LDS (Mormon) Family History Library (FHL). Rosemary Chorzempa, in her 1993 book, *Korzenie Polskie: Polish Roots*, briefly discusses the LDS holdings of military records. According to Chorzempa, if you have a definite location and year of birth for your ancestor, check film #1186632, item 1

("Distribution Location Index of the Austro-Hungarian Empire Army and Navy Troops, Regiments, etc."), which lists the Austrian units that recruited in each area and when they were in each locality. Then you can check that unit's records for your ancestor.

Another useful book at the FHL, according to Ellen Sadove Renck, is *Gesischichte der K. und Wehrmacht*, published in 1901. One can use the *Qualifikationslisten Index des K.U.K. Herres und K.U.K. Marine, 1761–1900*, to follow the locations of the various military units, which remained fairly stable in their deployment, except during a war. After fighting ceased, they generally returned to their original site. The Austrian Army Records are found in the FHL catalog under Austria—Civil Registration. The *Austrian History Yearbook*, vols. 6–7 explains the Kriegsarchiv that began in 1711.

In what seems to be a finding aid to an extensive collection of service records of officers and other military officials of the Austro-Hungarian Empire, *Dienstbeschreibungen und Qualifikationslisten*, 1761–1918, surnames (and some first names) are arranged alphabetically by film number. The English description of the finding aid indicates that the beginning name on each film is shown in this description. Thus, Glaas is the first name on film #1257095, Glanzer is the first name on film #1257096, and so forth. It is listed in the FHL's Locality Search Catalog under "Austria (see Military)."

Ada Greenblatt researched the Hapsburg Military Records for World War I and discovered that for each year there is an alphabetical index of surnames, with a page number after each name. When you find a name, turn to the page that gives details about the person's service.

Film #1506282. The microfilm is labeled 1912–14, but it actually covers 1911 and 1912. Alphabetical index for 1911 on pages 1479–1737; alphabetical index for 1912, pages 1551–1823.

Film #1506283. Alphabetical index for 1914 on pages 1353–1579; alphabetical index (A-R) for 1916, pages 1711–1843.

Film #1506284. Alphabetical index (Q-Z) for 1916 on pages 1342–1421; alphabetical index (A-N) for 1917, pages 1527–1719.

Film #1506285. Alphabetical index (N-Z) for 1917, pages 1718–1853; alphabetical index for 1918, pages 661–777.

Holdings of Specific Repositories

Ivano-Frankovsk Archives

Stanisławów, now Ivano-Frankovsk, was a large Jewish population center. Nat Abramowitz in *The Galitizianer*, vol. 4, no. 2, reported that professional researcher Alexander Dunai found no vital records in the Ivano-Frankovsk Archives, but did find other types of records in the archives and elsewhere in the city. A partial inventory of what Dunai found follows:

- Census of the Jewish population in Stanisławów for 1857, a 1,200-page list written in Gothic German.
- A portion of the 1900 census of the Jewish population in Stanisławów, written in Polish.
- List of real estate owned by Jews.
- Population information from Stanisławów district, 1923.
- Census of the Jewish population in Stanisławów, August 1939. It consists of about 10,000 pages, each of which contains information about the people in a household: birth dates, occupation, place of work, relationship and, in some cases, property holdings. The census is organized by street, and, within each apartment building, the records are in alphabetical order.

Stanisławów, Poland (now Ivano-Frankovsk, Ukraine). View of Sapierżyńska Street circa 1915.

Pozdrowienie ze Stanisławówa. — Ulica Sapierżyńska
Gruß aus Stanislau. — Sapierżyńskagasse.

- List of lawyers, doctors and merchants. The list includes all religious denominations, but most are Jews.
- Lists of Jews deported by the Germans.

Other documents exist from the Nazi occupation period, but they are under study.

Most of these documents are from the 20th century. Dunai has access to another institution that has one book of Jewish births from 1919 to 1924. Dunai's services are described in Chapter 6.

Ukraine Central State Historical Archives in Lviv

This section, developed by Julian and Fay Bussgang, originally appeared in vol. 4, no. 2 of *The Galitizianer*. It has been supplemented here by new information supplied by Alexander Dunai.

Fond 44. Magistracy of the town of Sanok, Sanok lands, *Rusynian Wojewódstwo* (province of Rusynia) since 1783. Sanok region: 1366–1939. Sanok received the Magdeburg Right of self-government in 1366. The Sanok Magistracy had jurisdiction over legislative, civil, commercial and criminal affairs. The fond contains documents for 1685–1864, written in Latin, Polish and German. The holdings include court documents, contracts for sale and purchase of land and chattel, testaments, settlements, real estate affairs and account books for 1787–90.

Fond 141. 26 files 1667–1854. Collection of documents about finances and properties of the Jewish population in Galicia. Town and district implementation of new taxes; benefits to various population groups from towns of Chełm, Bełż, and Czchów; rabbinical court decrees; register of debts and payments of the Jewish population of Belz.

Fond 186. Documents of the Lemberg Regional Lands and Taxes Commission, 1821–1934. Inventories of land holdings of villages; land registers and land maps of villages; lists of landowners in alphabetical order; lists of real estate owners in villages. According to Alexander Dunai:

> The greater part of the fond consists of the land registers and maps of villages, including Bochnia, Chortków, Berezhany, Jasło, Kolomyya, Kraków, Lemberg, Nowy Sącz, Przemyśl, Rzeszów, Sambor, Sanok, Stanisławów, Stryj, Tarnopol, Tarnów, Wadowice, Złoczów and Zolkiew. The other part consists of inventories of land with

their owners from Berezhany, Kolomyya, Lemberg, Przemyśl, Sambor, Stanisławów, Stryj, Tarnopol, Złoczów and Zolkiew. Additionally, there are lists of landholders for a small number of villages, including the (now Ukrainian) town of Staremiasto (1853) and the Polish town of Lutowiska (1855–95).

Fond 300. 350 files, 1921–39: Records of the private warehouse of iron tubes and hardware belonging to Szymon Soltz of Lwów.

Fond 332. 128 files, 1924–39. Lwów Branch of Zionist Organization for Immigration to Palestine (headquarters in Warsaw). Letters, documents, statistical data, list of immigrants and members.

Fond 334. 161 files, 1920, 1922–39. Lwów Branch of Central Immigration Society (EAC), covered four voivodeships around Lwów. Activities: gave information to immigrants, prepared documents, helped with employment, gave legal help and funds, scheduled transport to Canada and South America. List of immigrants and members.

Fond 335. 225 files, 1920–39. *Keren Haesod* (Society to Build Palestine). Covers Eastern Galicia branch of worldwide organization. Correspondence, minutes of meetings, lists of members and contributors.

Fond 336. 243 files, 1922–23, 1928–39. Regional Commission for Eastern Małopolska in Lwów. Group raised and distributed funds, organized Jews to go to Palestine, provided public education. List of delegates to 1897 Zionist Congress in Basel.

Fond 337. 123 files, 1919–39. *Hanoar Hatzion* (Young Zionists Organization), which had branches in Galician towns. Rules, correspondence, membership list.

Fond 338. 1,635 files, 1895, 1902–40. Regional Zionist Organization of Lwów. Political party of Jewish bourgeoisie in Eastern Galicia. From 1920 to 1939, active in three voivodeships to buy and sell land in Palestine. List of leaders, members, voting places.

Fond 339. 32 files, 1926–39. Society *Keren Kayemet* (Jewish National Fund) of Lwów established in Galicia, 1914. Headquarters in Warsaw. Its purpose was to raise funds for colonization of Palestine. Rules and regulations of society in Lwów and Kraków, correspondence, list of members, 1936–39.

Fond 341. 17 files, 1931–37. Publication and administration of *Zionist Weekly*, newspaper of the worldwide Zionist movement. List of subscribers and ledger book of receipts.

Fond 342. 129 files, 1926–39. *Achba* (Jewish Youth Organization) of Lwów, Eastern Małopolska. Closely tied to Zionist organizations in Poland, Western Europe, America and Palestine. Correspondence with Warsaw, Jerusalem, Tel Aviv, London and Prague. List and application forms of members. List of delegates to conventions.

Fond 346. 288 files, 1929–39. Lwów Branch of Association of Jewish Veterans who Fought for Polish Independence. Covered three voivodeships, reported to headquarters in Warsaw and branches in Poland, Denmark and elsewhere. Employment and financial assistance, loans, care of veterans' graves, Youth Cadre, rules/regulations, projects, memoranda, protocols, news bulletins, conditions in Poland, membership dues and lists and correspondence.

Fond 432. 49 files, 1924–39. Central Jewish Cooperative Bank of Lwów. Bank documents and activity reports.

Fond 441. 17 files, 1928–32. *Hanoar Haivri* (Jewish Boy Scouts) in Lwów and voivodeship. After 1930, it covered all of Małopolska and Silesia. In 1932, it was closed by decision of committees of Zionist organizations in Kraków and joined with *Agudat Hanoar Haivri* in Kraków. Files, correspondence and reports.

Fond 454. 41 files, 1933–39. *Tzion Baoley Miktzoa* (Central Committee of Jewish Zionist Craftsmen) in Małopolska. Activities: educated Jewish craftsmen, promoted Jewish culture, offered lectures. List and card files of members.

Fond 455. 82 files, 1930–39. *Hechalutz HaKlal Tzion* (Jewish Society of Zionist Youth). In 1935, joined with another society, General Zionist *Halutz*, which was active in Eastern Galicia and all of Poland. Correspondence, application forms, membership lists, card file of members going to work on the *kibbutz*.

Fond 456. 15 files, 1930–33. *Gmilat Chesed*. Headquarters for Eastern Galicia. Provided financial aid for poor Jewish craftsmen and merchants. Financial documents.

Fond 457. 10 files, 1925–39. *Hechalutz* (Pioneer) of Lwów (Society for the Education and Training of Jewish Youth for Immigration to Palestine). Card files of members.

Fond 458. 47 files, 1926–39. Lwów Branch of Jewish Cooperative Association. Reported to Warsaw, activities throughout Galicia. Correspondence, reports and financial documents.

Fond 496. 5 files, 1926, 1937–39. Society of Jewish Private Enterprise in Lwów. Payroll records of Geller, president of the society.

Fond 497. 243 files, 1873–1928. Synagogue schools of the Jewish community, chartered under Belgrade statute of 1866. Original founders were Jews expelled from Spain and Portugal during the Inquisition. Goal was to support religion, charity and education of Jews. Drafts of laws regarding religious societies, work plans, memoranda from clergy in Serbia, Croatia and Slovenia; financial activities. List of electors and abstracts of some metrical data.

Fond 498. 5 files, 1929–38. *Ahavat Chesed* (Society of Credit, Self-Help). Was active in three voivodeships in Eastern Małopolska. Applications of members for loans.

Fond 499. 5 files, 1929–38. Society for Assistance to Jewish Students in Poland, Lwów Branch. Applications for financial aid, financial reports.

Fond 500. 9 files, 1930–33. *Hanoteach* (Lwów Society of Farmers to Work in Palestine). Help with care of citrus trees in Palestine for owners in Poland; maintained a citrus plantation in Natanya.

Fond 501. 5 files, 1931–39. *Makkabi* (cultural and physical growth of Jewish youth, summer camp). Documents, audit.

Fond 502. 9 files, 1925–39. Society of Jewish Women, Eastern Małopolska. Office of job search and placement, shelters for working women, kindergartens, child care, help to runaways.

Fond 503. 222 files, 1921–39. *TOZ* (Health Care Society for Jews, Society for Promoting Good Health Among Jews). Lwów branch of organization headquartered in Warsaw. List of members of committee, medical card files.

Fond 505. 296 files, 1898–1931. Committee for Assistance of Jewish Population in Lwów. Active in Lwów after pogroms there on November 22–23, 1918. In 1923, changed name to Central Jewish Rescue Committee. List of committee members.

Fond 639. Handwritten and illegible.

Fond 701. 5,672 files 1785–1942. Jewish Religious Community of Lwów.

- Metrical Books. Births, marriages and deaths of Jewish communities in Galicia. (Note: These are the records that are listed above under vital records.) Documents are organized alphabetically by town. Within a town, events are listed in chronological order. Sets are incomplete. Most common are birth, marriage and deaths in Lwów and vicinity (56 books), Tarnopol (29 books), Narajew (28 books), Podhajce (21 books) and Mikulince (21 books). Seven books are alphabetical indexes.
  - One book lists Jews living in Tarnopol 1850–1900, with indication of birth date and profession.
  - One book includes drafts of abstracts from metrical records of Horodenka from the second half of the 19th century to the beginning of the 20th century.
  - Seven books are copies of metrical records, 1789–1942 (oldest documents are from a marriage book from Kamionka Strumiłowa, 1781–1861, and marriages from Stanisławów, 1789–1871).

- Correspondence between Lwów voivodeships about various activities: permits for marriage, dowries, taxes; selling kosher meat at auction; assistance to poor; construction and repair of synagogues; establishment of Jewish morgue; Jewish population census; Jewish goods and money for charity; applications from Jewish immigrants from Russia, 1785–1907; Jewish activities with hospitals and synagogues; list of Jewish families with debts (in 18 books), 1791–95, 1796–1850 (still in cataloguing stage).
- Financial documents, applications for aid, financial assistance, reports. List of committee reports. Case files. (Still in cataloguing stage)
- Reports and a list of members of an organization relating to financial assistance (still in cataloguing stage).
- List of deaths. Case files (Still in cataloguing stage).

YIVO Institute for Jewish Research

YIVO Institute for Jewish Research, which has the world's largest library and archival collection pertaining to Eastern European Jews, is located at 555 West 57th Street, Suite 1100, New York, NY 10019; phone: (212) 246-6080; fax: (212) 292-1892) YIVO's hours are Monday–Thursday, 9:30 a.m–5:30 p.m. The library and archives are closed Friday.

YIVO has the largest collection of *yizkor* books in the United States, lists of Holocaust survivors who registered with various agencies, and hundreds of volumes of books that were rescued from its original location in Vilnius (Vilna), Lithuania.

One aspect of YIVO that is less well known is its archival collection, which includes an extensive photo collection on laser disk and a *landsmanschaftn* archive.

Landsmanschaft organizations were burial, social, religious and welfare societies established in the late 19th and early 20th centuries by people who emigrated from Eastern European towns and wanted to continue their association with others from their old towns in their new countries. In the U.S., these *landsmanschaftn* were established in a few large cities, New York most prominent among them. Several of these groups served all Galician Jews. Additionally, many were composed of Jews from particular Galician towns or regions.

Rosaline Schwartz, a YIVO staff person, became alarmed when she learned that New York-based *landsmanschaftn*, which were going out of business because their members were dying out or no longer interested, were simply throwing away their records.

YIVO published a catalogue of their then current holdings in 1986, *A Guide to YIVO's Landsmanschaftn Archive* by Rosaline Schwartz and Susan Milamed. While most records consist of minutes and lists of those who paid or owed dues, some information may lead to new sources. No doubt, the collection has grown since 1986. Write to YIVO to inquire about specific places.

Towns are listed with current names; be sure to include that name when inquiring. Although these societies started in the 1890s, most of the records at YIVO begin after 1920.

Central Archives for the History of the Jewish People

The Central Archives for the History of the Jewish People, located in the Sprinzak building on the Givat Ram campus of Hebrew University (address: P.O. Box 1149, Jerusalem 91010), holds material from communities that may be relevant to researchers of Galicia. Much of the material listed in the guide is historically interesting, but not genealogically relevant. The following list was excerpted from *Guide to the Sources for the*

*History of the Jews in Poland in the Central Archives: Polish Jewry: Bibliographical Series,
4.* The documents noted are among the most genealogically relevant.

Brzesko. Inventory of the town and inhabitants, 1708

Brzeżany. Inventory of the town and inhabitants, 1666; inventory of the district, 1698

Brzozów. Inventory of the district, 1748

Chrzanów. Minutes of *bet din* (religious court) and synagogue record book, 1707–1825

Chyrów. Inventory of the town and inhabitants

Dynów. Inventory of estates, 1782

Dzwinograd. Inventory of *starostwo* (subprefecture) and inhabitants, 1762

Jaryczów Nowy. Circumcision register, 1790–1835

Jezierzany. Inventory of area inhabitants, 18th–19th centuries

Kolbuszowa. Inventory of district, 1832

Kraków. Many items, including fragmentary vital records 1788–1855; records of furrier's guild, 1837–40; Jewish guild records; Jewish court records; 1790–1972 census records

Kraciczyn. Inventory of estates, 1730–35

Lesko. Extracts from local court records, 1611–61

Nowy Sącz. Court case, 1751; records, privileges and inventories of the Jews, 1785–87

Nowy Targ. Fragmentary village records regarding Jews, 1710–12

Podhajce. Supplication by Jewish *arendarz* (leaseholder), 1750

Przemyśl. Fragmentary court records; inventory of the town and its inhabitants; list of Jewish houses and their owners, 1595–1790

Ropczyce. Inventory of inhabitants, 1760

Rzeczyca (near Tarnobrzeg). Contract involving Jews; inventory of *starostwo* (subprefecture), 1755–69

Sambor. Extract from inventory of royal estates, 1760

Sanok. Assessment record of Jewish inhabitants, 1692

Sokal. Fragmentary legal records, 1635–45; municipal records, 1768–62

Szczucin. Mishnah Study Society Book, 1889; fragmentary vital records, 1826–65

Tarnobrzeg. Extracts from municipal records concerning Jews, 1695–1830; contracts concerning *arendas*; list of Jewish taxpayers

Tarnów. Birth records, 1808–49; death records, 1800–55; records of various *arendas*, 1735–85

Trembowla. Inventories, 1626–1778

Witków. *Pinkas* (minutes book) of burial society, 1820–68

Zarnowiec (near Krosno). Fragmentary vital records, 1826–68

Zolkiew. Fragmentary *pinkas* (minutes book) of burial society, 1930s; extracts from municipal records

Żydaczów. Excerpts from official court records concerning Jews, 1701–66

Jeffrey Cymbler, who has used this resource, indicates that the Central Archives card catalog does not offer a complete description of material on their microfilms. Researchers are advised to view the whole film for a community to determine its usefulness.

The Galitzianer, vol. 2, no. 4, presented a list of Galician towns, compiled and submitted by Gershon Lauer, for which 1870 voting lists of males have been microfilmed. Galician towns included in the collection are: Brody, Buczacz, Dubiecko, Gródek, Grybów, Jasło, Jazłowice (now Pomortsy), Kuty, Lubaczów, Mosciska, Oświęcim, Podhajce, Rohatyń, Sambor and Śniatyn. Lauer advised caution when requesting copies of the lists from the Central Archives because they are large and expensive. Explore the possibility of having a copy of the microfilm made; it may cost less.

Wallace Witkowski, a retired attorney who does translating tasks for the U.S. Holocaust Memorial Museum, translated the following descriptions of two documents from this collection to illustrate the kind of information contained in inventory and tax documents. See Chapter 6 for contact information.

Przemyśl tax records, 1661. The handwritten document appears to be a modern copy of a seven-page entry in the 18th-century *hipoteka* (land registry) or *lustracja* (description of real property for tax assessment purposes) from the town of Przemyśl, Poland. The first page of the original bears a seal of the Ossolineum Library in Poland. [This library was moved from Lwów to Wrocław after World War II—Ed.] The following is a verbatim translation of the initial paragraph of the document.

> Taken from the ancient Jewish Protocols, in accordance with the descriptive assessments of the Jewish houses on these lands, from the beginning of the Przemyśl Jewish *Kahal*; owned by the Jews, which houses were built and land bought from the Polish lords; on which lands houses were erected, which by the privileges of old from the Polish kings are confirmed, and by Deputy Voivode Slotminski (?) assessed, pursuant to an order of His Excellency Szarmicki, Voivode of Ruthenia, in the reign of King Michal, which assessment was done after the conflagration of the Town of Przemyśl, in order that the dispute that arose between the local city hall and the Przemyśl synagogue be settled. This took place in the year 1661 and was entered into the records by [order of] Deputy Voivode.

There follows a seven-page list, by streets and by house numbers of properties, improved and unimproved, with names of the owners, sometimes with additional information about the owner or the property. The surnames, when provided, are primarily patronymics and, oddly, many of the buildings were owned by Jews from distant towns. It is not clear if the property was owned by absentee landlords or the people living on the property had moved to Przemyśl from these other places. For instance, a house with shops and basements belonging to Smichel Szaj, a merchant of various herbs and furs from Płock, a town quite some distance from Przemyśl and a large homestead belonging to "the Jew Calow [Polish for Caleb] from Rybotycze." Down the street from the latter were two other houses owned by a Mendel from Grodzisk and a Hersek Wolff from Gdańsk. In addition to furriers, barbers, tailors, a stall keeper and cloth dealers, there were several saloons noted among the real properties. The final building, opposite the sugar factory, belonged to Sawel Izrael and his brother-in-law.

The first street is Szkolna where the first building listed was the synagogue. The plot was bought from the Bishop of Przemyśl.

At the end of the list is a statement of a translator that reads:

> I, Jewish Sworn Translator, hereby state righteously [Witkowsky's note: form of an oath in old Polish] that these are all the homesteads that have been taken by the Extract from the ancient Protocols in Przemyśl . . . in the year 1783. Herszel Szymon, Jewish Sworn Translator.

Sanok, 1692. The document, a contemporary copy of a three-page handwritten extract from *lustracja* (literal meaning is "bringing to light") on ul. Lwówska Zydowska, for the year 1692, in a town identified only in a handwritten marginal note as Sanok. The document is primarily in Polish with some Latin words. The document . . . consists of a listing, without house numbers, of parcels of land, improved and unimproved. Limited information provides only the names of the owners or their successors. In some cases, the usage of the property or other data about the owner is included.

[Because the handwriting is poorly reproduced and the references not always known to me,] I was able to identify only a few items and names . . . here are the first four entries and the extent to which I was able to decipher them:

- A corner tenement house of the successors of Jeb (?), on one half of the parcel
- A tenement house, major part masonry, part wood, [owned by] [Boruchowski], on the whole parcel; rear empty"
- A tenement house of Mendel Solski, . . . now in possession of His Excellency Castellan Zinowski, in which tenement house lives the Jewish widow selling mead in a saloon occupying the whole place
- A tenement house of . . . [title] Michal Strojoski (?) on the whole parcel, rear empty, saloon, beer (?) sold by . . . [name undecipherable]

In addition, the other names deciphered are:

Marek Korzenek, Alexander Moszkowicz, Chocimski, Mojszek Czopownik, Jakub Medycki (?), Mendel Skoczylas, Lewko Dawidowicz, Zajkiel (?) Slomonowicz, Prygier Family and Prygier's son-in-law, Jakub, Jozef Sabceporow (?), Hertz Aronowicz, Szlomo Sukiennik, Szymon, Dawidowski, Dawid, Rybotycki, Szmul Moszkowicz, Abraham the Barber, Aron Muhatowicz, Moszek Blawatnik, Aron Berlinski (?), Bednarzewski, Majer, Chruscielski, Kwiatkiewicz, Teodor Bronislowicz (?) and brothers, Mendel, Aron ("the same parcel of land as the slaughterhouse"), and Marek Szmuklerz.

Jewish National and University Library

In an article in *ZichronNote*, vol. XIV, No.1, the newsletter of the San Francisco Bay Area Jewish Genealogical Society, Robert Weiss lists the *pinkassim*, or record books that, as of 1984, were held by the Jewish National and University Library in Jerusalem. Weiss's intent was to update Alsberg's 1981 *Guide to Jewish Archives*. A small number of holdings are for towns formerly in Galicia. Locations are listed by the current town name. Accession/location numbers follow the entry.

Community	Type of Record, Dates	Accession Number
Bukachevtsy	*Khevra kadisha*, 1750–1840	4'83
Ivano-Frankovsk	*Gemilut khasadi, hakhnasat orkhim*, 1813	4'348
Kozłów	*Khevra kadisha*, 1815–1948	4'1126
Kraków	Synagogue pulpit book, 1919	8'2417
	Record of deaths, synagogue of Rabbi Meir Dayan	(unknown)
Kraków	Memorial Book, 1631–1787	8'2382
Kraków	Memorial Book, 1713	8'2130
Śnyatyn	*Khevra Bikkur Kholim*, 1866	4'45

Jewish Historical Institute

The Ronald S. Lauder Foundation's Genealogy Project is housed at the Jewish Historical Institute. Yale Reisner is the Genealogy Project's executive director. The project's priorities have been to preserve the institute's archival material and to attend to inquiries from people who are Holocaust survivors or Poles who have discovered that they were either hidden children (during the Holocaust) or whose parents chose to hide the fact of their Judaism.

Most of the institute's holdings for Galicia concern Kraków and towns surrounding that city. Additionally, the Institute holds master's and doctoral theses on Jewish themes from the prewar and postwar periods among which are histories of Jewish communities. It also holds Jewish communal records, including cemetery records, documents from synagogue authorities that include lists of Jewish residents eligible to vote, and similar types of lists. The institute also has lists of Polish survivors compiled in 1945–46.

The institute's rich collection of material from Kraków, 1701–1942, includes marriage bann books for the liberal congregation of Kraków and twelve prewar *yahrzeit* (anniversary of death) calendars for the Remu synagogue that list the *yahrzeit* dates for members of the congregation each month.

The address for the Institute is:

Zydowski Instytut Historyczny w Polsce
00-900 Warszawa
ul. Tłomackie 3/5

The project welcomes financial assistance to continue its work in preservation and cataloging of fragile material. Be sure to note on your check that the money is intended for the Polish Genealogy Project. Send your checks to:

Ronald S. Lauder Foundation
767 Fifth Avenue, Suite 4200
New York, NY 10153

Drogobych, Poland (now Drohobych, Ukraine). Photo early 1920s.

❋ Chapter 4 ❋

Holocaust-Related Sources

Events during the Holocaust not only resulted in the destruction of approximately six million Jewish lives but also the destruction of a way of life. The once vital Jewish communities were crushed, especially those in Eastern Europe. It is no longer possible to visit towns in Ukraine and Poland to see living, thriving Jewish communities that produced our ancestors.

Jews engaged in researching their families find themselves confronting the reality that they lost relatives in the Holocaust. We do honor to ourselves and to the memory of our ancestors when we research the loves of those who were martyrs to the Nazi war machine. But there is the reality that records and other material relative to genealogical research were destroyed. Furthermore, we cannot easily learn from what we find today in ancestral towns what life was like before the Holocaust; therefore, our task in researching our ancestral heritage is made more difficult.

The resources for conducting such research are continually growing. Records maintained by the German government regarding military operations during World War II (including mass killing operations of Jews and other undesirables) and records of concentration camps have been available for some time. Many surviving records are at the U.S. National Archives and Records Administration. They exist on microfilm and are in German. The collapse of Communism has made available records of the former Soviet Union, microfilm copies of which have been acquired by the U.S. Holocaust Memorial Museum. Some of these newly available records are testimonies of eye witnesses; others are administrative records of German management of prisons, camps and other facilities located in Poland and Ukraine.

Many Jews who survived the Holocaust chose to be silent for decades about their experiences during that period. Now many are publishing memoirs or giving oral testimonies about these experiences. Although it was been more than 50 years since the Holocaust ended, new memorials and institutions are being created that house records—written, visual and oral—to assure that the world never forgets what happened.

Yizkor Books

Yizkor books are memorial books written by Holocaust survivors about the towns or regions from which they came. Of the known 1,000+ yizkor books, many have been written about Galician towns. Most are written entirely in Hebrew and/or Yiddish; few include English-language sections. Although most books were written within 20 years of the end of the war, some new *yizkor* books have been published within the past few years.

Yizkor books are variable in content, quality and style, but they generally include photos of places and people, hand-drawn maps of the town, personal memories of what it was like to live in the community, and a list of those who were killed in the Holocaust. Some books include information about community residents who survived and went to Israel, the United States, or South or Central America, or who remained in Europe. Most books include surname and/or topic indexes; even when they do not, however, the books are an important source of information.

Some of the books include some mention of, or even articles about, surrounding villages and towns. Another feature of many *yizkor* books is that they often include lists of residents or taxpayers or other types of listings that provide information from records of which one would not ordinarily have awareness, much less access. For instance, the *yizkor* book for Nowy Sącz includes an 1866 list of Jewish taxpayers.

Chapter 9 of this book includes information about Gesher Galicia members who have information to share about *yizkor* books for particular towns or regions.

Yad Vashem in Israel has the most complete set of *yizkor* books. In North America, large collections of these books are held by major Jewish libraries and some public and university libraries. YIVO Institute for Jewish Research in New York City has the most complete set; the Library of Congress, the second largest.

Many lists of *yizkor* books have been published. Since books are still being printed, the most current list is invariably the most comprehensive. Some such lists include:

• Zachary Baker, YIVO's chief librarian, over the years has compiled and maintained an extensive listing of *yizkor* books. His list was published originally in 1979/80. The most recent version is in Arthur Kurzweil's *From Generation to Generation*, 2nd edition, (New York: HarperCollins, 1994).

• *Genealogical Resources in the New York Metropolitan Area*, Estelle Guzik, (New York: Jewish Genealogical Society, Inc., 1989), included Zachary Baker's list of *yizkor* books then available in New York repositories.

• *From a Ruined Garden: Memorial Books of Polish Jewry* by Jack Kugelmass and Jonathan Boyarin (New York: Schocken Books, 1983) contains an annotated, alphabetical listing of towns for which there were *yizkor* books published to that date.

The Galician towns in the following list have *yizkor* books or are mentioned in the *yizkor* books given in parentheses. In addition, two memorial books cover many towns in Galicia: *Gedenkbuch Galicia* and *Pinkas Galicia*, both edited by N. Zucker and published in Buenos Aires, in 1964 and 1945 respectively.

Language code: H=Hebrew; Y=Yiddish; E=English; P=Polish; O=other

Andrychów (*see* Wadowice)
Baligród (*see* Lesko)
Baranów, 1964 (H/Y/E)
Baryłów near Brody (*see* Radziechów)
Bełż, 1974 (H/Y)
Biecz, 1960 (H/Y)
Bielsko Biała, 1973 (H/O)
Bóbrka, 1964 (H/Y/E)
Bolechów, 1957 (H/Y)
Borszczów, 1960 (H/Y)
Borysław (*see* Drohobycz)
Brody (*see* Arim, vol. 6)
Brzesko, 1980 (H/Y)
Brżezany, 1978 (H/Y/E)
Brzozów, about 1985 (E/Y/H)
Buczacz, 1956 (H)
Budzanów, 1968 (H/Y/E)
Bukowsko (*see* Sanok)
Bursztyn, 1960 (H/Y)
Busk, 1965 (H/Y/E/P)
Chołojów (*see* Radziechów)
Chorostków, 1968 (H/Y)
Chrzanów, 1948
Cieszanów, 1970 (H/Y)
Czarny Dunajec (*see* Nowy Targ)
Czortków, 1967 (H/Y/E)
Dębica, 1960 (H/Y)

Dobromil, 1964 (H/E)
Drohobycz, 1959 (H/Y)
Dubiecko (*see* Dynów)
Dynów, 1949/50 (Y)
Dynów, 1979 (H/Y)
Felsztyn, 1937 (Y/E)
Gliniany, 1945, 52 pages (Y);
   1950, 307 pages (H)
Gorlice, 1962 (H/Y)
Gródek Jagielloński, 1981 (H)
Hordenka, 1963 (H/Y)
Husiatyn, 1977 (H/Y)
Jabłonka (*see* Nowy Targ)
Janów (near Trembowla; see
   Budzanów and Trembowla)
Jarosław, 1978 (Y/E)
Jasło, 1953 (H)
Jaworów, 1950 (Y/E)
Jaworów, 1979 (H/Y)
Jezierzany, (H/Y)
Jordanów (*see* Nowy Targ)
Kalusz, 1980 (H/Y/E)
Kalwarja Zebrzydowice (*see*
   Wadowice)
Knihynicze (*see* Rohatyn)
Kolbuszowa, 1971 (H/Y/E)
Kolomyya, 1957
Kolomyya, 1971/2 (H)

Kopyczyńce (*see* Husiatyn)
Korczyna, 1967 (H/Y)
Kossów, 1964 (H/Y)
Kossów, 1981 (Y)
Kraków, 1959 (H)
Kraków (*see* Arim, vol. 3)
Krakówiec (*see* Jaworów)
Kuty, 1958
Łancut, 1963 (H/Y/E)
Lemberg (*see* Lvov)
Lesko/Lisko, 1965 (H/Y)
Leżajsk, 1970 (H/Y)
Łopatyn (*see* Radziechów)
Lutowiska (*see* Lesko)
Lvov (*see* Arim Vol. 1)
Lvov, 1956, (H)
Maków Podhalański (*see* Nowy
   Targ)
Medenice (*see* Drohobycz)
Mielec, 1979 (Y)
Mikałajów (*see* Radziechów)
Monasterzyska, 1974 (H/Y/E)
Mosty Wielki, 2 vols. 1975, 1977
   (H/Y/E)
Myślenice (*see* Wadowice)
Nadwórna, 1975 (H/Y/E)
Narajów (*see* Brzeżany)
Nowy Sącz, 1970 (H/Y)

Nowy Targ, 1979 (H/Y/E)
Oświecim, 1977 (H/Y)
Perehińsko (see Rozniatów)
Podhajce, 1972 (H/Y/E)
Przecław (see Radomysl Wielkie)
Przemyśl, 1964 (H/Y)
Rabka (see Nowy Targ)
Radomyśl Wielki, 1965 (H/Y/E)
Radziechów, 1976 (H/Y)
Rawa Ruska, 1973 (H/Y/E)
Rohatyń, 1962 (H/Y/E)
Rożniatów, 1974 (H/Y/E)
Rozwadów, 1968 (H/Y/E)
Rudki, 1978
Rymanów, 198? (H)
Rzeszów, 1967 (H/Y/E)
Sambor, 1970 (H)
Sambor, 1980 (H/Y/E)
Sanok (see Dynów)
Sanok, 1970 (H/Y)
Sassów, 1979 (Y)
Sienków (see Radziechów)
Skała, 1978 (H/Y/E)

Skałat, 1971 (H)
Skole (see Gedenkbukh Galicia)
Sokal, 1968 (H/Y)
Stanisławczyk (see Radziechów)
Stanisławów (see Arim vol. 5)
Stary Sambor (see Sambor)
Stojanów (see Kokal)
Strusów (see Trembowla)
Stryj, 1962 (H/Y/E)
Strzemilcze (see Radziechów)
Strzyżów, 1969 (H/Y)
Strzyżów, 198? English
    translation of and additions to
    above by Harry Langsam, 745
    N. Croft Avenue, Los Angeles,
    CA 90069
Sucha (see Wadowice)
Swaryczów (see Rozniatów)
Szczurowice (see Radziechów)
Tarnobrzeg, 1973 (H/Y)
Tarnopol, 1955 (H/Y/E)
Tarnów, vol. 1, 1954; vol. 2, 1968
    (H/Y)

Tłumacz, 1976 (H/Y/E)
Tłuste, 1965 (H/Y)
Toporów (see Radziechów)
Trembowla, 198? (H/E)
Trzebinia, 1969 (H/E)
Turka, 1966 (H/E)
Tyśmienica, 1974 (H/Y)
Uhnów, 1981 (H)
Ustrzyki Dolne (see Lesko)
Wadowice, 1967 (H/Y)
Wieliczka, 1980 (H/Y/E/P)
Wiszniew, 1972 (H/Y)
Wiśniowa, 1972 (H/Y)
Witków Nowy (see Radziechów)
Zabłotów, 1949 (H/Y)
Zagórz (see Sanok)
Zakopane (see Nowy Targ)
Zarszyn (see Sanok)
Zawidcze (near Brody) (see
    Radziechów)
Zborów, 1975 (H/Y)
Złoczów, 1967
Żółkiew, 1969 (H)

JewishGen *Yizkor* Book SIG

JewishGen sponsors a Special Interest Group that collects and disseminates information about *yizkor* books. For those with access to the Internet, you can contact the SIG in several ways. There is a World Wide Web site at <http://www.jewishgen.org/yizkor.html>. An information file about the SIG is available by e-mail at <yizkor-info@jewishgen.org>; another information file identifying libraries with collections of *yizkor* books is at <yizlibs@jewishgen.org>.

The SIG is trying to catalog all *yizkor* books known to exist and to determine who in the network of Jewish genealogists might have personal copies. They also have information about library collections of *yizkor* books, commercial book sellers who carry *yizkor* books, and translators who have expressed a willingness to assist with translations. Ideally, the SIG can help groups of people interested in the same towns find each other so that the cost of translation projects can be shared. If you own a *yizkor* book, have translated all or a portion of a book (including an index), need to find a book, or want to know who else is interested in financing a translation efforts, contact the SIG.

The current coordinator of the SIG is Martin Kessel. He can be contacted by writing to him at 43 Water Street, Natick MA 01760; e-mail: <mkessel@world.std.com>.

Pinkas Hakehillot

Yad Vashem has published more than 15 volumes of a series that describes the Jewish presence in Central and Eastern Europe from the earliest times to the Holocaust. Known as *Pinkas Hakehillot* (Encyclopedia of Towns), two are relevant to Galicia:
• Poland vol. 2 Eastern Galicia, 1980
• Poland vol. 3 Western Galicia and Silesia, 1984

The *Pinkas Hakehillot* series, according to the Summer 1993 issue of *Avotaynu*, can be purchased through Rubin Mass, Ltd., P.O. Box 990, Jerusalem 91009. Phone: (02) 632-565; fax: (02) 632-719.

Sources for *Yizkor* Books and Pinkas Hakehillot

The *Yizkor* Book Special Interest Group has compiled a list of sources for *yizkor* books in the United States and Israel. Most *yizkor* books are now out of print. The sources below make efforts to buy unwanted *yizkor* books or to obtain them from the heirs of deceased owners of *yizkor* books for resale. If you are seeking a particular book, it is best to contact every source to inquire about availability, condition of the book and price.

U.S. Sources

Aurora Fine Books
547 W. 27th Street, Suite 570
New York, NY 10001
phone: (212) 947-0422

Historicana
1200 Edgehill Drive
Burlingame, CA 94010
phone: (415) 343-9578

Ideal Book Store
1125 Amsterdam Avenue
New York, NY 10025
phone: (718) 662-1909

Judaix Art
P.O. Box 248
Monsey, NY 10952
phone: (914) 352-03592

Erich Chaim Kline
P.O. Box 829
Santa Monica, CA 90406
phone: (310) 395-4747

Isaac H. Mann
240 W. 98th Street
New York, NY 10025
phone: (212) 230-671

Schoen Books
7 Sugarloaf Street
S. Deerfield, MA 01373

Schwartz Judaica
1934 Pentuckett Avenue
San Diego, CA 92104
phone: (619) 233-5833
e-mail <Schwartz@cts.com>

Israeli Sources

Chaim E. Dzialowski
P.O. Box 6413
Jerusalem 91063, Israel

Nun Bet Books
6 Ben Yehuda Street
Tel Aviv 63801, Israel
phone: (03) 6204-81

Pinhat ha-Sefer
P.O. Box 46646
Haifa 31465, Israel

J. Robinson and Co.
31 Nachlat Benjamin Street
Tel Aviv 65162, Israel
phone: (03) 5605461
e-mail: rob_book@netvision.net.il

Moshe Schreiber
Mea Shearim Street 16
Jerusalem, Israel

Jacob Twersky
20 Sheinkin Street
P.O. Box 4356
Tel Aviv, Israel

National Yiddish Book Center

Gesher Galicia member Muriel Singer Friedman, a board member of the National Yiddish Book Center, has offered to help individuals find books they need through this organization. Write to her at 8994 S.W. 68 Place, Miami, FL 33156 USA; e-mail: <murielfriedman@msn.com>.

Holocaust-Related Institutions and Collections

[Jeffrey Cymbler contributed substantially to the information in this section]

Yad Vashem

A Guide to Jewish Genealogical Research in Israel: Revised Edition by Sallyann Amdur Sack and Israel Genealogical Society (Teaneck, N.J.: Avotaynu, 1993) offers excellent background on Yad Vashem and its holdings. In addition to an exhaustive collection of *yizkor* books and Holocaust testimonials, the library has acquired a modest collection of published and unpublished genealogies.

A list of 10,000 Jews who died in the Lwów ghetto has been acquired by Yad Vashem from the Ukrainian archives in Lviv. The list, Record Group M37/88, was prepared by officials of the Jewish cemetery during 1941–42. It is in chronological order and includes the descendent's age, date of death and residence in Lemberg (Lwów/Lviv).

Yad Vashem also has microfilms that list the names of concentration camp victims and survivors. The original material, compiled by the International Committee of the Red Cross from many sources, is now in Arolsen, Germany. The records can be viewed only at Yad Vashem. Write to Yad Vashem at Har Hazikaron, P.O. Box 3477, Jerusalem 91034.

U.S. Holocaust Memorial Museum

The U.S. Holocaust Memorial Museum in Washington, D.C., 100 Raoul Wallenberg Place SW, Washington DC 20024-2150, has an extensive collection of material about the Holocaust on microfilm and microfiche. The vast majority of this material came from the German records captured by the Allies as the war was ending, but some of it was generated by postwar investigations of Nazi war crimes. Of particular interest are sections of the archives collection for Ukraine (Record Group 31) and Poland (Record Group 15). The material can be accessed on the fifth floor of the Museum by visiting the archives located next to the library.

The library and archives are open seven days a week. However, if you plan to use the facilities on the weekend, you must notify the staff in advance because the material must be pulled for you on Friday. Weekend staffing is very limited. The facilities are excellent. Keep in mind that material from these collections are in languages other than English.

An agreement between the museum and the International Committee of the Red Cross (ICRC) has facilitated the transfer of microfilms of more than 25,000 pages of Holocaust-era material to the museum's archives. According to *Washington Jewish Week* (December 26, 1996, page 6), the documents "contain official reports on ICRC rescue missions, delegation visits to concentration camps and ghettos, deportation operations, and Jewish emigration before and after the war. Many of the pages include photographs relating to World War II and the postwar years in Europe." Microfilms of some documents were also deposited, under this agreement, with Yad Vashem and the Center for Jewish Documentation in Paris.

The U.S. Holocaust Memorial Archives website offers access to approximately 1,050 catalog entries describing manuscript collections and approximately 60 finding aids to microfilm collections, including records from the Main Commission for the Investigation of Crimes Against the Polish Nation, Warsaw, and various archives of the former Soviet Union. A full-word indexing search engine is available to query both the library and archives catalog. Contact the archives staff by e-mail at <archives@ushmm.org>. The website is: <http://www.ushmm.org>.

The Polish form of the towns names are used below.

Ukraine, Record Group 31

The Polish form of the towns names are used in describing this record group.

RG31.002M. Selected records from the Ukrainian Central State Archive in Kiev. Name lists of persons killed in various villages (in Russian). (14 reels)

RG31.003M. Selected records from what at the time of filming was the Lviv Oblast Archive (1 reel). This reel includes a list of names of about 13,000 Jews, most of whom were men born or resident in Lwów or neighboring towns. Plans have been cited for this list to be placed on the museum's website. These records were created when individuals applied for German passes to leave their ghettos to work in factories and other establishments, in an effort to prevent their deportation to camps. In most cases, the list provides only names and local addresses.

Fond 24. Records documenting the creation of ghettos on November 25, 1942, in Gródek, Jaworów, Rudki, Szczerzec, Bóbrka, Jaryczów Nowy and Zolkiew; disposition of registers for Jews in Lwów; correspondence; name lists of Jews (including birthplaces and dates from several towns in the vicinity of Lwów), 1942–43.

Fond 31. Order establishing Lwów ghetto, July 22, 1941.

Fond 35. List of Jewish physicians in Lwów.

Fond 37. Population statistics for Gródek Jagielloński, Janów, Jaworów, Sadowa Wiśnia, Rudki, Mosciska and Komarno regions, by community, nationality and Jewish population; Jews employed by Lwów city departments; labor utilization of POWs and Jews in labor camps and ghettos; Jewish workers in city agencies, etc.

Fond 56. Jews employed in Bolechów, Drohobycz, Skole and Broszniów.

Fond 85. Transit permission for Jews employed in Borysław and insurance matters for Jews working for German firms in Lwów.

Fonds 2042 and 1951. Records from the Drohobycz city administration.

Fond 1952. Material about Stryy and more transit passes for Jews in Drohobycz; work permits for Jews in Skole.

RG31.005*01. Records relating to Ukrainian Jews in Lwów.

RG31.006M. Selected records from what, at the time of filming, was the Czernovitz Oblast Archive (11 reels).

Poland, Record Group 15

RG15.003M. Records of the Office of the Gouvernment Kommissar for the Productivity of the Jewish Population (3 reels).

RG15.008M. Records of German occupation, 1939–45 (8 reels) (not yet available).

RG15.010M. Records of the Institut fur Deutsche Ostarbeit in Kraków. There is little about Jews, but for the town of Jarosław, the family Seitelbach was mentioned in 1943: Abraham, b. 1898; Maria, b. 1900; Sura, b. 1925; David, b. 1928. Numerous charts are included that list surnames taken from birth records dating 1777–1943, with the number of persons with those surnames for either every year, or, in some cases, every 10 years. For instance, for the town of Biecz: Gotfried, Kraus, Guter, Furst, First, Heller, Horn, Mayer, Muller, Rajman, Salamon, Saidel, Zaydel, Wolff and Schindler. In the town of Błazowa, an incident in 1943 resulted in the deaths of 23 Jews: Mayer Spiss, age 45, a rabbi; Baruch Wiesenfeld, age 65, merchant; Leib Sturm, age 43, merchant; Moses Katz, age 48, merchant; Ruchla Weiss, age 33, merchant; Leiba Leinhard, age 25, merchant; Symcha Heischuber, age 41; Moses Steppel, age 18; Kelman Wang, age 46; Efroim Sturm, age 39; Berl Horstein, age 45. Also included were 12 others whose names were unknown, with 2 Jews from Kalisz.

RG15.019M. Court inquiries about executions and graves in various places in Poland. A number of reels are of significance to Jews, but considerable effort is needed to extract the relevant information. Reels 3, 4, 10, 11, 14, 15 and 17 seem most pertinent. This record group is composed of questionnaires generated in 1945. Entirely in Polish, they document the knowledge of Poles and Ukrainians about the executions and mass killings of Jews and others. One item specifically seeks to identify, by ethnic group, those who had been victimized. Some of the questionnaires name individuals; others estimate the number killed in the action described. Where mass killings took place in cemeteries and elsewhere, the number of dead was estimated. Within each district, small towns are listed alphabetically. Not surprisingly, most of the individuals mentioned by name were not Jewish. When Jews are mentioned, some information is usually given beyond the name, such as age, occupation, and circumstances surrounding the person's death.

- *Reel 3.* Sections 8 and 9 refer to Kraków and the surrounding district: Bochnia, Biała Krakowska, Brzesko, Chrzanów, Dąbrowa Tarnowska, Limanowa and Miechów.
- *Reel 4.* Continues with Section 9 communities; Section 10: districts of Myślenice, Nowy Sącz and Nowy Targ; Section 11: districts of Olkusz, Tarnów, Wadowice and Żywiec.
- *Reel 10.* Section 33: districts of Rzeszów, Brzozów, Dębica, Gorlice and Jarosław; Section 34: districts of Jasło, Kolbuszowa, Krosno, Lesko and Lubaczów.
- *Reel 11.* Section 35: districts of Łancut, Mielec and Nisko; Section 36: districts of Przemyśl, Przeworsk, and Rzeszów; Section 37: districts of Sanok and Tarnobrzeg.

  From *Łancut powiat* (district): Symcha Safier; Izrael Wegier; Markus Weinberg; Golda Goldman; ? Kornblau; ? Mendel; Fass from Wysoka; Besenstock from Łancut; Weissman, age 60; Maria Wolkenfeld; Josef and Moses Fenig; Lazar Kestcher; Izrael Anmuth; Mendel Feuer; Moses Sauer; Maier Rozmarin and wife; Sara and Frimet Wurm; Kalman Walkenfeld and wife; Feiga Schwanenfeld and three children; Fiege Rosenfeld and two children; Boruch Reichard, his wife, Mala, and daughter Elka; Mira Low, Szulem Low and two children; Serla Speigel; Chana and Scheindel Rosenfeld. In another questionnaire: Josef Kanner, age 45; Mendel Lindenbaum, age 30; N. Bitner, age 40;

Majlech Lorberbaum, age 22; Mojeszez Lorberbaum, age 24; N. Cuker, age 26 from Sarzyna near Rudnik.

From town of Żołynia: ? Weiss, Isak Schuck, Joel Felter and wife.

From *Mielec* powiat: Town of *Borowa*: Moses Hirschfeld; Abraham Horowitz; Moses Birnbaum, his wife and three children; David Kupperman; Haskiel Bluth; Jakub Kass; Pinkas and Aron Spialter; Jakub and Maarkus Horn; Wolf and Joachim Storch; Isaak Klagsburn and wife; Abraham Storch; Leib Grun and wife; Moses Weiser, wife and three children; Josef Storch, wife and 3 children; Kahl family.

Town of *Czernia*: Mendel Mebsinger (one born 1910, the other born 1912); Raiza Gross, age 60; Matylda Gross, age 35; Hersch Braw, age 60, his wife, age 30; daughter, 15; and son, 12; Leib Kornbluth, age 40, and Cyla Kornbluth, age 60.

Town of *Przeclaw*: Jakob Jam; April Manes; Male Kopel; Fiege Silber.

From *Nisko powiat*: Josef Rothbard, born 1894; wife, born 1903; Markus and Yenta Krell.

From *Przemyśl powiat*: Town of Dubiecko: List of 80 people, mostly Jews, killed in Dubiecko, though many came from other communities in the vicinity, including Drohobycz, Kańczuga, Jawornik Polski, Iskan, Hucisko, Nienadowa. Surnames include Frieder, Rubinfeld, Lamper, Ringel, Hofner, Pechter, Kanner, Meller, Eisbart, Unger, Herfenist, Grudzewski, Domb, Baruch, Binder, Zeichner, Jaworniker, Gluksman and Tewel.

Town of Nienadowa, suburb of Dubiecko: Natan Unger, age 16; Etla Glucksman, age 61; Zeiger Gluksman, age 24; Markus Harfenist and numerous other Harfenist family members. Schimmel, Jaworniker, Adler and Hofner. Page 490: Sara and Isak Knoller; page 491: Samuel Landau and Jozef Schimmel; page 492: Aron, Sara and David Domb; Natan Meller; page 493: Simche Tisser, Samuel Strassler, N. and N. Dornbusch; page 495: Moses Harfenist; page 497: Leidnerow; page 498: Kańczuga and the Spitz family from Bacie.

From Przeworsk powiat: Town of Krzywcza: Rosner, Chaji Hersch; Aron and Srul Freifeld; David Wassner; Mendel and Jankiel Pelner; Moses Fast; Chaim Grumet.

Town of Orzechowice: page 501: Samuel Ehrenfreund.

Town of Rybotycze: David Rubenfeld, age 56; Moses Amster, age 60; Moses Rubenfeld, age 45; Michael Rubenfeld, age 58; Simche ?; Leib Dank.

Town of Kańczuga: Page 514: Berkowa Adler, age 43; Juda Harfenist, age 40; Jankiel Nadel, age 45; Hana Nadel, age 40; Josek Hoch, age 40, and Brandla ?, age 40.

Town of Frysztak: Chune Wolf Zanger, Josef Puderbeitel and Berisch Schlesinger.

Town of Markowa: Gartenhaus family: Kaila, age 38; Szmuel, age 20; Ryfka, age 17; Szmuel, age 15; Jankiel, age 13. Several additional lists.

Town of Jawornik Polski: Page 594: Springer family; Chaje Blau, age 50; Jacob Spitz, age 88; Leib Chiel, age 84; Chaskiel Speigel, age 60; Chaya and ? Speigel; Daniel Gerstler, age 50; Chaja Beck, age 48.

Town of Strzyżów: page 635: David Leiberman, b. August 1, 1884; Dr. Franciszek Rosenthal recte Koppleman, attorney, b. 1894; Samuel Zeinwel Grunblatt, b. June 18, 1893; Samul Grosskopf, b. May 6, 1872; Jakub Rosen, b. July 25, 1892; Moses Scheffler, b. December 6, 1877; Pinkas Klein, b. June 7, 1886; Chaim Salamon Flaumenhaft, b. May 21, 1884.

Town of Kolaczyce: page 636: Nates Stern.

Town of Bukowsko: page 661: 100 Jews listed.

From Rzeszów powiat: Town of Błazowa: page 535 describes an "action" resulting in the deaths of 23 Jews, among them were surnames: Spiss, Wiesenfeld, Sturm, Katz, Weiss, Leinhard, Heischuber, Steppel, Wang and Horstein.

From Sanok powiat:

Town of Rymanów: page 679: Hersch and Ester Pinkas; Josef and Dora Morchower; Ruchel
   Singer; Abraham and Moses Wolf; Markus Stoff and wife; Eisig Bobik; Jozel Sponder;
   Isaak Schamroth.
Town of Szczawne: page 690: families Kresch, Kornreich, Fall, Kessler, Feibus, Kiern and
   Symchowitz.
Town of Bażanówka: page 692: Henia Diller, b. 1922; Gizella Diller, b. 1927.
Town of Jacmierz: page 696: Abraham Wilner, b. 1876; Isela Sturn, b. 1910; Leon Sturm,
   b. 1938; Henie Sturm, b. 1939; Josef Brand, b. 1904; Abraham Spira, b. 1914; Regina
   Spira, b. 1919.
Town of Zarszyn: ? Wilner, b. 1902; David Goldstend, b. 193?; Moses Goldstend, b. 1932;
   Ruchel Brand, b. 1940. On page 790: Aron, Golda and Isak Strenger.
• *Reel 14*. Section 48: Kraków; Section 48a: Myślenice, Nowy Sącz, Nowy Targ, Olkusz,
   Tarnów, Wadowice and Żywiec.
• *Reel 15*. Continuation of reel 14.
• *Reel 17*. Section 58: the same districts as reel 10.

Specific Town Names

On Reel 10, there are some inquiries about Jewish deaths in towns in the Rzeszów area.
Mentioned as having died in one incident in Dukla: Helena Zajdel, David, Josef and Jakob Krill;
Jankiel and Israel Altholz; Benek Scherer; Moses Zehngut, age 48; Naftali Stein, age 32; Feitel
Stein, Isak Gutwirt; Israel and Tyla Fries; ? Zimerspitz; Majer Hechtschrifen; Chaim Spira.

In Nadole, near Dukla, Abraham and Herz Hendler, David Blechner and Josef Maum (?) were
mentioned. There were also names from other towns in the vicinity. There were numerous lists of
Jews with names, ages and occupations for towns around Lubaczów, including Oleszyce. One page
included photos of three Grief men and Aba Engel from Oleszyce.

A questionnaire from a Łancut court documented the deaths of Wachs family members along
with members of the Stein, Haftel, Leiberman, Gross, Blumenfeld and Turkenkopf families. On the
other hand, questionnaires from many towns merely noted the approximate numbers of Jews killed
in various *Actions*.

Another type of record on this reel charts the surnames of people born in various towns from
1777 to 1942, listing the number of individuals with each surname.

RG15.020M: Selected records from the Polish State Archive in Tarnów (11 reels; not yet
   available).
RG03.017*01 (flat file, drawer 1) consists of paper records relating to Jews from Mielnica, Poland.
RG15.024M: Records of Deutsche Strafanstalt Reichshof (German Prison in Rzeszów) and other
   prisons in the area, including Tarnów, Nowy Wiśnicz, Kraków and Jasło. Included are lists of
   Jews held in the Rzeszów prison (17 reels).

Other Holocaust-Related Materials

The Blackbook of Localities Whose Jewish Population was Exterminated by the Nazis (Jerusalem:
Yad Vashem, 1965). This book identifies some 32,000 towns in Central and Eastern Europe giving
town name and population before the Holocaust (exact year of census varies by country). The towns
are organized by district within each country. An consolidated alphabetical list of towns
independent of country/district is available on microfiche through Avotaynu, Inc.

*The Einsatzgruppen Reports: Selections from the Dispatches of the Nazi Death Squads' Campaign
Against the Jews, July 1941–January 1943*, edited by Yitzhak Arad, Shmuel Krakowski and Shmuel
Spector, was published in 1989 by The Holocaust Library of New York in cooperation with Yad
Vashem in Jersualem. This 370-page English-language book describes, from Germany's daily
reports, what the killing squads did to carry out the policy of annihilating the Jews in an area that
extended from the Caucasus, Crimea and Ukraine in the south through the Baltic states in the
north. Four main *Einsatzgruppen*—lettered A, B, C, and D—consisting of up to a thousand soldiers
each, killed nearly two million Jews in mass gassings, mass and individual shootings or hangings,

or other actions in or just outside of villages. Excerpts from translated German reports, which are arranged chronologically, describe what happened to many Jews during the Holocaust. These reports sometimes indicate that Russians and Ukrainians were deeply involved in killing each other in Ukraine and that Ukrainians, as well as Germans, actively participated in killing Jews.

B'Uvdan Moladity by Abraham Grussgott. Moishe Miller reported this book to be a good source of birth information for about 2,400 Jews who fled the Germans by going across the Tylicz Pass to Bardejov and Slovakian border towns and who were, for various reasons, not deported from Bardejov in 1942. The book contains name, birthdate, city of birth, occupation, and the reason they were not deported. Many Jews born in Nowy Sącz, Tylicz, Kańczuga, Oświęcim, Sanok and Gorlice, as well as other towns in Galicia are listed. Gerald Klafter reported that of four people mentioned in the book as survivors, he managed to find two relatives in the Chicago area. Klafter traced Abraham Grussgott's last known address to 1505 E. 49th Street, Brooklyn, NY 11234; phone: (718) 241-0600.

Poland's Jewish Heritage by Joram Kagan (New York: Hippocrene Books, 1992). This slim volume is spotty in its information about Holocaust-related events and memorials in certain communities in Poland. In addition to occasionally mentioning Jewish history in a community, the author sometimes notes the existence of mass graves and the condition of cemeteries and synagogues. Concentration and death camp sites are discussed at some length, and drawings and photos of memorials at these sites are presented. The book is valuable as a guide to travelers in Poland.

Accounts of the Holocaust in Galician Towns and Cities

Ambrozowicz, Józef and Janusz Klich. *Dębica i okolice* (Dębica and environs) (Rzeszów: Agencja Wydawniczo-Reklamowa JOTA, 1994).

Gilbert, Martin. *The Boys* (New York: Henry Holt and Company, 1997). This 500+ page book offers a rich and deeply disturbing examination of some of the experiences of 732 children and youth who had survived the Holocaust and were rehabilitated in England. It also includes a chapter describing everyday life in prewar Galicia. Those survivors from Galicia identified by their original names and towns are listed below.

Harry Balsam (Gorlice)
Ken Roman (Gorlice)
Aryeh Czeret (Budzanów)
Simon Lecker (later Gilbert) (Rymanów)
Jan Goldberger (Bielsko Biała)
David Hirszfeld (Biesna and Bobowa)
Leopold "Lipa" Tepper (Dukla)
Salek Orenstein (Opatów)
Michael Perlmutter (Opatów)
Moshe Rosenberg (Kraków)
Jack and Israel Rubinfeld (Bircza)
Zvi Brand (Ulucz near Bircza)
Zisha "Jack" Schwimmer (Stróżówka and Gorlice)
Witold Gutt (Przemyśl)
Toby Trompeter (Mielec)
Nathan and Kurt Lewin (Lvov)
Mark Goldfinger (Rabka Zdrój)
Joseph Moss (Krosno)

Michael Honey (formerly Misa Honigwachs) was one of "the boys." His is a moving account of the difficulties survivors encountered in adjusting to normal life after their horrendous experiences.

Gilbert's index is less than complete. Oddly, the author did not acknowledge the contributions of all of those who provided him with their written or verbal memories, and the index reflects the same sort of spotty organization. Even more surprising was Gilbert's sometimes peculiar characterization of geographical locations. In failing to remember that Galicia had ended following World

War I, Gilbert compounded his error by placing towns from what had been Western Galicia in Eastern Galicia. Moreover, he dubbed Ukraine "Ruthenia" and incorrectly placed 1930 communities that were in Czechoslovakia in this mythical land. While these are minor distractions to the overall purpose and theme of the book, Gilbert's extensive publication experience on the subject of geography would have suggested a more accurate account of this topic.

Horowitz, Irene and Carl. *Of Human Agony* (New York: Shengold Publishers, 1992) Survival in Borysław and Lwów.

Horowitz, Irene and Carl et al. *Holocaust Revisited* (New York: Shengold Publishers, 1994). Focus on Borysław and Drohobycz.

Kahane, David. *Lvov Ghetto Diary* (Amherst: Ma.: University of Massachusetts Press, 1990).

Kornbluth, William. *Sentenced to Remember: My Legacy of Life in Pre-1939 Poland and Sixty-Eight Months of Nazi Occupation* (Bethlehem, Pa.: Lehigh University Press), in conjunction with the Brookdale Holocaust Center; distributed by Copyright Associates University Presses, Inc., 440 Forsgate Drive, Cranbury, NJ 08512 in 1994. The focus of the book is on Tarnów.

Mayer, Bernard. *Entombed* (Self published: 2100 NE 207 Street, North Miami Beach, FL 33179). This is an account of how the author, as a teenager, along with others built and survived in a bunker under a house in Drohobycz. Photos and diagrams are included.

Mogilansky, Roman. *The Ghetto Anthology* (Los Angeles: American Congress of Jews from Poland and Survivors of Concentration Camps, 1985). Includes description of many places in Galicia.

Rosenberg, Blanca. *To Tell at Last: Survival Under False Identity* (Urbana, Ill.: University of Illinois Press, 1993). How two young women from Kolomyya survived the Nazis by masquerading as gentiles in Kolomyya, Lvov, Warsaw and Germany.

Rothenberg, Samuel. *List o Zagladzie Zydow w Drohobyczu* (Letters about the extermination of Jews in Drohobycz), (London: Poets and Painters Press, 1984). 14 pages.

Salsitz, Norman and Amalie Petranker. *Against All Odds* (New York: Holocaust Library, 1990). Describes Kolbuszowa, Stanisławów and Kraków under Russian and German occupation.

Schiff, Meilach. *Lost Borysław* (New York: Vantage, 1977).

Suslensky, Yakov. *True Heros* The book is a touching account of the Holocaust in Ukraine, during which many Jews were saved by Ukrainians at a risk (and often at the cost) of their own deaths. The book is a combination of oral history by real-life participants of the Holocaust drama and the author's analysis of the events. The book contains numerous photographs, letters, poems dated from the time of the war to the present. To order, contact Tanya Puchkova, 20 College Drive, Roscommon, MI 48653.

Szende, Stefan. *The Promise Hitler Kept* (New York: Roy Publishers, 1944). This book offers a detailed description of what happened to Jews in Lwów during the Russian and German occupations.

Thorne, Leon. *Out of the Ashes: The Story of a Survivor* (New York: Rosebern Press, 1961). Thorne, now a rabbi in the U.S., was in the Drohobycz and Sambor ghettos until liberation. He also discusses Schodnica and Lwów.

Well, Leon. *Janowska Road* (New York: Macmillan Company, 1963). Wells provided an excellent description of Janowska Concentration-Death Camp outside of Lwów.

January 1940: Radiogram

Victor Low of Hanover, New Hampshire, contributed the following information and Radiogram. Victor's father, Sol Low, was born in Sędziszów, near Kraków, in 1895. After emigrating to the United States in 1910, Sol Low became an active member of the *Ershte Shendishover Galitzianer Chevrah*, a *landsmanschaftn*.

The preamble to the *landsmanschaftn's* statement of purpose said, "The goal of the society is to maintain the spirit of fraternity . . . That ideal is to be kept alive among the younger generation born in this land and an attempt must be made to plant in them an awareness of our origins" (translated by Irving Howe).

With the rise of Fascism in Europe at the turn of the 1930s, Dad founded and became president of the United Galician Jews of America. By the late 1930s, it had some 80,000 members, who twice sent him to investigate the prospects of Galician Jews. On his second return, he urged the delegates to the annual convention to empty the organization's coffers and their own pockets and rescue as many Galitzianers as still could be saved from the gathering Holocaust. He was viewed as an alarmist, voted down and resigned to become an active Zionist.

Dad died in 1959 and Mom lived on until 1982. Among the memorabilia she left is an RCA radiogram sent to my folks by Dr. Abraham Silberschein, a Polish Jew and an ex-member of the Polish Parliament. Datelined Geneva, January 3, 1940, it said:

> Two hundred persons released by our action from co-camp leaving next German. Among them [20 names given]. Passage deposed here by American relatives. Information relatives but not papers. Other names follow. Accelerate action. Danger. Needing urgently passage for 350 other Polish Jews in co-camp and Western Galicia."

When I read this in 1983, I asked, "Why not inform the papers?" The answer was self-given. A majority of Americans polled in that decade were anti-Semitic and were hostile or indifferent to the chief future victims of the Germans. And almost all Polish Jews stayed home rather than heed the rare voices prophesying a systematic destruction of them if they failed to seek refuge—or failed to find it, as so often occurred—outside of Poland.

❊ Chapter 5 ❊

Other Books and Resource Materials

Materials cited in this chapter have come from a number of contributors over the years, including David Einsiedler, Laurence Krupnak, Lorin S. Weisenfeld, Elliott Bernstein, Barbara Urbanska-Yeager, Morey Altman and Georges Rosenfeld. Some materials in this chapter are simply presented, while others are reviewed or annotated in some detail. This is not an exhaustive list of material, but most books listed here include bibliographies that might lead the reader to other sources. Jewish encyclopedias also include articles about Galicia, as well as articles about specific towns and personalities. Additionally, Yad Vashem has compiled brief histories of towns that are available both on site and by mail.

General References

Baxter, Angus. *In Search of Your European Roots* (Baltimore: Genealogical Publishing Co., 1985). According to Elliot Bernstein, this book mentions many documents currently in Austria, including census returns, movement registration, military records.

Chorzempa, Rosemary. *Korzenie Polskie: Polish Roots* (Baltimore: Genealogical Publishing Co., 1993). This book is a worthwhile investment for anyone interested in research in Poland. Little in Chapters 1–3 is useful to the Jewish researcher. They focus on information of interest to non-Jewish genealogists. Chapter 4 discusses the social and class structure of Polish society, which offers insights into Polish attitudes toward Jews. Chapters 5 and 6 discuss ethnic groups and geography in relation to these groups. Chapter 7 offers a useful, if elementary, discussion about using maps and gazetteers.

Chapters 10, 11, 13 and 14 comprise the heart of this book for Jewish genealogists. Chapter 10 covers civil and military records. Addresses for every branch office of the Polish National Archives are listed. Chapter 11 briefly touches on the highlights of surnames in the region. Chapter 13 provides an excellent guide to pronounciation of letters and letter combinations, grammatical peculiarities of the Polish language and a helpful, if overly brief, genealogical dictionary in Polish, Latin and German. Judith Frazin's 1989 book, *A Translation Guide to 19th Century Polish-Language Civil-Registration Documents* offers a far superior genealogical dictionary in Polish and a specific translation guide to documents written in the narrative style used in Russian Poland. Chapter 13 also includes terms commonly used in vital records, including terms for illnesses associated with deaths. Chapter 14 offers a good letter-writing guide. Most chapters end with a brief reading list.

Jewish References

Sack, Sallyann Amdur and the Israel Genealogical Society. *A Guide to Jewish Genealogical Research in Israel: Revised Edition* (Teaneck, N.J.: Avotaynu, NJ, 1993). This revised and expanded edition is a basic guide to research resources in Israel.

Avotaynu: The International Review of Jewish Genealogy is published quarterly. Address: P.O. Box 900, Teaneck, NJ 07666; e-mail: <info@avotaynu.com>; web: <http://www.avotaynu.com>. Since 1985, this quarterly has published numerous articles about researching Galician ancestry. Back issues are available including a CD-ROM version of all issues published from 1985 to 1996. The CD-ROM version includes a search engine with full-word indexing.

General Historical References

Austria. Statistische Zentralkommission. *Orts: Reportorium des Konigreiches Galizien und Lodomerien mit dem Grossherzogthume Krakau: aug Grunlage der Volszahlung vom Jahre 1869 bearbeitet von der k. k. statistischen Central-Commision* (Vienna: Gerold's, 1874). Reprinted in Berlin by H. Scherer, 1989 (OCLC: 26523709). This book provides summary census data for Galicia administrative districts.

Dohrn, Verena. *Reise durch Galizien: Grenlandschaften des alten Europa* (Frankfurt: Fischer Verlag). This book has a chapter describing Przemyśl.

History of Towns and Villages of the Ukrainian SSR: Lviv Oblast. The September 1992 issue of *East European Genealogist,* published by the East European Branch, Manitoba Genealogical Society, noted that a copy of this book, published in Kiev in 1968, is located in the library of the Ukrainian Cultural and Educational Centre in Winnipeg. The book is written entirely in Ukrainian. For additional information or to arrange to have material translated, write to the Manitoba Genealogical Centre, 420-167 Lombard Avenue, Winnipeg, Manitoba R3B OT6, Canada.

Subtelny, Orest. *Ukraine: A History* (Toronto: Toronto University Press, 1988). This 600+ page book throughly discusses the complex history of Ukraine over the centuries, with substantial consideration to the role that Jews have played. There is a good discussion of Western Ukraine when it was part of Galicia with respect to its economic, social and cultural status in relation to surrounding territories. The book is available from Travel Books and Language Center, 4437 Wisconsin Avenue NW, Washington, DC 20016; phone: (202) 237-1322.

Bezirk, Gemeinde, Ortschaft	Zahl der Häuser	Bevölkerung		
		Männlich	Weiblich	Zusammen
Wiśniowa (Mycielski)	10	53	49	102
Witkowice	6	25	34	59
Zagorzyce	2	8	5	13
Zawadka	2	6	9	15
Zdziary	2	8	11	19
Summe der Gutsgebiete . . .	299	1352	1213	2565

Recapitulation:

Summe der Ortsgemeinden . .	8981	25555	27373	52928
Summe der Gutsgebiete	299	1352	1213	2565
Gesammtsumme der Bezirkshauptmann- schaft Ropczyce	9280	26907	28586	55493

Bezirks-Hauptmannschaft Rzeszów:
Ortsgemeinden:

Babica	98	298	303	601
Baryczka	126	307	379	686
Biała	177	482	574	1056
Białka	139	369	414	783
Błazowa	664	1897	2032	3929
Błędowa bei Zgłobień	66	171	190	361
Błędowa słocinska . .	118	331	345	676
Blizianka	86	207	227	434
Boguchwała	147	338	381	719
Borek nowy	199	543	569	1112
Borek stary	215	511	627	1138
Bratkowice	444	1153	1199	2352
Brzeżanka	68	194	200	394
Brzezówka	64	180	202	382
Budy	256	617	638	1255
Budziwój	275	748	825	1573
Bzianka	56	136	149	285
Chmielnik	294	823	947	1770
Cierpisz	67	174	213	387
Czudec				
Stadt	162	400	427	827
Vorstadt	170	511	534	1045
Summe . .	332	911	961	1872
Dobrzechów	103	317	346	663
Drabinianka	109	292	320	612
Dylęgówka	139	373	395	768
Futoma	244	568	692	1260
Gbiska	30	73	85	158
Glinik charzewski . .	59	179	181	360
Głogów	363	1166	1298	2464
Godowa	237	732	803	1535
Grodzisko	127	394	421	815
Grzegorzówka	68	204	187	391
Gwoździanka	61	192	170	362
Hadle szklarskie . .	93	270	272	542
Hermanowa	187	507	511	1048
Hucisko	86	246	262	508

Sample page from Orts: Reportorium des Konigreiches Galizien und Lodomerien mit dem Grossherzogthume Krakau: aug Grunlage der Volszahlung vom Jahre 1869 bearbeitet von der k. k. statistischen Central-Commision.

Jewish Historical References

The eminent-Polish Jewish historian Professor Majer Bałaban (1877–1942) wrote primarily in Polish, Russian and German, with a few books in Yiddish and Hebrew. He used authentic data from Polish and Jewish archival sources and was a reliable historian and genealogist. In 45 years, he published about 70 historical studies and some 200 short papers and reviews. His works on Galicia, all in the Polish language, are as follows:

• *Dzieje Żydów w Galicji i w Rzeczpospolitej Krakowskiej, 1772–1868* (History of Jews in Galicia and in the Kraków Republic) (Lwów, 1916). Bałaban presents a candid picture of the life of Jews in Austrian Galicia and their political and cultural struggles; much history, no genealogy.

• *Dzieje Żydów w Krakowie i w Kazimierzu, 1304–1868* (History of Jews in Kraków and Kazimierz, 1304–1868) (Kraków, 1913) Library of Congress, DS 135 P6 K72. (Republished in

Yiddish in about 1990.) The two volumes of history include 49 family trees of prominent rabbinic and non-rabbinic families. Excellent description of the organization and function of the *Kahal*, the official organization of the Jewish community. Geoffrey Weisgard (*Shemot*, vol. 5, no. 1) notes that Bałaban includes an 1809 map of Kazimierz that shows house numbers. An 1815 map in the book clearly shows the new Jewish cemetery, separated from the town of Kazimierz by a farm and fields.

* *Żydzi Lwowscy na Przełomie XVI i XVII Wieku* (The Jews of Lwów at the turn of the 16th and 17th centuries) (Lwów, 1906).

* *Zabytki Historyczne Żydów w Polsce* (Historical antiquities of the Jews in Poland) (Warsaw, 1929). This book is an inventory of Jewish art and artifacts between the two wars, most of which were ultimately destroyed. Bałaban describes the treasures of Galician towns and those of the Jews: exhibits, museums, libraries, archives, synagogues and cemeteries, and secular memorabilia and family relics (portraits, papers, ritual objects, prayer books, bibles, Talmuds). The illustrations include one of the Eastern Wall in the synagogue of Chodorów (circa 1642). Call number at the University of Judaism, Los Angeles, is 937.2 B 1712 1929.

Books by other authors include the following:

Eisenbach, Arthur. *The Emancipation of the Jews in Poland, 1780–1870* (Oxford: Basil Blackwell, 1991). Sections on Galicia appear on pages 201–06 and 504–13.

Fuks, Marian, Zygmunt Hoffman, Maurycy Horn and Jerzy Tomaszewski. *Polish Jewry: History and Culture* (Warsaw: Interpress Publishers, 1982) ISBN: 83-223-2002-7. While much of this book concerns Russian Poland, the authors do an admirable scholarly job of presenting Jewish culture, education, art, religious customs and family life. The second part of the book focuses on Jews in various industries and cultural pursuits in the 19th and 20th centuries. The illustrations that accompany the written text are impressive. The book, in English, purchased in Warsaw in 1986, may be difficult to obtain elsewhere.

Hausler, Wolfgang. *Das galizische Judentum in der Habsurgermonarchie: Im Lichte de zeitgenossischen Publizistik und Reiseliteratur Von 1772–1848* (Munich: R. Oldebourg Verlag, 1979), ISBN: 3-486-49511-9.

Heshel, Rabbi J., "The History of Hassidism in Austria" in *The Jews of Austria: Essays on Their Life, History and Destruction*, 2d ed. Edited by Josef Fraenkel (London: Valentine Mitchell, 1970).

Mahler, Raphael. *History of Modern Jewry, 1780–1815* (New York: Schocken Books, 1971). The chapter on Galician Jews is found on pages 314–40.

McCagg, William O., Jr. *History of Habsburg Jews, 1670–1918* (Bloomington: Indiana University Press, 1989). Discussion of Galician Jews appears on pages 105–22, 181–226.

Mendelsohn, Ezra. *The Jews of East Central Europe Between the World Wars* (Bloomington: Indiana University Press, 1983). Chapter on Poland, including Galicia, pages 11–83.

Sanders, Ronald. *Shores of Refuge: A Hundred Years of Jewish Emigration* (New York: Henry Holt and Company, 1987). This book focuses mostly on Russian emigration, but there is much rich description of Galicia and the condition of Galician Jews, as well as a detailed study of the Jewish exodus from Europe to the United States, Palestine and elsewhere.

Schorr, Mojzesz. *Żydzi w Przemyślu do Końca XVIII Wieku* (Jews in Przemyśl until the end of the 18th century) (Lwów, 1903). This is an early history, in Polish, of the Jews in Przemyśl.

Schmidl, Erwin A. *Jews in the Habsburg Armed Forces* (Eisenstadt, Germany: Osterreichisches Judisches Museum, 1989). The address: A-70 Eisenstadt, Unterbergstr. 6, Austria. German text pages 19–91; English translation, pages 93–189. Photographs are included.

Geography

Kubijouyc, W. *Atlas of the Ukraine and Ethnic Groups of Southwestern Ukraine* (Berlin: Selbst-verlagdern Publikationsstelle, 1942). Includes Jewish population figures for every town in the Ukraine ethnographic region in 1937.

Lenius, Brian J. *Genealogical Gazetteer of Galicia*. Lenius is an organizer of the Federation of East European Family History Societies. This 375-page book includes 22 maps and more than 13,500 place names. Administrative and judical district information, alternative names for villages, and sources for genealogical records are presented.

Lenius's book, unlike *The Galician Gazetteer* (see Appendix G), includes all towns in Galicia. *The Galician Gazetteer* represents only those towns where Jews were known to be living in 1877 when the Austrian government compiled the book. Lenius's book also includes a table of administrative and judicial districts for Christian parishes at various points in time. The judicial districts closely overlap the administrative entities where Jewish vital records were collected and stored. Lenius notes administrative district changes in 1906 and judicial district changes in 1914, both of which appear to be consistent with changes in the administration districts for Jewish records.

Lenius used *Church in Ruin* by O.W. Iwanusiw, a book that includes a gazetteer of Galician villages, as well as other sources, to guide him. The book has a large section of regional maps. Each map includes the boundaries of the administrative districts within the region and the major town or city within the district.

This highly recommended book is available from Brian J. Lenius, Box 18 Grp. 4 RR #1, Anola, Manitoba, Canada R0E 0A0.

East European Genealogist, published by the East European Branch of the Manitoba Genealogical Society, Inc. Write for membership information to P.O. Box 2536, Winnipeg, Manitoba R3C 4A7.

Magosci, Paul Robert. *Historical Atlas of East Central Europe* (Toronto: University of Toronto Press, 1993).

Mokotoff, Gary, and Sallyann Amdur Sack. *Where Once We Walked* (Teaneck, N.J.: Avotaynu, 1991). This book is a treasure and a major resource for serious genealogists, with one caveat for those with Galician roots. Although a complete list of the towns from *The Galician Gazetteer* was available to the authors, not all towns from that source were included in *Where Once We Walked*. For the more than 21,000 Central and Eastern European towns listed, however, there are sources, exact latitude and longitude, and other location information. The form used for the names of towns was that of the U.S. Board on Geographic Names, the current international standard.

Pogonowski, Iwo Cyprian. *Poland: A Historical Atlas*, (New York: Hippocrene Books, 1987). Although this book emphasizes the history of Russian Poland, interesting maps and facts cover the existence of Austrian-ruled Galicia.

Biographical Compilations

Almanach Żydowski (Jewish almanac). This book reads like a Jewish *Who's Who* of pre-World War II Lwów. It includes biographies of people and lists Jewish communal societies and religious organizations. Fay Bussgang, who has a photocopy of this book, will respond to inquiries if you send a self-addressed, stamped envelope to her at 2 Forest Street, Lexington, MA 02173.

Bader, Gershom. *Medinah V'Chachmeyah* (Galician-Jewish celebrities), (New York: National Booksellers, 1934). The book is written mostly in Hebrew, with liberal use of Yiddish. Only one volume was published, with the surnames *aleph* to *lamed* (A-L in the Hebrew alphabet). Brief biographies; for authors, their book titles. This book has been exhaustively indexed in English by Faigy Spitzer and Nick Martin with assistance from Alan Hirshfeld. The results of their efforts are being arranged for publication by Gesher Galicia.

Buber, Solomon. Buber, a grandfather of Martin Buber, was a scholar and researcher of note. One of the "enlightened" Hebraists in Poland, he wrote two books of interest in Hebrew:

• *Anshei Shem* (Men of renown) (Kraków, 1895). This book presents biographical sketches of 564 rabbis who served the Lwów community from 1550 to 1890. Some distinguished lay leaders are included in this list. Many biographies include family genealogies.

• *Kirya Nisgava* (Lofty city) (Kraków, 1900) is a similar book about Zolkiew.

• Dembitzer, Chaim Nathan. *Klilat Yoffi* (Perfection of beauty) (Kraków, 1888). Dembitzer, a Kraków rabbi, was a historian of Lwów rabbis. In Hebrew, the book contains biographies of 21 Lwów rabbis and other figures.

Wunder, Rabbi Meir. *Meorei Galicia* (Encyclopedia of Galician rabbis and scholars), 5 vols. This series offers detailed biographical information about rabbis and scholars and their families. Each volume includes indexes in English and Hebrew to family names and the towns mentioned in the biographical sketches. Rabbi Wunder also cites *yizkor* books and bibliographical sources. The Hebrew alphabet is the organizing framework for the volumes.

Gideon Rath transliterated and published the surname index to the first four volumes in *Chronicles*, the newsletter of the Jewish Genealogical Society of Philadelphia. He gave his permission to reprint the names in *The Galitzianer* (vol. 1, nos. 1–3). Some problems exist with the transliteration; therefore, Rabbi Wunder's own index of surnames should be consulted.

These volumes are held by major Jewish libraries and the U.S. Library of Congress. To purchase copies, write to Rabbi Wunder, Institute for Commemoration of Galician Jewry, 13 Panim Meiroth Street, 94473 Jerusalem, Israel.

Socioeconomic References

Gay, Ruth. *Unfinished People: Eastern European Jews Encounter America* (New York: W.W. Norton, 1996). This book is an often amusing and touching analysis of the culture that grew up among Eastern European Jews who came to New York in the late 19th and early 20th centuries. The author offers the perspective of a first-generation American from the Bronx, using such themes as laughter, the Catskills, food, work, Florida, hats, corsets, *landsmanschaftn*, marriage, girls and winter to frame her discussion of the unique culture that arose as young immigrants struggled to make peace with mainstream American culture. The central thesis is that many immigrants, particularly those who came alone or without their parents, were, themselves, "unfinished people," and this impacted their general knowledge and what they transmitted to their children. She cites numerous examples of holes in her own fund of general knowledge of the world around her as she was growing up.

Mahler, R. *Jewish Social Studies*, vol. 1, 1939:97. This article discusses socioeconomic issues among the 250,000 Jews in what had been Galicia in 1930. Most of the Jews were traders, shopkeepers and artisans. Most lived in small towns which, in Eastern Galicia, were the property of the Polish nobility. Innkeeping had long been a Jewish occupation, but the laws of 1785 and 1789 forbade Jews from engaging in this trade. Although the practice continued, it required Jews to hide their true occupations.

Moore, Deborah, ed. *East European Jews in Two Worlds: Studies from the YIVO Annual* (Evanston, Ill.: Northwestern University Press; New York: YIVO Institute for Jewish Research, 1990). This book includes a discussion of the economic background of Jewish emigrants from Galicia.

Opalski, Magdalena. *The Jewish Tavern Keeper and His Tavern in 19th-Century Polish Literature*, published in 1986 by The Zalman Shazar Center, Center for Research on History and Culture of Polish Jews, P.O. Box 4179, 91041 Jerusalem, Israel. This book includes a discussion of Galician Jews.

Potich, Peter J. and Howard Aster, eds. *Ukrainian-Jewish Relations in Historical Perspective* (Edmonton, Alberta: Canadian Institute of Ukrainian Studies, University of Alberta, 1990).

Schwartz, Rosaline and Susan Milamed. *From Alexandrovsk to Żyrardów: A Guide to YIVO's Landsmanschaften Archive* (New York: YIVO Institute for Jewish Research, 1986). Many Galician towns are included in this guide.

Historical Travel Guides

Baedeker, K. *Handbook for Travellers for Austria*. Martha Burg of Houston, Texas, found an 1896 edition of this work in her local library. The 10-page section on Galicia and part of the introduction includes background on money, travel and hotels. The brief section on Galicia offers valuable historical information on rail travel in the region.

In the opening "General Remarks," the author comments that the region is:

> rich in corn, wood, salt and petroleum, but poor in industries, which are chiefly in the hands of the Jews (660,000 out of a population of 6 million), to whom most of the inns, taverns, and shops belong. The horse dealers and carriage owners are always Jews. They differ in their dress and the mode of wearing their hair from the other inhabitants, who despise them but are financially dependent on them.

The author judged that good hotels were in "Cracow, Lemberg, Przemyśl and Czernowitz (in Bukowina). Otherwise, in the smaller towns and in the country, the inns are generally very primitive and dirty, while in the villages as a rule, the only house of call is the brandy shop." Unsaid was that these shops were usually owned by Jews.

At that time, two railways, one going east and west, the other north and south, ran through Galicia. One line went from Bielitz to Czernowitz and the other from Oświęcim to Tarnopol. The 212-mile trip from Kraków to Lemberg (Lwów) took 7½–10 hours. The 164 miles from there to Czernowitz took 6½ to more than 8 hours. Several branches from towns along the way extended out to towns in the vicinity. At that time, one-third of the population of Kraków were Jews. A small, general map of the town is included. Lemberg then had 21,900 Jews, of a total of 127,638 inhabitants, and was said to have two synagogues.

In describing Stanislau (Stanisławów, now Ivano-Frankovsk), Baedeker mentioned that the town had been "handsomely rebuilt since a great fire in 1868." Both restaurants recommended were owned by Jews. Borysław was known for its petroleum and ozocerite beds, and Truskawice for its sulphur and salt baths. Travel times for other legs of north-south journeys are listed with interesting local features and data.

Bonar, Andrew A., and Robert Murray M'Cheyne. *Narrative of a Mission of Inquiry to the Jews from the Church of Scotland* (Philadelphia: Presbyterian Board of Publishing, 1842). This book is an account of the travels of two Church of Scotland missionaries in 1839. The two men, who were authorized to visit Jewish communities, traveled through North Africa, Palestine, Turkey, the Balkans, territory now in Ukraine, Galicia, France and Germany. Gesher Galicia arranged for the 1997 republication of the book's chapter on the authors' travels through Galicia. To obtain a copy, send $15 payable to Gesher Galicia to Rita Permut, 7505 Democracy Blvd #136, Bethesda, MD 20817.

Modern Travel Guides

Gruber, Ruth Ellen. *Upon the Doorposts of Thy House: Jewish Life in East-Central Europe, Yesterday and Today* (New York: John Wiley and Sons, 1994). A review of the book was originally published in *The Galitzianer* (vol. 3, no. 3).

Though limited in scope, this book is deeply satisfying because the author infuses every page with her very personal reactions and observations. The book reads like a journal of Gruber's travels. For some places she has visited several times, she shares the changes that she sees, her own changed perspectives and, sometimes, the frustrations that can accompany travel in that part of the world.

Much of this book covers Galician territory. Gruber became snowbound while visiting Auschwitz and had to become a guest at the convent. We listen in on her conversations about the controversies swirling around the very existence of the convent. She shares her heartbreaking visits to Kraków, where Kazimierz, the ancient Jewish community on the outskirts of the city is crumbling, and no one quite knows what to do about the problem. The author also takes us through her motor tour of northeastern Hungary and southern Poland as she makes clear the vital connection between those places because of the cultivation of the tokaj grape, which was used in making wine for ritual and commercial purposes by some of our ancestors.

Gruber visits a few remaining Jews in villages, crumbling and desecrated synagogues, and the occasional cemetery to bear witness in our behalf. We cry with her. Her ear is wonderful and, although a photo is absent, we see the person she is talking to. This book is valuable to those who want to understand where they came from and where so few of us now live.

Gruber, Ruth Ellen. *Jewish Heritage Travel: A Guide to Central and Eastern Europe* (New York: John Wiley and Sons, 1992). Poland is included in this guide, but not Ukraine.

Kagan, Joram. *Poland's Jewish Heritage* (New York: Hippocrene Books, 1992).

Salter, Mark, and Gordon McLachlen. *Poland: The Rough Guide* (London: Rough Guides Ltd, 1996). Good sections are included on Kraków and what had been Galician territory in southern Poland.

Bibliographic Aids

Bacon, Gershon C., and Gershon David Hundert. *The Jews in Poland and Russia: Bibliographical Essays* (Bloomington: Indiana University Press, 1984). Bibliographical essays are organized by historical period and by aspects of life, referenced to a bibliographical checklist. Galicia is integrated in sections on Poland.

Magosci, Paul Robert. *Galicia: A Historical Survey and Bibliographic Guide*. Published in association with the Canadian Institute of Ukrainian Studies and the Harvard University Ukrainian Research Institute (Toronto: University of Toronto Press, 1985). Morey Altman recommended this book whose main focus is on Ukrainian history. There are good maps and a chapter on Jewish life. The bibliographical references are excellent and include materials on Jews in the Polish, Yiddish and Ukrainian languages.

Language Aids

Judith Frazin's marvelous book will aid you in crafting a letter: *A Translation Guide to 19th-Century Polish-Language Civil-Registration Documents*. Pages 33–41 are designed to provide phrases that you can use in your letter writing. The book may be ordered from Frazin, 1025 Antique Lane, Northbrook, IL 60062.

Pre-World War II Directories

Jeffrey Cymbler describes the results of his efforts to locate pre-World War I Polish directories in a lengthy article in *Avotaynu* (Spring 1997). The article is entitled, "Nineteenth- and Twentieth-Century Polish Directories As Resources for Genealogical Information." These directories include city, phone and business directories. For instance, the New York Public Library has a microfilm of the Polish telephone directory for 1936–37. The microfilm was made in 1964 and is marked "Ratio 15." The image is fuzzy, and not too many people had phones during that period, but the directory may provide valuable information about a relative. The directory, issued by the Polish government, included all phone subscribers in all districts except the city of Warsaw. Districts included Bydgoszcz, Katowice, Kraków, Lublin, Lwów, Poznan, suburban Warsaw and Wilno (Vilnius, Lithuania, today). Within each district, towns are listed alphabetically, and subscribers from those towns are listed with their names, phone numbers, occupations and addresses.

Gesher Galicia holds a two-reel microfilm of the 1929 *Księga Adresowa Polski* (Polish address register) from the University of Illinois. This is an all-Poland business directory in Polish and French. Morty Miller reported its existence.

A 1916 city directory for Lwów on microfilm is held by the Library of Congress (film #506331). Pages 1–360 contain an alphabetical list of male residents. On pages 361–78 is a list by professions and businesses, followed by a list of all streets in Lwów with their boundaries. Libraries, archives, schools and other institutions are then listed before a section of paid advertisements.

The Library of Congress also has microfilmed a 1930 phone directory (film #506171) for Kraków and Katowice districts. Copies of the microfilms can be purchased from the Library of Congress.

Request the numbers noted here: The Library of Congress, Photoduplication Service, Washington, DC 20540-5234.

Art

Ciagle Widze Ich Twarze (And I can still see their faces) (Warsaw: Shalom Foundation, 1996). In Polish and English, this book was based on an exhibition of 400 photos by the Shalom Foundation in Warsaw, April–May 1996. When word was issued about the planned exhibition of prewar photos, the foundation was flooded with 8,000 photographs of Polish Jews before and during World War II.

Hoshen, Sarah Harel, ed. *Treasures of Jewish Galicia: Judaica from the Museum of Ethnography and Crafts in Lvov, Ukraine* (Tel Aviv: Nahum Goldmann Museum of the Jewish Diaspora, 1996). This book is the catalog of an exhibition, "Rediscovered Treasures: Judaica Collections from Galicia," held at Beth Hatefutsoth July 1994–January 1995. This magnificently produced, 195-page book includes 11 chapters by various authors, beginning with a historical overview of Galicia by Israel Bartel. Hoshen's article, "Research and Collection of Judaica in Lvov: 1874–1942," describes the origins of the collection of Maksymilian Goldstein from Lemberg, which, combined with the collection of the Jewish Community Museum of Lviv, composes most of the Jewish holdings of the Museum of Ethnography and Crafts at the Ethnology Institute of the Academy of Sciences of Ukraine in Lviv. The book includes maps, paintings and photos of Jewish life, buildings and characters, including synagogues, tombstones, ritual objects, papercuts and everyday objects worn and used by Jewish residents of Galicia. It may be purchased from Beth Hatefutsoth, Ramat Aviv, P.O. Box 39359, 61363 Tel Aviv, Israel.

Photo Collections and Video Resources

Salaminder, Rachael. *The Jewish World of Yesterday, 1860–1938* (New York: Rizzoli International, 1993). Richard Schwarzstein comments that this 320-page book contains "fascinating photos of life in Central Europe, including Galicia"

A Time to Gather Stones. This is a moving 30-minute video of Miriam Weiner's group trip to Poland and Ukraine in 1993. A number of genealogy societies have shown the video at meetings. Copies can be purchased from Ergo Media, P.O. Box 2037, Teaneck, NJ 07666.

Return to My Shtetl Delatyn. Dutch filmmaker Willy Lindwer documented his father's trip to Poland and Ukraine in 1991. His father, Berl Nachim Lindwer, was born in Delatyn but left before World War II. In the film, Berl and his granddaughter walk the streets of the towns, interview the local population, and visit some of the remnants of Jewish culture. In addition to Delatyn, towns visited include Bolekhov, Kraków, Lvov, Przemyśl and Stryj.

Marian Rubin saw videos of Rzeszów and Łancut at Beth Hatefutsoth (Museum of the Diaspora) in Tel Aviv. The videos provided some history of the Jewish community and mention prominent members of the community. The videos combine current footage with scenes of the Jewish community before World War II. The Beth Hatefutsoth catalogue reveals that among the varied collection of videos are short, 1939 films about Jewish life in Kraków and Lwów and a 1988 filmed dialogue between former Jewish residents of Tarnow and a group of Poles.

Marcia Meyers saw a video at Beth Hatefutsoth about the synagogue ceiling of Chodorów and was able to buy a copy, in English formatted for American video machines. The cost was $15. Marcia pointed out, however, that the museum gift shop knew nothing about buying it. They purchased it by going to the office area and inquiring. She wrote to say, "It is a very moving 11 minutes on the painting of the beautiful ceiling."

Brandeis Jewish Film Center at Brandeis University in Waltham, Massachusetts, has a 1939 film depicting Jewish life in Warsaw, Lwów, Kraków, Białystok and Wilno (now Vilnius, Lithuania), according to Fay and Julian Bussgang.

Geography and Maps

Useful maps can be obtained from the following sources:
- A reproduction of an 1875 map of the Austrian Empire is sold by Avotaynu, Inc., P.O. Box 900, Teaneck, NJ 07666.
- Map Series G6480 S75.A8 described in Appendix G is on microfiche at the Library of Congress. The map series was created in 1878 by the Austrian government. The numbers within each square are linked to the main districts for various administrative purposes. A town may be located within an adjacent square, because the districts were not drawn to be entirely contiguous with the squares. There will be a modest charge for this service. Write to:

> The Library of Congress
> Geography & Map Division
> Washington, DC 20540

This map series, which was created for military purposes, is also part of the LDS (Mormon) Family History Library collection on microfiche, numbers 6,000,198 through 6,000,339. The index is on fiche 6,000,198.
- *Galizien German Descendants* (July 1995). John Pihach notes that Vienna's Kriegsarchiv is a source of Josephinian (*Josephinische Landesaufnahme*) military maps from 1779 to 1782. Send the latitude and longitude of the town or region for which you need a map or send a photocopy of a map showing your village to Kriegsarchiv, Nottendorffer 2, 1030 Wien, Austria, to order or to inquire about fees and postage.
- Omni Resources distributes a wide range of Polish maps and a lesser collection of Ukrainian maps. The Polish maps include a 97-page atlas, a historical atlas, a topographic map series and travel maps. Ukrainian maps appear to be useful mostly for travel purposes, although Omni Resources has an administrative district map that is several years old. One map is the official administrative district map of Poland (catalog #65-1948 PPWK), *Rzeczpospolita Polska mapa administryjna*. The districts are distinguished by different colors. The back of this map, well-marked and easy to use, lists hundreds of towns with location information. Omni Resources also sells a one-page map with administrative districts on one side and the map of Poland on the other. Order by contacting Omni Resources at <http://www.omnimap.com/catalog> or phone (800) 742-2677.
- Travel Books and Language Center. This store is located at 4437 Wisconsin Avenue NW, Washington, DC 20016; phone: (202) 237-1322.
- Robert Krengel and Michael Buczaczer suggest a source for old and new maps of Eastern Europe, including new maps of Ukraine: East View Publications, 3020 Harbor Lane North, S. 1-10, Minneapolis, MN 55447. Contact: Shannon J. Birge; phone: (800) 477-1005 or (612) 550-0961; fax: (612) 559-2931; e-mail: <eastview@mr.net>.
- Dobromil map. Faigy Spitzer has translated a map of Dobromil from Yiddish to English. She mentions that she could not quite get the meaning of *vilink* and would be grateful if someone could tell her what this means. To cover the copying cost, send $2 and a self-addressed, stamped envelope to her at 603 Bedford Avenue, Brooklyn, NY 11211.

U.S. Library of Congress and National Archives Resources

Miriam Weiner has published a helpful guide to the map collections of the Library of Congress and the U.S. National Archives entitled *In the Footsteps of Our Ancestors*. The guide includes information about the town plans of Poland held by the Geography and Map Division of the Library of Congress and World War II aerial photos taken of towns by the Germans, now located at the National Archives II in College Park, Maryland. The town plans of Poland series includes communities in Ukraine, since at the time the series was created, part of Ukraine was in Polish territory. The guide includes a list of all towns included in each of the two series. Some Galician towns are mentioned in two of the three series. Contact Miriam Weiner, 136 Sandpiper Key, Secaucus, NJ 07094; phone: (201) 866-4075.

❋ Chapter 6 ❋

Additional Resources

World Wide Web

JewishGen

JewishGen, Inc., a nonprofit organization that is the principal presence of Jewish genealogy on the Internet, includes a discussion group, information files, searchable databases, online education programs, and other useful functions. Its home page is <http://www.jewishgen.org>. From this page, a researcher can branch to many locations within the JewishGen umbrella or other sites on use in Jewish genealogical research.

A major database of JewishGen is the JewishGen Family Finder (JGFF). It contains tens of thousands of surnames/towns being researched by more than 7,000 (as of early 1998) genealogists throughout the world. If you have not submitted your surnames and towns to JGFF, use the online data entry page. Those who have contributed their research can maintain their entries directly online. Although submissions are free of charge, donations are welcome. Financial assistance helps JewishGen to expand its services. Contributions are tax deductible in the U.S.

Gesher Galicia

Gesher Galicia has a presence on the Internet. An InfoFile can be retrieved by sending an e-mail message to <ggalicia@jewishgen.org>. The subject line and message text can contain anything.

Sites by Individuals

Jonathan Eisenberg has created a website relating to Wojnilow (now Voynilov). The site also references other nearby towns, including Kalush and Bolshovtsy. Names referenced are Eisenberg, Fingerhut, Kierschner and Rotker. Site address: <http://members.aol.com/Seisenberg/voynilov. htm>

Moishe Miller has created a website for his Miller/Eckstein family. You can enter this website through JewishGen, <http://www.jewishgen.org>. Some people will be able to access this website through: <http://www.ics.uci.edu/~dan/genealogy/Miller/langsam.html>.

Israel Preker has set up a website on the town of Dębica. His web address is <http://www. netvision.net.il/php/pisrael> and the home page for Dębica site is: <http://www.goecities.com/ ~pisrael>. His address is P.O. Box 43276, 61430 Tel Aviv, Israel.

Gayle Schlissel Riley has set up a website on Tarnobrzeg. The address is <http://www.jewishgen. org/shtetlinks/tarnobrzeg/tarnobrzeg.html>.

Organizations

Jewish Preservation Committee of Ukraine

This committee is a part of the Union of Jewish Religion of Ukraine. Dmitry Surovtsev and Yulia Zeveleva offer their services in searching for records in Ukrainian and local archives. The typical fee to cover their time and expenses is about $50, plus $4–6 per hour for searching in Kiev and $80–100 plus $6 per hour to search in other cities. "Of course the cost varies depending on search difficulties." They have devised an order form that aids them in their research. Payment is made through an account established by Rabbi Bleich of Kiev.

Contact the committee at <jul@jpcu.freenet.kiev.ua> or Box 391-1, Kiev, 252034, Ukraine. The phone number is 380 44 416 07 84.

New Cracow Friendship Society

The New Cracow Friendship Society has published a 260-page journal that includes information on the city's Jewish life and history before World War II. There are approximately 50 pages of memorial notices, many of which are for victims of the Holocaust. Contact Max Hilfstein, 1523 Dwight Place, Bronx, NY 10465. (This notice was originally in the newsletter of the Jewish Genealogy Society of Rochester (Fall 1993). Reprinted in *The Galitzianer* (Winter 1994), this contact information has recently been updated by Geoffrey Weisgard.)

Śnyatyn

The United Sniatyner Sick and Benevolent Association had more than 30 members when the president wrote to Gesher Galicia to offer assistance to members with roots in Śnyatyn and surrounding towns. Contact Dr. Benjamin Solomowitz, 75-25 210 Street, Apt. 4H, Bayside, NY 11364.

Judaic Studies in Kraków

Several organizations are working to preserve and understand Jewish culture in Poland, as reported by Phyllis Simon. The Research Center on Jewish History and Culture in Poland, established in 1986, is a department of the Jagellonian University. This department channels and expands the growing interest in Jewish history and culture in Poland through research, publications and education.

Professor Dr. Jozef A. Gierowski, historian, organizer and director of the Research Center, is also the originator of the Center for Jewish Culture, an organization that drew support from many sources within Poland and abroad. These two entities combined to form the Polish-American Joint Commission, which sponsors the project. The Center for Jewish Culture's main tasks are to "help physically preserve the Jewish heritage and to make it more accessible to all" by sponsoring cultural events, a library, research, and publications, and by organizing restoration efforts. In addition, the Center for Jewish Culture arranges for heritage tours.

The Center is located in the former Bene Emuna prayer house, founded in 1886, at ul. Meiselsa 17. The site was originally a smelter belonging to the Kraków goldsmiths' guild until the 17th century. It had fallen into complete disrepair, and extensive renovations were necessary before it could be used for its new purpose.

The Center for Jewish Culture operates under the auspices of the Judaica Foundation, an organization founded by Mark Talisman, long-time U.S. Jewish activist and communal leader. Joachim Russek, the foundation's director, plans to build a second facility next door to expand space for offices, guest rooms and a kosher restaurant.

Translators

Erwin Biskup translates short documents from Gothic German, modern German and Polish. His address is 6614 Onyx Trail, Pollock Pines, CA 95726-9732; phone: (916) 644-1458; e-mail <gierejb@thegrid.net>.

Lawrence Feldman is fluent in Spanish and is familiar with Central America. He does some work for the U.S. Holocaust Memorial Museum's Archives and can assist people with research in that institution. Feldman recently examined documents relating to people who went to Spain to escape the Holocaust, some of whom were from the area that had been Galicia. He can be reached through P.O. Box 2493, Wheaton, MD 20915-2493; phone: (301) 933-2616; e-mail: <Lawrence846@aol.com>.

David E. Goldman has worked as a translator since 1988. He is a native English speaker who especially enjoys genealogical work. He translates into English from Yiddish, Hebrew, Russian,

Spanish and French. His address is 1644 58th Street, Brooklyn, NY 11204; phone/fax: (718) 331-3790; e-mail <davic@erols.com>.

Piotr Graff, originally from central Poland, can translate English into Polish and Polish into English. He is certified by both the American Translators Association and the Polish equivalent Stowarzyszenie Tłumaczy Polskich. He charges 15 cents per word. His address is RR3 Box 397, Bullock Road, Guilford, VT 05301.

Ronald Kleinman is a translator of Polish. You may request a price estimate by sending him a copy of the material you wish to have translated with a self-addressed, stamped envelope. He translated some 17th-century tax records from Przemyśl obtained from the Central Archives of the History of the Jewish People in Israel for Suzan Wynne. Kleinman may be contacted by writing to 10 Greg Lane, East Northport, NY 11731.

Alex Kysym, a Ukrainian who went to England in 1946 at age eight, having spent much of the war in a German camp, can both read and write Ukrainian. He also knows a smattering of Russian. His address is 1355 Tyneburn Crescent, Mississauga, Ontario L4X 1P6, Canada. He was referred by Jewish Genealogical Society of Canada members Mel and Renee Stein.

Yehoshua Leiman, a professional translator recommended by Darla Stone, translates material in Yiddish or Hebrew. He also translates from English into those languages. His address is 1746 East 21 Street, Brooklyn, NY 11229; phone: (718) 376-3715.

Peter Rafalowicz, recommended by Judith S. Langer Caplan, knows Polish and has translated the modern Polish letters she has been receiving from the Polish Archives. His address is 315 Atlantic Avenue #2, East Rockaway, NY 11518.

Rita Schorr-Germain is a trained historian and linguist who can assist with translation of a number of languages. Her fees are negotiable according to the project. Her address is 1306 Rose Avenue, Lancaster, PA 17601.

Barry Silver and Dorota Rzymska advertise their translation services, which include modern printed material in Polish, Czech, Russian, Ukrainian and other Slavic languages. They handle handwritten documents and scripts as well. They are able to do records research in Poland, Russia, Ukraine and Belarus. Contact their company, Genealogy Research Service, P.O. Box 341197, Los Angeles, CA 90034; phone (310) 390-3075; fax (310) 836-7306; e-mail <102217.3654@compuserve.com>.

Darla Stone offers her assistance with translating brief items from Hebrew and Yiddish. Write to her at 2302 Avenue U, P.O. Box 498, Brooklyn, NY 11229-0498.

Grazyna Vincunas, Polish Language Services, 20 Oakwood Place, Longmeadow, MA 01106-1528; phone and fax: (413) 567-9900.

Wallace A. Witkowski often translates from Polish to English for the U.S. Holocaust Memorial Museum. He can be contacted at 2703 N. 18th Street, Arlington, VA 22201-4027; phone: (703) 524-7149.

Aryeh Zurinam translates to and from Ukrainian. Write to him at Quick Print, 1662 W. 3rd Street, Brooklyn, NY 11223.

Research Services and Strategies

Alexander Dunai is a highly recommended researcher who lives in Lviv. He has performed extensive services at the Lviv Archives for Nat Abramowitz and other Gesher Galicia members. He has also investigated the holdings of the Archives in Ivano-Frankovsk and is available to travel elsewhere in Ukraine or Poland. His rate, as of late 1997, is $12 for each record researched, including all research, a copy of the record and the translation. Postage, usually by Air Express, is extra. He speaks English. He can be reached by phone: 38-0322-337769 on weekdays only between 7 a.m. and 12 p.m. Ukrainian time (between 12 noon and 5 p.m. Eastern Time); fax: 011-380-322 334316; e-mail: <dunai@iname.com>. Postal mail is a much less certain way of reaching him; he lives at ul. O. Stepanivny 17/2, Lviv 290016, Ukraine.

The most efficient way to reimburse him for his services is to wire funds through your nearest Western Union office. Western Union in Ukraine does not deliver messages or telephone people who have messages. For this reason, it is essential that you include Dunai's passport number, KA 124254, on the Western Union form. Then, you *must* fax or e-mail Dunai to tell him when you have wired money. Be sure to include the 10-digit Money Control Number of your wire transfer in your fax. Dunai then goes to Western Union, shows his passport, and retrieves the money. If you have trouble finding a Western Union office or need clarification about their procedures, call 1-800-325-6000 in the U.S.

FAST is directed by Boris Feldblyum, a Russian emigré to the U.S., who uses persons living in the former Soviet Union to do research. Feldblyum also translates from Russian, Ukrainian, Polish and Lithuanian and can provide additional services such as photography and assistance with obtaining specialized information. Write to FAST, 8510 Wild Olive Drive, Potomac, MD 20854; e-mail: <bfeldbly@capaccess.org>.

Laurence Krupnak, a former steering committee member of Gesher Galicia, has conducted research at facilities within the Polish National Archives system and in Ukraine. He lists an impressive array of records that his organization has found, including census, military and emigration records. Krupnak has resources for translating Russian, Ukrainian, Polish, Slovak, German and Latin documents. You can request an estimate for most projects. His address is 1711 Corwin Drive, Silver Spring, MD 20910; phone and fax: (301) 585-0117.

RAGAS (Russian-American Genealogical Archival Service) is an outgrowth of an agreement between the U.S. National Archives and the countries that are part of the Commonwealth of Independent States (see *Avotaynu*, vol. 8, no. 1). Now a private venture, the address is 1929 18th Street NW, Suite 1112, Washington, DC 20009; it is best to contact him by e-mail at <vladrag@ glas.apc.org>.

Miriam Weiner is president of Routes to Roots, a customized tour and archival research service in Poland and the former Soviet Union. Weiner maintains offices in Poland and Ukraine, from which she visits ancestral towns and works in numerous archives on behalf of clients. As a result of her archival research, many clients have received hundreds of entries for their family names. During town visits to the former Soviet Union, Weiner often finds clients' previously unknown relatives. Weiner was co-editor of the *Encyclopedia of Jewish Genealogy* and author of *Jewish Roots in Poland: Pages from the Past and Archival Inventories*, the first officially sanctioned publication of the holdings of the Polish National Archives, with documents in the Jewish Historical Institute and local town halls, town by town, in one volume. Further information, phone Weiner at (201) 866-4075; fax: (201) 864-9222; Routes to Roots website at <http://www.routestoroots.com>.

Nancy Weisman researches and photographs towns and cemeteries in the Czech Republic, Poland, Russia and Germany. Her address is P.O. Box 1274, Boston, MA 02104-1274; phone: (617) 739-2797. No Shabbat calls.

Henry Wolanczyk is a local history specialist for Narol, Poland. He is willing to transmit and collect facts about the town. His address is 37-610 Narol, ul. Lwówska 10, Poland.

Postcards from Ukraine

Tomek Wisniewski of Białystok, Poland, has a collection of old postcards which includes Eastern Galicia. The six Galician postcards are part of a set of 16 cards that make up the Jewish Rare Series, which includes the following:

- Synagogue in Dubno, Volhynia, circa 1910
- Old synagogue in Ostróg, circa 1910
- City synagogue in Drohobycz, Galicia, circa 1910
- Synagogue-Kenessa in Hałicz, Galicia, circa 1910
- Old synagogue in Tarnopol, Galicia, circa 1908
- Synagogue; Rebbai Palace in Czortków, Galicia, circa 1910, circa 1930
- Great old synagogue in Brody, Galicia, circa 1910

- Great synagogue in Nowogrodek, Belarus, circa 1930
- Great synagogue in Neiswierz (Nishvish), Belarus, circa 1930
- Synagogue in Brzesc (Brest, Brisk), Belarus, circa 1930
- Synagogue and Yeshiva in Lida, Belarus, circa 1910
- Great synagogue in Pinsk, Belarus, circa 1930
- Synagogue in Sveksna, Lithuania, circa 1920
- Synagogue in Svencionys, Lithuania, circa 1916
- Synagogue in Kielce, Poland, circa 1916
- Great synagogue in Bialystok, Poland, circa 1920

The whole set of postcards is $8. Each card is 70 cents. There is a 10 percent discount for more than 10 sets. Contact Tomek Wisniewski, Box 351, 1 Bialystok, Poland; e-mail: <tomekwisniewski @telbank.pl>.

❀ Chapter 7 ❀

Travel Tips and Notes

Poland

Travel conditions in Poland today are much improved over those that existed before Poland achieved independence from the Soviet Union. Outside of major cities, however, hotels are basic. It is easy to rent cars and other vehicles, and it is possible to find taxi drivers willing to take tourists to out-of-town locations for less than it would cost to rent a car. Those who adhere to Jewish dietary laws must bring their own food. Kraków has kosher restaurants, but kosher food is not available elsewhere in southern Poland.

Roads are usually two lanes, and one may expect to find local roads occupied by horse-drawn carts. As one person put it, "The driving is fierce and crowded; the roads are not well marked. The roads are frequently marked by town instead of route number." This traveler recommended hiring a local driver.

Be respectful of local customs. Offering payment for services is an art in Poland. You cannot be expected to understand the nuances of the often-elaborate negotiations surrounding such payment. It is helpful to have assistance from a local guide in conducting negotiations for access to records. If you do not, come equipped with small packages of note cards, chocolates, scented soap, cosmetics, small jars of coffee, plastic lemons or limes or other such items. Flowers are viewed as a nice gesture of appreciation. Money, of course, is always welcome, but you must take care not to offend by offering it.

The **Polish National Tourist Office** (formerly known as ORBIS) has several publications about Jewish-oriented travel in Poland. Their *Map of Jewish Heritage* highlights sites of interest, including centers of Hasidism, death and concentration camps and cemeteries and synagogues. *They Lived Among Us: Jewish Heritage in Poland* notes that the synagogue in Lisko (Lesko), which was built in the 18th century, is now an exhibition hall. Scenes from a handful of Galician cemeteries and other notable sites are mentioned and portrayed. The Polish National Tourist Office is located at 275 Madison Avenue, New York, NY 10016.

Mendel Reichberg heads a travel agency and frequently leads tours in Poland. A Hasid, he has managed to provide kosher food to participants on his tours. Reichberg can be reached by phone at (718) 436-1001.

Ukraine

Max Mermelstein of AJS Travel Consultants in Queens, New York, recommends Melech Shochet, a tour guide who speaks Yiddish and English. He has also used Michael Chernilevski, whose phone number is 521-388 in Lviv. Call Mermelstein at (800) 822-1321 for more information.

First-hand Reports on Travel in Ukraine

Debra Braverman, a member of the Jewish Genealogical Society, Inc., in New York, wrote a useful article about traveling in Ukraine. The article, which appeared in the Winter 1993–94 issue of *Dorot*, dealt primarily with travel conditions and stops in Ukrainian towns that were not once part of Galicia. However, she visited Ladyczyn (now Ladyzhin), which:

has a population of 23,000 and 25 Jews, all of whom are very old. There are no synagogues left, although the former site of one was pointed out. Visiting the cemetery was a shock, not because of the terrible condition, not even because of the grazing goats, but because the neighbors use it for farming. This cemetery has been officially closed since 1958, although there had been two illegal burials since then. Based on a forty-year rule for land reclamation, in 1998, the cemetery land can be built on. There was, however, a monument to the Jews killed by the Germans and buried there.

They also spent a day in Śniatyn, which has a population of 14,000, of whom eight are Jews. Braverman reports:

> The synagogue site is now a field. During the Holocaust, the Jews of the town were burned alive in the synagogue. The war memorial is to all the war dead, and there is no memorial specifically to the Jews. The remains of the cemetery are in the woods behind the Christian cemetery and there is but a single path to get through the woods. There are pieces of many gravestones there, very few of which can be read.

Pearl Atkin's article in the Winter 1993 issue of *Avotaynu* describes a summer 1992 trip to Ukraine and Poland that mentions several communities in Galicia. The town of Uścieczko (now Ustechko), on the Dneister River near Zaleschiki, was a primary focus of the trip. Pearl and her mother had made a trip together in 1982, but had been unable to travel beyond a bridge at Horodenka (now Gorodenka). On her 1992 trip, Pearl planned to take advantage of the lifting of travel restrictions to visit Ustechko and relevant archives to seek information about her family, the Prufer-Blechers. On the way, she also visited a number of communities, among them Drogobych, where she found a small Jewish community in which everyone "literally seemed to be sitting on his or her suitcase" waiting to leave.

Pearl and her driver drove to Ustechko from Lviv, a slow and difficult trip because the roads are still primitive. The Ternopol archives was the first stop. There Pearl was told that Uściescku's documents would be in Gorodenka or Ivano-Frankovsk. In Chortkov, she noted that the town's bakeries sold challah on Friday out of tradition, though there are no Jews for hundreds of miles around. The major cemetery had row after row of broken and leaning tombstones. She found another, smaller cemetery behind the Christian cemetery "in a dark forest behind a stone wall with a broken doorway and was practically unmarked." The large synagogue in the center of town has been converted to another use.

No Jews were left in Ustechko, and both synagogue and cemetery had been destroyed. A town resident told Pearl what had happened to the Jews.

> The Jews had fled before the Germans arrived and had gotten as far as the Gorodenka Bridge [the Uściescku Bridge had been out that day]. The Jews were shot as they crossed the bridge. The ones who made it through the hail of bullets to the other side were thrown down a ravine towards the water into pre-dug pits and were covered over with earth.

The woman who told the story still was disturbed by the memory. "The earth was still moving; the earth was still moving," she commented. Pearl left the town immediately without doing much of what she had come for.

When Pearl and her driver crossed the bridge at Gorodenka, she remembered that this was where she and her mother had had tea in 1982, and was grateful that her mother had not known what had occurred at the site.

The vital records of the Jews of Ustechko had been collected and stored in the town under the administration of the main district in Zaleshchiki. Apparently, these records were not among those transferred to Warsaw, and, presumably, they remain in Ukraine. Pearl arrived too late in both Ivano-Frankovsk and Gorodenka to check with the records offices there.

Visiting Ancestral Towns in Ukraine: A Report by Miriam Weiner

Miriam Weiner, a certified genealogist, author and lecturer in the field of Jewish genealogy and Holocaust research, has worked in archives throughout Poland since 1989 and in the former Soviet

Union since 1991. Weiner is the president of Routes to Roots, a firm offering customized tours to ancestral towns, archival research and "town visits" on behalf of clients. She is the author of *Jewish Roots in Poland: Pages from the Past and Archival Inventories*. For information on town visits and/or archival research, send a stamped, self-addressed envelope to Weiner, 136 Sandpiper Key, Secaucus, NJ 07094. Her phone number is (201) 866-4075 or fax (201) 864-9222 or visit the Routes to Roots website <http://www.routestoroots.com>. If you write, be sure to include the name(s) of your ancestral town(s).

[The following article is loosely based upon, but substantially revised and updated from, an article that originally appeared in *The Galitzianer* (vol. 2, no. 1, Fall 1994)]

During the past eight years, I have visited more than 100 towns and villages in Poland and Ukraine, many of which were once part of Galicia. There are vast differences between these two countries today. The focus of this article is on Eastern Galicia, specifically the Ukraine *oblasts* (districts) of Ternopol, Lviv and Ivano-Frankovsk (formerly Stanisławów).

When I first began to visit Ukraine on a regular basis in 1991, it soon became evident that I would need to pack differently and carry goods we take for granted in America. Because I now spend almost half my time in Eastern Europe, I bought an apartment in Ukraine in order to leave my office equipment (computer, fax, printer, cameras, video cameras, copy machines, etc.), reference books, clothing and other essentials in one secure place.

When I go to Poland, I think nothing of renting a car and driving myself, traveling only with my translator. In Ukraine, I do not go anywhere without both my translator and a driver/security guard. The road conditions are not near U.S. standards. The economic situation is such that highways are not repaired, and one must be ever vigilant for potholes as well as free-ranging animals that wander along the roads. Also, highways are not well lit (or lit at all) for night driving.

The police still stop cars at will—generally for no infraction of the law, but for the purpose of inspecting the car's engine number and to inquire about destination. This is unsettling to those of us who have enjoyed and take for granted the democratic country in which we live, where, unless one makes a driving mistake, one can drive literally for years (or a whole lifetime) without having a conversation with a policeman.

For the first few years in Ukraine, I carried gasoline in cannisters in the trunk of the car because it was almost impossible to find gas stations open. Gasoline is no longer a deficit item, and I am now free of the gas fumes and the ever-present danger of carrying several gallons in the trunk.

Travelers should be aware, however, that frequent service areas along the highway do not exist as we know them, and there are inadequate directional signs in the towns and along the roads. Toilet facilities along the highway could be an occasional outhouse, but more often, they consist of a short walk into the woods. Do not expect to find public telephones or convenience stores along the roadways.

The single most important thing to bring with you is extra patience—more than you ever dreamed you had. Everything takes longer to accomplish: phone calls, restaurant service, hotel registration/check out and document inspection at checkpoints on the highway and at border crossings.

Some handy items to pack are small tissue packets, film and batteries for cameras, packets of wet towelettes, aspirin or similar pain medication, first aid supplies, sugar substitutes (if you use them) and other food products needed for dietary restrictions. Sufficient supplies of any medications and a spare pair of eyeglasses should also be with you.

Another important consideration in planning your trip should be the reliability of your transportation in Ukraine; whether your driver is a good mechanic and if he carries spare parts with him. My frequent trips to Ukraine have forced me to learn more about automobile maintenance and repairs than I ever knew or wanted to know. Most cars used for tour transport are Russian made and one must think about their condition. Until recently, I carried a set of spark plugs, a tow rope, tire inflator, a spare set of windshield wipers, a can of WD-40, flares, motor oil (I brought a case from the United States) and a strong flashlight. However, in early 1997, I bought a 1997 Dodge minivan that I shipped by boat to Gdańsk. I then picked it up there and personally drove it through Poland and across the Ukrainian border (with my translator, of course). I felt it was important for the people who booked town tours with me to have a strong and reliable vehicle in which to travel. My adventures in crossing the Polish/Ukraine border in a new American car with New Jersey license plates, New Jersey car registration, and International driver's license, all in English, would provide material for a stand-up comedian's entire act.

Another item that goes everywhere with me is a small bag, similar in size to carry-on luggage. In this bag, I carry a first-aid kit and an assortment of presents for the many helpful people I continually meet in my travels. These souvenirs from America, consisting of office supplies, gifts for children (dolls, crayons, toy trucks), cosmetics, watches, etc., are one method of returning the many kindnesses I receive from government officials, the local people on the street and members of Jewish communities throughout Ukraine.

Although some people choose to do archival research personally, the lack of familiarity with local procedures in the former Soviet Union, the difficult living and travel conditions, the time-consuming research process itself, and problems with language and naming patterns cause many more to hire professionals for this job.

Some people have asked me to do archival research that can be conducted in as many as five archives for one town. For example, Jewish documents for Ivano-Frankovsk (Stanisławów) are located in the local ZAGs (civil registration) archive in the town, the Lviv Historical Archives and in two separate archives in Warsaw. Additionally, civil records and 20th-century Jewish records are located in the Ivano-Frankovsk *oblast* (district) archives. It is not uncommon for me to find Jewish documents dating a particular family back into the 1700s. For example, one assignment produced 700 documents on family names from Melnitsa Podolskaya. Research for another client resulted in more than 500 documents about his ancestors who had once lived in Ozeryany, Korolówka, Skala Podolskaya and Borshchev (formerly Borszczów). For the last few years, I have been doing research for a client that has resulted in locating more than 2,000 documents with his family names.

When I first began working with these very old Jewish record books, it was clear that some of the books had not been opened for perhaps 50 years. The pages were stuck together, and the books are very fragile. Since copy machines are the exception in Ukraine, I travel with a Canon copier, transformer/converter, extra cartridge and paper. Since it is not advisable to leave valuables in the car, I must carry all of this equipment in and out of hotels and offices where I travel, along with the two cameras, two video cameras and other equipment that are part of each trip.

I have visited and worked in many towns in Ukraine, including Berezhany, Bolekhov, Borshchev, Brody, Buchach, Chortkov, Dolina, Drogobych, Gorodek, Gusyatin, Ivano-Frankovsk, Jaworów, Korolówka, Lviv, Monastyriska, Mostiska, Ozeryany, Podgaysty, Probezhna, Peremyshlyany, Rohatyń, Rozniatów, Sambor, Skala Podolskaya, Snyatyn, Sudovaya Vishnaya, Ternopol, Ugnev, Zabolotov and Zolochev.

My town visits include taking photographs and videos of general views and remaining Jewish sites (cemeteries, synagogues, new Holocaust monuments, Jewish schools and hospitals). I also conduct interviews with government officials and people in the Jewish community, perform local archival research and hold meetings with town historians. Where possible, I obtain maps of the town and mark the Jewish sites, along with any former ancestral homes described during local interviews.

To date, I have worked in more than a dozen *oblast* archives throughout Ukraine. In the winter, heating is scarce, and people often wear coats inside. In the summer, there is no air conditioning, and heat can be stifling. I remember once finding my driver, a man of many talents, on a ladder at the Lviv Archives. He was repairing the wiring. Within a short time, the lights came back on.

Perhaps the most rewarding and fulfilling part of this work is that about 20 percent of the time I find previously unknown living relatives (in the former Soviet Union) for clients. Often the clients then plan a trip to Ukraine to meet their newly discovered cousins. All of this makes me regret that I never purchased stock in Kodak.

Recent Travel in Ukraine by Susan Gelber Cannon

In August 1996, I traveled with my husband and two sons (ages 10 and 17) to the two small towns in Ukraine that I had discovered, through researching family histories and maps from early in the century, to have been the homes of my grandparents, George and Sarah Poliner.

Articles and maps published in the back issues of *The Galitzianer* were instrumental to the success of our trip. Additionally, my request for information published in *The Galitzianer* resulted in advice from several knowledgeable people. We followed much of their advice—especially about bringing dried fruits and snacks. As vegetarians, we ate a lot of *vareniky* and blintzes and yogurt. (We actually brought a small plug-in pot with an electrical adapter with which to make instant dried soups each evening in our hotel room—a real help to vegetarians!)

We found that bringing a travel kit of silver duct tape, wire, needle and thread, batteries for cameras, and over-the-counter and prescription medicines was a very practical idea. We got the Hepatitis A vaccine, which eased our minds about eating salads, if nothing else. We brought backpacks in which to carry with us everywhere the 1½ liter bottles of spring water we each purchased twice daily.

We highly recommend bringing a compact video camera with a battery recharging system compatible with Ukraine's 220-volt electrical current. Samsung makes one that can adapt from 110 to 220 volts. We used it and were satisfied with its performance. (We have already presented several "video showings" of our travels to eager relatives who were fascinated by the footage even more than by still photographs.)

A guide book we found extremely useful is *Hippocrene Language and Travel Guide to Ukraine* by Linda Hodges and George Chumak (New York: Hippocrene Books, 1994). We also used sections of *Let's Go: Eastern Europe*. The section on Lviv is very descriptive. We had been told to bring lots of one dollar bills. However, we found it much more useful to exchange about $30 each day for use in small bakeries, shops and taxis. Dollars were not accepted anywhere except the artists' market in Lviv. Then, it was useful to have new, crisp, unmarked bills. Every store or restaurant asked for *coupons*, which is the local Ukrainian currency. Credit cards were not an option, except in the Grand Hotel in Lviv. We had also been advised to be as wary as one would in any big U.S. city, but frankly, we felt safer in Ukraine than in cities in the U.S. Of course, we were careful with our belongings and money and did not appear flashy; except, of course, for our numerous cameras (bring lots of film and videotape).

We were searching for our roots in Ukraine and found them, quite literally, in the form of a 150-year-old poplar tree that we believe was planted by my great-greatgrandfather Katz in the town of Shchurovichi, Ukraine (Szczurowice was the name when the territory was in Galicia; the Jews called it Shtervitz, 88 km northeast of Lviv). It was the only trace of my family's line that we had discovered with the help of both prearranged and impromtu guides—but what an impact this living, enduring symbol had on me and my family!

Our travel agent at Diaspora Enterprises (220 South 20th Street, Philadelphia, PA 19103) had arranged for our transportation and guide. Although we had some trouble with one of our drivers, we had an energetic and intrepid translator, Luba Kos from the Sputnik agency (which may now be called Planeta). She freely questioned people on the streets in Lviv, as well as in the small towns we visited, often obtaining leads and information. We found the *babushkas* (local slang for old ladies) in the countryside the most eager and willing to talk about the Jews who were no longer part of the communities. One old woman bemoaned the loss of the Jewish community in 1942. "I liked it better when the Jews lived here. We helped each other; we all shared." Another old woman told us that the Germans had burned the Jewish homes and stores in 1942, but pointed out the synagogue, still standing and now used as a music school in Berestchko (near Galicia). Even the Jewish cemetery had been bulldozed and a house built atop it.

In Schchurovichi, the streets were not paved, and there was no evidence of a synagogue. Perhaps 200 Jews, about 30 percent of the population, lived there before the war. Two Ukrainian men in their sixties, Ivan and Mychael, helped us find the Jewish cemetery at our guide's request. It was overgrown with brambles, nettles and brush. The only stone we found was face down and too heavy to turn.

Ivan remembered several Jewish families. "I went to school with Jewish children," he said. "The town was beautiful before the war." Ivan pointed to the few standing homes of the Jews who had lived there: Reiss, Halpern, Freedman, Katz.

When we told him that my great-grandmother was Esther Katz, Ivan confirmed that Mr. Katz was involved in growing hops and milling. He had planted a tree, known in the town as Katz's tree—it was a poplar—so old and tall. We adopted Katz's tree as the Family Tree.

Finally, Ivan pointed over the fields in the direction of the farm of Anton Lukasiewicz, a Christian farmer who had hidden my grandmother Sarah's cousin, Simon Sterling, and his wife, Sophie, from the Germans in 1943. "Everyone knew that Lukasiewicz had Jews at his place," Ivan confided.

No Jews remain there today. Those few who survived, like Simon and Sophie, left the country for the United States and Israel. The others were killed at various death camps in the surrounding area, at towns named Lopatyn, Łoczów and Brody. We had gathered this information from Simon Sterling's haunting account of his experiences in *A Survivor's Story*, transcribed by his daughter, Phyllis Sterling Jacobs. The town today bears little resemblance to the one described by my grandmother, Sarah Bodek, to her daughters. Brody (Brot, in Yiddish), a large important city in the late 1800s, is still a large city. There was a sizeable Jewish population. In 1942, the synagogue was destroyed. The shell of the building remains standing and has been under "reconstruction" for about eight years. The task seems daunting. According to Simon's account, about 12,000 Jews were killed in Brody's ghetto and many thousands more in the surrounding towns.

Lviv is still a gem of a city. Untouched by bombs during the world wars, buildings remain standing from the 1500s, with an intact town center and market square. Sarah Bodek had told her daughters about trips to Lemberg to attend dances. There is a lovely opera house in the center of town and historical churches of various denominations.

The Jewish ghetto of Lviv was liquidated in 1942. After Ukrainian independence, a monument was erected near the site. There were three major synagogues in Lviv. One, the Golden Rose, was destroyed by the Germans in 1942. A plaque, written in English, Ukrainian and Hebrew, now marks the site. Another synagogue is used today as an active Jewish community center. The third, used as a stable during the war, is now a 300-family synagogue led by Rabbi Bald from Brooklyn! We visited this beautiful synagogue and spoke at length with the rabbi's wife. She can arrange for guides and translators and encourages congregations elsewhere to arrange food and clothing drives to benefit the community there. There are beautiful paintings all around the high ceiling depicting the Twelve Tribes of Israel. Bullet holes are also visible.

We had not gone to Ukraine with the intention of doing archival research and did not do any. We were interested in visiting the towns and cities important to my grandparents, who had come to the U.S. in 1904. In a way, the visit raised more questions than it answered, in that any evidence of the Jewish communities my grandparents had described was so often missing. However, with every bit of our beings, we absorbed the days we spent in Ukraine, a fascinating country full of the feeling of history, age and transition. The intangible impact on our family, especially our sons, was strong and totally worthwhile. Whether you go with an organized tour or on your own, travel to Ukraine for family research purposes may be rewarding for you as well.

Another Brief Travel Saga by William Fern

In 1992, a friend and I took a trip to Drogobych, Borysław, Truskawiec and Lviv. We boarded an Aeroflot flight in Warsaw for Lviv. In midair, an announcement was made that the plane would land at Ivano-Frankovsk. The plane was filthy and in need of serious repair. We were glad to land safely anywhere. Passengers had to find their own way to Lviv.

After taking a taxi to Drogobych for about $30, we found that the only hotel in the town was the Tuston. We preferred to stay at the Hotel Beskid in nearby Truskawiec for $10 per day in U.S. currency, meals included. Travelers are advised to come with U.S. dollars in denominations of $1 and $5. Dollars open many doors.

On the return trip to Warsaw, the plane again left from Ivano-Frankovsk instead of Lviv as planned. The only hotel in Ivano-Frankovsk was filthy. At the airport, luggage was tagged with stubs of cardboard with only a number and no indication of flight, place of origin or destination. When we arrived, we were told that my luggage was lost. My friend refused to accept this verdict and insisted on going into the luggage area to check despite the loud protests of the attendant. There, in a corner, neatly tucked aside, was my luggage, officially "lost." Apparently, it is not uncommon for luggage to be "lost" in this fashion.

❀ Chapter 8 ❀

Indexes to Selected Books and Collections

Town Name Index to *Pinkas Hakehillot*

The following list includes the Galician towns described in the *Pinkas Hakehillot* (Encyclopedia of towns) published by Yad Vashem as a series on Jewish communities or areas in Central and Eastern Europe. Five of the volumes cover Poland, of which three include towns that were once in Galicia. The articles focus on Jewish life in these towns. George Sackheim translated and published a list of the towns mentioned in *Search* vol. 8, no. 3 in 1988. He designated in which volume on Poland the article appeared: volume 1 (Łódź and its Region), 2 (Eastern Galicia) or 3 (Western Galicia). In some cases, there appears to be more than one article.

Sackheim's translation (or perhaps that of the *Pinkas* authors, since some books include English-language indexes) spells the name of the town as it was spelled by the Austrian government. While not generally a problem for towns in Poland, many towns in Ukraine are now spelled differently in their transliterated form. Since there are multiple towns of the same name in Poland and Ukraine, there may be confusion for some towns. Some towns may have been missed from Sackheim's original list.

Table 8.1. Galician Towns Described in *Pinkas Hakehillot*

Baligród 3	Bukaczowce 2	Dukla 3	Jaworów 2 and 3
Baranów 3	Chodorów/Khodorov 2	Dunajów 2	Jazłowice 1 and 2
Barycz 2	Chołojów 2	Dynów 3	Jedlicze 3
Bełż 2	Chorostków 2	Stary Dzików 2	Jezierzany 2
Bełżc 1 and 2	Chrzanów 3	Dzików 1	Jeżow 3
Bialy Kamień 2	Chyrów 2	Gliniany 1 and 2	Jezupol 2
Biecz 3	Cieszanów 1 and 2	Gołogóry 2	Jordanów 3
Bielsko 1	Cisna 3	Gorlice 3	Kalusz 2
Bielsko Biała 3	Czarny Dunajec 3	Grabów 1	Kamionka Strumiłowa 2
Bircza 2	Czchów 3	Grebów 3	Kańczuga 3
Błazowa 3	Czortków 2	Grójec 1	Kęty 3
Bóbrka 2	Czortowiec 2	Gromnik Grybów 3	Kłodowa 1
Bochnia 1 and 3	Czuduc 3	Grzymałów 2	Kolaczyce 3
Bohorodczany 2	Dąbie 1	Halicz 2	Kolbuszowa 3
Bolechów 2	Dąbrowa 1	Horodenka 2	Kołomea 2
Bolszowce 2	Dąbrowa Tarnowska 3	Ilnik 2	Kopyczyńce 2
Borysław 2	Dębica 1 and 3	Iwanowice 1	Korczyna 3
Brody 1 and 2	Delatyn 2	Jankowice 1	Kozłów 2
Broszniów 2	Dobczyce 3	Janów 1 and 2	Kozowa 2
Brzesko 3	Dobra 1	Jarosław 1	Kraków 1 and 3
Brzeżany 2	Dobromil 2	Jaryczów 2	Krechowice 2
Brzeżnica Stara 1	Dobrotwór 2	Jasienica Rosielna 3	Krościenko 2
Brzostek	Dolina 2	Jasliska 3	Krosno 3
Brzozów 3	Domaradz 3	Jasło 3	Krukienice 2
Buchach 2	Drohobycz 2	Jawornik Polski 3	Krynica 3
Budzanów/Budanow 1, 2	Dubiecko 3	Jawornik Szklarski 3	Krystynopol 2

Krzeszowice 3
Krzywcza 3
Kulików 2
Kuty 2
Łabowa 3
Łacko 3
Łańcut 3
Lanczyn 2
Lesko 2
Lesniów
Lezhanovka 2
Leżajsk 3
Limanowa 3
Lipsko 2
Lomna 2
Lopatyn 2
Lutowiska 2
Lemberg 1 and 2
Magierów 2
Mielec 3
Mielnica 2
Mikołajów 2
Mikuliczyn 2
Mikulińce 2
Monasterzyska 2
Mosciska 2
Mszana Dolna 3
Muszyna 3
Myślenice 3
Nakło 1
Narajów 2
Narol 2
Niebylec 3
Niemirów 1 and 2
Niepolomice 3
Nowy Dwór 1
Nowy Sącz 3
Nowy Targ 3
Obertyn 2
Olesko 2
Oleszyce 2
Olpiny 3

Osiek 1 and 3
Otrówek 1
Oświęcim 3
Peczeniżyn 2
Pilzno 3
Piwniczna 3
Plazów 1
Podbuż 3
Podhajce 2
Podwołoczyska 2
Pomorzany 2
Potok 2
Probuzna 2
Pruchnik 3
Przecław 3
Przedbórz 1
Przemyślany 2
Przemyśl 2
Przewórsk 3
Rabka 3
Radgoszcz 3
Radlow 3
Radomyśl nad Sanem 3
Radomyśl Wielkie 3
Radoszyce 1
Radymno 3
Radziechów 2
Raków 1
Rawa Ruska 2
Romanów 1
Ropczyce 3
Równe 1
Rożniatów 2
Roznów 2
Rozwadów 3
Rybnik 3
Rybotycze 2
Ryglice 3
Rymanów 3
Rzepiennik Strzyżowski 3
Rzeszów 1 and 3
Sambor 2

Sanniki 1
Skała 2
Skałat 2
Skawina 3
Skole 2
Śniatyn 2
Sokal 2
Sokołów 2 and 3
Sokolówka 2
Solotwina 2
Sosnowice 1
Stanisławczyk 2
Stanisławów 2
Stara Sól 2
Starachowice 1
Stary Sącz 3
Stary Sambor 2
Stebnik 2
Stojanów 2
Stratyń 2
Strusów 2
Stryj 2
Strzeliska Nowe 2
Strzyżów 3
Suchostaw 2
Swięciany 1
Świrz 2
Szczakowa 3
Szczawnica Wyżna 3
Szczerzec 2
Szczurowice 2
Tartaków 2
Tarnobrzeg 3
Tarnopol 1 and 2
Tarnoruda 3
Tarnów 1 and 3
Tłumacz 2
Tłumaczyk 2
Tłuste 2
Touste 2
Trembowla 2
Truskawiec 2

Trzebina 3
Tuchów 3
Turka 2
Tyczyn 3
Tylicz 3
Tyrawa Woloska 3
Uhnów 2
Ujazd 1
Ulanów 3
Ulaszkowce 2
Urycz 2
Uście Zielone 2
Uścieczko 2
Ustrzyki Dolne 2
Wesola 1
Wieliczka 3
Wielkie Oczy 1/2
Winniki 2
Wiśnicz Nowy 2/3
Witów 1
Żabie 2
Zabłotów 2
Zabno 3
Zagórz 3
Zagórze 1
Zakliczyn 3
Zakopane 3
Zaleszczyki 2
Założce 2
Zarnowiec 1
Zator 3
Zawada 1
Zawalów 2
Zbaraż 2
Złoczów 2
Zlotniki 2
Żmigród Nowy 3
Żołkiew 1 and 2
Żołynia 3
Żurawno 2
Żywiec 3

Town Name Index to *Le Toledot ha-Kehillot be Polin*

Rabbi Zevi Horowitz, born in Kraków in 1872, was the son of the chief rabbi there. Zevi Horowitz himself became the chief rabbi in Dresden in 1920 and remained there until 1939, when he took refuge in Nice. He lived through the war, but died in Nice just after the war ended in 1945. His book, published posthumously by his son, was entitled *Le Toledot ha-Kehilot be Polin* (On the history of the Jewish communities of Poland). He seems to have used the term "Poland" to describe Eastern Europe generally, since some of the towns were never in Poland.

The book is a compilation of articles, some very brief and some very long, about the communities, with an emphasis on the rabbinic history of the town.

The list below represents the work of David Einsiedler, who corrected the list initially published in *The Galitzianer* (vol. 1, no. 2). The entire list of Galician towns and the page number in the Horowitz book follows.

Suzan Wynne has a personal copy of *Le Toldedot ha-Kehillot be Polin*. The book, which may still be in print, was published in 1978 by Mosad Harav Kook in Jerusalem. David Einsiedler, the Library of Congress and the New York Public Library each has a copy. Try Jewish bookstores, Jewish libraries or, if all else fails, send Suzan Wynne a self-addressed stamped envelope, and you will be told the cost for a copy of the article(s) of interest. Her address is 3603 Littledale Road, Kensington, MD 20895. For towns in present-day Ukraine, the current name is included after the slash, if it has changed. Each entry shows the town name and the page (in parentheses) in the book where the town description appears.

Bełż, N of Lviv (132)

Biały Kamień/Belyy Kamen, ENE of Lviv (130)

Bóbrka, SE of Lviv (99)

Bochnia, E of Kraków (104)

Bohorodczany/Bogorodchany, S of Lviv (151)

Bolechów/Bolekhov, S of Lviv (105)

Brzesko (Brigel), E of Kraków (154)

Brzeżany/Berezhany, NE of Lviv (155)

Brzostek, W of Przemyśl (157)

Buczacz/Buchach, SE of Lviv (101)

Budzanów/Budanov, SE of Ternopol (100)

Bursztyn/Burshtyn, SE of Lviv (126)

Busk, NE of Lviv (112)

Dobromil, SW of Lviv (195)

Drohobycz/Drogobych, SW of Lviv (229)

Dukla, SW of Przemyśl (199)

Gołogóry, E of Lviv (166)

Janów, near Lviv (360)

Jarosław, NNW of Przemyśl (366)

Jaryczów Nowy/Novyy Yarychev, NE of Lviv(361)

Jazłowice/Pomortsy (356)

Kamionka near Przemyśl (491)

Komarno, SW of Lviv (493)

Lesko (Linsk, Lisko), SE of Sanok (379)

Leszniów/Leshnev, NE of Lviv (382)

Narol, NNE of Przemyśl (391)

Niemirów, WNW of Lviv (392)

Nowy Sącz (Sanz), SE of Kraków (477)

Olesko, ENE of Lviv (7)

Oświęcim/Auschwitz, W of Kraków (4)

Podhajce/Podgaytsy, SE of Lviv (432)

Podkamień, ENE of Lviv (437)

Pomorzany/Pomoryany, ESE of Lviv (439)

Przemyśl, E of Kraków (464)

Rawa Ruska/Rava Russkaya, NW of Lviv (516)

Rohatyń/Rogatin, SE of Lviv (508)

Skole, S of Lviv (405)

Stryy, S of Lviv (403)

Swirż, 45 mi. ESE of Lviv (400)

Tarnopol/Ternapol, E of Lviv (324)

Tarnów, E of Kraków (321)

Tyśmienica/Tysmenitsa, near Tlumacz (332)

Ulanów, N of Kraków (1)

Uście Zielone/Uste Zelene, SE of Lviv (2)

Wisnicz Nowy near Kraków (265)

Wojsławice, near Sokal, N of Lviv (262)

Jaworów, W of Lviv (351)

Załoźce/Zalozhtsy, E of Lviv (301)

Zbaraż/Zbarazh, N of Ternopol (298)

Zborów, E of Lviv (299)

Złoczów/Zolochev, E of Lviv (304)

Żmigród Nowy, SE of Kraków (307)

Żurawno/Zhuravno, SE of Lviv (300)

Zuzmir (Kazimierz, Jewish suburb of Kraków) (481)

United States Passenger Lists

Family Finding (vol. 5, no. 3), the newsletter of the Jewish Genealogy Society of Wisconsin, discussed an important resource relating to Rotterdam passenger lists. Rotterdam was a major port of exit from Europe for Galician Jews. Norman Ross Publishing (300 W. 58th Street, New York, NY 10019) has put the Holland-American Line passenger lists for 1900–40 on microfiche. Part 1 of the collection is a set of 272 fiche containing an alphabetized list of passengers with their ticket numbers, ships and departure dates. These are divided into several fiche for periods of several months. For example, one group covers December 6, 1900, to August 8, 1901. Part 2 is a set of 781 fiche containing the names of passengers on each ship, with information about their booking agents, ticket types and prices, and information on train travel after arriving in the U.S. The publisher sells the whole collection for $7,900, but is willing to sell portions of Parts 1 and 2. The index may be ordered separately.

U.S. State Department Resources

An important index of surnames mentioned in U.S. State Department records in the National Archives exists for the records of requests for assistance and information made by U.S. citizens on behalf of relatives living in Austria-Hungary in the years before and during World War I. The prewar correspondence most often concerned missing family members and procedures for sending money; war brought a sense of urgency to the correspondence. Letters reflect the frantic concern about family members who had been visiting in Europe when war broke out, relatives who had not been heard from, and relatives who had been heard from and were without funds.

This index, which was created by volunteers from the Jewish Genealogy Society of Greater Washington, includes names from all parts of the Austro-Hungarian Empire, including Austria proper, Romania, Moravia, Hungary and Bukowina; about half of the names were of people living in Galicia. The index includes the names of the U.S. citizens (usually naturalized) making the request, as well as the person(s) being inquired about.

The index is part of the microfiche series entitled "Index to Department of State Records Found in U.S. National Archives" which may be ordered from Avotaynu, Inc., P.O. Box 900, Teaneck, NJ 07666. If you find a name of interest and are unable to travel to Washington to visit the National Archives, you may ask for assistance in obtaining a copy of the relevant material by writing to the National Archives, Washington, DC 20408. Provide all of the information listed in the index notation. A small fee is charged for research and copying. See also Appendix E for names of Galitzianers appearing in these records.

State Department Records Reveal Eighty-Year-Old Family Drama
by Saul Lindenbaum

When World War I began, my grandfather, Selig Lindenbaum, was in New York City. However, my father, Sam, and his sister, Regina (then ages 6 and 14, respectively), as well as my grandmother, Etel, were still living in Uście Biskupie, a small town in Eastern Galicia. After the Russians burned down their home, the three of them became refugees in a series of small towns around Borszczów (now Borshchev). When the United States entered the war against Austria in 1917, communication between people in the two countries appears to have been difficult to impossible. Conditions in the new country of Poland were chaotic right after the war, too, and Selig lost track of his family for many months. My father has often spoken of Selig's determined letter-writing efforts to locate them in postwar Poland and bring them to America. But my grandfather was a quiet, unassuming man who never seemed quite at ease in America. Though learned in Hebrew and Yiddish, he never mastered English, so I had always wondered just how, exactly, he had gone about trying to find his family.

About a year ago, I discovered that Avotaynu, Inc. (P.O. Box 900, Teaneck, NJ 07666) sells on microfiche an index of people who had written to the State Department on behalf of relatives in post-World War I Poland. It was clear that this could be an opportunity to separate family myth from reality, so I bought a copy of the microfiche. When it arrived, I hastened to the local library, slipped the fiche on "Jewish Names in Protection of U.S. Citizens in Austria-Hungary, 1914–1920" into the machine, ran rapidly through the alphabet to "L" and there it was, a file with my grandfather's name. Next, I inserted the microfiche called, "Jewish Names in Protection of Interests of U.S. Citizens in Romania, Germany and Poland, 1917–1920" and was thrilled to find two more files under the names of my grandfather, father and aunt.

I went home and wrote a letter to the National Archives as indicated on the microfiche, requesting copies of the three files. I don't know why, but I expected to receive nothing or, at best, two or three pages of correspondence. But, in less than three weeks, a thick manila envelope arrived from the Archives, containing 37 pages of correspondence between Selig and the State Department that covered an eight-month period in 1919–20. An unexpected bonus was a copy of Selig's naturalization papers, which he had had to provide before the government would consider his case. The correspondence was rich with detail, including the fact that when he began to write, Selig clearly did not know that his wife had died in a typhus epidemic three months earlier.

The first letter, dated August 9, 1919, was obviously written by another immigrant. It was handwritten and filled with misspelled words, even of the towns in Galicia where Selig thought the family might be. It would not have been hard to figure out what was meant, but within two weeks, the State Department wrote back saying that they could not help him because they had never heard of the towns.

Selig found someone better to write the next letter. It was typed, and everything was spelled correctly. The State Department agreed to send $60 (at least a month's salary, I'm sure), to the American Consul in Warsaw on receipt of a money order from Selig. In December, he sent another money order for $40, but several letters then followed in which Selig said that the children told him that they had not received the money, while the State Department insisted that they had. By March 1920, everyone agreed that Regina and Sam had received the $100.

Now the biggest struggle began. Regina and Sam, then living in Kozaczyne, a shtetl near Borszczów, had obtained Polish passports and permission to emigrate, but they needed money for overland travel and for passage on a ship. Selig wanted to cable another $200 to them, but the State Department refused to help. They wanted him to go through a bank or through the Joint Distribution Committee (JDC). "My children are starving," Selig writes, and the banks and the JDC are taking six months to contact people. But the government, polite as ever and acknowledging the "abnormal conditions" in Poland, was unmoved. One man circulated an internal memo asking if an exception could be made in this case, but no exception was made.

At this point, Selig played his last card. The final letter in his behalf was dated April 1920 from Reuben Fink. The letterhead identified him as the Washington correspondent for *Der Tag* (The Day), a Yiddish newspaper in New York. His plea also fell on deaf ears, and an internal memo notes that Fink was "prejudiced" against the JDC. The correspondence ended here.

After reading these letters, it was clear to me, at last, that the stories about my grandfather's efforts to save his family were accurate and that the reality was far more dramatic and touching than anything I had imagined. His anguish and desperation are evident on every page, but in the end, he was successful. However he did it, he finally got the money to his children and was there to meet them when they arrived at Ellis Island on August 5, 1920, after a harrowing journey across Europe and the Atlantic Ocean. But that's another story.

❀ Chapter 9 ❀

Notes About Specific Galician Towns

Over the years, Gesher Galicia members have pooled their resources and knowledge of specific towns. Listed below are some of their offerings. If you contact the individual contributors noted below, be sure to enclose a self-addressed, stamped envelope or compensation for the equivalent postage.

Eastern Galicia
(The old Galician name is given in parentheses following the current name.)

Berezhany (Brzeżany)
Bill Feuerstein (24710 Calle Altamira, Calabassas, CA 91302-3004) has a map of the Berezhany burial plots in Mt. Zion Cemetery, Maspeth, NY, that covers burials for the years 1900–79.

Bolekhov (Bolechów)
Donald Meyers (160-63 25th Drive, Flushing, NY 11358-1003; phone: (718) 767-1087) has some recent information about this town and is interested in exchanging information with others.

Gershon Lauer suggests that researchers with an interest in Bolekhov read the memoirs of *Ber of Bolechov* (1723–1805). "He did a great deal of traveling; his memoirs can prove very useful to all Galician researchers." The book was published in three languages (Hebrew, Yiddish and English) in 1922 from a manuscript by Dr. M. Vishnitzer. "All three editions are available in Jews College Library in London and, presumably, in other western libraries." The English edition was published by Oxford University Press.

Brody
Gershon Lauer (8 Paget Road, London N16 5NQ, England) submitted information about Brody. There are two *yizkor* books. The first is volume 6 of a series entitled *Arim v'Imahot b'Israel*, published by Mossad Harav Kook. The volume, published independently in 1955 and titled *Sefer Brody*, was compiled by Dr. Nathan Gelber, who traces the community from 1584 until its tragic end in 1943. This 400-page book includes "excellent references to archives and other prewar books and materials" that he consulted. There is also a name index and a list of gravestone inscriptions that he culled from the pre–1831 cemetery records.

The second book, published in 1994 by the organization of former Brody residents in Israel, is entitled *Ner Tamid: Yizkor L'Brody* (An eternal light: Brody in memoriam). This book includes personal recollections of Brody survivors, a Holocaust memorial list, a list of *landsmanschaftn* members who died in Israel, and various articles about the town's history. The editor also translated the table of contents and the book's town history section into English.

For Polish-language readers, a book about Brody was published in 1935 by David Wurm entitled *Z dziejów żydostwa brodzkiego* (From the history of Brody's Jews). Both the Klaus and Jerusalem libraries have copies of this book. Wurm was among the Jews who were murdered when the Germans arrived in Brody in 1941.

Brody researchers should note that Fond 701 in the Lviv Archives (Religious Community in Lviv) has many records of the Brody Jewish community. There were two cemeteries in Brody. The pre-1831 cemetery has been destroyed. Efforts are being made to fence in the newer one and to have it listed as a protected site. (See Appendix C for additional information about a cemetery project concerning Brody.)

There are early 1800s Jewish court (*bet din*) records on microfilm for Brody at both the Central Archives for the History of the Jewish People in Jerusalem and the Jewish Theological Seminary in New York. Lauer also recommends two books about the great fire in Brody that were written by Mordechai Trelisker and published in Zolkiew in 1835: *Haserayfoh* (The fire), which describes the fire and its results, and *Koyss HaTarayloh* (The poisonous cup), a collection of songs and poems about the fire.

Lauer also has additional information and would like to exchange information with others with roots in Brody. In particular, he is seeking information about a pre-World War II Hebrew-language book about the five sages of Brody called *Chamisha Chachmei Brody*.

Chortkov (Chortków)

Sidney C. Gelb (32 Brook Path, Plainview, NY 11803) has translated the table of contents of the Chortkov *yizkor* book and has copied the map of Chortkov and the English section on the history of the Jews in Chortkov. He is willing to share his efforts. He will send it through the mail if he receives a self-addressed, 9"x12" envelope with 78 cents postage. For those from outside the U.S., please send $2.50 instead.

Dolgoye (Dołhe)

Theodore Klein found a map, a history and the 1944 census in the United States Holocaust Museum Archives. The call number for these materials is RG-03.013*0.

Drogobych (Drohobycz)

William Fern (4 Edgewater Hillside, Westport, CT 06880) has made English translations of the following works and will send a photocopy of any of them for the cost of copying and postage.
- Summary of the chapter on the history of the Jews of Drohobycz from the *yizkor* book of Drohobycz-Borysław, edited by N.M. Gelber, *Memorial to the Jews of Drohobycz-Borysław and Surroundings* (Tel Aviv, 1959). This book deals with general historical background.
- Wikler, Jakuh. "*Z Dziejów Żydów w Drohobyczu*" (History of the Jews of Drohobycz), *Bulletin of Jewish Historical Institute* 71–72 (Warsaw, 1969).

Glinyany (Gliniany)

Anne Halpern reports there are three *yizkor* books for Gliniany. One is *Kehilat Glina, 1473–1943: Tolodoteha ve-Hurbana* (The community of Glina 1473–1943: Its history and destruction) by Asher Korech (Jerusalem, 1950) (in Hebrew). The Library of Congress call number is DS135.R93 G564 1950. The other two books (published in 1945 and 1950) were edited by Halpern's grandfather, Henoch Halpern. One, in Yiddish and 52 pages long, has been translated on tape, and Anne Halpern is in the process of transcribing the book. If she can obtain permission from the translator, she will share it with others. Furthermore, Anne and her father are exploring ways that the longer, 307-page book can be translated from the Yiddish. If you are interested in participating in this translation, please contact Anne Halpern at 3305 Liberty Parkway, Dundalk, MD 21222; e-mail <labraholic@aol.com>.

Khorostkov (Chorostków)

Andrew Tanenbaum (Van Nijenrodeweg 875, 1081 BG Amsterdam, Holland) arranged to have part of the *yizkor* book translated into English. The translation is on disk in ASCII.

Mosty Velikieye (Gross Mosty)

Yvette Scharf (165 Howard Drive, Hamden, CT 06514-1803) has compiled a surname list for the English section of the *yizkor* book, which was published without a name index. To date, she has not done the same for the Hebrew and Yiddish sections. She also has a translated version of the book's table of contents. The book deals primarily with the families of those who provided the information for the book. To obtain information, send a self-addressed, stamped envelope.

Podgaytsy (Podhajce)

Dr. A. Rozkowski, who visited this town, says there are no Jews left in Podgatsy. He was told that "one Jew came back after the war but died a few years ago. He had said that after his death, the synagogue would collapse, and this has happened. One corner (very thick) of the building has collapsed, but it is still standing and is used as a magazine [store]." The Jewish cemetery of Podgatsy lost about 85 percent of its tombstones; the Germans forced the local population to build a road using them. The cemetery is clearly visible; cows graze there.

Sassów (see Zolochev)

Stryy (see Turka)

Ternopol (Tarnopol)

Dr. A. Rozkowski visited Ternopol. There are a few Jews there, but we did not meet any personally. He was told that a Jewish society, *Aleph*, exists there. The Jewish cemetery is overgrown with weeds and a lot of tombstones are lost, but at least it has an iron fence from the main street. It is located opposite a Christian cemetery. He visited a provincial archives in Ternopol and was told that they have some Jewish documents.

Turka (and Stryy)

Gloria Klehr Frey has a photocopy of the *yizkor* book that covers Turka and Stryy. Her address is 211-5 Gibson Blvd., Clark, NY 07066; e-mail: <G.klehrfrey@worldnet.att.net>.

Zabolotov (Zabłotów)

David Fox (969 Placid Court, Arnold, MD 21012; e-mail: <fox@erols.com>) has acquired a number of sources about Zabołotov and some of the very small shtetls in the vicinity (Pipielniki and Dzurów). These include a photocopy of the *yizkor* book published in 1949. An original copy of the book is in the Harvard University Library and, through the generosity of the late Herb Unger, a photocopy is in the Library of Congress. It does not appear to have an index, but the table of contents has been translated into English. Fox also has an excellent biography about growing up in Zabołotov: *God's Water Carriers* by Manes Sperber (New York: Holmes and Meir, 1987). Fox also has a rough translation of the Zabolotov entry in *Pinkas Hakehillot*, Poland (Eastern Galicia), vol. 2.

Zolochev (Złoczów)

Brian Neil Burg (2673 Renz Circle, Fullerton, CA 92833-2055; e-mail: <enfjbri@aol.com>) has the book *Złoczów Memorial, 1939–1944: A Chronicle of Survival* by Samuel Lipa Tennenbaum. The book mentions Sassów and other towns and some names.

Western Galicia

Błazowa and Rymanów

Suzan Wynne (3603 Littledale Road, Kensington, MD 20895; e-mail: <srwynne@erols.com>) has *yizkor* records from the Blazower Society in Lower Manhattan, New York. The society merged with the *landsmanschaftn* from Rymanów; there are also names with origins from that town. There is no index, and the records have not been translated. Those associated with the Blazower Society are buried in that section at Mt. Zion Cemetery, 594-63 54th Avenue, Maspeth, NY 11378; phone: (718) 335-2500.

Brzozów

Suzan Wynne (3603 Littledale Road, Kensington, MD 20895; e-mail: srwynne@erols.com) has a copy of the Brzozów *yizkor* book. The authors did not create an index of surnames, but Suzan developed one for the English section.

Dębica

Ronald Miller (Image Analytics Corporation, 275-D Marcus Blvd., Hauppage, NY 11788; e-mail: <miller@iacsoft.com>) has the *yizkor* book for Dębica (Dembitz, in Yiddish).

Mark Taub's father, David Taub, a Holocaust survivor, was born in Dębica. Mark Taub reported that he and his father have traveled there twice, in 1991 and 1993, to do research and visit the area. He notes he was fortunate to obtain copies of elementary school report cards, voter registration lists, business/occupation license journals, etc. He found the house his father was born in. The synagogue still stands, though it is a flea market today, and the cemetery, while 95 percent destroyed, still has 40–50 stones remaining.

Dobromil

David Fox (969 Placid Court, Arnold, MD 21012; e-mail: <fox@erols.com>) holds the *yizkor* book for Dobromil edited by Saul Miller. The book is entitled *Dobromil: Life in a Galician Shtetl, 1890–1907*. The English section of the book is 83 pages, and the Yiddish section 50 pages. It was published in 1980 by Lowenthal Press. Library of Congress Catalog Card Number 80-81470. The book is not indexed and has no table of contents, but contains valuable information about the town.

Głogów

In *The Galitzianer* (vol. 3, no. 1), Marian Rubin (36 Iris Avenue, San Francisco, CA 94118; <e-mail: merubin@aol.com>) wrote the following:

In the Bor forest of Głogów Małopolska, where many Jews from the Rzeszów ghetto—including Jews from towns such as Tyczyn, Czudec, Niebylec, Głogów and Kolbuszowa—were slaughtered by the Germans in 1942, a memorial ceremony was held on June 26, 1995 (see also *The Galitzianer* [vol. 1, no. 4], "Letter from Rzeszów").

Under pouring rain, the nearly 200 people who came to remember the victims and to dedicate a stone and tablets to their memory, walked about a third of a mile into the woods to the memorial site. The area is situated between two mass graves, where, according to Klara Ma'ayan, president of the Rzeszów *landsmanschaft* in Tel Aviv, 5,000 Jews had been murdered.

Among those gathered for the ceremony were officials and academicians from the area and representatives from the Catholic Church. Among the Jews attending were thirty Israelis, the eldest of whom had been born in Rzeszów. They were accompanied by their children and, in some cases, by their grandchildren. I had made arrangements to join the group in Warsaw. My father's family had emigrated from Rzeszów to the U.S. in 1858, so my connection to the town was removed from the immediate, painful connection of the others. However, as I stood at the ceremony, I was keenly aware of something that many genealogists learn. Relatives, whose names I have not yet learned, probably remained in Rzeszów and were perhaps among those for whom *kaddish* was being said.

Prayers were read by Avraham Beck, who was born in Rzeszów and now lives in Israel. The memorial project was initiated by Mrs. Ma'ayan, who worked closely with Bogusław Kotula. Kotula, the son of the late distinguished historian Franciszek Kotula, is a resident of Rzeszów. He and his brother Sławomir have continued the close, warm ties with the Jewish community that their father had enjoyed. Mrs. Ma'ayan praised the efforts of Rzeszow mayor, Mieczysław Janowski, who had arranged for local funding of the project. Other funds came from the *landsmanschaft*, the Polish Embassy in Israel, and the Israeli Embassy in Poland.

Gorlice

Sidney Charles Gelb (32 Brook Path, Plainview, NY 11803) has translated the table of contents of the Gorlice *yizkor* book, as well as page 16 of the text. He is willing to share his efforts. He can fax the information in the United States or send it through the mail if he receives a self-addressed, 9"x12" envelope with 78 cents postage. For those outside the U.S., please send $2.50.

Kanczuga (see Rzeszów)

Kolbuszowa

For a detailed account of prewar Kolbuszowa, see *A Jewish Boyhood in Poland: Remembering Kolbuszowa* by Norman Salsitz (Syracuse, N.Y.: Syracuse University Press, 1992).

Phil Birnbaum returned from Poland in August 1997 and filed this report: He met an 83-year-old, Mr. Pochinsky, who was born into the Jewish family of kosher butchers named Plawker. After the war, he married a Catholic and converted to his wife's faith. Today, no one else of Jewish heritage lives in the town of 10,000. All pre-1948 records were destroyed. The synagogue is now the town's historical museum, and a few items from the synagogue are on display. The *mikvah* (ritual bath) next to the synagogue is now used as a construction office. It is reported that the cemetery is reasonably large and overgrown, but headstones are intact and not desecrated. Contact Jacek Baren, Town Historian, 36-100 Kolbuszowa, ul. Koscuiski 2. The fax number at the town hall is 48 17 227 2939. Though he is willing to assist people at the rate of $60 per hour for up to three hours, he does not speak English.

Łancut

Suzan Wynne (3603 Littledale Road, Kensington, MD 20895; e-mail: <srwynne@erols.com> has a copy of the name index to the *yizkor* book for Łancut.

Mielec

Yvette Scharf (165 Howard Drive, Hamden, CT 06514-1803) had the 288-page *Mielecer Idn* translated by Martin Koenigsberg. The *yizkor* book was written in Yiddish and published by Solomon Klagsbrun in Israel in 1979. The translated version is 223 pages. From the English version, Scharf was able to extract surnames, nicknames, occupations and relationships to each other. She also extracted information about where a person came from other than Mielec. Scharf also had the table of contents translated.

Przemyśl

Suzan Wynne (3603 Littledale Road, Kensington, MD 20895; e-mail: <srwynne@erols.com>) has the *yizkor* book and a translated version of the table of contents and the name index, as well as other relevant materials about the city.

Radomyśl Wielkie

Morty Miller (6508 Hubbardton Way, Springfield, VA 22150-4275) and Carole Rosofsky Fox acquired a booklet in Polish entitled *The Martyrdom of the Jewish Population of Radomyśl Wielki and the Surrounding Areas During the Second World War* by Antoni Balaryn (1989), which lists a number of former residents who were in the town at the time of the Holocaust. Balaryn, who is not Jewish but who has maintained friendships with boyhood schoolmates who are, compiled the record of events in Radomyśl Wielkie from his own memories and from written documents. The names mentioned in the booklet include: Aloni, Amsterdam, Appel-Brand, Eisig, Feder, Feuerestein, Fisch, Geldzeller, Gold, Grin, Gutwirt, Hand, Ici, Kanengiser, Keller, Kelman/Kalman, Klein, Koch, Leibowicz, Leiman, Mechowicz, Natowicz, Padawer, Plafkier, Rabin, Schimeleib, Schlesinger, Schwartz, Spatz, Spiegel, Trau, Trompeter, Wind, Windstrauch, Zerlo, Ziss.

Rymanów (see Błazówa)

Rzeszów

Darla Stone (200 Corbin Place, Suite 3V, Brooklyn, NY 11235) has a list of subscribers for a Hebrew book published in 1927. The subscribers were from Tarnów, Kańczuga and Rzeszów.

Nat Abramowitz obtained a copy of a handwritten letter written on January 13, 1946, by a priest from a town near Rzeszów to the authorities investigating Nazi atrocities. The priest, Father Andrzej Mikołajczyk, offered the following testimony:

> In the forest, in Rudno, between Rzeszów and Głogów, 10 km [6 miles] north of Rzeszów, on the road from Rzeszów to Kolbuszowa, there are Jewish mass graves that were seeded with trees following the mass killings. Ten thousand Jews and Poles from the Rzeszów ghetto are interred there. Among them are Jews from Rzeszów, Tyczyn, Czudec, Niebylec, Strzyżow, Sokolów, Głogów, Kolbuszowa and many surrounding villages. They were also from transports overcrowded with Jews who were destined for the death camp of Bełzec, behind the town of Rawa Ruska, which at this time belongs to the Soviets. To the best of my knowledge, trees were seeded on top of the graves. In case these graves have not yet been registered, I ask you to investigate this case and I guarantee the truth of this statement.

Sanok

Suzan Wynne (3603 Littledale Road, Kensington, MD 20895; e-mail: <srwynne@erols.com>) has a copy of the Sanok *yizkor* book and a translated table of contents as well as a translated index of surnames.

Tarnobrzeg

Gayle Schlissel Riley (612 E. Live Oak, #A, San Gabriel, CA 91776) has a booklet by the town's historical society about Jewish life there. The booklet lists marriage records and the names of high school graduates. Gayle also has 77 names from birth records for 1896–1900 and a 19th century registration of citizens. She has set up a website about Tarnobrzeg. The address is <http://www.jewishgen.org/shtetlinks/tarnobrzeg/tarnobrzeg.html>.

Tarnów, Kańczuga and Rzeszów

Darla Stone (200 Corbin Place, Suite 3V, Brooklyn, NY 11235) has a list of subscribers for a Hebrew book published in 1927 for Tarnów, Kańczuga and Rzeszów.

Tyczyn

Nat Abramowitz found an article in Polish about the administrators of Tyczyn's Jewish community. The article appears to have been taken from a larger book after World War I, but before World War II, since it referred to the existence of 1,000 Jewish residents. Pictured were Dr. Speiser, an attorney who was head of the Gemilas Chesed (a cooperative bank); M. Hollander, a leading administrator; H. Horn, deputy leader; J. Tuchman; A. Bernstein; I. Dorlich (official rabbi of the community); M. Goldfuss, an engineer; and Sz. Schneeweiss. The article mentioned the stone synagogue built in 1795 which replaced the wooden synagogue that had burned. Rabbi Jacob Shapiro, author of *Ohel Jacob*, settled in the town during the rampage of the Cossack Chmielnicki in 1648. Rabbi Shapiro was buried in the town's cemetery. To obtain a copy of the article, write to Suzan Wynne (3603 Littledale Road, Kensington, MD 20895) and enclose $2.

Ulanów

Richard Schwarzstein (1300 Dove Street, Suite 200, Newport Beach, CA 92660) has a 1992 chapter of a Polish book by Tadeusz Kumik about this town. The chapter includes the information that the Jewish cemetery is well maintained. The book has a photo of the cemetery and information about some of the former Jewish residents of the town. Schwatrzstein has an English translation of a book on Ulanow that deals with the Jews of the village. Kumik noted that the synagogue was burned by the Germans in the fall of 1941, and it appears that the Jewish records may have been destroyed at that point since they have not been found in any other logical place. [Ulanów was a subdistrict within the major district of Nisko]

Schwarzstein adds that the book also has a list of various Jewish tradespeople in 1895, 1899 and 1938, based on records of the Basic School in Ulanów. The fathers of school children are listed by name and trade. It also fixes October 4, 1942, as the date for the extermination of the Jews. The book further gives statistics on Jewish inhabitants and total inhabitants of Ulanów for various years starting in 1857 (based on official Austrian censuses). As noted elsewhere in this guide, Schwarzstein has had some success in locating 19th-century Polish handwritten documents from ancestors who lived in Ulanów and Nisko. These documents were notarized and are now housed in the Przemyśl branch of the Polish Archives.

Schwarzstein also learned from Elaine Miller of Miami, Florida, that a Ulanów survivor, David Koegel (41 Stradford Road, Harrison, NY 10528; phone: (914) 967-4809) wrote a book that is partly about Ulanów and can be purchased from him. The book deals with his personal experiences during World War II in Rudnik, Lwów and Ulanów, and in work camps in Janiszów, Budzyn and Rzeszów.

❀ Appendix A ❀

Pronouncing and Recognizing Your Polish Town and Family Names
by Fay Vogel Bussgang[1]

Polish can be a very difficult language to master, but learning to pronounce correctly the names of towns and family names one is researching and to recognize them in their various grammatical forms ought to be manageable. One could then recognize that "Brzeziny" and "w Brzezinach" refer to the same town but that "Brzeżany" is something totally different. A guide to Polish pronunciation and basic rules of Polish grammar relevant to genealogical research are presented below.

Polish Pronunciation Guide

The following guide gives the essentials for learning to sound out family or town names. When you practice, go slowly, sound all the letters, and put the accent on the next to last syllable.

Polish	English	Sounds Most Like	Polish Example
a	short ah	ha! ha!	Kraków, Radom
ą[2]	on [om before b/p]	song [trombone]	Nowy Sącz, [Dąbrowa]
e	eh	bet	Mazowiecki, Przemyśl
ę[2]	en [em before b/p]	Bengal [hemp]	Będzin, [Dębicy]
i	ee	feet	Katowice, Wieliczka
o	o	bought	Drohobycz, Horodenka
ó/u	oo/u (or, see below)	boot, flute	Jelenia Góra, Lublin, Kuźnica
ó/u	short oo/u	book, put	Łódź, Lwów, Kraków
y	short i	fit	Gdynia, Drohobycz
c	ts	eats	Katowice, Kielce, Płock, Siedlce
ć/ci	ch (softened)	cello/cheat	Chęciny, Ciechanów, Tykocin
cz	ch	church	Łowicz, Wieliczka
ch/h	h (aspirated)	Helen	Chęciny, Chelm, Częstochowa
dz	ds	suds	Dzbanów, Radzanów
dzi	dgy	fudgy	Będzin, Działoszyce, Radziejów
j	y	year	Jarosław, Kolomyja, Radziejów
ł	w	wood	Łódź, Białystok, Wrocław
ń	nn	onion	Gdańsk, Poznań, Toruń
prz	psh	pshah!	Przedbórz, Przemyśl
r	r (rolled)	rrroar!	Radom, Rawa Ruska
ś/si	sh (softened)	sh!	Przemyśl, Siedlce, Śląsk
sz	sh	shop	Kalisz, Kolbuszowa

---

[1] © 1998, Fay Vogel Bussgang

[2] ą and ę are nasalized before s, ś, sz, rz, z, ż, ź, f, w, ch; ą is also nasalized at the end of a word. In these instances, such as in Śląsk or Częstochowa, there is no n or m sound after the ą or ę.

szcz	shch	<u>sh</u> children	Bydogo<u>szcz</u>, <u>Szcz</u>ecin
w	v	<u>v</u>an	L<u>w</u>ów, <u>W</u>arszawa, <u>W</u>rocław
ź/zi	zh (softened)	ca<u>sh</u>mere	Ku<u>ź</u>nica, <u>Zi</u>elona Góra
ż/rz	zh	vi<u>si</u>on	Łom<u>ż</u>a, <u>Rz</u>eszów, <u>r</u>ychlin

Beware: The **final consonant** of a word is **unvoiced**, that is, the larynx (voice box) is not used in craeting the sound. The following letters change to their unvoiced counterpart: *b → p, d → t, g → k, w → f, z → ś, ź → s, dz→ c, dź → ć, rz/ż → sz, dż → cz.* Therefore Kraków sounds like "Krakoo<u>f</u>," and Brzeg, sounds like "Bzhe<u>k</u>."

Rules of Polish Grammar Useful for Genealogists

Even if you cannot translate a Polish document, understanding the most common forms of the names of people and towns will help you determine if a person or place of interest to you is mentioned in the document.

There are three important concepts to note in learning the Polish language that may be new to English-language speakers: case, gender, and stem. Each of these, explained below, as well as whether the noun is singular or plural, influences the ending (suffix) of the noun.

The *case* of a noun indicates its function in a sentence; it shows whether the noun is the subject, the direct or indirect object or is in a prepositional phrase. There are seven different cases in Polish, but only those commonly seen in genealogical research are described below: nominative, genitive, instrumental (used mainly in marriage documents) and locative. Table A2 gives examples of town named in the most frequently encountered cases.

Town names, like other nouns in Polish, come in different varieties; they have *gender* (feminine, masculine or neuter), and some are even plural.

The *stem* is the basically unchangeable part of a word to which endings are added. The stem is termed soft, velar or hard, depending on the pronunciation of its last letter.

This may sound confusing, but it will make more sense as you go along. It is not necessary to learn all the grammar presented here. Try to get a general understanding of the concepts and then write down the endings that apply to your particular town and family names and become familiar with them.

Nominative Case

The nominative case is used to denote the subject of a sentence. The name of a town or person in the nominative case is spelled as you commonly know it: Płock, Radom, Glasman.

Genitive Case

The genitive case denotes "of" or possession, follows certain prepositions, or is the direct object after a negative verb. In vital records, the genitive is most often used following *z/ze* (from) to identify the town someone is from, as in *z Krakowa*, and to indicate maiden name, as in *z Bussgangów* (literally, from the Bussgangs).

Forming the Genitive Case from the Nominative for Town Names

- Feminine town names usually end in *a* in the nominative case: Warszawa, Warta, Horodenka. (A few towns ending in double consonants or *ew* are also feminine: Bydgoszcz, Łódź, Żółkiew.) The genitive ending for all feminine towns is *y* or *i*: Warszaw<u>y</u>, Wart<u>y</u>, Horodenk<u>i</u>, Bydgoszcz<u>y</u>, Łodz<u>i</u>, Żółkw<u>i</u>. (Note that *ie* before a final letter, as in Żółki<u>ew</u>, is dropped in the genitive case before the ending is added.
- Masculine town names end in a consonant in the nominative: Lwów, Gdańsk, Płock, Włocławek. The genitive ending is *a* or *u* for towns with masculine names:
  - The genitive of most Polish masculine town names is formed by adding *a* at the end: Lwow<u>a</u>, Gdańsk<u>a</u>, Płock<u>a</u>, Włocławk<u>a</u> Note that *e* before a final letter is dropped before the genitive ending is added.
  - If the town name ends in a soft consonant such as *ń* or a hidden softening (which you learn by usage), *ia* is added: Poznań → Poznan<u>ia</u>; Radom → Radom<u>ia</u>; Wrocław → Wrocław<u>ia</u>.
  - Most foreign cities and a few Polish towns have the ending *u*: Londyn<u>u</u>, Boston<u>u</u>, Tarnobrzeg<u>u</u>, Żmigrod<u>u</u>.

- **Neuter town names** end in *o* or sometimes *e* in the nominative: Brzesko, Radomsko, Opole. Neuter town names form the genitive by adding *a* to the stem: Brzeska, Radomska, Opola.
- **Plural town names** end in *y*, *i*, and with a few exceptions, *e*, in the nominative: Chęciny, Suwałki, Działoszyce, Katowice. To form the genitive, the final letter is dropped to form Chęcin, Suwałek, Działoszyc, Katowic. (If the word thus formed ends in two consonants that make pronunciation difficult, an *e* is often added before the final letter to separate the two consonants, as in Suwałek.)

Forming the Genitive Case from the Nominative for Women's Surnames

To indicate the maiden name of a married woman, the genitive plural is used after *z/ze*. The usual genetive plural ending is *ów*: Bussgang → *z* Bussgangów; Spiro → *ze* Spirów. If the name ends in *cka/ ska* (feminine of names ending in *cki/ski*), the ending is *ich*: Sawicka → *z* Sawickich, Kowalska → *z* Kowalskich. To indicate that a woman is unmarried, *ówna* is added to her surname in the nominative, *ównej* in the genitive: Glasman → Glasmanówna/Glasmanównej (Miss Glasman). To indicate a woman is married, *owa* is added in the nominative or *owej* in the genitive to her husband's surname: Glasmanowa/Glasmanowej (Mrs. Glasman).

Instrumental Case

In general, the instrumental case is used to show with whom or by what means something is done. In a marriage record, it may be used for the groom who appears *with* the Rabbi. It is formed simply by adding *em* for a man (to both first and last names or just to the first name): Szmuel Kron → *wraz ze* (together with) Szmuelem Kronem. For names ending in *cki/ski*, the ending is *m*: Aron Laski → *z* Aronem Laskim.[3] The instrumental case is also used after "*między*" (between) to indicate an agreement between the bride and groom. For a woman, *ą* is added to the stem of her first name (Ruchla → Ruchlą): *między* Aronem Laskim i Ruchlą Wolf, also to the surname of the *ówna* form is used: Ruchlą Wolfówną.

Locative Case

The locative case, which tells where something is located, is used only after certain prepositions, the most common in vital records being *w/we* (in).[4] The rules for forming the locative seem very complicated, because there are changes in the stem of the word, not just the ending. If you go through your list of towns one by one and apply the rules, however, it should not be too difficult. First, you must determine the gender of the name and also its type of stem (hard, velar, soft).

- **Hard stems**. If the last consonant of the word is hard, regardless of gender, it must be softened and then an *e* ending is added.
  - Hard stems ending is *p*, *b*, *f*, *w*, *m*, *n*, *s* and *z* are softened by adding *i* before the *e* ending: Warszawa → *w* Warszawie; Kraków → *w* Krakowie; Chełmno → *w* Chełmnie; Lublin → *w* Lublinie.
  - Stem endings *t*, *d*, *r*, and *ł* are softened according to the following pattern before adding *e*: *t* → *ci*, *d* → *dzi*, *r* → *rz*, *ł* → *l*: Łańcut → *w* Łańcucie; Rajgród → *w* Rajgrodzie; Zielona Góra → *w* Zielonej Górze.
- **Velar stems**. The final consonant of a velar stem has a gutteral sound (k, g, ch).
  - Feminine nouns soften velar stems (*k* → *c*, *g* → *dz*, *ch* → *sz*) before adding an *e* ending: Horodenka → *w* Horodence; Struga → *w* Strudze; Bierwicha → *w* Bierwisze.
  - Masculine and neuter names with velar stems simply add *u* to the stem: Płock → *w* Płocku; Przemyśl → *w* Przemyślu; Tarnobrzeg → *w* Tarnobrzegu; Włocławek → *w* Włocławku (drop *e* before final *k*); Radomsko → *w* Radomsku.
- **Soft stems**. Soft stems end with the consonants *i*, *j*, *l*, *c*, *ć*, *cz*, *ś*, *sz*, *ź*, *ż*, *rz*)

---

[3] The word *ze* is used instead of *z* to indicate "from" or "with" when the word following it begins with a cluster of consonants which would make it difficult to pronounce without the added *e*. This is why the instrumental *ze* is used before Szmuel, but only *z* is used before Aron.

[4] For the same reason, *we* is used instead of *w*. Therefore, it is *we Lwowie*, but *w Warszawie*. However, what we think would be difficult may not necessarily be what Poles consider difficult. We might want *we* before Przemyśl, but they don't consider the *Prze* sound to cause any problems!! Thus, it is *w Przemyślu*.

– Feminine names ending in *ia* or with a soft stem add *i* or *y* to the stem: Bochnia → w Bochni, Łódź → w Łodzi, Bydgoszcz → w Bydgoszczy, Dębica → w Dębicy.

– Masculine and neuter names ending in a soft stem consonant add *u* to the stem: Drohobycz → w Drohobyczu; Mielec → w Mielcu; Opole →w Opolu; Zgierz → w Zgierzu.

• **Plural names** of towns all form the locative case by adding *ach* to the stem: Brzeziny → w Brzezinach; Katowice → w Katowicach; Chęciny → w Chęcinach; Suwałki → w Suwałkach.

Table A1. Sample Declensions of Town Names (Arranged by Type of Stem)

Type of Stem	Nominative	Genitive	Locative
Fem hard stem	Warszawa	Warszawy	Warszawie
Fem hard stem	Indura	Indury	Indurze
Fem velar stem	Wieliczka	Wieliczki	Wieliczce
Fem soft stem	Dębica	Dębicy	Dębicy
Fem soft stem	Łomża	Łomży	Łomży
Fem soft stem	Kołomyja	Kołomyji	Kołomyji
Fem soft stem	Łódź	Łodzi	Łodzi
Masc hard stem	Kraków	Krakowa	Krakowie
Masc hard stem	Lublin	Lublina	Lublinie
Masc hard stem	Żmigród	Żmigrodu*	Żmigrodzie
Masc velar stem	Gdańsk	Gdańska	Gdańsku
Masc velar stem	Chmielnik	Chmielnika	Chmielniku
Masc velar stem	Tarnobrzeg	Tarnobrzegu*	Tarnobrzegu
Masc soft stem (hidden)	Jarosław	Jarosławia	Jarosławiu
Masc soft stem (hidden)	Radom	Radomia	Radomiu
Masc soft stem	Mielec	Mielca	Mielcu
Masc soft stem	Lubraniec	Lubrańca	Lubrańcu
Masc soft stem	Zamość	Zamościa	Zamościu
Masc soft stem	Tarnopol	Tarnopola	Tarnopolu
Neut hard stem	Grodno	Grodna	Grodnie
Neut velar stem	Radomsko	Radomska	Radomsku
Neut soft stem	Opole	Opola	Opolu
Plural	Chęciny	Chęcin	Chęcinach
Plural	Katowice	Katowic	Katowicach
Plural	Kielce	Kielc	Kielcach
Plural	Suwałki	Suwałek	Suwałkach

For towns with compound names—composed of a noun plus a modifier—the nouns follow the rules above, but the adjectives, such as Nowy (new), Zielona (green), or Mazowiecki (in Mazowiecki region), however, follow the rules for adjectival endings, depending on gender, case, and number. Adjectival endings are underlined in the compound names below to show the pattern of the endings.

Table A2. Declention of Adjectives Associated With Town Names

Adjective	Nominative	Genitive	Locative
Zielona (f)	Zielona Góra	z Zielonej Góry	w Zielonej Górze
Zduńska (f)	Zduńska Wola	ze Zduńskiej Woli	w Zduńskiej Woli
Mazowiecka (f)	Rawa Mazowiecka	z Rawy Mazowieckiej	w Rawie Mazowieckiej
Mazowiecki (m)	Mińsk Mazowiecki	z Mińska Mazowieckiego	w Mińsku Mazowieckim
Nowy (m)	Nowy Sącz	z Nowego Sącza	w Nowym Sączu
Nowe (n)	Nowe Miasto	z Nowego Miasta	w Nowym Mieście
Biały (m)	Białystok	z Białegostoku	w Białymstoku

[Białystok (m) is treated like a compound word made up of *Biały* (white) and *stok* (slope).]

❀ Appendix B ❀

Sample Letter to Polish Archives

The following is a letter in Polish adapted from Judith Frazin's book, *A Translation Guide to 19th-Century Polish Language Civil-Registration Documents*. (See Chapter 5 for ordering information.) Her book offers a much greater variety of phrases, but the letter below should suffice as an adequate explanation of what most researchers seek.

Poland today is divided into 49 provinces, which are abbreviated *woj.* for voivodeships. When writing to small towns in Poland, it is best to use these designations in the address because there may be more than one town of that name.

The provinces listed below include towns that were once part of Western Galicia. Because of the complexities of the Polish language, they are to be written as follows:

Bielsko-Biała = *woj. bielskie*
Katowice = *woj. katowickie*
Krosno = *woj. krosnienskie*
Nowy Sącz = *woj. nowosadeckie*
Przemyśl = *woj. przemyśkie*
Rzeszów = *woj. rzeszówskie*
Tarnobrzeg = *woj. tarnobrzeskie*
Tarnów = *woj. tarnówskie*

Send your letter to the town civil records office (*Urząd Stanu Cywilnego*):

Urząd Stanu Cywilnego	Civil Registration Office
Name of the province (if you know it)	Name of province (if you know it)
Name of town, Poland	Name of town, Poland
szanowny Panie,	Dear Sir:
W celu uzupełnienia historii mojej rodziny, potrzebne mi są dane z żydowskich ksiąg urodzin, ślubów i zgonow z [name of town].	In order to prepare a history of my family, I need information from the Jewish records of birth, marriage and death from [name of town].)
Jeśli te akta nie są w Waszym posiadaniu, proszę o podanie mi adresu, gdzie się one znajdują.	If you do not have the records, I request that you provide the address where the records may be found.
imię i nazwisko:	Given name and surname:
data urodzenia (w przybliżeniu):	Date of birth (approximately):
miejsce urodzenia:	Place of birth:
imię i nazwisko ojca:	Full name of father:
panieńskie nazwisko matki:	Maiden name of mother:

imię matki:	First name of mother:
imię i nazwisko męża:	First name of husband:
imię i panieńskie nazwisko żony:	First and maiden name of wife:
data ślubu:	Date of marriage:
miejsce ślubu:	Place of marriage:
data emigracji:	Date of emigration:
wyzanie (żydowskie):	Religion: (Jewish)

Interesuje mnie rodzina tej osoby i **byłbym** wdzięczny [**byłabym** wdzie**czna** if you are female] za podanie mi imion, nazwisk, oraz dat i miejsc urodzenia rodzenstwa, jak rowneż przesłanie mi odpisu aktu ślubu rodzicow.

I would like to know more about the family of this person, and if you would provide the names and birth dates of the brothers and sisters, and an extract of the marriage record of the parents, I would be very grateful.

Z góry dziękuję.

I thank you in advance for your assistance.

Z poważaniem,

Respectfully,

Polish Date Styles

Dates in Polish can present major challenges to those who are unfamiliar with the pecularities of the Polish language. Dates and, indeed, numbers sometimes appear written out in Polish. In other words, instead of writing a number such as 1899, you might encounter "one thousand eight hundred ninety-nine." Judith Frazin's book includes a good list of numbers to help translate records with examples of how to read them.

Dates follow the European style with the day first, the month next and then the year, as in 2 November 1997. Months in Polish are as follows:

January: stycznia	May: maja	September: września
February: lutego	June: czerwca	October: pażdziernika
March: marca	July: lipca	November: listopada
April: kwietnia	August: sierpnia	December: grudnia

❀ Appendix C ❀

Synagogues and Cemeteries

Surveys of Polish Jewish Cemeteries and Synagogues

Efforts to document the current condition of Jewish cemeteries, synagogues and other monuments in several European countries, including Poland and Ukraine, have been the focus of the Survey of Historic Jewish Monuments, spearheaded by the United States Commission for the Preservation of America's Heritage Abroad. The second and substantially revised summary report on Poland, entitled *The Survey of Historic Jewish Monuments in Poland*, includes brief information about the condition of almost 700 Jewish cemeteries and about 250 synagogues. A more complete database of information about each site has been installed at the U.S. Holocaust Memorial Museum in Washington, D.C. Written reports on survey efforts can be obtained from the United States Commission for the Preservation of America's Heritage Abroad, 1101 15th Street NW, Suite 1040, Washington, DC 20005; fax: (202) 254-3934. Detailed data is also available on line at <http://www.jewishgen.org/cemetery>.

Eastern Galicia

The Jewish Preservation Committee (JPC) of Ukraine is, according to Dmitry Surovtsev in Kiev, "a noncommercial organization founded under the Union of Jewish Religion Organisation of Ukraine. For the last three years, JPC has prepared the most complete existing lists of Jewish landmarks, cemeteries, monuments and mass burial sites all over Ukraine." The committee offers its information to others for a fee. See also information about their genealogical search service in Chapter 6. Contact Dmitry Surovtsev, Box 391-1, Kiev 252034, Ukraine; phone and fax: 380 44 416 07 84; e-mail: <jul@jpcu.freenet.kiev.ua>.

Institute for the Investigation of the Jewish Diaspora Studies, St. Petersburg

The Institute for the Investigation of the Jewish Diaspora Studies at St. Petersburg's (Russia) Jewish University, directed by Valery A. Dymshits, has spent six years investigating Jewish monuments in 700 towns in the former Soviet Union. In an article in *Avotaynu* (Fall 1994), Dymshits notes they found 100 Jewish cemeteries and dozens of synagogues. Of note was that in July and August 1994, the Institute planned to visit towns in the formerly Galician towns of Bolekhov, Brody, Busk, Pechenezhin and Yablonov. The cemetery in Tluste was documented and the results published later in 1994 by the Center for Jewish Art, Hebrew University in Jerusalem.

Among the former Galician towns surveyed are Bełż, Bolekhov, Borislav, Borschov, Buchach, Busk, Brody, Drogobych, Gusyatin, Javorov, Kamenka-Bugskaya, Khodorov, Kolomyya, Komarno, Kosov, Kuty, Lvov, Monastyriska, Mostiska, Peremyshlyany, Podkamen, Rudki, Rozdol, Sambor, Sasov, Skole, Sokal, Stanisławów (Ivano-Frankovsk), Stryy, Tchortchov, Ternopol, Tłuste/Tolstoye, Turka, Zydachów, Zolkiew and Zolochev.

Rabbi Meir Wunder of Jerusalem has been involved with this project, and now he and Dr. Dymshits are seeking a publisher. Dr. Dymshits may be contacted at P.O. Box 10, St. Petersburg, 196247, Russia; phone: 7-812-292-2830 or 233-5095; fax: 7-812-268-7568.

The article also mentions that a guidebook covering more than 130 towns in Ukraine, which was to be written in English, Hebrew and Russian, will be published. To memorialize relatives in this book with a small donation, contact the Institute's Israeli representatives: Russian Jewish Heritage Center, Klal Center 74, Yaffo Street 97, Jerusalem.

Brody

As reported *The Galitzianer*, vol. 4, no. 3, Drs. Neil Rosenstein and Benjamin Solomowitz have undertaken a massive project to index the 5,000 remaining gravestones in the Brody cemetery. All gravestones have been photographed, and the two men are now creating an English-language index. They plan to publish the results.

Podkamien

Howard Blue visited this town in 1989. There are no remains of the synagogue or the Jewish cemetery.

Western Galicia

Pamiatki i Zabytki Kultury Zydowskiy w Polsce

John Pihach, a member of the East European Branch of the Manitoba Genealogical Society, excerpted *Pamiątki i Zabytki Kultury Żydowskiej w Polsce* (Memorabilia and monuments of Jewish culture in Poland), written by Przemysław Burchard and published in 1990 in Warsaw. Completely in Polish, the nine-page excerpt discusses the condition of Jewish cemeteries and synagogues in the voivodeships of Krosno, Przemysl and Rzeszów—three voivodeships where many Western Galician towns were located.

Krosno voivod: Baligród, Barwinek, Biecz, Brzozów, Bukowsko, Cisna, Dukla, Halbów, Iwonicz, Jasienica Rosielna, Jasło, Jasliska, Korczyna, Krosno, Lesko, Lutowiska, Mrzyglód, Nowotaniec, Nowy Żmigród, Ropienka, Rymanów, Sanok, Tyrawa Woloska, Ustrzyki Dolne, Wola Michowa, Zagórz.

Przemysl voivod: Bircza, Bobrówka, Borownica, Cieszanów, Dubiecko, Dynów, Grochowce, Jarosław, Jawornik Polski, Kańczuga, Kaszyce, Krasiczyn, Krzywcza, Lubaszów, Medyka, Nienadowa, Oleszyce, Pruchnik, Przemysl, Przeworsk, Radymno, Rybotycze, Siedliska, Sieniawa, Stary Dzików, Wielkie Oczy.

Rzeszow voivoid: Błazowa, Czudec, Frysztak, Giedlarowa, Glinik Dolny, Głogów Małopolski, Grodzisko Dolne, Kobuszowa, Leżajsk, Łancut, Mielec, Niebylec, Ranizów, Ropczyce, Rzeszów, Sędziszów Małopolski, Sokolów Małopolski, Strzyżów, Tyczyn, Wielopole Skrzyńskie, Wierzawice, Żołynia.

Suzan Wynne has copies of these nine pages. To obtain a copy, send $2 to her at 3603 Littledale Road, Kensington, MD 20895.

Report from Dov Rubin

Dov Rubin traveled to southern Poland during July 1997, in part to investigate the condition of cemeteries in his ancestral towns and those of collateral relatives. He found the following:

Baligród: The cemetery is about 300 meters to the northwest of the Rynek (town center) at the top of the hill above the city. Only 20 gravestones exist among the brambles. None have last names and contain long acrostics based on first names. Dates range from 1870 to 1920. The cemetery path into the plowed field yielded other gravestone remnants.

Brzozów: The cemetery is about five blocks east of the civil registration office and consists of two to three acres of land, moved recently and fenced in with a locked gate. The gatekeeper lives directly opposite the cemetery entrance. There were no full-standing gravestones, just a monument in the middle containing 18 gravestone fragments.

Krzywcza: The cemetery is located behind the last houses on the western side of the Rynek, up the hill. It is totally overgrown with branches. Only two or three gravestones exist, which are no longer readable.

Lutowiska: The cemetery is located southeast of town and is not accessible by car. Just after the civil registration office and the library, walk behind the houses and follow a long cow path. Because cows graze there, the cemetery does not suffer from overgrowth. The cemetery has many gravestones, but there are no surnames. The dates range from 1850 to 1925. The daughter of Rabbi Naftali from Rymanów is buried there.

Pilzno: Located to the south of the town, the cemetery is fenced, the grass is mowed, and there is a respectable entrance. Four monuments are standing; two are for members of the Kornheiser family and one is for Sara Storch. The fourth is a monument to those area residents killed in the Holocaust. The names on the mass grave plaque are Chilowicz: Iszk, 32; Reizla, 30; Izak, 7; Beno, 5; Furman: Lazar, 33; Gitka, 28; Apfel: Hirsch, 28; Ezriel, 23; Pinter: Meier, 48; Bochner: Lazar, 35; Resla, 32; Grumet: Baruch, 35; List: Leib, 55; Gedalie, 30; Jozef, 11; Einspruch: Wolf, 55; Kunwald: Abram, 31; Rosenbaum: Pinkas, 25; Kampf: Sara, 28; Amalja, 6; Rywka, 3; Tanenbaum: Mozes, 24. All were killed between April 14, 1943, and November 22, 1943, in Pilzno, Jaworze, Budyn, Warowicz and Hulczówka.

Tyrawa Woloska: The overgrown cemetery had about five gravestones under such heavy growth, it was too dark to read the writing on the stones.

Wola Michowa: The cemetery is about 0.75 km northeast of the central bus stop in town. You must climb the hill just before the second bridge outside of town. The walk is very scenic, along the top of a meadow. About 50 gravestones are still standing. Most are readable, though the Hebrew is written in the archaic form with no spaces between words, and lines wrap in midword. No last names are given. Dates range from 1874 to 1915.

Other Towns in Western Galicia

Bircza. The town cemetery is beyond a little foot bridge across from the central bus stop in town. The Jewish section of the cemetery is the first section on the right just over the bridge. In 1986, when Suzan Wynne visited this cemetery, it had about 75 standing gravestones, some of which were readable. There were no surnames on the gravestones. The low wall was breached in places, and there was considerable evidence that gravestones had been removed.

Błazowa. Estelle Guzik and Suzan Wynne visited the cemetery in 1986. Located at the top of a steep hill about a half mile from the town square, the low cemetery wall was crumbling, and there were signs that animals and local residents had been there. Men and women were buried separately in this cemetery. A large number of gravestones for women were visible and readable, but there were no last names, and the brambles and forest were beginning to swallow that section of the cemetery. The men's section was in poor condition.

Kańczuga. Suzan Wynne visited this cemetery in 1986. It is located on the edge of a small farm just outside of town. A path leads from the farmhouse to the cemetery; the path was constructed by the farm family from fragments of headstones. This distressing sight was compounded by the equally dismal condition of the cemetery. Most headstones in 1986 were devoid of readable words due to erosion.

Kombornia. In 1986, Estelle Guzik reported that half the cemetery still exists, but it was so overgrown and dark that it was impossible to see the writing on the stones.

Kraków. In the Summer 1994 issue of *Lineage* (vol. 6, no. 2), the newsletter of the Jewish Genealogical Society of Long Island, Linda Cantor wrote about efforts by the World Monument Fund's Jewish Heritage Council to restore the Tempel Synagogue in Kazimierz, the old Jewish quarter of Kraków. The project, which began in 1992, has involved reinforcing the foundation, refurbishing the interior, and putting on a new roof. Built in 1862 by the Association of Progressive Jews, the Tempel Synagogue is the only intact 19th-century synagogue still standing in Poland. To contribute financially to this effort, write to JHC director Samuel Gruber, 174 East 80th Street, New York, NY 10021.

Łancut. Mendel Reichberg, owner of a travel company, is actively working to restore the Łancut cemetery. If you are interested in contributing or finding out more about his efforts, contact him at 4820 13th Avenue, Brooklyn, NY 11219.

Mielec (see Tyczyn)

Rzeszów. Marian Rubin has stated that the Rzeszów *landsmanschaft* in Tel Aviv has announced plans to renew the synagogue at ul. Kazimierza 18. The synagogue building, which once also served as a home of the aged and a kitchen, will be renovated in order to create a prayer site for anyone who might arrive in Rzeszów from Israel or the Diaspora and who wants to say *kaddish* and to remember his family from Reisha (the Yiddish name for Rzeszów). Plans include establishment of a memory room and museum. The *landsmanschaft* will erect a monument at the site of the main Jewish cemetery in Rzeszów, at the spot from which the Jews were transported to the death camp at Belzec. The *landsmanschaft* is asking for contributions for these projects, which will cost $10,000. Those interested in making a contribution should make a check payable to "Rzeszów Landsmanschaft" and mail it to the treasurer, Mrs. Lutka Goldberg, Horkanos Str. 6, Tel Aviv. Please include a note to the attention of Mrs. Ma'ayan, who is collecting such information, with the names of your families from the Rzeszów area, and include the names, addresses and phone numbers of your children, grandchildren and cousins, since the *landsmanschaft* is making an effort to ensure continuing contact with the second and third generations of the "Reisha" community. In Israel, members of the second generation are now actively involved in projects. After the project is completed, the *landsmanschaft* plans a dedication ceremony.

Rubin traveled with members of the Reisha Landsmanschaft in June 1995 to the dedication of a monument in the woods of Głogów, the site of the mass graves of Holocaust victims from Rzeszów and nearby communities (see "Memorial in Głogów" in *The Galitzianer* Fall 1995).

Sanok. The cemetery was destroyed during the Holocaust. There is a monument to those who were killed during the Holocaust and buried there. Additionally, there are a small number of graves of people who remained in Sanok and have died since the war. A handful of Jews still live in Sanok.

Sieniawa. The LDS (Mormon) Family History Library has eight pages of "Transcriptions of Jewish Gravestones" in the Jewish cemetery in Sienawa. It is on microfilm #1,573,074, item 2.

Tyczyn. Phyllis Simon sent *The Galitzianer* a copy of an article from *AMIT Woman* (September 1994) by Micheline Ratzersdorfer. The article describes the author's June 1994 visit to Mielec and Tyczyn and surrounding areas. These were the towns of her parents' youth.

> Rolling farmlands gave way to heavy woods as we neared Mielec (from Kraków), which now boasts two factories, one manufacturing helicopters and the other, small planes. Modern housing developments greeted us at the edge of town, but the center seemed unchanged from my father's descriptions, with two-story, old-fashioned houses. We reached my grandparents' street, where a memorial to the murdered Jews of Mielec stands on a small plot of grass. We met two elderly Poles who showed us where the grandparents' house stood and the place across the street where 600 Jews were murdered by the Germans. The site of the Jewish cemetery is now a small park "surrounded by a fence with three large *magen davids* (stars of David)." A simple sign inside the park is all that identifies the site as a cemetery. There was not a tombstone in sight.

> In Tyczyn, a town where, in 1923, one third of the population had been Jewish and 4 of the 12 members of the town's council had been Jewish, Ratzersdorfer was to find more disappointment. Tyczyn's Jewish cemetery has been cleaned up (by Rabbi Mendel Reichberg of New York) and "a beautiful new fence surrounds its asymmetric perimeter. Approximately the area of four city blocks, it climbs up and down a hill, as everything in Tyczyn does. But there are few gravestones visible, perhaps 20 in the whole expanse. Gingerly, we made our way along the slopes, deciphering names when possible. Not one stone for me, no vestige of my family. . . . For

the first time, I understood what the total destruction of the Jewry of Eastern Europe meant.

Nat Abramowitz has had translated a Polish news article dated November 11, 1993, about Rabbi Reichberg's cemetery restoration efforts. An edited version appears here:

> Yesterday, Rabbi Reichberg arrived in Tyczyn in order to inspect the results of these efforts. Removal of brush was in progress at the cemetery by public works workers employed by the municipality. At the rabbi's request, a worker, Czesław Dyjak of Dąbrowa Tarnowska, erected a small building in the center of the cemetery, to be used as a house of worship. The cost of the work on the cemetery to date is estimated at about 400 million zlotys. The workers also succeeded in cleaning up several hidden gravestones. Rabbi Reichberg prayed for the souls of the interred.
>
> The Jewish population began settling in Tyczyn in the 17th century. In 1939, the town was populated by about 1,000 Jews. In mid-1942, they were transported by the Germans to death camps. The cemetery was destroyed, and the gravestones were used as paving for the Tyczyn market square.
>
> Rabbi Reichberg, age 71, comes from Bochnia. . . . He manages a collection of funds among the Jewish population and has organized the work involved with restoring cemeteries in Dynów, Mielec, Dąbrowa Tarnowska and Bochnia. The rabbi also has plans for the work on cemeteries in Łancut, Sienawa and Dębica.

If you would like to contribute to Rabbi Reichberg's efforts in Tyczyn, contact him at 4820 13th Avenue, Brooklyn, NY 11219.

Jawornik Polski. In 1986, the Jewish cemetery was bulldozed to make way for a new housing development.

❀ Appendix D ❀

Examples of Vital Records

Galician Documents in the 18th and 19th Centuries

A form of this article originally appeared in an issue of *The Galtizianer*. It is included here to illustrate changes, over time, in official vital records documents.

During the years of Communist rule in Poland, efforts to obtain information from the branch of the Polish Archives in Przemyśl were unsuccessful. Soon after Poland achieved independence, I tried again and, this time, my efforts were rewarded with a long list of names with identifying information. After selecting the most likely records, I was billed for them, and about six weeks later, a large packet of photocopied documents arrived. The information in the documents was rich with details.

The oldest record requested (though not the oldest record on the list) was a March 1795 marriage record for Zacharia Metzger and Scheindel (whose surname was not mentioned). The document showed that the marriage took place at house number 129. Also included was a 1798 birth record for their son, Moses Metzker, born at house number 222 (Figure D-1). The form of these documents was printed in German and provided much less information than those which came later.

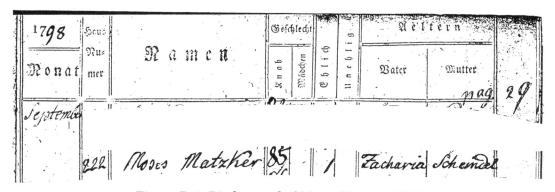

Figure D-1. Birth record of Moses Metzger, 1798.

A death record for 96-year-old Leib Metzger in 1812 (Figure D-2), also in German, included the house number but did not have columns for the names of the parents. However, the cause of death had been added.

Birth records from 1870 to 1875 were recorded on forms in Latin that had space for name, dates of birth and baptism (this space was used by Jews for the date of circumcision), the house number, whether the child was Catholic or non-Catholic, sex, whether the infant was "legitimate," names of parents and the godparents (Figure D-3).

An 1877 birth document reflects the new Austrian law which standardized the recording and maintenance of civil records. The form has 12 columns in both German and Polish. This form was changed in minor ways over the years, but the type of information captured apparently remained the same until after Galician territory reverted to Polish rule (Figure D-4).

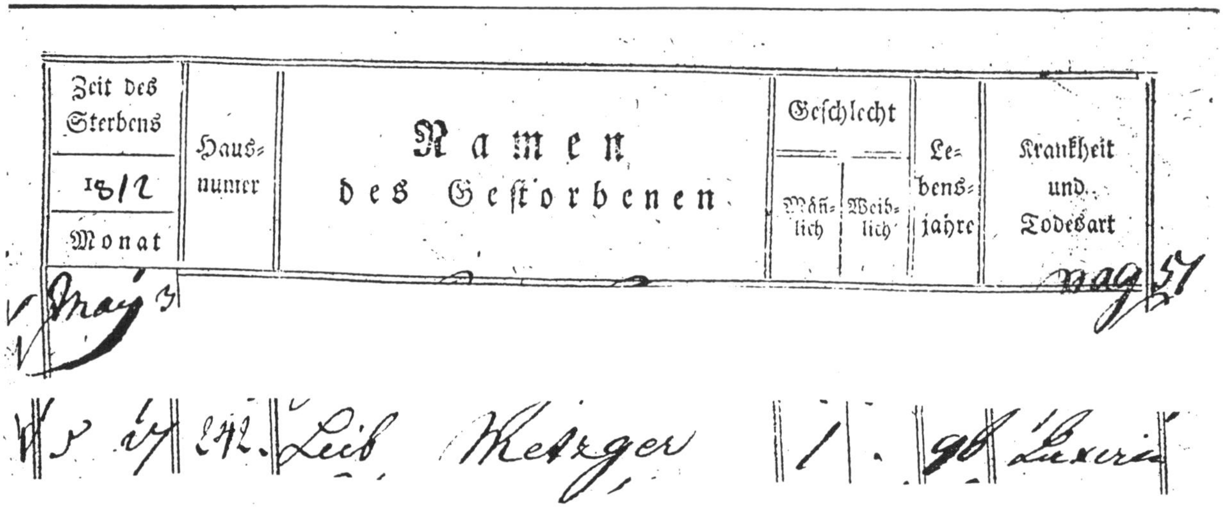

Figure D-2. Death record of Leib Metzger, 1812.

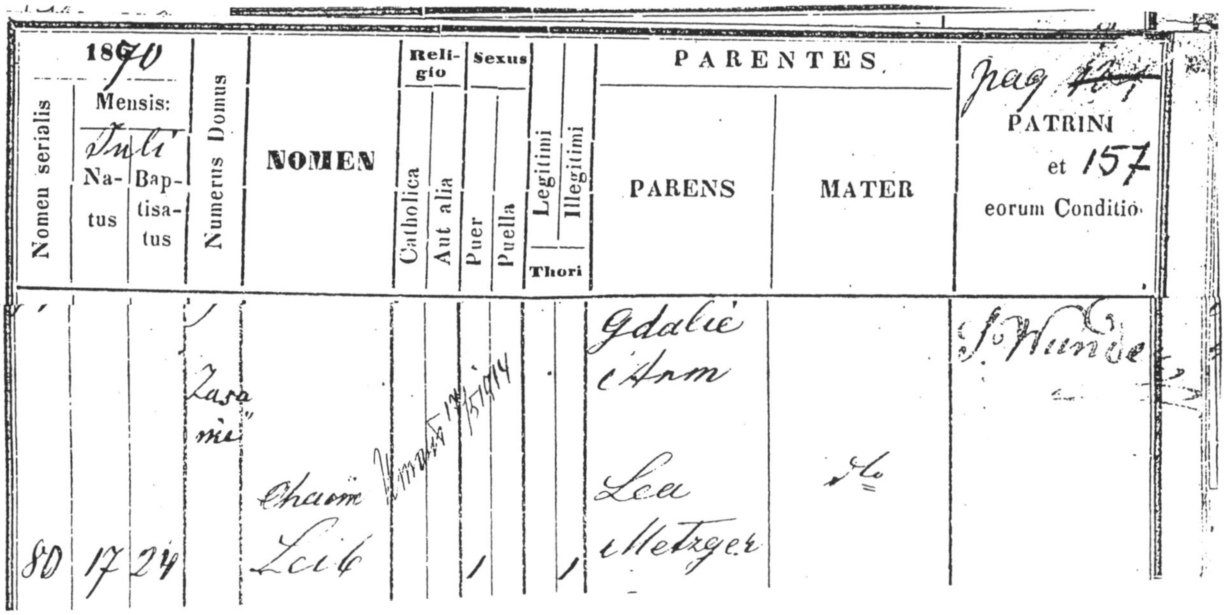

Figure D-3. Birth record from 1870 with headings in Latin.

106 • *Finding Your Jewish Roots in Galicia: A Resource Guide*

1	2 Der Geburt / Urodzenia						3 Der Beschneidung oder Namens-Beilegung / Obrzezania lub nadania imienia						4 des Kindes / Dziecięcia		5 Eheliche, angeblich eheliche oder uneheliche Geburt / Ślubne, rzekomo ślubne lub nieślubne	6 Vor- und Zuname des Vaters sowie Stand, Beschäftigung Wohnort / Imię i nazwisko, stan, zatrudnienie i miejsce zamieszkania ojca
Fortlaufende Zahl Liczba porządkowa	Tag Dzień	Monat Miesiąc	Jahr Rok	Ort Miejsce	Haus-Nr. Nr. domu		Tag Dzień	Monat Miesiąc	Jahr Rok	Ort Miejsce	Haus-Nr. Nr. domu	Name Imię	Geschlecht Płeć — mänlich męzka / weiblich żeńska		
264	4	October	1878	Rozdół	106		8	October	1878	Rozdół	106	Chane Gittle Östreicher	1	unehelich	

7 Vor- und Zuname der Mutter, ihr Stand und Wohnort dann Vor- und Zuname, Beschäftigung und Wohnort ihrer Eltern / Imię i nazwisko, stan, miejsce zamieszkania matki i jej rodziców	8 Eigenhändige Unterschrift, Beschäftigung und Wohnort / Własnoręczny podpis, zatrudnienie i miejsce zamieszkania	9	10	11 Tod geborene Kinder / Dzieci nieżywo urodzone	12 Anmerkung UWAGA
	der Pathen oder Zeugen des Sandeks oder Schemes / kumów lub świadków Sandeka lub Schemes	des oder der Besshneidenden / obrzezującego lub obrzezujących	Der Hebamme oder des Geburtshelfers / akuszera lub akuszerki		
Sara Riwke Östreicher Tochter des Baruch Meier u. Chaje Grumet.	Abraham Wach, selberg. —		Elle Mauer		

Figure D-4. Standard birth register form.

1 Fortlaufende Zahl Liczba bieżąca	2 Datum und Zahl des obrigkeitlich dibirten Lodtenbeschauzettels und Name des Todtenbeschauers Data i liczba karty oględzin pośmiertnych potwierdzonej przez zwierzchność i nazwisko oglądającego zwłoki	3 Des Absterbens Śmierci					4 Der Beerdigung Pogrzebu				5 Des Verstorbenen Zmarłego Vor- und Zuname, Stand, Beschäftigung, ferner Name, Beschäftigung und Wohnort der Aeltern Imie i nazwisko, stan, zatrudnienie i imiona, zatrudnienie i zamieszkanie rodziców	Wohnort Miejsce zamieszkania
		Stunde Godzina	Tag Dzień	Monat Miesiąc	Jahr Rok	Ort Haus-Nr. Miejsce i Nr. domu	Tag Dzień	Monat Miesiąc	Jahr Rok	Ort Miejsce		
6	Ho Sokol am 15t Jänner 1882 32. Lichenbeschau J. Zarzycki	14		Jänner	1882	Sokal Bezg. Spital		Jänner	1882	Sokal	David Langer Ledig Sohn des Chosen und Sara Langer mit Linere	Linere

6 Geschlecht Płeć		7 Alter Wiek		8 Stand Stan			9 Krankheit und Todesart Choroba i rodzaj śmierci	10 Anmerkung Uwaga
mänlich męzka	weiblich żeńska	Jahre Lat	Monate Miesięcy	ledig wolny	verheiratet żonaty, zamężna	verwitwet wdowiec wdowa		
1	—	17	—	1	—		Geschwür	Für Zustandsschein desselben würde an das Matriken Amt in Warez übersandt. Langweber

Figure D-5. Standard death register form.

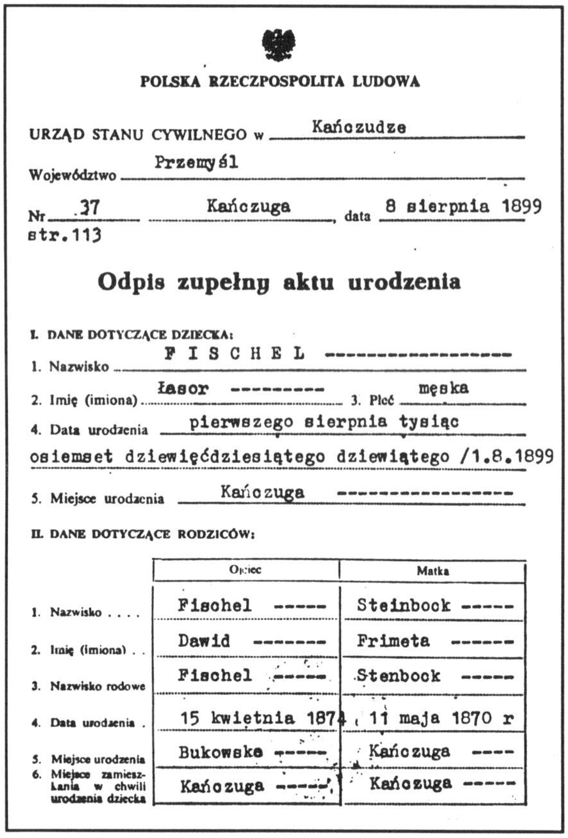

Birth transcript (top left)

POLSKA RZECZPOSPOLITA LUDOWA

URZĄD STANU CYWILNEGO w _Kańczudze_

Województwo _Przemyśl_

Nr _37_ _Kańczuga_ data _8 sierpnia 1899_
str.113

Odpis zupełny aktu urodzenia

I. DANE DOTYCZĄCE DZIECKA:

1. Nazwisko _F I S C H E L ------------------_
2. Imię (imiona) _Łasor ---------_ 3. Płeć _męska_
4. Data urodzenia _pierwszego sierpnia tysiąc osiemset dziewięćdziesiątego dziewiątego /1.8.1899_
5. Miejsce urodzenia _Kańczuga -----------------_

II. DANE DOTYCZĄCE RODZICÓW:

	Ojciec	Matka
1. Nazwisko	Fischel -----	Steinbock -----
2. Imię (imiona)	Dawid -------	Frimeta ------
3. Nazwisko rodowe	Fischel -----	Stenbook -----
4. Data urodzenia	15 kwietnia 1874	11 maja 1870 r
5. Miejsce urodzenia	Bukowsko -----	Kańczuga -----
6. Miejsce zamieszkania w chwili urodzenia dziecka	Kańczuga -----	Kańczuga ------

Marriage transcript (top right)

POLSKA RZECZPOSPOLITA LUDOWA

Województwo _Przemyśl_
URZĄD STANU CYWILNEGO w _Kańczudze_

Odpis skrócony aktu małżeństwa

I. DANE DOTYCZĄCE OSÓB ZAWIERAJĄCYCH MAŁŻEŃSTWO:

	Mężczyzna	Kobieta
1. Nazwisko	Fischel -------	Steinbock -----
2. Imię (imiona)	Dawid ---------	Frimeta -------
3. Nazwisko rodowe	Fischel	Steinbock
4. Data urodzenia	15 kwietnia 1874	11 maja 1870 r
5. Miejsce urodzenia	Bukowsko ----	Kańczuga ----

II. DANE DOTYCZĄCE DATY I MIEJSCA ZAWARCIA MAŁŻEŃSTWA:
1. Data _szesnastego lipca tysiąc dziewięćset szesnastego /16.7.1916/roku_
2. Miejsce _Kańczuga_

III. NAZWISKO NOSZONE PO ZAWARCIU MAŁŻEŃSTWA:
1. Mężczyzny _Fischel -----------------_
2. Kobiety _Fischel -----------------_
3. Dzieci _Fischel -----------------_

IV. DANE DOTYCZĄCE RODZICÓW:
A. Ojciec
1. Nazwisko rodowe _Fischel -----_ _Steinbock -----_
2. Imię _Leisor ------_ _Izak ---------_
B. Matka
1. Nazwisko rodowe _Langsam ------_ _Frieder ------_
2. Imię _Gitli -------_ _Rywa --------_

V. ADNOTACJE O USTANIU LUB O UNIEWAŻNIENIU MAŁŻEŃSTWA:

Miejsce na opłatę skarbową

20/1916
1990-09-08

KIEROWNIK
Urzędu Stanu Cywilnego

Death transcript (bottom left)

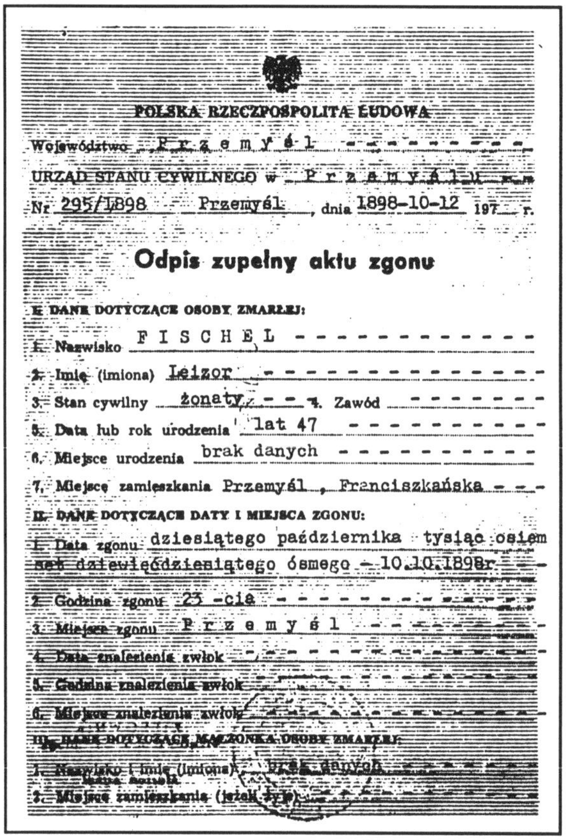

POLSKA RZECZPOSPOLITA LUDOWA

Województwo _Przemyśl_
URZĄD STANU CYWILNEGO w _Przemyślu_
Nr _295/1898_ _Przemyśl_, dnia _1898-10-12_ 197 r.

Odpis zupełny aktu zgonu

I. DANE DOTYCZĄCE OSOBY ZMARŁEJ:
1. Nazwisko _F I S C H E L - - - - - - - - - - -_
2. Imię (imiona) _Leizor - - - - - - - - - - -_
3. Stan cywilny _żonaty_ - - 4. Zawód - - - - - - - -
5. Data lub rok urodzenia _lat 47_ - - - - - - - -
6. Miejsce urodzenia _brak danych_ - - - - - - - -
7. Miejsce zamieszkania _Przemyśl, Franciszkańska_ - -

II. DANE DOTYCZĄCE DATY I MIEJSCA ZGONU:
1. Data zgonu _dziesiątego października tysiąc osiemset dziewięćdziesiątego ósmego - 10.10.1898r._
2. Godzina zgonu _23 -cia_
3. Miejsce zgonu _P r z e m y ś l_ - - - - -
4. Data znalezienia zwłok - - - - - - - -
5. Godzina znalezienia zwłok - - - - - - -
6. Miejsce znalezienia zwłok - - - - - - -

III. DANE DOTYCZĄCE MAŁŻONKA OSOBY ZMARŁEJ:
1. Nazwisko i imię (imiona) _Frau genannt_
2. Miejsce zamieszkania (jeżeli żyje)

Caption (bottom right)

**Typical Transcripts from
Town Civil Registration Offices
(Urząd Stanu Ciwilnego)**

(From left to right, top to bottom): Birth,
marriage and death transcripts. Some local
offices now have copying machines and
provide a copy of the actual document
rather than transcripts.

Jewish Registry Office BORSZCZOW

L 103/913

Marriage Certificate

Excerpt from book of marriages, Jewish Registry District of BORSZCZOW | Volume III, Page 109

1	Ordinal Number 3	
2	**Bridegroom**	Name and surname, occupation, place of birth, place of residence, address, names and occupation of his parents	Jakob Jeruchim [unknown] Rosenblum, born in Tluste, resident of Borszczow [tax district] No. 502, tailor, son of Abraham and Matel Babcia Rosenblum from the home of Teber, a tailor in Borszczow.
		Age:	24 years 8½ months
		Status: Single	1
		Widower	--
3	**Bride**	Name and surname, occupation, place of birth, place of residence, address, names and occupation of parents	Keile Schkolnik, Born in Buczacz, resident of Borszczow [tax district] No. 502, Daughter of the now deceased Schulim Schkolnik, and Sara Henie [unknown] from the home of Struber in Borszczow
		Age:	20 years, 11 months
		Status: Single	1
		Widowed	--
4	**Marriage Ceremony**	Day	21 / Twenty first day
		Month	January *
		Year	1912 / Nineteen hundred and twelve
		Place	Borszczow
5	**Signature and indication of residence**	Rabbi officiating at marriage ceremony	Majer Leibisch Neuberger, Resident of Borszczow
		Witnesses and their occupation	Samson Ch. Bergman, shamash in Borszczow; Moses Leinweber, shamash in Borszczow

6
R
e
m
r
k
s

Announcements made on 23 December and 30 December 1911 and 6 January 1912. Written announcement made by the representative Rabbi Majer Leibisch Neuberger, Officiating, on 21 January 1912. Groom's birth certificate from Tluste, 16 January 1912 [page] 18. Certificate [of] the c.k. council of eldermen] in Buczacz issued 3 January 1912. -- Bride's birth certificate from Buczacz, 15 June 1910 [page] 387, permission from the c.k. district office in Buczacz dated 22 June 1910, [illegible] IV. 259/10 for the marriage contract of a minor [female] in documenis 138/911.--

Most recent extract complies with appropriate entry in book of marriage certificates, certified this day.
[Stamp]: DISTRICT JEWISH REGISTRY OFFICE, 20 March 1913
[Remainder of stamp illegible]
[Tax stamp and round seal]: Jewish Registry Office, Borszczow. [Signature]: Ojser Rosenblum

❀ Appendix E ❀

United States Government Sources

U.S. State Department Records:
Protection of Interests of U.S. Citizens in the Decimal File (RG59)

U.S. State Department records held at the National Archives and Records Administration include a section of correspondence about U.S. citizens—and the relatives of citizens concerned with the welfare of family members—living or visiting abroad. This correspondence is part of the Decimal File in Record Group 59.

The material is particularly compelling reading for the World War I years, when communication between the United States and the countries of Eastern Europe was extremely difficult. Relatives living in the United States were distressed about the welfare of family members in Eastern Europe, and the correspondence in this record group reflects their efforts to locate them, and to send food, money and clothing to them through the U.S. State Department.

Some files are huge, while other include no more than a letter or two. Jewish Genealogy Society of Greater Washington volunteers extracted apparently Jewish names from this record group, and the resulting "Index to Department of State Records Found in U.S. National Archives" is available through Avotaynu, Inc. The index is sold as a set of nine microfiche, which includes a section entitled, "Protection of Interests of U.S. Citizens in Germany, Poland and Romania, 1910–29; Austria-Hungary, 1910–39."

The State Department records themselves are held in Archives II in College Park, Maryland. For information or to obtain copies of the records, write to U.S. National Archives and Records Administration, Washington, DC 20408.

U.S. Emergency Passport Applications, 1919–26

Emergency passports were issued primarily to U.S. citizens who had lost their passports while traveling abroad. A second group of applicants included individuals who were traveling without a passport who decided that they needed one, either to prove U.S. citizenship or for some related purpose. The primary interest of genealogical researchers is a third group of applicants—those who qualified without ever stepping on U.S. soil because of the laws governing citizenship prior to the 1920s.

Before 1922, women generally could not become citizens in their own right. With some exceptions, women became citizens by virtue of being the daughter or wife of a U.S. citizen. Thus, the wife and minor children of a man who came to this country, who resided here for five years and who became a citizen, automatically derived citizenship from him. If the family of the new citizen still lived abroad, they were able to enter the U.S. with full rights of citizenship. This curious situation meant that people who had concerns about not being admitted to the U.S.—because of physical, mental or medical conditions that might otherwise have disqualified them at the port of entry—could enter unquestioned. This strategy was put to good use by some Jews.

American citizens caught in Europe when World War I broke out also applied for emergency passports. In order to ensure that they, as U.S. citizens, were under continuous U.S. protection and would not experience difficulties because they carried an expired passport, they renewed their passports at the nearest U.S. consulate.

The U.S. National Archives holds passport applications for the period 1789–1926. Bound in volumes, they are filed according to the country in which the U.S. consulate was located. Typically, there are several books in an archival box. The applications are rich in genealogical information and include beautifully preserved photos.

Because the official index to the 1915–26 series of applications was lost, a group of volunteers from the Jewish Genealogy Society of Greater Washington compiled an index of the names of Jews that appeared in the material for the time period.

To access the collection, go to the National Archives II, located on the campus of the University of Maryland in College Park, Maryland, or write to U.S. National Archives and Records Administration, Washington, DC 20408. Provide the information listed in the index. You will receive a bill and a photocopy of the record(s). If you want a reproduction of the photograph, mention this in the letter. This service can be expected to be provided at a very reasonable cost.

Remember that the National Archives has all other indexes for regular and emergency passports up to and after 1926. If you want a researcher to check, make that request at the same time. Include the time frame when an application might have been made since these applications are grouped in several series.

All existing indexes for the period 1797–1906 have been microfilmed and are available through your nearest LDS (Mormon) Family History Center as well as in Room 400 of the main building of the National Archives in Washington, D.C. Since passports were generally not required by the United States for reentry into the country until World War I, this collection is rather small, but includes a large percentage of Jews.

The names of Jews from Galicia from the index and location information are given in Table E.1. Note that some birthplaces are not in Galicia; they are included if any member of the family was born in a Galician town. Issue is the country where the emergency passport was issued. The location code is divided into three numeric parts, representing the box, book and page number where the record is located. For example, the first entry in the table identifies Adel Adasse, born in Szczucin (Poland), passport issued in Poland, whose file is located in box 1737, book 1, page 385. Do not be put off by the country code. Remember that persons may have been displaced during the war. After the war, Galicia was no more than a memory, and virtually all of Galician territory reverted to Poland until World War II.

Table E-1. Names of Galician Jews in Emergency Passport Applications

Surname	Given Name	Birthplace	Issue	Location Code
Adasse	Adel	Szczucin	Pol	1737 0001 00385
Addasse	Ida	Szczucin	Pol	1737 0001 00392
Alexander	Annie	Zolkiew	Aus	1585 0177 01481
Alexander	Celia	Zolkiew	Aus	1585 0177 01481
Alexander	Esther	Zolkiew	Aus	1585 0177 01481
Alexander	Samuel	Zolkiew	Aus	1585 0177 01481
Alexander	Sara	Zolkiew	Aus	1585 0177 01481
Alter	Chaim	Grebów	Pol	1740 0006 02149
Anderman	Abraham	Buczacz	Pol	1737 0001 00146
Anderman	Abraham	Buczacz	Pol	1738 0003 00807
Anderman	Hanna	Buczacz	Pol	1738 0003 00807
Antler	Isador	Jazłowice	Swt	1759 0178 04394
Antler	Minke	Jazłowice	Swt	1759 0178 04395
Antler	Rubin	Monasterzyska	Aus	1585 0177 01313
Antler	Sadie	Jasłowice	Swt	1759 0173 04396
Ashkenazi	Anna	Tyczyn	Pol	1738 0003 00955
Ashkenazi	Joseph	Tyczyn	Pol	1738 0003 00955
Ausbel	Frimet	Galicia	Aus	1584 0147 00583
Ausbel	Sheva	Galicia	Aus	1584 0147 00584
Ax	Blanche	Stanisławów	Aus	1585 0177 01355
Bader	Chana	Borysław	Pol	1739 0004 01334

Surname	Given Name	Birthplace	Issue	Location Code
Bader	Jenny	Dynów	Aus	1584 0147 00724
Bader	Markus	Borysław	Pol	1739 0004 01334
Balamut	Anna	Wielopole	Pol	1738 0002 00528
Balamut	Chaim	Wielopole	Pol	1738 0002 00528
Balamut	Isak	Wielopole	Pol	1738 0002 00528
Balamut	Rachel	Wielopole	Pol	1738 0002 00528
Balamut	Wolff	Wielopole	Pol	1738 0002 00528
Balamuth	Annie	Rokszyce	Aus	1585 0176 01039
Balamuth	Isaac	Rokszyce	Aus	1585 0176 01039
Balamuth	Isaac	Galicia	Ger	1676 0175 08190
Baldash	Isidor	Tarnopol	Pol	1738 0003 01157
Baldash	Mina	Tarnopol	Pol	1738 0003 01157
Barer	Israel	Turza Wielka	Pol	1737 0001 00043
Barer	Cyllie	Turza Wielka	Pol	1737 0001 00043
Baron	Pauline	Obertyn	Aus	1585 0176 00947
Bau	Abraham	Dombrowa	Aus	1584 0147 00734
Bau	Beile	Dombrowa	Aus	1584 0147 00734
Bau	Breindl	Dombrowa	Aus	1584 0147 00734
Bau	Chaskel	Dombrowa	Aus	1584 0147 00734
Bau	Chiel	Dombrowa	Aus	1584 0147 00734
Baumel	David	Grzymałów	Aus	1584 0147 00716
Baumel	Max	Grzymałów	Aus	1584 0147 00716
Baumel	Regina	Grzymałów	Aus	1584 0147 00716
Bebczuk	Malka	Jezierzany	Pol	1739 0004 01528
Bebczuk	Morris	Jezierzany	Pol	1739 0004 01528
Berg	Malka Kramer	Rawa Ruska	Pol	1741 0009 04443
Berg	Malka Kramer	Rawa Ruska	Pol	1737 0001 04443
Berman	Anna	Radomysl	Fin	1651 0001 00087
Berman	Elisabeth	Radomysl	Fin	1651 0001 00087
Berman	Harry	Radomysl	Fin	1651 0001 00087
Berman	Louis	Radomysl	Fin	1651 0001 00087
Bernhang	Rosie	Galicia	Aus	1584 0147 00573
Bernzweig	Emilia	Stanisławów	Pol	1738 0003 00884
Beyman	Buncha	Czortków	Fr	1660 0165 02887
Beyman	Buncha	Czortków	Fr	1702 0001 00037
Bienenstock	Jacob	Tarnobrzeg	Pol	1737 0001 00302
Bienenstock	Schyfra	Tarnobrzeg	Pol	1737 0001 00302
Biller	Isaac	Zabłotów	Pol	1737 0001 00246
Biller	Molly	Zabłotów	Pol	1737 0001 00246
Birnbaum	Beppi	Widynów	Pol	1738 0002 00491
Birnbaum	Bessie Gewitz	Frysztak	Pol	1741 0009 04638
Birnbaum	David	Widinów	Pol	1738 0002 00491
Birnbaum	David	Zaleszczyki	Aus	1585 0176 01280
Birnbaum	Nathan	Widynów	Pol	1738 0002 00491
Bisgier	Minnie	Galicia	Aus	1585 0176 01083
Bisgier	Pauline	Galicia	Aus	1585 0176 01083
Bisgier	Ruth	Galicia	Aus	1585 0176 01083
Blatt	Anna	Kozowa	Pol	1740 0006 02024
Blatt	Jonas	Brzeżany	Pol	1740 0006 02024
Bloch	Samuel	Dobrowa	Ger	1676 0176 10536
Bloomfield	Clara	Lemberg	Aus	1585 0176 00967
Blustin	Annie	Sanok	Aus	1585 0177 01414
Blustin	Mary	Sanok	Aus	1585 0177 01414
Bodner	Anna	Radomysl Wielkie	Ger	1740 0006 02333
Bodner	Aron	Radomysl Wielkie	Ger	1740 0006 02333
Brandes	Baruch	Swidowa	Pol	1737 0001 00371
Brandes	Yetta	Swidowa	Pol	1737 0001 00371
Brandriss	Sara	Brody	Aus	1585 0176 00877
Brenner	Kalman	Kraków	Ger	1679 0183 00421
Brodofsky	Annie	Nowy Dwor	Pol	1737 0001 00196
Brodofsky	Max	Nowy Dwor	Pol	1737 0001 00196
Brown	Harry	Kraków	Ger	1674 0172 04226
Bruck	Solomon	Złoczów	Aus	1585 0177 04720
Buchner	Irving	Kraków	Aus	1585 0177 00018

Surname	Given Name	Birthplace	Issue	Location Code
Burn	Emilia	Stanisławów	Pol	1738 0003 00884
Burn	Samuel	Stanisławów	Pol	1738 0003 00884
Calvary	Dora	Tarnów	Bel	1590 0003 00842
Chapkiewicz	Chana	Rzeszów	Pol	1739 0004 01523
Chapkiewicz	Philip	Rzeszów	Pol	1739 0004 01523
Charapp	Drezel	Jezierzany	Pol	1739 0004 01234
Charapp	Max	Jezierzany	Pol	1739 0004 01234
Cohen	Braina	Lemberg	Aus	1585 0177 01415
Cohen	Fannie	Lemberg	Aus	1585 0177 01415
Cohen	Gusia	Galicia	Cz	1644 0001 00205
Cohen	Harry	Lemberg	Aus	1585 0177 01415
Cohen	Mary	Lemberg	Aus	1585 0177 01415
Cohen	Wolf	Galicia	Cz	1644 0001 11205
Cohn	Eva	Brody	Aus	1585 0177 01387
Cohn	Eva	Brody	Aus	1585 0177 01545
Conay	Daniel	Zagórze	Fr	1667 0180 00831
Dachs	Mendel	Delatyn	Fr	1673 0169 01757
Degen	Renie	Galicia	Aus	1585 0176 01092
Deitel	Yetta	Lemberg	Pol	1741 0008 04182
Dembitzer	Emma	Wash DC	Den	1648 0004 00318
Dembitzer	Louis	Kraków	Den	1648 0004 00317
Diamond	Abraham	Miedzyrzecz	Egy	1650 0002 00015
Diamond	Max	Miedzyrzecz	Egy	1650 0002 00014
Diamond	Max	Miedzyrzecz	Egy	1650 0002 00119
Dicker	Joel	Brzeżany	Aus	1585 0177 01354
Dicker	Leah	Brzeżany	Aus	1585 0177 01354
Dinner	Lewis	Bełż	Aus	1584 0147 00704
Dramin	Pauline	Tarnów	Aus	1584 0147 00661
Dreiblatt	Morris	Kraków	Hol	1706 0001 00035
Drucker	Max	Galicia	Aus	1585 0176 01122
Dub	Basia	Bukaczowce	Pol	1741 0009 04597
Dub	Genia	Sędziszów	Pol	1741 0009 04597
Dub	Mechel	Sędziszów	Pol	1741 0009 04597
Eckstein	Feige	Sokolki	Pol	1737 0001 00037
Eckstein	Gershon	Sokolki	Pol	1737 0001 00037
Edelman	Jacob	Włodzimierz	Pol	1739 0004 01493
Edelman	Rose	Włodzimierz	Pol	1739 0004 01493
Eder	Lottie	Mielec	Pol	1749 0005 01883
Eder	Sam	Mielec	Pol	1749 0005 01883
Einhorn	Benny	Kraków	Hol	1707 0003 00793
Eis	Elias	Miechów	Aus	1585 0176 01250
Eis	Malka	Miechów	Aus	1585 0176 01250
Eis	Pinkas	Miechów	Aus	1585 0176 01250
Eis	Ryfka	Miechów	Aus	1585 0176 01250
Eisenberg	Chaja Mincia	Bursztyn	Aus	1585 0177 01309
Eisenberg	Juda Chaim	Bursztyn	Aus	1585 0177 01309
Eisenberg	Leah	Bursztyn	Aus	1585 0177 01309
Eisenberg	Sadie	Bursztyn	Aus	1585 0177 01309
Eisenkraft	Chaim	Russów	Aus	1585 0176 01211
Eisner	Bernard	Kołomea	Pol	1738 0002 00629
Eisner	Max	Kołomea	Pol	1738 0002 00629
Eisner	Fannie	Kołomea	Pol	1738 0002 00629
Elifant	Dora	Poździmierz	Aus	1585 0176 01274
Elifant	Joseph	Poździmierz	Aus	1585 0176 01274
Elifant	Minnie	Poździmierz	Aus	1585 0176 01274
Ettinger	Arnold	Tarnów	Ger	1674 0172 04882
Ettinger	Arnold	Tarnów	Ger	1674 0178 04276
Ettinger	Sabine	Tarnów	Ger	1674 0178 04276
Ettinger	Sabine	Tarnów	Swt	1759 0178 04279
Ewig	Adolph	Stryy	Hun	1708 0001 00279
Ewig	Israel	Stryy	Hun	1708 0001 00279
Fassman	Bertha	Krzywcza	Pol	1738 0002 00427
Fassman	Nathan	Krzywcza	Pol	1738 0002 00427
Fassman	Sarah	Krzywcza	Pol	1738 0002 00427

Surname	Given Name	Birthplace	Issue	Location Code
Faust	Abraham	Zaleszczyki	Pol	1737 0001 00368
Faust	Bessie	Zaleszczyki	Pol	1737 0001 00368
Faust	Rachel	New York	Pol	1737 0001 00368
Feid	Joseph	Dubowica	Pol	1737 0001 00378
Feid	Sarah	Dubowica	Pol	1737 0001 00378
Feingold	Hirsch	Kolbuszowa	Ger	1678 0180 15610
Feld	Sara	Dubowica	Aus	1585 0177 01365
Feld	Sarah	Dubowica	Hun	1709 0162 00850
Feuer	Moritz	Galicia	Aus	1585 0176 01001
Feuer	Rosa	Galicia	Aus	1585 0176 01090
Fink	Chaim	Slone	Pol	1738 0003 01079
Fink	Rosa	Galicia	Aus	1584 0147 00629
Finkel	Julius	Sielce	Pol	1738 0003 01068
Finkel	Rywka	Sielce	Pol	1738 0003 01068
Fishman	Rose	Lemberg	Ger	1674 0171 03480
Flam	Bernard	Tarnów	Pol	1738 0002 00689
Flam	Bernard	Tarnów	Pol	1737 0001 00118
Flam	Camil	Tarnów	Pol	1737 0001 00118
Flam	Celia	Pilzno	Pol	1737 0001 00118
Flam	Joseph	Pilzno	Pol	1737 0001 00118
Flam	Pinkus	Tarnów	Pol	1737 0001 00118
Flam	Camil	Tarnów	Pol	1738 0002 00689
Flam	Celia	Pilzno	Pol	1738 0002 00689
Flam	Pinkus	Tarnów	Pol	1738 0002 00689
Fliegelman	Chiel	Majdan	Pol	1737 0001 00282
Fliegelman	Chiel	Majdan	Pol	1737 0001 00283
Fliegelman	Ethel	Majdan	Pol	1737 0001 00282
Fliegelman	Markus	Majdan	Pol	1737 0001 00283
Fliegelmann	Biele	Majdan	Pol	1737 0176 01273
Fliegelmann	David	Majdan	Pol	1737 0176 01273
Fliegelmann	Elka	Majdan	Pol	1737 0176 01273
Fliegelmann	Golda	Majdan	Pol	1737 0176 01273
Fliegelmann	Jakob	Majdan	Pol	1737 0176 01273
Freimaurer	Anna	Lysaków	Pol	1737 0001 00237
Freimaurer	Louis	Kuty	Pol	1737 0001 00237
Freimaurer	Harry	New York	Pol	1737 0001 00238
Freimaurer	Rosie	New York	Pol	1737 0001 00239
Fried	Isidore	Galicia	Egy	1650 0002 00083
Fried	Tille	Ciechanów	Pol	1737 0001 00075
Friedlander	Cyrla	Woloska Wieś	Pol	1738 0002 00581
Friedlander	Herman	Woloska Wieś	Pol	1738 0002 00581
Friedman	Esther	Radomysl	Pol	1738 0003 01024
Friedman	Morris	Radomysl	Pol	1738 0003 01024
Friedman	Rive	Horodenka	Pol	1737 0001 00169
Friedman	Sam	Horodenka	Pol	1737 0001 00169
Fuchs	Perl	Leszniów	Aus	1585 0177 01303
Fuerman	Dasia	Sieniawa	Pol	1738 0003 00983
Fuerman	Isidore	Sieniawa	Pol	1738 0003 00983
Gaffner	May	Buczacz	Pol	1741 0008 04397
Garfinkel	Mina	Galicia	Cz	1644 0001 00261
Gebel	Rachel	Rymanów	Pol	1741 0009 04603
Gebel	Sadie	New York	Pol	1741 0009 04603
Geffner	Paul	Buczacz	Aus	1585 0177 01435
Geller	Emanuel	Wróblik	Aus	1585 0176 01277
Geller	Joseph	Wróblik	Aus	1585 0176 01277
Geller	Paulina	Wróblik	Aus	1585 0176 01277
Geschwind	Morris	Mielec	Hol	1729 0003 01224
Gevirtz	Malvina	Kalusz	Ger	1674 0172 04307
Gewurz	Bertha	Dębica	Aus	1584 0147 00576
Gewurz	Elias	Dębica	Aus	1584 0147 00576
Gewurz	Elias	Dębica	Aus	1584 0147 00576
Gewurz	Henoch	Dębica	Aus	1584 0147 00576
Gewurz	Joseph	Dębica	Aus	1584 0147 00576
Gewurz	Lena	Dębica	Aus	1584 0147 00576

Surname	Given Name	Birthplace	Issue	Location Code
Gewurz	Sarah	Dębica	Aus	1584 0147 00576
Ginsberg	William	Sambor	Pol	1738 0003 00889
Glatt	Leah	Galicia	Ger	1678 0181 06719
Gluckman	Aron	Sambor	Fr	1664 0174 05295
Gluckman	Golde	Sambor	Fr	1664 0174 05295
Gluckman	Mendel	Sambor	Fr	1664 0174 05295
Gluckman	Golde	Sambor	Eng	1699 0174 07234
Gold	Esther	Galicia	Aus	1584 0147 00784
Gold	Isaac	Baligród	Pol	1749 0005 01933
Gold	Jacob	Lemberg	Ger	1675 0173 05100
Gold	Rose	Baligród	Pol	1749 0005 01933
Goldberg	Cipra Esther	Muszyna	Pol	1739 0004 01494
Goldberg	Rifka	Obertyn	Pol	1740 0006 02025
Goldhirsh	Fanny	Jezierzany	Egy	1650 0002 00052
Goldhirsh	William	Jezierzany	Egy	1650 0002 00052
Goldik	Chaim	Torski	Pol	1738 0002 00563
Goldik	Sophie	Torskie	Pol	1738 0002 00563
Goldmuntz	Michael	Kraków	Hol	1706 0001 00282
Goldmuntz	Michael	Kraków	Hol	1707 0002 00435
Goldmuntz	Sophie	Lemberg	Bel	1590 0003 00658
Goldmuntz	Sylvan	Kraków	Hol	1705 0001 00283
Gottfried	Fannie	Kołomea	Hun	1708 0161 00470
Gottfried	Bessie	New York	Hun	1708 0161 00470
Gottfried	Irene	Corona NY	Hun	1708 0161 00470
Gottfried	Rosie	Tarnopol	Pol	1737 0001 00224
Gottfried	Samuel	Galicia	Egy	1649 0001 50/19
Gottfried	Simon	Tarnopol	Pol	1737 0001 00224
Gottlieb	Adolph	Bochnia	Aus	1585 0176 01002
Gredinger	Adele	Galicia	Aus	1584 0147 00695
Gredinger	Dora	Galicia	Aus	1584 0147 00695
Gredinger	Fanny	Galicia	Aus	1584 0147 00695
Gredinger	Herman	Galicia	Aus	1584 0147 00695
Gredinger	Jetty	Galicia	Aus	1584 0147 00695
Gredinger	Moritz	Galicia	Aus	1584 0147 00695
Gredinger	Rebecca	Galicia	Aus	1584 0147 00695
Green	Bessie	Rokitno	Aus	1585 0176 01257
Greenbaum	Morris	Podwołoczyska	Pol	1741 0009 00036
Greenberg	Annie	Glinyany	Pol	1738 0002 00658
Greenbaum	Zelig	Sokolniki	Rus	1744 0003 00035
Greenbaum	Freida	Sokolniki	Rus	1744 0003 00035
Greenbaum	Samuel	Sokolniki	Rus	1744 0003 00035
Greenberg	Louis	Glinyany	Pol	1738 0002 00658
Greenberg	Sophie	Galicia	Pol	1737 0001 00078
Greene	Jacob	Galicia	Aus	1585 0177 01470
Greene	Tillie	Galicia	Aus	1585 0177 01470
Grinberg	Harry	Strzyżów	Pol	1737 0001 00220
Grinberg	Necha	Strzyżów	Pol	1737 0001 00220
Gutreich	Blume	Galicia	Aus	1585 0176 01138
Habenstrut	Anna	Rawa Ruska	Pol	1738 0002 00678
Habenstrut	Joseph	Rawa Ruska	Pol	1738 0002 00678
Habenstrut	Rebecca	Rawa Ruska	Pol	1738 0002 00678
Habenstrut	Samuel	Rawa Ruska	Pol	1738 0002 00678
Haber	Mateusz	Brzozowce	Pol	1738 0004 01034
Haber	Sofia	Brzozowce	Pol	1738 0004 01034
Halpern	Henoch	Lemberg	Pol	1741 0009 04549
Halpern	Sam	Lemberg	Pol	1741 0009 04549
Hauser	Izik	Borysław	Fr	1650 0160 01754
Hecht	Lois	Horodenka	Aus	1584 0147 00515
Hecker	Jennie	Kolbuszowa	Ger	1675 0174 07215
Heischuber	Esther	Tyczyn	Pol	1740 0006 02382
Heischuber	Max	Tyczyn	Pol	1740 0006 02382
Heller	Max	Halicz	Pol	1737 0001 00263
Heller	Rose	Halicz	Pol	1737 0001 00263
Hellman	Osias	Dolina	Aus	1585 0176 00991

Surname	Given Name	Birthplace	Issue	Location Code
Heuschuber	Anna	Rzeszów	Aus	1584 0147 00740
Heuschuber	Esther	Rzeszów	Aus	1584 0147 00740
Heuschuber	Herman	Rzeszów	Aus	1584 0147 00740
Heuschuber	Moses	Rzeszów	Aus	1584 0147 00740
Hitzig	Becky	Galicia	Aus	1585 0177 01512
Hitzig	Eni	Galicia	Aus	1585 0177 01512
Hochaus	Lillian	Kraków	Bel	1590 0003 00841
Hochaus	Samuel	Kraków	Bel	1590 0003 00841
Hochaus	Samuel	Kraków	Bel	1589 0001 00032
Hoffman	Minnie	Chorostków	Pol	1737 0001 00206
Hoffman	Sam	Chorostków	Pol	1737 0001 00206
Hollander	Irving	Lemberg	Rus	1744 0008 00034
Hollander	Lena	Lemberg	Rus	1744 0008 00034
Jalb	George	Dukla	Aus	1585 0176 01298
Jonas	Leon	Galicia	Aus	1585 0176 01025
Jonas	Minna	Galicia	Aus	1585 0176 01025
Kudd	Isidor Israel	Kraków	Aus	1585 0176 01025
Judd	Josephine	Kraków	Aus	1585 0176 01025
Judd	Isidore	Kraków	Fr	1662 0170 03885
Kahn	Sarah	Galicia	Aus	1585 0176 01172
Kalb	David Leib	Rymanów	Pol	1737 0001 00173
Kalb	Bessie	Rymanów	Pol	1737 0001 00172
Kalb	David Leib	Komorniki	Swt	1758 0176 03629
Kalb	Liba	Haber, Czech	Pol	1737 0001 00173
Kalb	Benjamin	Haber, Czech	Pol	1737 0001 00173
Kanner	Bennie	Galicia	Aus	1584 0147 00593
Kanner	Bertha	New York	Aus	1584 0147 00593
Kanner	Bine	New York	Aus	1584 0147 00593
Kanner	Leopold	New York	Aus	1584 0147 00593
Kanner	Marcus	Galicia	Aus	1584 0147 00593
Kanon	Lilly	Radomysl	Aus	1584 0147 00659
Kanon	Tessie	Radomysl	Aus	1584 0147 00659
Kantor	Pauline	Lemberg	Pol	1738 0003 01176
Kantor	Tadeusz	Lemberg	Pol	1738 0003 01176
Kaplan	Pesa	Radomysl	Lat	1577 0146 00143
Karol	Julia	Podhajce	Pol	1737 0001 00214
Karol	Adele	New York	Pol	1737 0001 00214
Karol	Justyn	Podhajce	Pol	1737 0001 00214
Karpen	Florence	Kraków	Pol	1741 0008 04192
Karpen	Jennie	Kraków	Pol	1741 0008 04192
Karpen	Lawrence	Kraków	Pol	1741 0008 04192
Katz	Max	Korczyna	Fr	1666 0177 06585
Klein	Rosa	Galicia	Aus	1585 0176 01064
Konig	Benny	Stanisławów	Aus	1585 0177 01431
Konig	Betty	Stanisławów	Aus	1585 0177 01431
Konig	Louis	Kalusz	Aus	1585 0177 01430
Kornhabe	Fannie	Lemberg	Aus	1585 0177 00510
Kornhabe	Julius	Lemberg	Aus	1585 0177 00510
Kornhabe	Samuel	Lemberg	Aus	1585 0177 00510
Kornstein	Annie	Galicia	Aus	1584 0147 00609
Kornstein	Dora	Galicia	Aus	1584 0147 00609
Kornstein	Fannie	Galicia	Aus	1584 0147 00609
Kornstein	Morris	Grzymałów	Aus	1584 0147 00609
Kornstein	Morris	Grzymałów	Aus	1585 0177 01406
Kreiger	Abraham	Tyczyn	Pol	1749 0005 01954
Kreiger	Sally	Tyczyn	Pol	1749 0005 01954
Kruleck	Fannie	Narol	Aus	1584 0147 00725
Kruleck	Israel	Narol	Aus	1584 0147 00725
Kruleck	Sarah	Narol	Aus	1584 0147 00725
Kronstein	Isadore	Żurawno	Aus	1586 0173 00118
Kurzrok	Gitla	Sassów	Pol	1738 0002 00531
Kurzrok	Raphael	Sassów	Pol	1738 0002 00531
Lachner	Celia	Brody	It	1715 0172 00835
Lachner	Henry	Brody	It	1715 0172 00835

Surname	Given Name	Birthplace	Issue	Location Code
Last	Moses	Tarnobrzeg	Ger	1677 0178 00881
Leidner	Golda	Mielec	Hol	1707 0002 00580
Leidner	Samuel	Mielec	Hol	1707 0002 00580
Leidner	Samuel	Mielec	Pol	1737 0001 00123
Leidner	Golda	Mielec	Pol	1737 0001 00122
Leistyna	Bertha	Grybów	Pol	1738 0002 00780
Leistyna	Sophie	Grybów	Pol	1738 0002 00780
Leistyna	Morris	Grybów	Pol	1738 0002 00780
Lechner	Mary	Nisko	Pol	1737 0001 00229
Lechner	Morris	Nisko	Pol	1737 0001 00229
Lerner	Hyman	Krystynopol	Pol	1738 0002 00680
Lerner	Sadie	Ciechanów	Pol	1737 0001 00048
Lewkowitz	Annie	Jaszczurowa	Ger	1679 0183 00350
Lichtenberg	Tachel	Bledowa	Pol	1737 0001 00049
Lieberman	Annie	Tyczyn	Aus	1584 0147 00712
Lieberman	Jacob	Raków	Pol	1740 0006 02152
Lieberman	Regina	Galicia	Aus	1584 0147 00761
Lieberman	Sam	Galicia	Aus	1584 0147 00761
Lieblich	Max	Rzeszów	Aus	1585 0176 01215
Lifscheitz	Morris	Monastyriska	Pol	1740 0006 02261
Lifscheitz	Yenta	Monastyriska	Pol	1740 0006 02261
Linder	Nettie	Rymanów	Aus	1585 0176 01173
Lippman	Ettel	Buczacz	Aus	1585 0177 01513
Low	Anna	Bóbrka	Pol	1739 0004 01347
Low	Berl	Bóbrka	Pol	1739 0004 01347
Low	Heni	Bóbrka	Pol	1739 0004 01347
Lowenthal	Dora	Galicia	Aus	1584 0147 00602
Lowenthal	Lillian	Galicia	Aus	1584 0147 00602
Luks	Pinkas	Wasylkowce	Pol	1738 0002 00575
Luks	Rachel	Wasylkowce	Pol	1738 0002 00575
Mages	Annie	Drohobycz	Pol	1738 0002 00782
Mages	Fannie	Drohobycz	Pol	1738 0002 00782
Mages	Jennie	Drohobycz	Pol	1738 0002 00782
Mages	Nathan	Drohobycz	Pol	1738 0002 00782
Mages	Timothy	Drohobycz	Pol	1738 0002 00782
Mandel	Joseph	Pruchnik	Aus	1585 0176 01143
Manheim	Daniel	Szczakowa	Pol	1738 0003 00924
Manheim	Jacob	Szczakowa	Pol	1738 0003 00924
Manheim	Rose	Szczakowa	Pol	1738 0003 00924
Manheim	Taube	Szczakowa	Pol	1738 0003 00924
Manheim	Wolf	Szczakowa	Pol	1738 0003 00924
Margulias	Abraham	Galicia	Aus	1584 0147 00598
Margulias	Broni	Galicia	Aus	1584 0147 00598
Margulias	Israel	Galicia	Aus	1584 0147 00598
Margulias	Jacob	Galicia	Aus	1584 0147 00598
Margulies	Abraham	Galicia	Aus	1584 0147 00657
Margulies	Broni	Galicia	Aus	1584 0147 00657
Margulies	Clara	Galicia	Cz	1684 0003 00085
Margulies	Mary	Tarnopol	Pol	1737 0001 00054
Margulies	Mary	Tarnopol	Aus	1584 0147 00664
Margulies	Mary	Tarnopol	Pol	1737 0001 00055
Margulies	Rosa	Mikulince	Pol	1737 0001 00054
Margulies	Simon	Mikulince	Pol	1737 0001 00054
Margulies	Simon	Tarnopol	Aus	1584 0147 00664
Messer	Annie	Lubaczów	Pol	1737 0001 00216
Messer	Carl	Lubaczów	Pol	1737 0001 00216
Meyerowitz	David	Glinik	Aus	1584 0147 00708
Meyerowitz	Eva	Glinik	Aus	1584 0147 00708
Meyerowitz	Sophie	Glinik	Aus	1584 0147 00708
Mielnik	Anna	Rohatyń	Pol	1738 0002 00423
Mielnik	Helen	Rohatyń	Pol	1738 0002 00423
Mielnik	John	Rohatyń	Pol	1738 0002 00423
Muschel	Alte	Dąbrowa	Aus	1584 0147 00532
Muschel	Markus	Dąbrowa	Aus	1584 0147 00532

Surname	Given Name	Birthplace	Issue	Location Code
Nagel	Anna	Złoczów	Aus	1585 0176 01275
Nagel	Eva	Złoczów	Aus	1585 0176 01275
Nagel	Harry	New York	Aus	1585 0176 01275
Nathanson	Ida	Grodzisko	Fr	1656 0157 00605
Papernik	Samuel	Zolocze	Aus	1585 0177 01582
Pavlotsky	Boris	Radomysl	Pol	1739 0004 01534
Pavlotsky	Etla	Radomysl	Pol	1739 0004 01534
Perlman	Abraham	Galicia	Hol	1707 0003 00864
Perlman	Abraham	Wieliczka	Aus	1585 0176 01239
Perlman	Abraham	Galicia	Hol	1707 0003 01104
Perlman	Chaskell	Boston	Aus	1585 0176 01240
Perlman	Dora	Brzesko	Aus	1584 0147 00579
Perlman	Fannie	Galicia	Aus	1585 0176 01240
Perlman	Hanna	Boston	Aus	1585 0176 01240
Perlman	Samuel	Galicia	Aus	1585 0176 01240
Perlman	Stefina	Boston	Aus	1585 0176 01240
Perlman	Theresa	Wieliczka	Aus	1585 0176 01240
Perlstein	Sima Parciak	Rzeszów	Pol	1741 0008 04370
Pitzele	Fanny	Kraków	Fr	1658 0162 02388
Pitzele	Rosa	Kraków	Fr	1658 0162 02389
Pitzele	Rubin	Kraków	Fr	1658 0162 02390
Polikuk	Jacob	Buczacz	Pol	1749 0005 01885
Polikuk	Liebe	Zoloty Potok	Pol	1749 0005 01885
Posner	Blima	Nowy Dwor	Pol	1737 0001 00304
Posner	Joseph	Nowy Dwor	Pol	1737 0001 00304
Postaz	Charlotte	Tarnopol	Ger	1676 0175 08676
Postaz	Frieda	Tarnopol	Ger	1676 0175 08676
Postaz	Mollie	Tarnopol	Ger	1676 0175 08676
Potsteve	Clara	Nowy Dwor	Pol	1737 0001 00314
Propper	Gussie	Mokre	Pol	1737 0001 00388
Propper	Hyman	Mokre	Pol	1737 0001 00388
Rabinowitz	Nasia	Radomysl	Pol	1749 0005 01910
Rabinowitz	Chaim	Radomysl	Pol	1749 0005 01910
Rabinowitz	Leiser	Stanisławow	Pol	1738 0002 00608
Rabinowitz	Meshulam	Stanisławow	Pol	1738 0002 00608
Rakower	Fannie Wertheim	Nowy Sącz	Bel	1589 0001 00315
Rakower	Josef	Podgórze	Bel	1589 0001 00269
Rakower	Josef	Podgórze	Bel	1589 0001 00315
Rakower	Sabine	Podgórze	Bel	1589 0001 00315
Rand	Gussie	Sanok	Aus	1584 0147 00711
Rappaport	Ascher Schaye	Strzyżów	Pol	1737 0001 00185
Rappaport	Cyvie	Strzyżów	Pol	1737 0001 00185
Reichenstein	Ethel	Lemberg	Aus	1585 0176 00957
Reisner	Harry	Rzeszów	Aus	1585 0176 00873
Reiss	Joseph	Lemberg	Lat	1577 0147 00055
Renner	Jacob	Stanisławów	Bel	1590 0003 00828
Richter	Max	Lemberg	Aus	1584 0147 00644
Richter	Moses	Lemberg	Aus	1584 0147 00644
Richter	Nettie	Lemberg	Aus	1584 0147 00644
Rine	Victor	Kudryńce	Egy	1650 0002 00156
Ringelheim	Chaje	Jarosław	Aus	1585 0176 04633
Ringelheim	David	Jarosław	Aus	1585 0176 04633
Ringelheim	Osias	Jarosław	Aus	1585 0176 04633
Ringelheim	Mary	Galicia	Aus	1585 0176 04633
Ringelheim	Jacob	Kanczuga	Aus	1585 0176 04633
Ritterman	Abraham	Trzebina	Aus	1584 0147 00683
Ritterman	Abraham	Trzebina	Swt	1759 0173 04397
Rodner	Anna	Radomysl Wielkie	Pol	1740 0006 02333
Rosen	Morris	Lesko	Aus	1584 0147 00656
Rosenbach	Sophia	Mikulince	Ger	1673 0169 01400
Rosenbluth	Frederick	Galicia	Eng	1696 0163 04922
Rosenbluth	Hanna	Galicia	Eng	1696 0163 04922
Rosenbluth	Herman	Galicia	Eng	1696 0163 04922

Surname	Given Name	Birthplace	Issue	Location Code
Rosenbluth	Gussie	New York	Aus	1585 0176 01210
Rosenbluth	Minia	Śniatyn	Aus	1585 0176 01210
Rosenfeld	Johanna	Stanisławów	Pol	1738 0002 00615
Rosenfeld	Oscar	Stanisławów	Pol	1738 0002 00615
Rosenfeld	Oscar	Stanisławów	Aus	1585 0176 01183
Rosenfeld	Rose	Stanisławów	Aus	1585 0176 01184
Rosenfeld	Rose	Stanisławów	Pol	1738 0002 00650
Rosenfeld	Salomon	Stanisławów	Pol	1738 0002 00614
Rosenfeld	Salomon	Stanisławów	Pol	1738 0002 00615
Rosenfeld	Taube/Toni	Stanisławów	Pol	1738 0002 00614
Rosenfeld	Taube/Toni	Stanisławów	Aus	1585 0176 01183
Rosenman	Celia	Maków	Hol	1707 0003 00979
Rosenstrauch	Sam	Podhajce	Aus	1584 0147 00587
Rosiner	Clara	Sielce	Pol	1738 0002 00697
Rosiner	Max	Sielce	Pol	1738 0002 00697
Roth	Fanny	Tarnów	Ger	1677 0178 14343
Roth	Pauline	Sanok	Aus	1584 0147 00615
Rothman	Henry	Lezajsk	Swt	1759 0178 04469
Rothman	Henry	Lezajsk	Aus	1706 0176 01021
Rubin	David	Kolbuszowa	Aus	1585 0176 01272
Rudolph	Nettie	Galicia	Aus	1584 0147 00604
Sacher	Joseph	Kuty	Ger	1676 0177 12505
Saifer	Anna	Felsztyn	Pol	1738 0003 00986
Saifer	Paisy	Felsztyn	Pol	1738 0003 00986
Salzman	Israel	Niebylec	Rus	1744 0008 00043
Sattler	Annie	Galicia	Aus	1585 0176 01127
Schaffer	Hyman	Dora	Pol	1740 0006 02301
Schafler	Elias	Radymno	Hol	1706 0001 00453
Schatz	Anna	Bialy Kamień	Pol	1741 0008 04155
Schatz	Bronia	Bialy Kamień	Pol	1741 0008 04155
Schein	Cecilia	Stanisławów	Pol	1738 0002 00717
Schiffer	Bruche	Majdan	Pol	1737 0001 00309
Schiffer	Salamon	Majdan	Pol	1737 0001 00309
Schindler	Poli	Galicia	Hun	1708 0161 00482
Schindler	Jack	New York	Hun	1708 0161 00482
Schindler	Meyer	New York	Hun	1708 0161 00482
Schlaff	Frandel	Ropczyce	Pol	1738 0002 00533
Schlaff	Lewis	Ropczyce	Pol	1738 0002 00533
Schlanger	Moses	Rzeszów	Aus	1585 0176 00857
Schmertzler	Fannie	Zaleszczyki	Rom	1743 0001 00002
Schmertzler	Morris	Kasperowce	Rom	1743 0001 00002
Schnall	Max	Galicia	Aus	1585 0176 01101
Schnapp	Rose	Podhajce	Aus	1584 0147 00554
Schwartz	Clara	Lemberg	Aus	1586 0178 00153
Schwartz	Zacharia	Dolina	Pol	1749 0005 01875
Schwarz	Anna	Szczerzec	Pol	1738 0003 01029
Schwarz	Harris	Szczerzec	Pol	1738 0003 01029
Scitumer	Kopie	New York	Aus	1585 0176 01261
Scitumer	Lena	Stanisławów	Aus	1585 0176 01261
Segal	David	Roznów	Pol	1740 0006 02007
Segal	Gertrude	Roznów	Pol	1740 0006 02007
Seidmann	Fannie	Raków	Pol	1741 0009 04613
Seinfeld	Herman	Stanisławów	En	1696 0168 00472
Shuelander	Mariem	Sokolów	Pol	1737 0001 00221
Shuelander	Morris	Sokolów	Pol	1737 0001 00221
Siegel	Regina	Borysław	Pol	1738 0002 00786
Singer	Esther	Gorlice	Ger	1679 0183 00290
Sitzer	Clara	Kalusz	Pol	1738 0003 01154
Sitzer	Leib	Kalusz	Pol	1738 0003 01154
Sojfer	Anna	Felsztyn	Pol	1738 0003 00986
Sojfer	Paisy	Felsztyn	Pol	1738 0003 00986
Sonnenfeld	Mary Goldhirsh	Jezierzany	Pol	1650 0003 00334
Speigel	Helen	Buczacz	Aus	1585 0176 01250
Speilvogel	Chaim	Tarnobrzeg	Ger	1676 0177 13276

Surname	Given Name	Birthplace	Issue	Location Code
Speilvogel	Jacob	Tarnobrzeg	Ger	1676 0177 13276
Speilvogel	Schiffra	Tarnobrzeg	Ger	1676 0177 13276
Sprunk	Rosa	Galicia	Aus	1585 0176 00925
Stanger	Malka Kramer	Rawa Ruska	Pol	1741 0009 04443
Starer	Brina	Ottynia	Pol	1738 0003 01165
Starer	Pinkus	Ottynia	Pol	1738 0003 01165
Stark	Celia Keller	Kraków	Eng	1699 0175 0139A
Stein	Adele	Kołomea	Aus	1585 0177 01438
Stein	Harry	Kołomea	Aus	1585 0177 01360
Stein	Chaja Feider	Kołomea	Pol	1738 0003 00848
Stein	Samuel	Kołomea	Pol	1738 0003 00848
Steinhauser	Esther	Bochnia	Bel	1590 0003 00880
Steinhauser	Esther	Bochnia	Bel	1589 0001 00282
Sternbach	Isidor	Borysław	Aus	1584 5449 00483
Sternbach	Isidor	Borysław	Cz	1644 0001 00327
Sternfeld	Barney	Sandomierz	Eng	1699 0175 00068
Stevenson	Abe	Nowy Dwor	Pol	1737 0001 00314
Stone	Fannie	Kraków	Pol	1740 0005 01797
Stein	Fannie	Kraków	Pol	1740 0005 01797
Stein	Salo	Kraków	Pol	1740 0005 01797
Stone	Salo	Kraków	Pol	1740 0005 01797
Streich	Clara	Stanisławów	Pol	1741 0008 04362
Streicher	Beril	Kołomea	Pol	1739 0004 01408
Streicher	Sara	Kołomea	Pol	1739 0004 01408
Sturtz	Annie	Jasło	Pol	1737 0001 00264
Sturtz	Elsie	Jasło	Pol	1737 0001 00264
Sturtz	Elsie	New York	Pol	1737 0001 00264
Sturtz	Sophie	Jasło	Pol	1737 0001 00264
Sussman	Fannie	Ruda	Aus	1585 0177 01458
Sussman	Samuel	Ruda	Aus	1585 0177 01458
Sussman	Nehama Glatstein	Tarnopol	Ger	1673 0170 02158
Swartz	Elika	Radomysl	Lat	1577 0147 00061
Teitel	Hyman	Tarnobrzeg	Aus	1584 0147 00729
Thau	Bertha	Galicia	Aus	1585 0177 01583
Thau	Mauritz	Galicia	Aus	1585 0177 01583
Thau	Phillip	Galicia	Aus	1585 0177 01583
Thau	Tilli	Galicia	Aus	1585 0177 01583
Thurshwel	Albert	Galicia	Cz	1644 0001 00395
Thurshwel	Eidel	Galicia	Cz	1644 0001 00395
Thurshwel	Rebecca	Galicia	Cz	1644 0001 00395
Traun	Joseph	Galicia	Aus	1585 0176 01228
Trauring	Aron Benjamin	Galicia	Aus	1585 0176 01103
Tischler	Bertha	Zakliczyn	Aus	1585 0177 01134
Tischler	Katie	Zakliczyn	Aus	1585 0177 01134
Tischler	Rosie	Zakliczyn	Aus	1585 0177 01134
Trauring	Isak	Kanczuga	Aus	1584 0147 00589
Tuchschneider	Joseph	Radomysl	Pol	1737 0001 00297
Tuchschneider	Sarah	Radomysl	Pol	1737 0001 00297
Tuerk	Beatrice	Posada Chyrowska	Ger	1675 0174 06200
Tuerk	Moses	Posada Chyrowska	Ger	1675 0174 06200
Tuerk	Rose Francis	Posada Chyrowska	Ger	1675 0174 06200
Unger	Ida	Korczyna	Aus	1585 0177 01530
Uram	Henry	Maniów	Bel	1590 0003 00756
Viertel	Anna	Stanisławów	Aus	1585 0176 01074
Viertel	Bertha	Stanisławów	Aus	1585 0176 01074
Viertel	Calel	Stanisławów	Aus	1585 0176 01074
Viertel	Simon	Stanisławów	Aus	1585 0176 01074
Viertel	Zofia	Stanisławów	Aus	1585 0176 01074
Vogel	Pinkas	Kossów	Aus	1585 0147 00728
Wachtel	Max	Rzeszów	Ger	1676 0173 11383
Wadler	Anna	Kraków	Ger	1673 0169 01020
Wadler	Lucille	Kraków	Ger	1673 0169 01020
Wadler	Mayer	Kraków	Ger	1673 0169 01020
Wadler	Ruth	Kraków	Ger	1673 0169 01020

Surname	Given Name	Birthplace	Issue	Location Code
Wadler	Seymour	Kraków	Ger	1673 0169 01020
Wasser	Bertie	Lemberg	Aus	1585 0176 01071
Wasser	Bertie	Lemberg	Aus	1585 0176 01260
Wasser	Jacob	Lemberg	Aus	1585 0176 01260
Wasser	Jacob	Lemberg	Aus	1585 0176 01071
Wasser	Jacob	Lemberg	Aus	1585 0177 01441
Wasser	Willie	Lemberg	Aus	1585 0176 01260
Weber	Arthur	Slopnice	Aus	1584 0147 00685
Weber	Elias	Slopnice	Aus	1584 0147 00685
Wiedman	Lena	Jezierzany	Pol	1738 0002 00739
Wiedman	Max	Jezierzany	Pol	1738 0002 00739
Weichsel	Tobias	Rzeszów	Pol	1738 0002 00716
Weiner	Emanuel	Kraków	Eng	1699 0175 00048
Weiner	Emanuel	Kraków	Eng	1690 0156 09385
Weisgray	Dina	Rohatyń	Aus	1585 0177 01384
Weisgray	Morris	Rohatyń	Aus	1585 0177 01384
Weisgray	Mortimer	Rohatyń	Aus	1585 0177 01384
Weiss	Leah	Krościenko	Aus	1585 0177 01488
Weiss	Marcus	Krościenko	Aus	1585 0177 01487
Weissberg	Bernard	Leżajsk	Bel	1590 0002 00384
Welczer	Max	Galicia	Pol	1738 0002 00518
Welczer	Sara	Galicia	Pol	1738 0002 00518
Werner	Louis	Galicia	Ger	1673 0169 01017
Wilson	Minnie	Nowy Sącz	Ger	1680 0186 01092
Wilson	Emanuel	Philadelphia	Ger	1680 0186 01092
Wohlman	Beatrixe	New York	Hun	1708 0001 00212
Wohlman	Max	Stryj	Hug	1708 0001 00212
Wolfenstein	Clara	Czortków	Aus	1585 0177 00002
Wolfenstein	Philip	Czortków	Aus	1585 0177 00002
Wolkenheim	Amalia	Rzeszów	Pol	1737 0001 00183
Yamenfeld	Basia	Kołomea	Pol	1741 0009 00050
Yamenfeld	Clara	Kołomea	Pol	1741 0009 00050
Yamenfeld	Wolf	Kołomea	Pol	1741 0009 00050
Zahler	Louis	Radomysl	Aus	1585 0177 01408
Zahler	Louis	Radomysl	Aus	1585 0177 01063
Zeichner	Elias	Niżniów	Aus	1584 0147 00673

❀ Appendix F ❀

Documents About Kraków Jews: 18th and 19th Centuries

by Geoffrey M. Weisgard

For several centuries until 1939, Kraków was a major center of Jewish life and influence. It is not surprising, then, that numerous books have been published that describe Kraków's Jewish community. In recent years, most new books have concentrated on the Holocaust period but resources do exist for genealogists and historians interested in Kraków Jews of the 19th and 20th centuries. Little is available about the 18th and earlier centuries, however, largely due to fires that destroyed the mostly wooden structures of Kraków. In his *Jewish Monuments of Kraków's Kazimierz: A Short Guide*, Michael Rozek refers to the *Kehillah* (Jewish community) scribe, Pinchas Szijowicz Horowitz, noting that, in 1773, *Kehillah* archives were destroyed by fire in his house, along with many valuable documents of the Jews from Kazimierz (the Jewish quarter of Kraków).

By the 18th century, the major center of Kraków's Jewish population and activity was firmly established in Kazimierz, then still considered a separate town. Jews were prohibited from practicing trade and crafts in Kraków and its environs, but these prohibitions did not extend to Kazimierz.

Maps

Maps from the 18th century show that Jews lived in only a part of Kazimierz. A number of maps may be of interest to genealogists and historians, though only one is from the 18th century.

The first is a map that appears in *Miasto Kazimierz* (Town of Kazimierz) by E. Ekielski. This map, which appears to have been dated 1703, illustrates various features of Kazimierz from the 14th to the 17th centuries. The second map, found in Majer Bałaban's book *Kraków, Wedrówki w Przeszłosc: Kazimierz* (Kraków: A journey in the past), is an Austrian map from 1786. Though small in scale, it shows the city's surrounding rivers and the city walls and identifies the *Judenstadt* (Jewish city) in the northeast corner.

The third map, which appears in Bałaban's leading academic work, *Historja Zydów w Krakówie i ma Kazimierz, 1304-1868* (History of the Jews of Kraków and Kazimierz, 1304–1868), was probably prepared around 1809. This map is particularly useful because it shows house numbers that correspond to the censuses of 1790 and 1795. A fourth map, published in 1815, shows the new Jewish cemetery separated from Kazimierz by a farm and fields. Kazimierz is clearly shown, virtually surrounded by rivers. In particular, the map shows the Stara Visła (Old Vistula), which ran along the route of what is now ul. J. Dietła. At the time of the first partition of Poland in 1772, Austria occupied the area to the south of the Old Vistula, including Kazimierz, but not the area to the north, Kraków. This map is located in the Kraków archives on ul. Lubcicz.

A fifth map, published in Kraków in 1930 by the *Polska akademia umiejętności*, is of Kraków province, but it includes as an inset a plan of the city of Kraków. This map is in the LDS (Mormon) Family History Library collection under the title *Atlas historyczny Polsky: nr. 1. Mapa wojewodztwa krakowskiego z doby sejmu czteroletnego (1788–92)*/Karol Buczek. The call number in the Europe Book Area is 943.8, E7h, Ser. A.

Records of Births, Marriages and Deaths

In 1784, the Austrian administration introduced the requirement to register births, marriages and deaths with civil authorities. Some registrations for the end of the 18th century are among the records held on microfilm by the LDS Family History Library. The reader is cautioned, however, that the records for 1798–1800 are incomplete and also that family names were not widely used among Jews at the time.

The Jewish community is likely to have maintained records of births, marriages and deaths prior to 1784, but few have been found. An example of 18th-century death records can be seen in a manuscript that is held by the Jewish National and University Library in Jerusalem, which has two manuscripts concerning Kraków. The first (Heb. 8'2332) is a *pinkas hazkarat neshamot* (Book of memorial services for the dead) from the synagogue of Rabbi Meir Dayan in Kraków. This is a 34-page, mostly parchment document from the 17th–18th centuries. The other manuscript is a similar document from another synagogue. The entries in the 19-page *pinkas hazkarat neshamot* begin in the 19th century and end in 1919.

Burials prior to 1800 took place at the cemetery adjacent to the Remu synagogue. It appears that burial records for the cemetery have not survived, and, in addition, its tombstones suffered extensive destruction during the German occupation. Nevertheless, a number of books list information relating to the surviving gravestones. Further research is being conducted by a team at the Jagiellonian University in Kraków. The team, headed by Dr. Pilarczyk of the Department of Jewish Studies, has undertaken to record the inscriptions on the surviving stones; particularly important work because of continuing damage from erosion and environmental pollution.

The "new" cemetery on ul. Miodowa opened in 1800. A book exists that lists burials from about the 1880s to the present time. This was one of three or four such books, but the others apparently did not survive the Holocaust. The original book is held at the Jewish community office at ul. Skawinska 2, but the staff has no copy machine. Copies can be obtained from the New Cracow Friendship Society (a society of Holocaust survivors and their families), c/o Max Hilfstein, 1523 Dwight Place, Bronx, NY 10465; phone: (718) 972-2224. The society welcomes donations in exchange for information.

Censuses

In 1765 a census was taken of the entire Jewish community of Poland, but the results of that census appear to survive only in aggregate data. In *Historia Żydów w Krakówie i w Kazimierz, 1304–1868* (History of the Jews of Kraków and Kazimierz, 1304–1868), Bałaban maintains that the data resulting from the 1765 census were less accurate than that from the subsequent 1773 census. When Bałaban wrote his book in 1936, the 1765 census was in the main archives in Kraków, but searches there, as well as in other archives, have been conducted without success; its fate is unknown. It may have been destroyed during World War II, or it is buried somewhere at that same archives.

The Roman Catholic Church collected information about the Jewish community of Kraków as described in *Sources for Jewish History in the 18th Century in Church Archives* by Stanisław Litak of the Catholic University in Lublin. One such census was carried out in 1787, but, though it provides general information about the community, no names are included. Copies of this census are believed to be held at the Archives of the Bishop of Kraków.

A 1790 census does not show great detail, but, nevertheless, I was able to find my ancestors in that census using the 1795 census described below as a starting point. Living at house number 96 was Szmul Świecarz (*swiecarz* means candlemaker in Polish), age 45; his wife, Dwora, age 40; and their family, including Isaac, who is featured in the 1795 return.

The first census useful to genealogists was taken by the Austrians in 1795; however, a major difficulty for genealogists with this census is that most of the people listed did not have surnames.

The German-language book, *A List of the Jews of the Jewish Town of Kazimierz and the Surrounding Suburbs and Villages*, contains this census. Copies of this book are held by the Centre for Research on the History and Culture of Polish Jews of the Central Archives for the History of the Jewish People at Hebrew University in Jerusalem. A copy of this book is also held by the Archiwum Panstwowe (National Archives), ul. Sienna in Kraków.

As an example, entry number 508 shows that my ancestor, Isaac, son of Samuel, lived at house number 96, and that he was 30 years old. The previously referenced map in Bałaban's book shows that house number 96 was on ul. Ciemna. The entry also shows that Isaac's wife, Ester, age 36, was the daughter of Chaim. They lived with their children, Blume, age 8, and Gittel Lea, age 3. The record of Blume's marriage in 1805 is in my possession.

Central Archives for the History of the Jewish People

The Central Archives for the History of the Jewish People in Jerusalem holds many documents relating to Kraków in the 18th century and even earlier, but few are of genealogical significance. However, the inventory shows that the Central Archives holds fragmentary birth, marriage and death records from the 1788–1855 period, as well as court records concerning the Jews of 1624–1765.

Jewish Historical Institute

The Jewish Historical Institute in Warsaw (as of 1996) has the largest and most accessible number of documents of any collection relating to the Jewish community of Kraków. Although the institute's holdings relate primarily to post-18th-century Poland, they also have 45 files of 18th-century documents. Each file includes a brief index written in Polish. The documents, also written in Polish, contain a large number of names, which could be of particular interest to genealogists. A list of the 45 documents is available. Send three international reply coupons to Geoffrey M. Weisgard, 18 Daylesford Crescent, Cheadle, Cheshire 5K8 1LH, England.

National Archives in Kraków

The National Archives (*Archiwum Panstwowe*) in Kraków is divided among a number of buildings located in different parts of the city. The map archives is located at ul. Lubicz; 20th century documents are to be found at ul. Grunwaldzka 8; the bulk of 18th- and 19th-century documents are held at ul. Sienna 16. Non-Polish-speaking researchers are advised to enlist the assistance of someone who speaks Polish. In addition to the censuses for Kraków and the district for 1790–92 and 1795–96, the archives holds a list of Jewish inhabitants compiled for the army in 1795; a list of Jewish doorkeepers in Kraków, 1796–1808; and a list of property owners in Kazimierz, 1790–94.

Selected Books on the History of Kraków Jewry

The following works may be helpful to the genealogist or historian:

Bałaban, M. *Historia Zydów w Krakówie i w Kazimierz, 1204–1868* (History of the Jews of Kraków and Kazimierz, 1204–1868), 2 vols. This is the leading work on the history of the Jewish community of Kraków. Published in Kraków from 1931 to 1936, the volumes were an update of Bałaban's *Dzreje Zydów Krakówie i w Kazimierz, 1304–1868*, published before World War I. The volumes were reprinted in Poland in Polish and Yiddish in the 1990s. The second volume contains several chapters on the 18th century, which include a lengthy index of names, a number of family trees and illustrations and maps.

Bałaban, M. *Przewodnik po Żdowskich Zabytkach Krakowa* (Guide to Jewish monuments of Kraków), 1935 (republished 1990). The book includes descriptions and plans of the Remu cemetery.

Duda, Eugenieusz. *Krakowskie Judaica* (Kraków Judaica). The book is written largely in Polish, but an English section sets out the history of the Jewish community in Kraków. The book also contains modern maps and photos.

Rozek, Michael. *Jewish Monuments of Kraków's Kazimierz: A Short Guide.* Kraków, 1990. This book may be found in Great Britain through Orbis Books Ltd., 68 Kenway Road, London SW5 ORD, or Earl's Court Publications, Ltd., 192 Chiswick High Road, London W4 1PP.

Exielski, Eustachy. *Miasto Kazimierz i Budowle Akademickie w tym mieśce* (Town of Kazimierz and its university buildings), Kraków, 1869. This book includes a map from 1793.

Friedberg, ?. *Luchot Zikaron.* Drohobycz, 1897. The book offers 122 biographies of rabbis and leaders in the Talmudic Academy of Kraków.

Wettstein, F.N. *Luchot Zikaron.* Frankfurt, 1904, reprinted Jerusalem, 1968/9. Biographies of rabbis and other community leaders.

Zunz, J.M. *Ir Hatzedek.* Lemberg, 1874. In Hebrew, this book offers a history of the Kraków rabbinate from 1500 to 1856.

Bibliographies of Polish Judaica, 1993. This book reproduces a number of papers presented at an international symposium in Kraków, July 1988. The symposium was sponsored by the Jagiellonian University, the centre of research on Jewish history and culture in Poland.

Guide to Bibliographies of Polish Judaica edited by Krzystof Pilarczyk. This book lists a number of books worthy of examination. It also contains an inventory of the archives of Kazimierz, entitled, *Inwentarz Archiwum Miasta Kazimierza pod Krakowem, 1335–1802* (Inventory of the town of Kazimierz near Kraków, 1365–1802) by Marian Friedberg, published by the National Archives of Poland, Warsaw, 1996.

Another book relevant to 18th-century research is a catalogue of art monuments in Poland (vol. 4, part 6), issued by the Polish Academy of Sciences Institute of Art in 1995. The text, largely in Polish, includes short sections in English, an index of names mentioned in the volumes and a number of photographs, some of which include 18th-century tombstones in the Remu cemetery.

Several *yizkor* books have been published for Kraków. One, *Sefer Kroke*, includes a section on the history of the Jews in Kraków from 1304 to 1815.

Two Hasidic Jews on the streets of Kraków. Photo early 1900s.

❀ Appendix G ❀

Towns and Administrative Districts Where Jews Lived in 1877 Galicia

The two lists in this appendix will permit you to identify the jurisdiction of your Galician towns of ancestry.

The 1875 Austrian law governing the collection and maintenance of vital records is described in Chapter 2. The 1877 manual that described the administrative procedures for carrying out the law included a list of towns where Jews were known to live as recorded in the 1870 census, and the administrative districts to which the towns were assigned. The following is a complete list of the main districts and subdistricts that the Austrian government designated in 1877 for the purpose of collecting records of Jewish births, marriages and deaths.

Also included is a designation of whether the town is in current-day Poland (POL) or Ukraine (UKR). The four-digit number refers to the 1878 Austrian index map that Gesher Galicia prints on the back of its Family Finder and is reproduced at the end of this section of the appendix (Figure G-1). You may use this four-digit number to order the map for that area from the Library of Congress, Geography and Map Division, Washington, DC 20540. The map series reference number is: G6480 S75.A8.

To determine which district your ancestral town was in, refer to *The Galician Gazetteer* which follows the index map.

Biała 4062 POL
  Oświęcim
  Kęty
  Lipnik

Bircza 4169 POL
  Nowemiasto
  Dobromil
  Rybotycze
  Bircza

Bóbrka 4172 UKR
  Bóbrka
  Strzeliska Nowe (now Strilychi Novi)
  Chodorów (now Khodoriv)
  Mikołajów (now Mykolaiv)
  Brzozdowiec (now Berezdivtsi)

Bochnia 4065 POL
  Wiśnicz Nowy
  Bochnia

Bohorodczany (now Bogorodchany) 4572 UKR
  Bohorodczany (now Bogorodchany)
  Lysiec (now Lisets)
  Solotwina (now Slotvina)

Borszczów (now Borshchev) 4476 UKR
  Borszczów (now Borshchev)
  Skała (now Skala Podolskaya)
  Mielnica (now Melnytsia)

Brody 3974 UKR
  Brody
  Leszniów (now Leshnev)
  Podkamien (now Podkamen)
  Załoźce (now Zalozhtsy)
  Sokolówka (now Sokolivka)
  Szczurowice (now Shchurovychi)
  Stanisławczyk (now Stanislavchick)
  Toporów (now Toporov)

Brzesko 4065 POL
Brzesko
Wojnicz
Czchów
Szczurowa
Radłów

Brzeżany (now Berezhany) 4274 UKR
Brzeżany (now Berezhany)
Kozowa (now Kosova)
Kozłów
Narajów (now Narayev)

Brzozów 4168 POL
Brzozów
Dynów 4069
Jasienica

Buczacz (now Buchach) 4375 UKR
Buczacz (now Buchach)
Jazłowice (now Pomortsy)
Potok (now Potik Zoloty)
Barysz (now Barysh)
Monasterzyska (now Manastryska)

Chrzanów 3963 POL
Chrzanów
Trzebinia

Cieszanów 3970 POL
Cieszanów
Lubaczów
Lipsko
Narol
Oleszyce

Czortków (now Chortkov) 4375 UKR
Czortków (now Chortkov)
Budzanów (now Budanov)
Jagielnica (now Yagelnitsa)
Ulaszkowce (now Ulashkovtsy)

Dabrowa 3966 POL
Dąbrowa
Szczucin 3866

Dolina 4472 UKR
Dolina
Bolechów (now Bolekhov)
Rożniatów (now Rozhnyuv)

Drohobycz (now Drogobych) 4271 UKR
Drohobycz (now Drogobych)
Borysław (now Borislav)

Gorlice 4166 POL
Biecz
Rzepiennik Strzyewski

Gródek Jagielloński (now Gorodok) 4071 UKR
Gródek Jagielloński (now Gorodok)
Janów (now Janiv)

Grybów 4166 POL
Grybów
Bobowa

Horodenka (now Gorodenka) 4575 UKR
Horodenka (now Gorodenka)
Czernelica (now Chernilitsa)
Obertyn (now Obertin)

Husiatyn (now Gusyatin) 4376 UKR
Chorostków (now Khorostkov)
Husiatyn (now Gusiatyn)
Kopyczyńce (now Kopychintsy)
Probużna (now Probezhna)

Jarosław 3969 POL
Jarosław
Radymno
Sieniawa
Pruchnik

Jasło 4167 POL
Jasło
Olpiny
Frysztak

Jaworów (now Yavorov) 4071 UKR
Jaworów (now Yavorov) (UKR)
Krakówiec (POL)
Wielkie Oczy (POL)

Kalusz (now Kalush) 4373 UKR
Kalusz (now Kalush)
Wojnilów (now Voynilov)

Kamionka (also Kamionka Strumiłowa; now Kamenka Bugskaya) 3973 UKR
Kamionka (also Kamionka Strumiłowa; now Kamenka Bugskaya)
Busk
Witków Nowy (now Novyy Witkiv)
Radiechów (now Radekhov)
Chołojów (now Uzlovoye)
Stojanów (now Stoyaniv)

Dobrotwór (now Dobrotvor)

Kolbuszowa 3867 POL
Kolbuszowa
Majdan 3867
Ranizów 3868
Sokolów (now Sokolow Małopolski)

Kołomea (now Kolomyya) 4574 UKR
Kołomea (now Kolomyya)
Jabłanów (now Yablonov)
Peczenizyn (now Pechenezhin)
Gwoździec (now Hvizdets)

Kossow (now Kosov) 4674 UKR
Kuty
Żabie (now Verkhovina) 4774
Kossów (now Kosov)
Pistyn

Krakow 3964 POL

Krosno 4161 POL
Dukla
Korczyna
Żmigród (now Zmigrod Nowy or Stary)

Łancut 3968 POL
Łancut
Leżajsk 3969
Przeworsk 3969
Żołynia
Kańczuga 3969

Lesko/Lisko 4268 POL
Baligród
Lisko/Lesko
Lutowiska
Ustrzyki Dolne 4269
Wola Michowa

Limanowa 4165 POL
Limanowa
Mszana Dolna

Lwów (also known as Lemberg; now Lviv) 4072 UKR
Lemberg/Lwów/Lviv
Jaryczów (now Novyy Yarychev)
Nawarya (now Naviriya)
Szczerzec (now Shchyrets)
Winniki (now Vinniki)
Zniesienie

Mielec 3867 POL
Mielec
Radomyśl Wielkie

Mosciska (now Mostistka) 4070 UKR
Mosciska (now Mostistka)
Sądowa Wiśnia (now Sudovaya Vishnya)
Hussaków (now Gusakov)

Myślenice 4064 POL
Maków
Myślenice
Jordanów

Nadworna (now Nadvorna) 4573 UKR
Nadworna (now Nadvorna)
Delatyn (now Delyatin)
Lanczyn (now Lanchyn)

Nisko 3768 POL
Nisko
Ulanów
Rudnik 3868

Nowy Sącz 4165 POL
Nowy Sącz
Stary Sącz
Piwniczna
Łabowa
Krynica
Muszyna 4266
Łacko
Szczawnica 4265

Nowy Targ 4264 POL
Nowy Targ
Krościenko

Pilzno 4066 POL
Pilzno
Dębica 3967
Jadłowa/Jodłowa
Brzostek 4067

Podhajce (now Podgaytsy) 4274 UKR
Podhajce (now Podgaytsy)
Zawalów (now Zavaliv)
Złotniki (now Zolotnyky)

Przemysl 4069 POL
Sosnica
Niżankowice
Krzywcza
Przemyśl
Dubiecko (now Dubetsko)

Przemyslany (now Peremyshlyany) 4173
UKR
Przemyślany (now Peremyshlyany)
Gliniany (now Glinyany)
Dunajowce (now Dunaiv)
Swirz (now Svirzh)

Rawa (also known as Rawa Ruska; now Rava Russkaya) 3971 UKR
Rawa (Rawa Ruska; now Rava Russkaya)
Magierów (now Mageriv)
Niemirów (now Niemirov)
Uhnów (now Ugnev)
Lubycza Krolewska (now Liubycha)

Rohatyń (now Rogatin) 4273 UKR
Rohatyń (now Rogatin)
Bursztyn (now Burshtyn)

Ropczyce 3967 POL
Ropczyce
Sędziszów
Wielopole

Rudki (still Rudki) 4171 UKR
Rudki
Komarno

Rzeszów 3968 POL
Rzeszów
Głogów
Tyczyn
Strzyżów
Czudec
Niebylec
Błazowa

Sambor (also known as Altstadt) 4170
UKR
Stare Miasto
Starasól (now Staraya Sil)
Chyrów (now Khirov)
Felsztyn (now Skeliva)

Sanok 4168 POL
Sanok
Rymanów
Bukowsko
Nowotaniec
Tyrawa Woloska

Skałat (still Skalat) 4276 UKR
Skałat
Grzymałów (now Grimaylov)
Podwołoczyska (now Pidvolochyska) 4176

Tarnoruda (now Ternoruda)
Touste (now Tovste)

Śniatyn (now Snyatyn) 4675 UKR
Śniatyn (now Snyatyn)
Zabłotów (now Zabolotiv)

Sokal 3872 UKR
Bełż (now Beltsy)
Krystynopol (now Krystonopil)
Sokal
Tartaków (now Tartakiv)
Warcż/also known as Warez (now Variazh)

Stanisławow (also known as Stanislav; now Ivano-Frankovsk) 4473 UKR
Stanisławów (now Ivano-Frankovsk)
Maryampol (now Mariampil Miasto) 4373
Jezupol (now Zhovten)
Hałicz (now Galich) 4373

Stryj (now Stryy) 4272 UKR
Stryj (now Stryy)
Skole (now Skolie)

Tarnobrzeg 3767 POL
Baranów
Tarnobrzeg
Radomyśl
Rozwadów

Tarnopol (Ternopol) 4175 UKR
Tarnopol (now Ternopol)
Mikulińce (now Mykulyntsi)

Tarnów 3966 POL
Tarnów
Zabno
Ryglice
Tuchów

Tłumacz (now Tlumach) 4474 UKR
Tłumacz (now Tlumach)
Tyśmienica (now Tysmenytsia)
Niżniów (now Nizhnev)
Ottynia (now Otynya)
Uście Zielone (now Ustia Zelene)
Chocimirz (now Khotimir)

Trembowla (now Terebovlya) 4275 UKR
Trembowla (now Terebovlya)
Janów (now Janiv)
Strusów (now Stusiv)

Turka 4370 UKR

Wieliczka 4064 POL
Klasno
Podgórze

Wadowice 4063 POL
Andrychów
Kalwarya
Wadowice
Zator

Zaleszczyki (now Zaleshchiki) 4575 UKR
Zaleszczyki (now Zaleshchiki)
Tłuste (now Tovste)
Korolówka (now Oleyevo Korolevka)
Uścieczko (now Ustechko)
Gródek (now Horodek)

Zbaraz (now Zbarazh) 4175 UKR

Złoczów (now Zolochev) 4074 UKR
Złoczów (now Zolochev)
Zborów (now Zboriv)
Jezierna (now Ozernyany)
Gologory (now Holohory)
Olesko (now Olesko)
Sassów (now Sasiv)
Biały Kamień (now Belyy Kamen)
Pomorzany (now Pomoryany)

Żolkiew (now Zhovka) 3972 UKR
Żolkiew (now Zhovka)
Kulików (now Kulikov)
Mosty Wielki (also called Gross Mosty; now Velikiye Mosty)

Żydaczow (now Zydachov) 4272 UKR
Żydaczów (now Zydachov)
Żurawno (now Zhuravno)
Rozdól (now Rozdil)

Żywiec 4063 POL
Zabłocie

Longitude conversion:
The Prime Meridian for this Map is
17° 40' West of the Greenwich Meridian

1878 Map showing Galicia, Austria

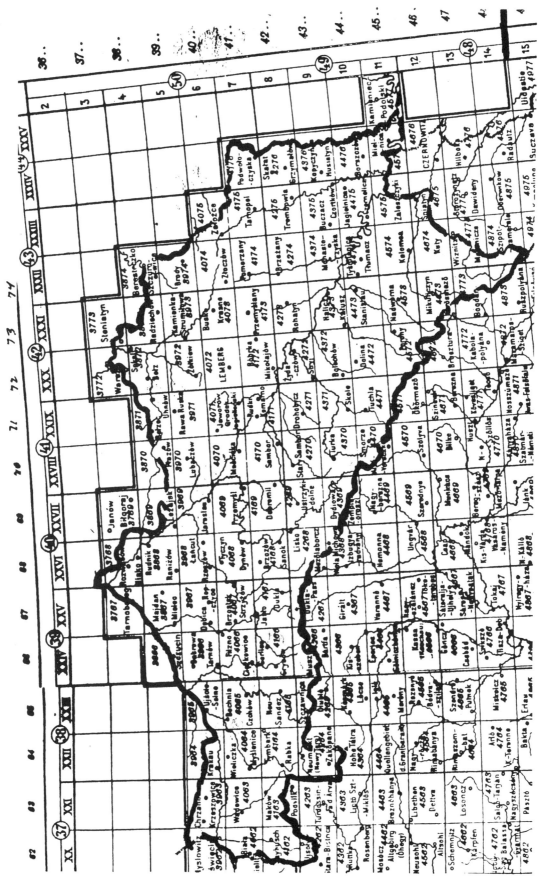

Figure G-1. 1878 map of Galicia showing grid numbers to order maps from the U.S. Library of Congress.

Administrative Districts of Towns in Galicia

The following was compiled from an 1877 manual published by the Justice Ministry of the Austrian government entitled *Fuhrung der Geburts-, Ehe- und Sterbematrikeln fur die Israeliten in Galizien*. While primarily the publication of regulations governing the collection and maintenance of vital records, the manual is useful as a gazetteer, a listing of communities where Jews were living at the time and their administrative districts.

The 1877 list was not a complete list of all towns in Galicia. The original document indicates that these were the towns where Jews were living at the time of the 1874 census. From then until 1919, Jews may have relocated into other communities. Brian Lenius' *Genealogical Gazetteer of Galicia* included a few towns which are not listed below. However, Lenius' book omitted a number of towns included here, though his sources were extensive, and he believed that his listing was complete. Perhaps some towns were so small that they were excluded from 19th-century gazetteers that Lenius relied on.

When you find your town name, you will see associated with the name the main district and subdistrict. Using these names, go to the first list in this appendix to determine (1) the present-day name of the main district and subdistrict, (2) the town's present-day country of jurisdiction, and (3) the map identification number.

Towns in Galicia sometimes carried descriptors. Under the Austrians, the German word *alt* (old) was used, as in Alt Sambor. The Polish equivalent is *stary* (old), *nowy* (new), *wielky* (large) and *mały* (small) as masculine forms (also *stare, nowe, wielke* and *małe)* or *stara, nowa, wielka* and *mała* as the feminine form. *Miasto* generally denotes the whole town or city. *Rynek* is the town center or market square. Sometimes towns were divided into sections and the words *dolny* (lower) and *górne* (upper) were used, as in Ustrzyki Dolne and Ustrzyki Górne.

Town	Main District	Subdistrict	Town	Main District	Subdistrict
Abramowice	Limanowa	Limanowa	Babice	Przemyśl	Krzywcza
Adamierz	Dąbrowa	Dąbrowa	Babice	Wadowice	Wadowice
Adamówka	Jarosław	Sienawa	Babin	Kalusz	Wojnilów
Adamy	Kam. Strumiłowa	Busk	Babin	Kam. Strumiłowa	Chołojów
Adzary	Dąbrowa	Dąbrowa	Babin	Kossów	Kossów
Agatówka	Tarnobrzeg	Rozwadów	Babina	Sambor	Sambor
Akreszory	Kossów	Pistyn	Babińce	Rohatyń	Rohatyń
Albigówa	Łańcut	Łańcut	Babińce	Sokal	Sokal
Albinówka	Śniatyn	Zabłotów	Babińce ad Krzywcze	Borszczów	Mielnica
Alfredówka	Przemyślany	Gliniany	Babińce ad Dżwinogród	Borszczów	Mielnica
Alfredówka	Tarnobrzeg	Tarnobrzeg	Babuchów	Rohatyń	Rohatyń
Alwernia	Chrzanów	Chrzanów	Babule	Mielec	Mielec
Andryanów	Rudki	Komarno	Bachlówa	Lisko	Lisko
Andrychów	Wadowice	Andrychów	Bachórz	Brzozów	Dynów
Andrzejówka	Nowy Sącz	Muszyna	Bachórze	Przemyśl	Dubiecko
Andrzejówka	Sokal	Tartaków	Bachów	Przemyśl	Krzywcza
Anielówka	Tarnopol	Tarnopol	Bachówice	Wadowice	Wadowice
Anielówka	Zaleszczyki	Tłuste	Bacza	Nowy Sącz	Łabowa
Annaberg	Stryj	Skole	Baczal Dolna	Jasło	Jasło
Antonin	Kam. Strumiłowa	Radziechów	Baczałka	Pilzno	Brzostek
Antoniów	Tarnobrzeg	Radomyśl	Baczów	Przemyślany	Przemyślany
Antonów	Czortków	Jagielnica	Baczyn	Wadowice	Kalwarya
Antonówka	Tłumacz	Niźniów	Baczyna	Staremiasto	Staremiasto
Arlamów	Bircza	Dobromil	Bagienica	Dąbrowa	Dąbrowa
Arlamowska	Mościska	Mościska	Bajdy	Krosno	Dukla
Armanice	Przemyśl	Niżankowice	Bajkowce	Tarnopol	Tarnopol
Artasów	Zolkiew	Kulików	Bajowice	Mościska	Hussaków
Artyszczów	Gródek	Gródek	Bakowce	Bóbrka	Strzeliska Nowe
Augustówka	Brzeżany	Kozowa	Bakowe	Tarnobrzeg	Rozwadów
Babcze	Borhodczany	Sołotwina	Bakowice	Staremiasto	Chyrów
Babianka	Tłumacz	Ottynia	Bałahorówka	Horodenka	Obertyn
Babica	Rzeszów	Czudec	Bałazówka	Limanowa	Limanowa
Babice	Biała	Oświęcim	Balice	Mościska	Hussaków
Babice	Chrzanów	Chrzanów	Balicze Podrozne	Żydachów	Żurawno

Town	Main District	Subdistrict	Town	Main District	Subdistrict
Balicze Pogórne	Żydachów	Żurawno	Bełejów	Dolina	Bolechów
Baligród	Lisko	Baligród	Bełeluja	Śniatyn	Śniatyn
Balin	Chrzanów	Chrzanów	Bełż	Sokal	Bełż
Balińce	Kołomea	Gwozdziec	Bełżec	Cieszanów	Lipsko
Balnica	Lisko	Wola Michowa	Bełżec	Rawa Ruska	Lubycza
Bałucianka	Sanok	Rymanów	Bełżec	Złoczów	Biały Kamień
Bandrów	Lisko	Ustrzyki Dolne	Benczyn	Wadowice	Zator
Bandrów Narodowy	Lisko	Ustrzyki Dolne	Berdechów	Tarnobrzeg	Rozwadów
Bania	Kalusz	Kalusz	Berdikau	Jaworów	Jaworów
Bania	Kołomea	Jabłonów	Berdychów	Gorlice	Gorlice
Bania Kotowska	Drohobycz	Drohobycz	Berdychów	Grybów	Bobowa
Banica	Gorlice	Gorlice	Berdychów	Jaworów	Jaworów
Banica	Grybów	Grybów	Berehy Dolne	Lisko	Ustrzyki Dolne
Banków	Bochnia	Bochnia	Berehy Górne	Lisko	Lutowiska
Banowice	Myślenice	Myślenice	Berenowce	Złoczów	Zborów
Bańska	Nowy Targ	Nowy Targ	Bereska	Lisko	Baligród
Banunin	Kam. Strumiłowa	Busk	Berest	Grybów	Grybów
Bar	Gródek	Gródek	Berestek	Zaleszczyki	Uścieczko
Bar	Mościska	Sądowa Wisznia	Bereżanka	Borszczów	Skała
Barańczyce	Sambor	Sambor	Berezki	Lisko	Lutowiska
Baranie	Sokal	Sokal	Bereżnica	Sambor	Sambor
Baranów	Buczacz	Monasterzyska	Bereżnica	Stryj	Stryj
Baranów	Tarnobrzeg	Baranów	Bereżnica Krolewska	Żydaczów	Żydaczów
Baranówka	Brzeżany	Brzeżany	Bereżnica Niżna	Lisko	Lisko
Baranówka	Nisko	Rudnik	Bereżnica Szlachecka	Kalusz	Kalusz
Barczków	Bochnia	Bochnia	Bereżnica Wyżna	Lisko	Baligród
Barczyce	Nowy Sącz	Piwniczna	Bereżów	Kołomea	Jabłonów
Barnowice	Nowy Sącz	Łabowa	Bereżów	Staremiasto	Starasól
Barszczowice	Lemberg	Jaryczów	Bereżów Nizny	Kołomea	Jabłonów
Bartatów	Gródek	Gródek	Bereżów Wyzny	Kołomea	Jabłonów
Bartkowa	Nowy Sącz	Nowy Sącz	Bereżówka Bortniki	Buczacz	Monasterzyska
Bartkówka	Brzozów	Dynów	Bereżówka Monasterzyska	Buczacz	Monasterzyska
Bartne	Gorlice	Gorlice	Berlin	Brody	Brody
Barwałd Dolny	Wadowice	Wadowice	Berłohy	Kalusz	Kalusz
Barwałd Średni	Wadowice	Wadowice	Bernadówka	Trembowla	Strusów
Barwinek	Krosno	Dukla	Berniany	Zaleszczyki	Uścieczko
Barycz	Przemyśl	Sosnica	Berteszów	Bóbrka	Strzeliska Nowe
Barycz	Rzeszów	Błazowa	Berwinkowa	Kossów	Żabie
Barycz	Wieliczka	Klasno	Berzowica Wielka	Tarnopol	Tarnopol
Barycza	Brzozów	Jasienica	Besko	Sanok	Rymanów
Baryłów	Brody	Szczurowice	Besów	Bochnia	Bochnia
Barysz	Buczacz	Barysz	Bestwina	Biała	Lipnik
Basiówka	Lemberg	Nawarya	Bestwinka	Biała	Oświęcim
Basznia Dolna	Cieszanów	Lubaczów	Betwin	Przemyśl	Przemyśl
Basznia Górna	Cieszanów	Lubaczów	Bezapy	Złoczów	Złoczów
Batiatysze	Zolkiew	Gross Mosty	Bezejów	Sokal	Bełż
Batków	Brody	Załoźce	Bezmiechowa Dolne	Lisko	Lisko
Batycze	Przemyśl	Przemyśl	Bezmiechowa Górne	Lisko	Lisko
Batyjów	Brody	Szczurowice	Biała	Biała	Lipnik
Baworów	Tarnopol	Mikulińce	Biała	Czortków	Czortków
Bayczka	Rzeszów	Niebylec	Biała	Myślenice	Maków
Bażanówka	Sanok	Rymanów	Biała	Nowy Sącz	Nowy Sącz
Bazar	Czortków	Jagielnica	Biała	Rawa Ruska	Magierów
Bęczarka	Myślenice	Myślenice	Biała	Rzeszów	Tyczyn
Bedinka	Sokal	Krystynpol	Biała	Tarnopol	Tarnopol
Bedinka Poturzycka	Sokal	Krystynopol	Biała	Tarnów	Tarnów
Bediuchy	Sokal	Sokal	Biała Niżna	Grybów	Grybów
Bednarka	Gorlice	Gorlice	Biała Wyżna	Grybów	Grybów
Bednarów	Stanisławów	Stanisławów	Białaskorka	Tarnopol	Tarnopol
Bedrykowce	Zaleszczyki	Zaleszczyki	Białdoliny Szlacheckie	Brzesko	Brzesko
Będziemyśl	Ropczyce	Sędziszów	Białe	Przemyślany	Dunajowce
Będzieszyna	Brzesko	Czchów	Białka	Nowy Targ	Nowy Targ
Bekersdorf	Podhajce	Podhajce	Białka	Rzeszów	Błazowa
Bełchówka	Sanok	Bukowsko	Białka Dunajec	Nowy Targ	Nowy Targ
Bełdno	Bochnia	Wiśnicz Nowy	Białkowce	Złoczów	Jezierna

Town	Main District	Subdistrict	Town	Main District	Subdistrict
Białobereska	Kossów	Kuty	Biskupice	Dąbrowa	Dąbrowa
Białobiernica	Złoczów	Zborów	Biskupice	Wieliczka	Klasno
Białoboki	Łańcut	Kańczuga	Biskupice Lanckoronskie	Brzesko	Czchów
Białoboznica	Czortków	Czortków	Błaszkowa	Pilzno	Jodłowa
Białobrzegi	Krosno	Dukla	Błazów	Sambor	Sambor
Białobrzegi	Łańcut	Żolynia	Błazowa	Rzeszów	Błazowa
Białodoliny Rodlowskie	Brzesko	Wojnicz	Blechnarka	Gorlice	Gorlice
Białokiernica	Podhajce	Podhajce	Bledowa ad Tyczyn	Rzeszów	Tyczyn
Białowoda	Nowy Sącz	Szczawnica	Blich	Brody	Załoźce
Białowoda Polska	Nowy Sącz	Nowy Sącz	Blicza	Brzesko	Brzesko
Biały Potok	Czortków	Budzanów	Blizianka	Rzeszów	Niebylec
Białykamień	Złoczów	Białykamień	Blizna	Ropczyce	Ropczyce
Biczyce Niemieckie	Nowy Sącz	Nowy Sącz	Blizno	Brzozów	Jasienica
Biczyce Polskie	Nowy Sącz	Nowy Sącz	Błonie	Mielec	Radomyśl Wielkie
Biecz	Gorlice	Gorlice	Błonie	Tarnów	Tarnów
Biedaczów	Łańcut	Żolynia	Błotnia	Przemyślany	Przemyślany
Biegonice	Nowy Sącz	Stary Sącz	Błotnia	Stryj	Stryj
Bielanka	Gorlice	Gorlice	Błozew Dolna	Rudki	Rudki
Bielanka	Myślenice	Jordanów	Błozew Górna	Sambor	Sambor
Bielany	Biała	Kęty	Błudniki	Stanisławów	Halicz
Bielawce	Brody	Brody	Blyszczanka	Zaleszczyki	Zaleszczyki
Bielawince	Buczacz	Buczacz	Błyszczywody	Żólkiew	Żólkiew
Bieliczna	Grybów	Grybów	Bobiatyn	Sokal	Tartaków
Bielina	Nisko	Ulanów	Bobowa	Grybów	Bobowa
Bielowce	Borszczów	Mielnica	Bobrek Dolny	Chrzanów	Chrzanów
Bielowy	Pilzno	Pilzno	Bobrek Górny	Chrzanów	Chrzanów
Bieniawa	Podhajce	Złotniki	Bóbrka	Bóbrka	Bóbrka
Bieniów	Złoczów	Złoczów	Bóbrka	Krosno	Dukla
Bienków	Kam. Strumiłowa	Kam. Strumiłowa	Bóbrka	Lisko	Lisko
Bieńkowa Wiznia	Rudki	Rudki	Bobrowa	Pilzno	Dębica
Bieńkowce	Rohatyń	Rohatyń	Bobrówka	Jarosław	Jarosław
Bieńkowice	Bochnia	Bochnia	Bobrowniki	Tłumacz	Uście Zielone
Bieńkowice	Wieliczka	Klasno	Bobrowniki Małe	Tarnów	Zabno
Bieńkówka	Myślenice	Maków	Bobrowniki Wielkie	Tarnów	Zabno
Bierlowice	Myślenice	Myślenice	Bobulińce	Buczacz	Buczacz
Bierna	Biała	Lipnik	Bochnia	Bochnia	Bochnia
Bierówka	Jasło	Jasło	Boczów	Bochnia	Wiśnicz Nowy
Bierzanów	Wieliczka	Klasno	Bodaki	Gorlice	Gorlice
Biesiadki	Brzesko	Brzesko	Bodnarówka	Rzeszów	Strzyżów
Biesiady	Żólkiew	Żólkiew	Bodzanów	Wieliczka	Klasno
Biesna	Gorlice	Gorlice	Bodziwoj	Rzeszów	Tyczyn
Bieśnik	Gorlice	Gorlice	Bodzów	Wieliczka	Podgórze
Bieżdziatka	Jasło	Frysztak	Bogdanówka	Myślenice	Jordanów
Bieżdziedza	Jasło	Frysztak	Bogdanówka	Złoczów	Jezierna
Bihałe	Cieszanów	Lubaczów	Bogoniowice	Grybów	Bobowa
Bilcze	Drohobycz	Drohobycz	Boguchwala	Rzeszów	Rzeszów
Bilcze	Zaleszczyki	Korolówka	Bogucice	Bochnia	Bochnia
Bilczyce	Wieliczka	Klasno	Bogucice	Wieliczka	Klasno
Bilicz	Staremiasto	Starasól	Bogumilowice	Brzesko	Wojnicz
Bilina	Sambor	Sambor	Bogusza	Grybów	Grybów
Bilinka	Sambor	Sambor	Boguszówka	Bircza	Bircza
Bilinka	Sambor	Sambor	Bohatkowce	Podhajce	Złotniki
Bilitówka	Skałat	Grzymałów	Bohordczany	Bohordczany	Bohordczany
Biłka	Przemyślany	Przemyślany	Bohordczany Stare	Bohordczany	Bohordczany
Biłka	Skałat	Touste	Bohordyczyn	Tłumacz	Chocimirz
Biłka Królewska	Lemberg	Jaryczów	Bohutyn	Złoczów	Pomorzany
Biłka Szlachecka	Lemberg	Jaryczów	Bojańczyce	Wieliczka	Klasno
Biłków	Borhodczany	Sołotwina	Bojanice	Sokal	Warez
Biłohorszcze	Lemberg	Zniesienie	Bojanice	Żólkiew	Gross Mosty
Bilsko	Nowy Sącz	Nowy Sącz	Bojanów	Nisko	Nisko
Binarowa	Gorlice	Gorlice	Boków	Podhajce	Zawałów
Binczarowa	Grybów	Grybów	Bolanowice	Mościska	Mościska
Biołoszowa	Tarnów	Ryglice	Boldury	Brody	Brody
Bircza	Bircza	Bircza	Bolechów	Dolina	Bolechów
Biskowice	Sambor	Sambor	Bolechów Ruski	Dolina	Bolechów

Town	Main District	Subdistrict	Town	Main District	Subdistrict
Bolechówce	Drohobycz	Drohobycz	Boża Wola	Jaworów	Wielkie Oczy
Bolęcin	Chrzanów	Chrzanów	Boznów	Nowy Sącz	Nowy Sącz
Bolesław	Dąbrowa	Dąbrowa	Braciejowa	Pilzno	Dębica
Bolestraszyce	Przemyśl	Przemyśl	Brandwica	Tarnobrzeg	Rozwadów
Bołochów	Dolina	Dolina	Bratkowce	Stanisławów	Stanisławów
Bolomyja	Rzeszów	Niebylec	Bratkowce	Stryj	Stryj
Bołozynów	Brody	Sokolówka	Bratkowce	Tłumacz	Tyśmienica
Bolszowce	Rohatyń	Bursztyn	Bratkowice	Gródek	Gródek
Bonarówka	Krosno	Korczyna	Bratkowice	Rzeszów	Rzeszów
Boniowice	Bircza	Dobromil	Bratówka	Krosno	Korczyna
Boniszyn	Złoczów	Złoczów	Bratucice	Bochnia	Bochnia
Bonów	Jaworów	Jaworów	Bratyszów	Tłumacz	Niźniów
Bór Łodygowski	Biała	Lipnik	Brelików	Lisko	Lisko
Bór Witkowski	Biała	Lipnik	Breń Osuchowski	Mielec	Radomyśl Wiel.
Boratycze	Mościska	Hussaków	Brigidyn	Drohobycz	Drohobycz
Boratycze	Przemyśl	Przemyśl	Brnik	Dąbrowa	Dąbrowa
Boratyn	Brody	Brody	Brodki	Lemberg	Szczerzec
Boratyn	Jarosław	Jarosław	Brodła	Chrzanów	Chrzanów
Boratyn	Sokal	Krystynopol	Brody	Brody	Brody
Borchów	Cieszanów	Oleszyce	Brody	Wadowice	Kalwarya
Bordulaki	Brody	Stanisławczyk	Brody Stare	Brody	Brody
Boreczek	Ropczyce	Sędziszów	Bronica	Drohobycz	Drohobycz
Borek	Bochnia	Bochnia	Bronisławówka	Złoczów	Zborów
Borek	Krosno	Dukla	Broniszów	Ropczyce	Ropczyce
Borek Fałecki	Wieliczka	Podgórze	Broszniów	Kalusz	Kalusz
Borek Mały	Ropczyce	Ropczyce	Browary	Buczacz	Jazłowice
Borek Nowy	Rzeszów	Tyczyn	Bruchnal	Jaworów	Jaworów
Borek Stary	Rzeszów	Tyczyn	Bruckenthal	Rawa Ruska	Uhnów
Borek Szlachecki	Wadowice	Zator	Brunndorf	Gródek	Gródek
Borek Wielki	Ropczyce	Sędziszów	Bruśnik	Brzesko	Czchów
Borkanów	Podhajce	Złotniki	Bruśnik	Grybów	Bobowa
Borki	Dąbrowa	Szczucin	Brusno Nowe	Cieszanów	Narol
Borki	Mielec	Mielec	Brusno Stare	Cieszanów	Lipsko
Borki	Nisko	Ulanów	Brustury	Kossów	Pistyn
Borki Dominikańskie	Gródek	Janów	Brykoń	Przemyślany	Przemyślany
Borki Janowskie	Gródek	Janów	Brykuta Nowa	Trembowla	Strusów
Borki Małe	Skałat	Touste	Brykuta Stara	Trembowla	Strusów
Borki Wielkie	Tarnopol	Tarnopol	Brylińce	Przemyśl	Przemyśl
Borodczyce	Bóbrka	Chodorów	Bryły	Jasło	Jasło
Borowa	Brzesko	Czchów	Bryńce Cerkiewne	Bóbrka	Bóbrka
Borowa	Mielec	Radomyśl Wiel.	Bryńce Zagóne	Bóbrka	Bóbrka
Borowa Gora	Cieszanów	Lubaczów	Bryszcze	Żólkiew	Żólkiew
Borowe	Żólkiew	Gross Mosty	Brzączowice	Wieliczka	Klasno
Borowna	Bochnia	Wiśnicz Nowy	Brzana Dolna	Grybów	Bobowa
Borownica	Bircza	Bircza	Brzana Górna	Grybów	Bobowa
Borszczów	Borszczów	Borszczów	Brzaza	Dolina	Bolechów
Borszczów	Śniatyn	Zabłotów	Brzczowa	Wieliczka	Klasno
Borszów	Przemyślany	Przemyślany	Brzeczyczany	Gródek	Gródek
Borszowice	Przemyśl	Niżankowice	Brzegi	Nowy Targ	Nowy Targ
Bortiatyn	Mościska	Sądowa Wisznia	Brzegi	Sambor	Sambor
Bortniki	Bóbrka	Chodorów	Brzegi	Wieliczka	Klasno
Bortniki	Tłumacz	Chocimirz	Brześciany	Sambor	Sambor
Borusowa	Dąbrowa	Dąbrowa	Brzesko	Brzesko	Brzesko
Borwałd Górny	Wadowice	Kalwarya	Brzeszcze	Biała	Oświęcim
Boryczówka	Trembowla	Trembowla	Brzeżanka	Rzeszów	Strzyżów
Boryków	Podhajce	Podhajce	Brzeżany	Brzeżany	Brzeżany
Borynicze	Bóbrka	Brzozdowce	Brzeżawa	Bircza	Bircza
Borysław	Drohobycz	Borysław	Brzezice	Rudki	Komarno
Borysławka	Bircza	Rybotycze	Brzezie	Wieliczka	Klasno
Boryszkowce	Borszczów	Mielnica	Brzezina	Żydaczów	Rozdół
Borzęcin	Brzesko	Radłów	Brzezinka	Biała	Oświęcim
Borzęta	Myślenice	Myślenice	Brzezinka	Chrzanów	Chrzanów
Boszyry	Husiatyn	Husiatyn	Brzezinka	Wadowice	Andrychów
Bouszów	Rohatyń	Bursztyn	Brzezinka ad Kopytówka	Wadowice	Zator
Bouszów	Stanisławów	Halicz	Brzeziny	Nowy Sącz	Nowy Sącz

Town	Main District	Subdistrict	Town	Main District	Subdistrict
Brzeziny	Ropczyce	Wielopole	Budzyn	Jaworów	Krakówiec
Brzezna	Nowy Sącz	Nowy Sącz	Budzyn	Tłumacz	Tłumacz
Brzeżnica	Bochnia	Wiśnicz Nowy	Bugaj	Dąbrowa	Dąbrowa
Brzeżnica	Pilzno	Dębica	Bugaj	Gorlice	Gorlice
Brzeżnica	Wadowice	Zator	Bugaj	Wadowice	Kalwarya
Brzezowa	Bochnia	Wiśnicz Nowy	Bugaj	Wieliczka	Klasno
Brzezowa	Brzesko	Czchów	Bujaków	Biała	Kęty
Brzezowa	Krosno	Dukla	Bujanów	Żydaczów	Żurawno
Brzezowice	Brzesko	Brzesko	Bujawa	Sokal	Tartaków
Brzezówka	Dąbrowa	Szczucin	Bujne	Nowy Sącz	Nowy Sącz
Brzezówka	Jasło	Jasło	Buk	Lisko	Baligród
Brzezówka	Kolbuszowa	Kolbuszowa	Bukaczowce	Rohatyń	Bursztyn
Brzezówka	Rzeszów	Tyczyn	Buków	Brzozów	Brzozów
Brzodzowce	Bóbrka	Brzozdowiec	Buków	Wieliczka	Podgórze
Brzostek	Pilzno	Brzostek	Bukowa	Pilzno	Brzostek
Brzostowa Gora	Kolbuszowa	Majdan	Bukowa	Sambor	Sambor
Brzoszkowice	Biała	Oświęcim	Bukowice	Lisko	Baligród
Brzoza	Tarnobrzeg	Radomyśl	Bukowiec	Grybów	Bobowa
Brzoza Królewska	Łańcut	Leżajsk	Bukowiec	Kolbuszowa	Kolbuszów
Brzoza Stadnicka	Łańcut	Żolynia	Bukowina	Bóbrka	Chodorów
Brzozów	Brzozów	Brzozów	Bukowina	Nisko	Ulanów
Brzozówa	Tarnów	Tuchów	Bukowina	Nowy Targ	Nowy Targ
Brzozowice ad Czaszyn	Sanok	Bukowsko	Bukówna	Tłumacz	Niżniów
Brzozówka	Ropczyce	Ropczyce	Bukowsko	Sanok	Bukowsko
Brzuchowice	Lemberg	Zniesienie	Bulowice	Biała	Kęty
Brzuchowice	Przemyślany	Przemyślany	Bunary Nizne	Grybów	Grybów
Brzuska	Bircza	Bircza	Bunary Wyzne	Grybów	Grybów
Brzusznik	Żywiec	Zabłocie	Burakówka	Zaleszczyki	Tłuste
Brzyna	Nowy Sącz	Łącko	Burcze	Rudki	Komarno
Brzyna	Ropczyce	Ropczyce	Burdziakowce	Borszczów	Skała
Brzyście	Jasło	Jasło	Burgthal	Gródek	Gródek
Brzyście	Mielec	Mielec	Burletka	Wieliczka	Klasno
Brzyska Wola	Łańcut	Leżajsk	Bursztyn	Rohatyń	Bursztyn
Bryski	Pilzno	Jodłowa	Burzyce	Rudki	Rudki
Brzyszczki	Jasło	Jasło	Burzyce Nowy	Rudki	Rudki
Brzyszyna Dolna	Wieliczka	Podgórze	Burzyce Stary	Rudki	Rudki
Bubniszcze	Dolina	Bolechów	Burzyn	Tarnów	Ryglice
Bubszczany	Złoczów	Pomorzany	Busk	Kam. Strumiłowa	Busk
Buchowice	Mościska	Mościska	Buskupice Radłowskie	Brzesko	Radłów
Bucniów	Tarnopol	Tarnopol	Busowisko	Staremiasto	Staremiasto
Buców	Przemyśl	Przemyśl	Buszcze	Brzeżany	Narajów
Buczacz	Buczacz	Buczacz	Buszkowice	Przemyśl	Przemyśl
Buczaczki	Kołomea	Gwozdzice	Buszkowiczki	Przemyśl	Przemyśl
Buczały	Rudki	Komarno	Butyny	Żólkiew	Gross Mosty
Bucze	Brzesko	Brzesko	Buzek	Złoczów	Białykamień
Buczki	Skałat	Grzymałów	Bybło	Przemyśl	Niżankowice
Buczków	Bochnia	Bochnia	Bybło	Rohatyń	Bursztyn
Buczkowce	Czortków	Budzanów	Byczyna	Chrzanów	Chrzanów
Buczkowice	Biała	Lipnik	Byków	Mościska	Hussaków
Buczyna	Bochnia	Wiśnicz Nowy	Byków	Przemyśl	Przemyśl
Buczyna	Brody	Brody	Byków	Sambor	Sambor
Buda	Nisko	Nisko	Bykowie	Sanok	Sanok
Budki Nieznanowski	Kam. Strumiłowa	Chołojów	Bylice	Sambor	Sambor
Budków	Bóbrka	Bóbrka	Bysina	Myślenice	Myślenice
Budomierz	Jaworów	Wielkie Oczy	Bystra	Biała	Lipnik
Budy	Rzeszów	Głogów	Bystra	Gorlice	Gorlice
Budy ad Rajsko	Biała	Oświęcim	Bystra	Myślenice	Jordanów
Budy Łancuckie	Łańcut	Łańcut	Bystra	Żywiec	Zabłocie
Budy Przeworskie	Łańcut	Przewórsk	Bystre	Lisko	Baligród
Budyłów	Brzeżany	Kozowa	Bystre	Staremiasto	Staremiasto
Budyłów	Śniatyn	Śniatyn	Bystrowice	Jarosław	Jarosław
Budynin	Sokal	Bełż	Bystrzyca	Drohobycz	Drohobycz
Budzanów	Czortków	Budzanów	Bystrzyca Dolna	Ropczyce	Sędziszów
Budzisz	Ropczyce	Wielopole	Bystrzyca Górna	Ropczyce	Sędziszów
Budzów	Wadowice	Kalwarya	Byszki	Brzeżany	Brzeżany

Town	Main District	Subdistrict	Town	Main District	Subdistrict
Byszów	Podhajce	Zawałów	Chochorowice	Nowy Sącz	Nowy Sącz
Byszów	Sokal	Tartaków	Chocimirz	Tłumacz	Chocimirz
Bytomska	Bochnia	Wiśnicz Nowy	Chocin	Kalusz	Kalusz
Bzianka	Sanok	Rymanów	Chocznia	Wadowice	Wadowice
Caporocz	Zaleszczyki	Tłuste	Chodaczków Mały	Tarnopol	Tarnopol
Caryńskie	Lisko	Lutowiska	Chodaczków Wielki	Tarnopol	Tarnopol
Cebłów	Sokal	Bełż	Chodaczów	Łańcut	Kańczuga
Cebrów	Tarnopol	Tarnopol	Chodaczów	Łańcut	Żołynia
Cecory	Brzeżany	Kozłów	Chodenice	Bochnia	Bochnia
Cecowa	Złoczów	Zborów	Chodnowice	Mościska	Hussaków
Celejów	Husiatyn	Chorostków	Chodnowice	Przemyśl	Przemyśl
Ceniawa	Dolina	Rożniatów	Chodorów	Bóbrka	Chodorów
Ceniawa	Kołomea	Kołomea	Chodorowa	Grybów	Bobowa
Ceniów	Brzeżany	Kozowa	Chodowice	Stryj	Stryj
Ceperów	Lemberg	Jaryczów	Chojnik	Tarnów	Tuchów
Cerekiew	Bochnia	Bochnia	Cholewiana Góra	Nisko	Nisko
Cergowa	Krosno	Dukla	Chołojów	Kam. Strumiłowa	Chołojów
Cerkowna	Dolina	Bolechów	Chołowice	Przemyśl	Przemyśl
Cetula	Jarosław	Sienawa	Chomczyn	Kossów	Kossów
Cetula	Jaworów	Jaworów	Chomiakówka	Czortków	Jagielnica
Cewków	Cieszanów	Oleszyce	Chomiakówka	Kołomea	Gwozdziec
Chabówka	Myślenice	Jordanów	Chomiakówka	Tłumacz	Tyśmienica
Chałupki	Łańcut	Przeworsk	Chomranice	Nowy Sącz	Nowy Sącz
Chałupki Dusowskie	Przemyśl	Sosnica	Chomrzyska	Nowy Sącz	Łabowa
Chartanowce	Zaleszczyki	Uścieczko	Chorągwica	Wieliczka	Klasno
Charzewice	Brzesko	Czchów	Chorderkowce	Bóbrka	Bóbrka
Charzewice	Tarnobrzeg	Rozwadów	Chorkówka	Krosno	Dukla
Chaszczowanie	Stryj	Skole	Chorobrów	Brzeżany	Kozłów
Chechly	Ropczyce	Ropczyce	Chorobrów	Sokal	Sokal
Chełm	Bochnia	Bochnia	Chorocowa	Kossów	Kuty
Chełm	Myślenice	Myślenice	Choronów	Rawa Ruska	Uhnów
Chełmek	Chrzanów	Chrzanów	Chorosiec	Brzeżany	Kozłów
Chełmice	Nowy Sącz	Nowy Sącz	Chorosnica	Mościska	Sądowa Wisznia
Chełmice Niemiecki	Nowy Sącz	Nowy Sącz	Chorostków	Husiatyn	Chorostków
Chełmice Polski	Nowy Sącz	Nowy Sącz	Chorostków	Rohatyń	Bursztyn
Chilczyce	Złoczów	Złoczów	Chorowiec	Wieliczka	Podgórze
Chiszewice	Rudki	Komarno	Chorzelów	Mielec	Mielec
Chlebiczyn	Śniatyn	Zabłotów	Chorzów	Jarosław	Pruchnik
Chlebiczyn Lesny	Kołomea	Kołomea	Chotowa	Pilzno	Pilzno
Chlebna	Krosno	Dukla	Chotowice	Przemyśl	Krzywcza
Chlebowice	Bóbrka	Bóbrka	Chotylub	Cieszanów	Cieszanów
Chlebowice Swirskie	Przemyślany	Świrz	Chotynice	Jarosław	Radymno
Chlewczany	Rawa Ruska	Uhnów	Chrabuzna	Złoczów	Zborów
Chlewiska	Cieszanów	Lipsko	Chraplice	Mościska	Hussaków
Chlewiska	Sambor	Sambor	Chraplice	Przemyśl	Przemyśl
Chliple	Rudki	Rudki	Chreniów	Kam. Strumiłowa	Busk
Chłopczyce	Rudki	Rudki	Chrewt	Lisko	Lutowiska
Chłopiatyn	Sokal	Bełż	Chromohorb	Stryj	Stryj
Chłopice	Jarosław	Jarosław	Chronów	Bochnia	Wiśnicz Nowy
Chłopówka	Husiatyn	Chorostków	Chrość	Wieliczka	Klasno
Chłopy	Rudki	Komarno	Chrostowa	Bochnia	Wiśnicz Nowy
Chmiel	Lisko	Lutowiska	Chruślice	Nowy Sącz	Nowy Sącz
Chmieliska	Skałat	Skałat	Chrusno Nowe	Lemberg	Szczerzec
Chmielnik	Rzeszów	Tyczyn	Chrusno Stare	Lemberg	Szczerzec
Chmielno	Brody	Stanisławczyk	Chryplin	Stanisławów	Stanisławów
Chmielów	Tarnobrzeg	Tarnobrzeg	Chrzanów	Chrzanów	Chrzanów
Chmielowa	Horodenka	Czernelica	Chrząstów	Mielec	Mielec
Chmielowa	Zaleszczyki	Uścieczko	Chrząstowice	Wadowice	Zator
Chmielówka	Borhodczany	Sołotwina	Chrząstówka	Jasło	Jasło
Chmielówka	Trembowla	Strusów	Chudykowce	Borszczów	Mielnica
Chobot	Bochnia	Bochnia	Chudyowce	Zaleszczyki	Korolówka
Chocen	Lisko	Lisko	Chwalibog	Kołomea	Gwozdziec
Chochłów	Sokal	Warez	Chwałowice	Tarnobrzeg	Radomyśl
Chochołów	Nowy Targ	Nowy Targ	Chwatów	Złoczów	Olesko
Chochoniów	Rohatyń	Bursztyn	Chyrów	Staremiasto	Chyrów

Town	Main District	Subdistrict	Town	Main District	Subdistrict
Chyrzyna Kortyniki	Przemyśl	Krzywcza	Czartorya	Bóbrka	Brzozdowiec
Chyszów	Tarnów	Tarnów	Czartorya	Tarnopol	Mikulińce
Chyżówka	Limanowa	Limanowa	Czasław	Wieliczka	Klasno
Cichawa	Wieliczka	Klasno	Cząstkowice	Jarosław	Jarosław
Cichawka	Bochnia	Wiśnicz Nowy	Czaszyn	Sanok	Bukowsko
Ciche Miętustwo	Nowy Targ	Nowy Targ	Czatkowice	Chrzanów	Trzebina
Ciechania	Krosno	Dukla	Czchów	Brzesko	Czchów
Cięcina	Żywiec	Zabłocie	Czechów	Buczacz	Monasterzyska
Cieczyna	Jasło	Frysztak	Czechowa	Kołomea	Gwozdziec
Cieląż	Sokal	Sokal	Czechówka	Wieliczka	Klasno
Ciemierzowice	Przemyśl	Sosnica	Czechy	Brody	Sokołówka
Ciemierzyńce	Przemyślany	Dunajowce	Czechy	Złoczów	Olesko
Ciemieżypce	Złoczów	Gologory	Czekaj Pniowski	Tarnobrzeg	Radomyśl
Cieniawa	Grybów	Grybów	Czekaj Wrzawski	Tarnobrzeg	Rozwadów
Cieplice	Jarosław	Sienawa	Czelatycze	Jarosław	Pruchnik
Cierpisz	Ropczyce	Sędziszów	Czelowice	Rudki	Komarno
Cieszanów	Cieszanów	Cieszanów	Czeluśnica	Jasło	Jasło
Ciezacin Mały	Jarosław	Jarosław	Czepiele	Brody	Podkamień
Ciezacin Wielki	Jarosław	Jarosław	Czerchawa	Sambor	Sambor
Ciężkowice	Chrzanów	Chrzanów	Czercze	Rohatyń	Rohatyń
Ciężkowice	Grybów	Bobowa	Czerczyk	Jaworów	Jaworów
Ciężów	Stanisławów	Stanisławów	Czeremcha	Sanok	Rymanów
Cikowice	Bochnia	Bochnia	Czeremchów	Bóbrka	Chodorów
Cisna	Lisko	Baligród	Czeremchów	Kołomea	Kołomea
Cisów	Dolina	Bolechów	Czeremosznia	Złoczów	Białykamień
Cisowa	Przemyśl	Przemyśl	Czerepin	Lemberg	Nawarya
Cisowiec	Lisko	Baligród	Czerhanówka	Kossów	Kossów
Cisowlas	Kolbuszowa	Raniżów	Czerkasy	Rudki	Komarno
Ciszec	Żywiec	Zabłocie	Czerkawszczyzna	Czortków	Czortków
Ciszki	Brody	Sokolówka	Czerkowatyce	Kam. Strumiłowa	Stajanów
Cmolas	Kolbuszowa	Kolbuszów	Czerlany	Gródek	Gródek
Cucułowce	Żydaczów	Żydaczów	Czermin	Mielec	Radomyśl Wiel.
Cucyłów	Nadwórna	Nadwórna	Czermna	Jasło	Olpiny
Cuniów	Gródek	Janów	Czerna	Chrzanów	Chrzanów
Ćwików	Dąbrowa	Dąbrowa	Czernelica	Horodenka	Czernelica
Ćwitowa	Buczacz	Jazłowice	Czerniatyn	Horodenka	Horodenka
Ćwitowa	Kalusz	Wojniłów	Czerniawa	Mościska	Mościska
Cygany	Borszczów	Skała	Czerniawka	Jarosław	Radymno
Cygany	Tarnobrzeg	Tarnobrzeg	Czernica	Brody	Podkamień
Cyranka	Mielec	Mielec	Czernica	Żydaczów	Rozdól
Czabalina	Brzesko	Czchów	Czernice	Nowy Sącz	Łącko
Czabarówka	Husiatyn	Husiatyn	Czernichów	Rudki	Rudki
Czaczów	Nowy Sącz	Łabowa	Czernichów	Tarnopol	Tarnopol
Czahrów	Rohatyń	Bursztyn	Czernichów	Żywiec	Zabłocie
Czajkowa	Mielec	Mielec	Czerniejów	Stanisławów	Stanisławów
Czajkowice	Rudki	Komarno	Czernilawa	Jaworów	Jaworów
Czaniec	Biała	Kęty	Czernilów Mazowiecki	Tarnopol	Tarnopol
Czanyż	Kam. Strumiłowa	Busk	Czernilów Ruski	Tarnopol	Tarnopol
Czaplaki	Jaworów	Wielkie Oczy	Czerniów	Rohatyń	Bursztyn
Czaple	Sambor	Sambor	Czerniszówka	Skałat	Skałat
Czarna	Grybów	Grybów	Czerteż	Sanok	Sanok
Czarna	Łańcut	Żolynia	Czerteż	Żydaczów	Żurawno
Czarna	Lisko	Ustrzyki Dolne	Czertynie	Żólkiew	Kulików
Czarna	Pilzno	Pilzno	Czertyżne	Grybów	Grybów
Czarna	Ropczyce	Sędziszów	Czerwonogród	Zaleszczyki	Uścieczko
Czarne	Gorlice	Gorlice	Czesniki	Rohatyń	Rohatyń
Czarnokońce Małe	Husiatyn	Probużna	Czołhańszczyzna	Tarnopol	Tarnopol
Czarnokońce Wielkie	Husiatyn	Probużna	Czołhany	Dolina	Bolechów
Czarnokońiecka Wola	Husiatyn	Probużna	Czołhynie	Jaworów	Jaworów
Czarnołożce	Tłumacz	Tyśmienica	Czorsztyn	Nowy Targ	Nowy Targ
Czarnorzeki	Krosno	Korczyna	Czortków	Czortków	Czortków
Czarnowoda	Nowy Sącz	Szczawnica	Czortków Stary	Czortków	Czortków
Czarnuchowice	Wieliczka	Klasno	Czortowiec	Horodenka	Obertyn
Czarnuszowice	Lemberg	Jaryczów	Czuczmany	Kam. Strumiłowa	Busk
Czarny Dunajec	Nowy Targ	Nowy Targ	Czudec	Rzeszów	Czudec

Town	Main District	Subdistrict	Town	Main District	Subdistrict
Czudowice	Jarosław	Pruchnik	Darów	Sanok	Nowtanice
Czukiew	Sambor	Sambor	Darowice	Przemyśl	Niżankowice
Czupernosów	Przemyślany	Przemyślany	Darszyce	Wieliczka	Klasno
Czyrna	Grybów	Grybów	Daszawa	Stryj	Stryj
Czystohorb	Sanok	Bukowsko	Daszówka	Lisko	Ustrzyki Dolne
Czystopady	Brody	Zaloczce	Dawidkowce	Czortków	Czortków
Czystopady	Brody	Zalocze	Dawidów	Lemberg	Winniki
Czystylów	Tarnopol	Tarnopol	Dęba	Tarnobrzeg	Tarnobrzeg
Czyszki	Lemberg	Winniki	Dębelówka	Dolina	Dolina
Czyszki	Mościska	Mościska	Dębesławce	Kołomea	Kołomea
Czyszki	Złoczów	Olesko	Dębica	Pilzno	Dębica
Czyżki	Sambor	Sambor	Dębina	Kam. Strumiłowa	Radziechów
Czyżów	Dąbrowa	Dąbrowa	Dębina	Łańcut	Łańcut
Czyżów	Wieliczka	Klasno	Dębina Letowska	Brzesko	Wojnicz
Czyżów	Złoczów	Pomorzany	Dębna	Sanok	Sanok
Czyżowice	Mościska	Mościska	Dębnik	Chrzanów	Trzebina
Czyżówka	Chrzanów	Chrzanów	Dębniki	Wieliczka	Podgórze
Czyżyce	Bóbrka	Bóbrka	Dębno	Brzesko	Brzesko
Czyżyków	Lemberg	Winniki	Dęborzyn	Pilzno	Jodłowa
Dąb	Chrzanów	Chrzanów	Dębów	Łańcut	Przeworsk
Dąbie	Wieliczka	Klasno	Dębowa	Pilzno	Jodłowa
Dąbki	Horodenka	Czernelica	Dębowice	Jasło	Jasło
Dąbrowa	Chrzanów	Chrzanów	Dębowiec	Tarnobrzeg	Rozwadów
Dąbrowa	Cieszanów	Lubaczów	Dębówka	Borszczów	Skała
Dąbrowa	Dąbrowa	Dąbrowa	Dehowa	Rohatyń	Rohatyń
Dąbrowa	Kalusz	Wojniłów	Delatyn	Nadwórna	Delatyn
Dąbrowa	Kam. Strumiłowa	Radziechów	Delawa	Drohobycz	Drohobycz
Dąbrowa	Łańcut	Żolynia	Delawa	Tłumacz	Tłumacz
Dąbrowa	Nowy Sącz	Nowy Sącz	Delejów	Stanisławów	Maryampol
Dąbrowa	Ropczyce	Sędziszów	Dembno	Nowy Targ	Nowy Targ
Dąbrowa	Sambor	Sambor	Dembów	Łańcut	Leżajsk
Dąbrowa	Wieliczka	Klasno	Demenka Lesna	Żydaczów	Rozdól
Dąbrowa Rzeczycka	Tarnobrzeg	Rozwadów	Demenka Poddniestrzańska	Żydaczów	Rozdól
Dąbrowa Wrzawska	Tarnobrzeg	Rozwadów	Demeszkowce	Rohatyń	Bursztyn
Dąbrowica	Dąbrowa	Szczucin	Demeszkowce	Stanisławów	Hałicz
Dąbrowica	Gródek	Janów	Demianów	Rohatyń	Bursztyn
Dąbrowica	Jarosław	Sienawa	Demianów	Stanisławów	Hałicz
Dąbrowica	Nisko	Ulanów	Demidów	Bóbrka	Chodorów
Dąbrowica	Tarnobrzeg	Baranów	Demków Grabie	Brzesko	Czchów
Dąbrowica Chrostowa	Bochnia	Wiśnicz Nowy	Demków Pusty	Brzesko	Czchów
Dąbrówka	Bochnia	Bochnia	Demnia	Brzeżany	Brzeżany
Dąbrówka	Borszczów	Borszczów	Demnia	Dolina	Rożniatów
Dąbrówka	Brzesko	Szczurowa	Demycze	Śniatyn	Zabłotów
Dąbrówka	Jasło	Jasło	Denysów	Tarnopol	Tarnopol
Dąbrówka	Nisko	Ulanów	Deputaty	Nisko	Ulanów
Dąbrówka	Wadowice	Wadowice	Derczyce	Drohobycz	Drohobycz
Dąbrówka Infułacka	Tarnów	Tarnów	Dereniówka	Trembowla	Janów
Dąbrówka Luchowska	Tarnów	Tuchów	Derewlany	Kam. Strumiłowa	Kam. Strumiłowa
Dąbrówka Pniowska	Tarnobrzeg	Radomyśl	Derewnia	Żólkiew	Żólkiew
Dąbrówka Polska	Sanok	Sanok	Dernów	Kam. Strumiłowa	Kam. Strumiłowa
Dąbrówka Ruska	Sanok	Sanok	Derzów	Żydaczów	Rozdól
Dąbrówka Starzeńska	Brzozów	Dynów	Desznica	Krosno	Dukla
Dąbrówka Szczepans.	Tarnów	Tarnów	Deszno	Sanok	Rymanów
Dąbrówki Górzyckie	Dąbrowa	Dąbrowa	Deutschbach	Cieszanów	Narol
Dąbrowkibreńskie	Dąbrowa	Dąbrowa	Diatkowce	Kołomea	Kołomea
Dachnów	Cieszanów	Cieszanów	Ditkowce	Brody	Brody
Dalastowice	Dąbrowa	Szczucin	Ditkowce	Tarnopol	Tarnopol
Daleszowa	Horodenka	Czernelica	Długie	Gorlice	Gorlice
Daliowa	Sanok	Rymanów	Długie	Krosno	Dukla
Dalnicz	Żólkiew	Gross Mosty	Długie	Sanok	Rymanów
Damienice	Bochnia	Bochnia	Długoleka	Nowy Sącz	Stary Sącz
Danilcze	Rohatyń	Rohatyń	Długopole	Nowy Targ	Nowy Targ
Daniłowce	Złoczów	Jezierna	Długoszyn	Chrzanów	Chrzanów
Danina	Żydaczów	Rozdól	Dłużniów	Sokal	Warez
Dankowice	Biała	Oświęcim	Dmuchawiec	Brzeżany	Kozłów

Town	Main District	Subdistrict	Town	Main District	Subdistrict
Dmytrów	Kam. Strumiłowa	Chołojów	Doły	Brzesko	Brzesko
Dmytrów Duzy	Tarnobrzeg	Baranów	Dołżanka	Tarnopol	Tarnopol
Dmytrów Mały	Tarnobrzeg	Baranów	Dołżka	Dolina	Bolechów
Dmytrowice	Lemberg	Winniki	Dołżka	Kalusz	Wojnilów
Dmytrowice	Mościska	Sądowa Wisznia	Dołżyca	Lisko	Baligród
Dmytrowice	Przemyśl	Sosnica	Dołżyce	Sanok	Bukowsko
Dmytrze	Lemberg	Szczerzec	Domacyny	Mielec	Mielec
Dobcza	Jarosław	Sienawa	Domalkówka Wola	Kolbuszowa	Kolbuszów
Dobczyce	Wieliczka	Klasno	Domaradz	Brzozów	Jasienica
Dobiczye	Tarnów	Zabno	Domaszer	Lemberg	Zniesienie
Dobieszyn	Krosno	Dukla	Domaszów	Rawa Ruska	Uhnów
Dobne	Nowy Sącz	Muszyna	Domatków	Ropczyce	Ropczyce
Doboków	Pilzno	Pilzno	Dominikowice	Gorlice	Gorlice
Dobra	Jarosław	Sienawa	Domosławice	Brzesko	Czchów
Dobra	Limanowa	Limanowa	Domostawa	Nisko	Ulanów
Dobra Rustykalna	Bircza	Bircza	Dora	Nadwórna	Delatyn
Dobra Szlachecka	Bircza	Bircza	Dorbrosin	Żólkiew	Żólkiew
Dobraczyn	Sokal	Krystynopol	Dornbach	Łańcut	Leżajsk
Dobranowice	Wieliczka	Klasno	Dornfeld	Lemberg	Szczerzec
Dobrocierz	Brzesko	Czchów	Dorochów	Trembowla	Strusów
Dobrohostów	Drohobycz	Drohobycz	Dorofijówka	Skałat	Podwołoczyska
Dobromil	Bircza	Dobromil	Dorohin	Stanisławów	Hałicz
Dobroniów	Limanowa	Limanowa	Doroszów Mały	Żólkiew	Kulików
Dobropole	Buczacz	Buczacz	Doroszów Wielkie	Żólkiew	Kulików
Dobrostany	Gródek	Janów	Dorozów	Sambor	Sambor
Dobrotwór	Kam. Strumiłowa	Dobrotwor	Doznamorycz	Tarnopol	Tarnopol
Dobrowlany	Bóbrka	Chodorów	Drabimanka	Rzeszów	Rzeszów
Dobrowlany	Drohobycz	Drohobycz	Draganowa	Krosno	Dukla
Dobrowlany	Kalusz	Kalusz	Draganówka	Tarnopol	Tarnopol
Dobrowlany	Stryj	Stryj	Drahasymów	Śniatyn	Śniatyn
Dobrowlany	Zaleszczyki	Zaleszczyki	Droginia	Myślenice	Myślenice
Dobrowódka	Kołomea	Kołomea	Drohiczówka	Zaleszczyki	Uścieczko
Dobrowody	Podhajce	Podhajce	Drohobycz	Drohobycz	Drohobycz
Dobrucowa	Jasło	Jasło	Drohobyczka	Przemyśl	Dubiecko
Dobrynin	Mielec	Mielec	Drohojów	Przemyśl	Sosnica
Dobrzanica	Przemyślany	Przemyślany	Drohomirczany	Bohordczany	Lysiec
Dobrzanka	Bircza	Bircza	Drohomyśl	Jaworów	Wielkie Oczy
Dobrzany	Gródek	Gródek	Drohowycze	Bóbrka	Brzozdowiec
Dobrzany	Lemberg	Szczerzec	Drohowyże	Żydaczów	Rozdól
Dobrzany	Mościska	Sądowa Wisznia	Drozdowice	Gródek	Gródek
Dobrzany	Stryj	Stryj	Drozdowice	Przemyśl	Niżankowice
Dobrzechów	Jasło	Frysztak	Drwinia	Bochnia	Bochnia
Dołega	Brzesko	Szczurowa	Dryszczów	Brzeżany	Brzeżany
Dołha Wojniłowska	Kalusz	Wojnilów	Dryszczów	Podhajce	Zawałów
Dołhe	Drohobycz	Borysław	Duba	Dolina	Rożniatów
Dołhe	Drohobycz	Drohobycz	Dubaniowice	Rudki	Rudki
Dołhe	Stryj	Stryj	Dubas	Kolbuszówa	Kolbuszów
Dołhe	Tłumacz	Uście Zielone	Dubie	Brody	Brody
Dołhe	Trembowla	Janów	Dubie	Chrzanów	Trzebina
Dołhe Kałuskie	Kalusz	Kalusz	Dubie	Złoczów	Olesko
Dołhomosciska	Gródek	Gródek	Dubiecko	Przemyśl	Dubiecko
Dołhomosciska	Mościska	Sądowa Wisznia	Dubienko	Buczacz	Monasterzyska
Dołhopol	Kossów	Żabie	Dubkowce	Skałat	Touste
Dolina	Czortków	Jagielnica	Dubkowice	Jarosław	Radymno
Dolina	Dolina	Dolina	Dublany	Lemberg	Zniesienie
Dolina	Sanok	Sanok	Dublany	Sambor	Sambor
Dolina	Tłumacz	Tłumacz	Dubowce	Tarnopol	Tarnopol
Dolina ad Zaluz	Sanok	Sanok	Dubowica	Kalusz	Wojnilów
Doliniany	Gródek	Gródek	Dubrawka	Żydaczów	Żurawno
Doliniany	Mościska	Sądowa Wisznia	Dubryniów	Rohatyń	Rohatyń
Doliniany	Rohatyń	Rohatyń	Dubszara	Dolina	Rożniatów
Dolnawieś	Myślenice	Myślenice	Dubszcze	Brzeżany	Kozowa
Dołobów	Rudki	Rudki	Dudyn	Brody	Podkamień
Dołpotów	Kalusz	Wojnilów	Dudynice	Sanok	Nowtanice
Dołuszyce	Bochnia	Wiśnicz Nowy	Dukla	Krosno	Dukla

Town	Main District	Subdistrict	Town	Main District	Subdistrict
Dulcza Mała	Mielec	Radomyśl Wiel.	Facimiech	Wadowice	Zator
Dulczówka	Pilzno	Pilzno	Falejówka	Sanok	Sanok
Duliby	Bóbrka	Strzeliska Nowe	Falisz	Stryj	Stryj
Duliby	Buczacz	Jazłowice	Faliszowice	Brzesko	Czchów
Duliby	Stryj	Stryj	Faliszówka	Krosno	Dukla
Dulowa	Chrzanów	Chrzanów	Falkenberg	Bircza	Dobromil
Dunajowce	Przemyślany	Dunajowce	Falkenstein	Lemberg	Szczerzec
Duninów	Zaleszczyki	Gródek	Falkowa	Grybów	Bobowa
Duńkowice	Jarosław	Radymno	Falkowa	Nowy Sącz	Nowy Sącz
Duńkowiczki	Przemyśl	Przemyśl	Falkowice	Wieliczka	Klasno
Dupliska	Zaleszczyki	Zaleszczyki	Faściszowa	Brzesko	Czchów
Durdy	Mielec	Mielec	Fehlbach	Cieszanów	Lubaczów
Dusanów	Przemyślany	Przemyślany	Feliksówka	Kam. Strumiłowa	Kam. Strumiłowa
Dusowce	Przemyśl	Sosnica	Feliksówka	Kam. Strumiłowa	Witków Nowy
Duszatyn	Sanok	Bukowsko	Felizienthal	Stryj	Skole
Dwerniaczek	Lisko	Lutowiska	Felsendorf	Cieszanów	Lubaczów
Dwernik	Lisko	Lutowiska	Felsztyn	Staremiasto	Felszytn
Dworce	Brzeżany	Narajów	Filipkowce	Borszczów	Mielnica
Dworce	Żółkiew	Gross Mosty	Filipowice	Brzesko	Czchów
Dwory	Biała	Oświęcim	Filipowice	Chrzanów	Chrzanów
Dybków	Jarosław	Sienawa	Firlejów	Przemyślany	Przemyślany
Dyczków	Tarnopol	Tarnopol	Fitków	Nadwórna	Nadwórna
Dydiatycze	Mościska	Sądowa Wisznia	Florynka	Grybów	Grybów
Dydnia	Brzozów	Brzozów	Fojna	Żółkiew	Żółkiew
Dylągowa	Brzozów	Dynów	Folwarki	Buczacz	Monasterzyska
Dylągówka	Rzeszów	Tyczyn	Folwarki	Złoczów	Złoczów
Dyniska	Rawa Ruska	Uhnów	Folwarki Małe	Brody	Brody
Dynów	Brzozów	Dynów	Folwarki Wielki	Brody	Brody
Dytiatyn	Rohatyń	Bursztyn	Folwarki Żydaczowskie	Żydaczów	Żydaczów
Dzial	Nowy Targ	Nowy Targ	Fox	Pilzno	Dębica
Dzianisz	Nowy Targ	Nowy Targ	Fraga	Rohatyń	Rohatyń
Dzibułki	Żółkiew	Kulików	Fredropol	Przemyśl	Niżankowice
Dzieduszyce Małe	Żydaczów	Żurawno	Freifield	Cieszanów	Cieszanów
Dzieduszyce Wielkie	Stryj	Stryj	Fron	Nowy Targ	Nowy Targ
Dziedziłów	Kam. Strumiłowa	Busk	Frycowa	Nowy Sącz	Łabowa
Dziekanowice	Wieliczka	Klasno	Frydrychowice	Wadowice	Andrychów
Dzierdziówka	Tarnobrzeg	Rozwadów	Frysztak	Jasło	Frysztak
Dzierzaniny	Brzesko	Czchów	Frywald	Chrzanów	Trzebina
Dziewięcirez	Rawa Ruska	Rawa Ruska	Furmany	Tarnobrzeg	Tarnobrzeg
Dziewiętniki	Bóbrka	Strzeliska Nowe	Futoma	Rzeszów	Błazowa
Dziewin	Bochnia	Bochnia	Futory	Cieszanów	Oleszyce
Dziezki	Rohatyń	Rohatyń	Gabon	Nowy Sącz	Stary Sącz
Dzików	Cieszanów	Oleszyce	Gabryelin	Tarnobrzeg	Tarnobrzeg
Dzików	Tarnobrzeg	Tarnobrzeg	Gać	Łańcut	Przeworsk
Dzikowice	Rzeszów	Głogów	Gaj	Nowy Sącz	Nowy Sącz
Dzikowiec	Kolbuszowa	Kolbuszowa	Gaj	Wieliczka	Podgórze
Dziurdziów	Lisko	Lisko	Gaje	Lemberg	Winniki
Dżurków	Brzesko	Czchów	Gaje Ditkowieckie	Brody	Brody
Dżurków	Kołomea	Gwozdziec	Gaje Niżne	Drohobycz	Drohobycz
Dżurów	Śniatyn	Zabłotów	Gaje Smoleńskie	Brody	Brody
Dżuryn	Czortków	Czortków	Gaje Starobrodzkie	Brody	Brody
Dźwiniacz	Zaleszczyki	Zaleszczyki	Gaje Wyżne	Drohobycz	Drohobycz
Dźwiniacz Dolny	Lisko	Ustrzyki Dolne	Gałówka	Staremiasto	Staremiasto
Dźwiniaczka	Borszczów	Mielnica	Gałyszów	Gorlice	Gorlice
Dźwinogród	Bóbrka	Mikalajów	Ganczary	Lemberg	Winniki
Dźwinogród	Borszczów	Mielnica	Garbek	Tarnów	Tuchów
Dźwinogród	Buczacz	Buczacz	Gasówka	Jasło	Jasło
Dzwonowa	Pilzno	Brzostek	Gassendorf Hurucko	Drohobycz	Drohobycz
Ebenau	Gródek	Gródek	Gawłów Nowy	Bochnia	Bochnia
Einsiedel	Lemberg	Szczerzec	Gawłów Stary	Bochnia	Bochnia
Einsingen	Rawa Ruska	Rawa Ruska	Gawłówek	Bochnia	Bochnia
Eleonorówka	Skałat	Grzymałów	Gawluszowice	Mielec	Mielec
Engelsberg	Dolina	Dolina	Gawrzyłowa	Pilzno	Dębica
Engelsbrunn	Bircza	Dobromil	Gbiska Tropie	Rzeszów	Strzyżów
Ernsdorf	Bóbrka	Bóbrka	Gdeszyce	Mościska	Hussaków

Town	Main District	Subdistrict	Town	Main District	Subdistrict
Gdeszyce	Przemyśl	Niżankowice	Gogolów I	Jasło	Frysztak
Gdów	Wieliczka	Klasno	Gogolów II	Jasło	Frysztak
Gebiczyna	Pilzno	Pilzno	Gołąbkowice	Nowy Sącz	Nowy Sącz
Gelsendorf	Stryj	Stryj	Golce	Nisko	Ulanów
Germakówka	Borszczów	Mielnica	Golcowa	Brzozów	Jasienica
Gerynia	Dolina	Bolechów	Goleszów	Mielec	Radomyśl Wiel.
Gesiówka	Bohordczany	Bohordczany	Gołkowice	Wieliczka	Klasno
Giedlarowa	Łańcut	Leżajsk	Gołogórki	Złoczów	Gologory
Gieraltowice	Wadowice	Zator	Gołogóry	Złoczów	Gologory
Gieraltowiczki	Wadowice	Zator	Gołonka	Tarnów	Tuchów
Gierczyce	Bochnia	Wiśnicz Nowy	Gołouchowice	Wadowice	Zator
Gierowa	Nowy Sącz	Nowy Sącz	Gontowa	Brody	Zalocze
Gillershof	Łańcut	Leżajsk	Góra Motyczna	Pilzno	Dębica
Gilowice	Żywiec	Zabłocie	Góra Ropczycka	Ropczyce	Sędziszów
Głęboczek	Borszczów	Borszczów	Górajec	Cieszanów	Cieszanów
Głęboka	Borhodczany	Sołotwina	Górajowice	Jasło	Jasło
Głęboka	Sambor	Sambor	Górka	Brzesko	Szczurowa
Głębokie	Sanok	Rymanów	Górka	Chrzanów	Chrzanów
Głęmbowice	Wadowice	Zator	Górki	Brzozów	Brzozów
Głęmieniec	Biała	Lipnik	Górki	Mielec	Radomyśl Wiel.
Glichów	Wieliczka	Klasno	Gorlice	Gorlice	Gorlice
Gliczarów	Nowy Targ	Nowy Targ	Gorliczyna	Łańcut	Przeworsk
Glinianka	Nisko	Ulanów	Górnawieś	Myślenice	Myślenice
Gliniany	Przemyślany	Gliniany	Górno	Kolbuszowa	Sokołów
Gliniczek	Jasło	Jasło	Gorowa	Nowy Sącz	Nowy Sącz
Glinik	Nowy Sącz	Nowy Sącz	Goruszów	Dąbrowa	Dąbrowa
Glinik	Ropczyce	Wielopole	Góry	Limanowa	Limanowa
Glinik Charzawski	Rzeszów	Strzyżów	Góry Luszowskie	Chrzanów	Chrzanów
Glinik Maryampolski	Gorlice	Gorlice	Gorzanka	Lisko	Baligród
Glinna	Brzeżany	Kozłów	Gorzejowa	Pilzno	Dębica
Glinna	Lemberg	Nawarya	Gorzejowa	Pilzno	Pilzno
Glinne	Lisko	Lisko	Gorzeń Dolny	Wadowice	Wadowice
Glinne	Sambor	Sambor	Gorzeń Górny	Wadowice	Wadowice
Glinnik Dolny	Jasło	Frysztak	Gorzków	Bochnia	Wiśnicz Nowy
Glinnik Górny	Jasło	Frysztak	Gorzków	Wieliczka	Klasno
Glinnik Niemiecki	Jasło	Jasło	Gorzów	Chrzanów	Chrzanów
Glinnik Polski	Jasło	Jasło	Gorzyce	Dąbrowa	Dąbrowa
Glinnik Średni	Jasło	Frysztak	Gorzyce	Łańcut	Przeworsk
Glińsko	Żólkiew	Żólkiew	Gorzyce	Tarnobrzeg	Tarnobrzeg
Gliny Małe	Mielec	Radomyśl Wiel.	Gosprzydowa	Brzesko	Brzesko
Gliny Wielkie	Mielec	Radomyśl Wiel.	Gostwica	Nowy Sącz	Stary Sącz
Glisne	Limanowa	Mszana dolna	Gotkowice Niemieckie	Nowy Sącz	Stary Sącz
Głogoczów	Myślenice	Myślenice	Gotkowice Polskie	Nowy Sącz	Stary Sącz
Glogów	Rzeszów	Głogów	Grab	Krosno	Dukla
Głogówiec	Łańcut	Przeworsk	Grabanina	Krosno	Dukla
Głojsce	Krosno	Dukla	Grabicz	Tłumacz	Ottynia
Głów	Tarnów	Zabno	Grabie	Wieliczka	Klasno
Głowienka	Krosno	Dukla	Grabieuznanskie	Bochnia	Wiśnicz Nowy
Głuchów	Łańcut	Łańcut	Grabina	Bochnia	Wiśnicz Nowy
Głuchów	Sokal	Krystynopol	Grabiny	Pilzno	Dębica
Głuchowice	Lemberg	Szczerzec	Grabkowce	Złoczów	Zborów
Głuchowice	Lemberg	Winniki	Grabnia	Nisko	Rudnik
Głuszków	Horodenka	Horodenka	Grabno	Brzesko	Wojnicz
Gniewczyna	Łańcut	Przeworsk	Graboszyce	Wadowice	Zator
Gniłowody	Podhajce	Podhajce	Grabów	Dolina	Dolina
Gnojnica	Jaworów	Krakówiec	Grabowa	Kam. Strumiłowa	Busk
Gnojnica	Ropczyce	Ropczyce	Grabowa	Nowy Sącz	Nowy Sącz
Gnojnik	Brzesko	Brzesko	Grabowce	Stryj	Skole
Goczałkowice	Tarnobrzeg	Rozwadów	Grabowce	Stryj	Stryj
Godowe	Rzeszów	Strzyżów	Grabowice	Bohordczany	Bohordczany
Godusza	Limanowa	Limanowa	Grabowice	Przemyśl	Sosnica
Gody	Kołomea	Kołomea	Grabowice	Tarnopol	Tarnopol
Godziska Nowa	Biała	Lipnik	Grabówka	Brzozów	Brzozów
Godziska Stara	Biała	Lipnik	Grabówka	Kalusz	Kalusz
Godziska Wilkowska	Biała	Lipnik	Grabownica	Bircza	Nowemiasto

Town	Main District	Subdistrict	Town	Main District	Subdistrict
Grabownica	Brzozów	Brzozów	Gwoździec Stary	Kołomea	Gwoździec
Grabowski	Wieliczka	Klasno	Gwoźnica Dolna	Brzozów	Jasienica
Grajów	Wieliczka	Klasno	Gwoźnica Dolna	Rzeszów	Niebylec
Grąziowa	Bircza	Rybotycze	Gwoźnica Górna	Brzozów	Jasienica
Grąziowa	Staremiasto	Staremiasto	Gwoźnica Górna	Rzeszów	Niebylec
Grebelki	Kam. Strumiłowa	Kam. Strumiłowa	Habkowce	Lisko	Baligród
Grębów	Tarnobrzeg	Rozwadów	Hacaki	Tarnobrzeg	Baranów
Grobla	Bochnia	Bochnia	Haczów	Brzozów	Jasienica
Grobla Jankowiecka	Tarnopol	Tarnopol	Hadle Kańczudzkie	Łańcut	Kańczuga
Groble	Nisko	Rudnik	Hadle Szklarskie	Rzeszów	Tyczyn
Grochowie	Mielec	Mielec	Hadykówka	Kolbuszowa	Kolbuszowa
Gródek	Gródek	Gródek	Hadynkowce	Husiatyn	Kopyczyńce
Gródek	Grybów	Grybów	Haiworonka	Podhajce	Złotniki
Gródek	Nowy Sącz	Nowy Sącz	Hałbów	Krosno	Dukla
Gródek	Zaleszczyki	Gródek	Halcnów	Biała	Lipnik
Grodkowice	Bochnia	Bochnia	Halicz	Podhajce	Podhajce
Grodowice	Staremiasto	Felsztyn	Halicz	Stanisławów	Halicz
Grodzisko	Bircza	Nowemiasto	Haliczanów	Gródek	Gródek
Grodzisko	Jasło	Frysztak	Haller	Wadowice	Zator
Grodzisko	Łańcut	Leżajsk	Halowice	Sokal	Warez
Grodzisko	Wadowice	Zator	Haluszczynce	Skałat	Skałat
Grodzisko Dolne	Łańcut	Leżajsk	Haluszowa	Nowy Targ	Nowy Targ
Grodzisko Górne	Łańcut	Leżajsk	Hamulec	Lemberg	Zniesienie
Grójec	Biała	Oświęcim	Hanaczów	Przemyślany	Gliniany
Grójec	Chrzanów	Trzebina	Hanaczówka	Przemyślany	Gliniany
Gromiec	Chrzanów	Chrzanów	Hanczarów	Horodenka	Obertyn
Gromnik	Tarnów	Tuchów	Hanczowa	Gorlice	Gorlice
Grondy	Brzesko	Brzesko	Handzlówka	Łańcut	Łańcut
Grondy	Dąbrowa	Dąbrowa	Haniowce	Rohatyń	Bursztyn
Gronków	Nowy Targ	Nowy Targ	Hańkowce	Śniatyn	Zabłotów
Gross Mosty	Żółkiew	Gross-Mosty	Hańkowice	Mościska	Hussaków
Grudna Dolna	Pilzno	Brzostek	Hankówka	Jasło	Jasło
Grudna Górna	Pilzno	Brzostek	Hanmowce	Stanisławów	Jezupol
Grudna Kępska	Jasło	Jasło	Hanowce	Żydaczów	Żydaczów
Grudza	Tarnobrzeg	Radomyśl	Hanunin	Kam. Strumiłowa	Radziechów
Gruszka	Tłumacz	Tłumacz	Harasymów	Horodenka	Obertyn
Gruszki	Wieliczka	Klasno	Harbutowice	Wadowice	Kalwarya
Gruszów	Limanowa	Limanowa	Harbuzów	Złoczów	Zborów
Gruszów	Wieliczka	Klasno	Harklowa	Nowy Targ	Nowy Targ
Gruszów Mały	Dąbrowa	Dąbrowa	Harmięże	Biała	Oświęcim
Gruszów Wielki	Dąbrowa	Dąbrowa	Harta	Brzozów	Dynów
Gruszowiec	Limanowa	Mszana dolna	Hartfield	Gródek	Gródek
Grybów	Grybów	Grybów	Haszcze	Trembowla	Trembowla
Grywałd	Nowy Targ	Krościenko	Hatki	Podhajce	Złotniki
Grzęda	Kam. Strumiłowa	Chołojów	Hawlowice Dolne	Jarosław	Pruchnik
Grzęda	Lemberg	Zniesienie	Hawlowice Górne	Jarosław	Pruchnik
Grzekhynia	Myślenice	Maków	Hawrylak	Horodenka	Obertyn
Grzeska	Łańcut	Przeworsk	Hawryłówka	Nadwórna	Nadwórna
Grzybów	Mielec	Radomyśl Wiel.	Hecznarowice	Biała	Kęty
Grzybowice	Lemberg	Zniesienie	Heinrichsdorf	Kam. Strumiłowa	Witków Nowy
Grzymałów	Skałat	Grzymałów	Helenków	Brzeżany	Kozowa
Grzymałówka	Brody	Szczurowice	Hemia	Dolina	Dolina
Guminska	Pilzno	Dębica	Herbutów	Rohatyń	Bursztyn
Guminska	Tarnów	Tarnów	Hermanów	Lemberg	Jaryczów
Gura	Sokal	Bełż	Hermanowa	Rzeszów	Tyczyn
Gusztyn	Borszczów	Skała	Hermanowice	Przemyśl	Przemyśl
Gusztynek	Borszczów	Skała	Hińkowce	Zaleszczyki	Uścieczko
Gutynka	Żydaczów	Żurawno	Hinowiec	Brzeżany	Brzeżany
Guzowa	Tarnów	Tarnów	Hladki	Tarnopol	Tarnopol
Gwizdów	Łańcut	Żolynia	Hlebówka	Borhodczany	Sołotwina
Gwoździanka	Rzeszów	Niebylec	Hleszczawa	Trembowla	Trembowla
Gwoździec	Brzesko	Wojnicz	Hlibów	Skałat	Grzymałów
Gwoździec	Kolbuszowa	Ranizów	Hłomcza	Bircza	Bircza
Gwoździec	Kołomea	Gwoździec	Hłuboczek Wielki	Tarnopol	Tarnopol
Gwoździec Nowy	Kołomea	Gwoździec	Hłudno	Brzozów	Dynów

Town	Main District	Subdistrict	Town	Main District	Subdistrict
Hnatkowice	Przemyśl	Sosnica	Hoszany	Rudki	Rudki
Hnidawa	Brody	Zalocze	Hoszów	Dolina	Bolechów
Hnizdyesów	Żydaczów	Żydaczów	Hoszów	Lisko	Ustrzyki Dolne
Hoczew	Lisko	Lisko	Hoszowczyk	Lisko	Ustrzyki Dolne
Hodów	Złoczów	Pomorzany	Hów	Żydaczów	Rozdól
Hodowice	Lemberg	Nawarya	Howiłów Wielki	Husiatyn	Chorostków
Hodwisznia	Rudki	Rudki	Howiłów Mały	Husiatyn	Chorostków
Hodynie	Mościska	Mościska	Hranki	Bóbrka	Brzozdowiec
Hoffnungsau	Dolina	Dolina	Hrebenne	Rawa Ruska	Rawa Ruska
Hohenbach	Mielec	Radomyśl Wiel.	Hrebenne	Żólkiew	Kulików
Hohołów	Sokal	Krystynopol	Hrebenów	Stryj	Skole
Holbocze	Podhajce	Podhajce	Hrehorów	Buczacz	Monasterzyska
Hołdowice	Bóbrka	Strzeliska Nowe	Hrehorów	Rohatyń	Rohatyń
Hołdówka	Rudki	Komarno	Hroszówka	Bircza	Bircza
Hołe Rawskie	Rawa Ruska	Rawa Ruska	Hrusiatycze	Bóbrka	Strzeliska Nowe
Holeszów	Bóbrka	Chodorów	Hruszatyce	Mościska	Hussaków
Holholuka	Stryj	Stryj	Hruszatyce	Przemyśl	Niżankowice
Holihrady	Zaleszczyki	Zaleszczyki	Hruszów	Drohobycz	Drohobycz
Hołobutów	Stryj	Stryj	Hruszów	Jaworów	Wielkie Oczy
Hołodówka	Mościska	Sądowa Wiszna	Hruszowice	Jarosław	Radymno
Hołodówska	Cieszanów	Lubaczów	Hrycówka	Trembowla	Janów
Hołosko Małe	Lemberg	Zniesienie	Hrycowola	Brody	Szczurowice
Hołosko Wielkie	Lemberg	Zniesienie	Hryniawa	Kossów	Żabie
Hołowczynce	Zaleszczyki	Tłuste	Hryniów	Bóbrka	Bóbrka
Hołowecko	Staremiasto	Staremiasto	Hryniowce	Tłumacz	Tłumacz
Hołowy	Kossów	Żabie	Hrynkowce	Husiatyn	Probużna
Hołozkowice	Brody	Brody	Huba	Nowy Targ	Nowy Targ
Hołsków	Nadwórna	Lanczyn	Hubenice	Dąbrowa	Dąbrowa
Hołubica	Brody	Podkamień	Hubice	Bircza	Dobromil
Hołubice	Złoczów	Olesko	Hubice	Bircza	Dobromil
Hołuczków	Sanok	Tyrawa woloska	Hubice	Drohobycz	Drohobycz
Hołwiecko	Stryj	Skole	Hubin	Buczacz	Potok
Hołyn	Kalusz	Kalusz	Hubinek	Rawa Ruska	Uhnów
Honiatycze	Rudki	Komarno	Hucisko	Bóbrka	Bóbrka
Honoratatówka	Rohatyń	Rohatyń	Hucisko	Brzeżany	Brzeżany
Horbacze	Rudki	Komarno	Hucisko	Rzeszów	Głogów
Horbków	Sokal	Tartaków	Hucisko	Wieliczka	Klasno
Hordynia	Sambor	Sambor	Hucisko	Żólkiew	Żólkiew
Horochowlina	Bohordczany	Bohordczany	Hucisko ad Niwiska	Kolbuszowa	Kolbuszowa
Horod	Kossów	Kossów	Hucisko ad Przewrotne	Kolbuszowa	Raniżów
Horodek	Lisko	Baligród	Hucisko Brodzkie	Brody	Podkamień
Horodelec	Sokal	Tartaków	Hucisko Jawornickie	Rzeszów	Tyczyn
Horodenka	Horodenka	Horodenka	Hucisko Łodygowskie	Biała	Lipnik
Horodlowice	Sokal	Sokal	Hucisko Oleskie	Złoczów	Olesko
Horodnica	Horodenka	Horodenka	Hucisko Żywieckie	Żywiec	Zabłocie
Horodnica	Husiatyn	Husiatyn	Huczko	Bircza	Dobromil
Horodnica	Skałat	Skałat	Hujcze	Rawa Ruska	Rawa Ruska
Horodyłów	Złoczów	Złoczów	Hukalowce	Złoczów	Zborów
Horodysławice	Bóbrka	Mikalajów	Huki	Jaworów	Krakówiec
Horodyszcze	Brzeżany	Kozłów	Hulcze	Sokal	Warez
Horodyszcze	Sambor	Sambor	Hulicze	Podhajce	Zawałów
Horodyszcze	Tarnopol	Tarnopol	Hulskie	Lisko	Lutowiska
Horodyszcze Bazy	Sokal	Krystynopol	Humenów	Kalusz	Kalusz
Horodyszcze Krol.	Bóbrka	Chodorów	Humienice	Lemberg	Szczerzec
Horodyszcze Warezskie	Sokal	Warez	Humienice	Sambor	Sambor
Horodzów	Rawa Ruska	Magierów	Humniska	Brzozów	Brzozów
Horoszowa	Borszczów	Mielnica	Humniska	Kam. Strumiłowa	Busk
Horożanka	Podhajce	Zawałów	Humniska	Trembowla	Trembowla
Horożanna Małe	Rudki	Komarno	Hureczko	Przemyśl	Przemyśl
Horożanna Wielka	Rudki	Komarno	Hurko	Przemyśl	Przemyśl
Horpin	Kam. Strumiłowa	Kam. Strumiłowa	Hurnie	Stryj	Stryj
Horyhlady	Tłumacz	Niźniów	Husiatyn	Husiatyn	Husiatyn
Horynice	Cieszanów	Cieszanów	Hussaków	Mościska	Hussaków
Horysławice	Mościska	Hussaków	Hussów	Łańcut	Łańcut
Hostów	Tłumacz	Ottynia	Huta	Bóbrka	Bóbrka

Town	Main District	Subdistrict	Town	Main District	Subdistrict
Huta	Brzozów	Dynów	Jabłonica	Jasło	Jasło
Huta	Ropczyce	Ropczyce	Jabłonica	Kossów	Żabie
Huta Brzuska	Bircza	Bircza	Jabłonica	Nadwórna	Delatyn
Huta Deręgowska	Nisko	Ulanów	Jabłonica Polska	Brzozów	Jasienica
Huta Gogolowska	Jasło	Frysztak	Jabłonica Ruska	Bircza	Bircza
Huta Komorowska	Kolbuszowa	Majdan	Jabłonka	Borhodczany	Sołotwina
Huta Krasnianska	Skałat	Touste	Jabłonka	Borhodczany	Sołotwina
Huta Krzysztalowa	Cieszanów	Lubaczów	Jabłonka	Brzozów	Brzozów
Huta Lubycka	Rawa Ruska	Lubycza	Jabłonki	Lisko	Baligród
Huta Nowa	Buczacz	Monasterzyska	Jabłonów	Husiatyn	Kopyczyńce
Huta Pieniacka	Brody	Podkamień	Jabłonów	Kołomea	Jabłonów
Huta Polańska	Krosno	Dukla	Jabłonów	Rohatyń	Bursztyn
Huta Połoniecka	Kam. Strumiłowa	Busk	Jabłonówka	Kam. Strumiłowa	Busk
Huta Roźaniecka	Cieszanów	Narol	Jabłonówka	Podhajce	Zawałów
Huta Stara	Buczacz	Monasterzyska	Jachówka	Myślenice	Maków
Huta Stara	Cieszanów	Lipsko	Jackowce	Złoczów	Jezierna
Huta Stara	Kam. Strumiłowa	Radziechów	Jackówka	Tłumacz	Tłumacz
Huta Szklana	Kam. Strumiłowa	Radziechów	Jacmanice	Przemyśl	Przemyśl
Huta Zielona	Rawa Ruska	Rawa Ruska	Jacmierz	Sanok	Rymanów
Hutar	Stryj	Skole	Jadachy	Tarnobrzeg	Tarnobrzeg
Hutka Obedynska	Rawa Ruska	Rawa Ruska	Jadamwola	Limanowa	Limanowa
Huwniki	Bircza	Rybotycze	Jadowniki	Brzesko	Brzesko
Huzele	Lisko	Lisko	Jagieła	Łańcut	Przeworsk
Huziejów Nowy	Dolina	Bolechów	Jagielnica	Czortków	Jagielnica
Huziejów Stary	Dolina	Bolechów	Jagielnica Stara	Czortków	Jagielnica
Hwozd	Borhodczany	Sołotwina	Jagodnik	Kolbuszowa	Kolbuszowa
Hybie	Brzesko	Wojnicz	Jagunia	Kam. Strumiłowa	Kam. Strumiłowa
Hyki et Dębiaki	Mielec	Mielec	Jahłusz	Rohatyń	Rohatyń
Hyrniówka	Bohordczany	Bohordczany	Jajkowce	Żydaczów	Żurawno
Hyrowa	Krosno	Dukla	Jakimczyce	Rudki	Komarno
Hyżne	Rzeszów	Tyczyn	Jakimów	Kam. Strumiłowa	Busk
Ilińce	Śniatyn	Zabłotów	Jaktorów	Przemyślany	Gliniany
Ilkowice	Sokal	Sokal	Jakubów	Dolina	Dolina
Ilkowice	Tarnów	Zabno	Jakubówka	Horodenka	Obertyn
Inwald	Wadowice	Andrychów	Jala	Nisko	Rudnik
Isaków	Horodenka	Obertyn	Jałowe	Lisko	Ustrzyki Dolne
Isep	Brzesko	Wojnicz	Jamda	Nisko	Rudnik
Isep	Żywiec	Zabłocie	Jamelna	Gródek	Janów
Iskan	Bircza	Bircza	Jamelnica	Stryj	Skole
Iskrzynia	Krosno	Korczyna	Jamna	Grybów	Bobowa
Ispas	Kołomea	Jabłonów	Jamna	Nadwórna	Delatyn
Isypowce	Tarnopol	Tarnopol	Jamna Dolna	Bircza	Rybotycze
Iszerków	Podhajce	Złotniki	Jamna Górna	Bircza	Rybotycze
Iwaczów	Złoczów	Zborów	Jamne	Kam. Strumiłowa	Kam. Strumiłowa
Iwaczów Dolny	Tarnopol	Tarnopol	Jamnica	Stanisławów	Stanisławów
Iwaczów Górny	Tarnopol	Tarnopol	Jamnica	Tarnobrzeg	Rozwadów
Iwańce	Borszczów	Mielnica	Jamy	Mielec	Radomyśl Wiel.
Iwanie	Zaleszczyki	Uścieczko	Janczowa	Nowy Sącz	Nowy Sącz
Iwanikówka	Bohordczany	Łysiec	Janczyn	Przemyślany	Przemyślany
Iwanków	Borszczów	Skała	Janikowice	Dąbrowa	Dąbrowa
Iwankówka	Husiatyn	Chorostków	Jankowce	Lisko	Lisko
Iwanowce	Kołomea	Peczeniżyn	Jankowce	Tarnopol	Tarnopol
Iwanowce	Żydaczów	Żydaczów	Jankowice	Chrzanów	Chrzanów
Iwanówka	Skałat	Skałat	Jankowice	Jarosław	Jarosław
Iwkowa	Brzesko	Czchów	Jankówka	Wieliczka	Klasno
Iwkowska	Brzesko	Czchów	Janów	Gródek	Janów
Iwla	Krosno	Dukla	Janów	Sambor	Sambor
Iwonicz	Krosno	Dukla	Janów	Trembowla	Janów
Izabelin	Buczacz	Monasterzyska	Janowice	Biała	Lipnik
Izbiska	Mielec	Radomyśl Wiel.	Janowice	Limanowa	Limanowa
Izby	Grybów	Grybów	Janowice	Tarnów	Tarnów
Izdebki	Brzozów	Dynów	Janowice	Wieliczka	Klasno
Izdebnik	Wadowice	Kalwarya	Janówka	Buczacz	Buczacz
Izlickie	Rudki	Komarno	Janówka	Tarnobrzeg	Tarnobrzeg
Izydorówka	Żydaczów	Żurawno	Janówka	Tarnopol	Tarnopol

Town	Main District	Subdistrict	Town	Main District	Subdistrict
Januszkowice	Pilzno	Brzostek	Jawornik	Myślenice	Myślenice
Januszowa	Nowy Sącz	Nowy Sącz	Jawornik	Tarnów	Zabno
Jarczowce	Złoczów	Zborów	Jawornik Górny	Sanok	Bukowsko
Jarhorów	Buczacz	Monasterzyska	Jawornik Niebyłecki	Rzeszów	Niebylec
Jarosin	Nisko	Ulanów	Jawornik Polski	Rzeszów	Tyczyn
Jarosław	Jarosław	Jarosław	Jawornik Ruski	Bircza	Bircza
Jarosławice	Złoczów	Zborów	Jaworów	Dolina	Dolina
Jaroszowice	Wadowice	Wadowice	Jaworów	Jaworów	Jaworów
Jaroszówka	Wieliczka	Klasno	Jaworów	Kossów	Kossów
Jaroszyce	Stryj	Stryj	Jaworów	Mościska	Mościska
Jaryczów	Lemberg	Jaryczów	Jaworówka	Kalusz	Kalusz
Jaryczów Nowy	Lemberg	Jaryczów	Jaworsko	Brzesko	Wojnicz
Jaryczów Stary	Lemberg	Jaryczów	Jaworze	Krosno	Dukla
Jarymówka	Jasło	Jasło	Jaworze	Pilzno	Pilzno
Jasiel	Sanok	Bukowsko	Jaworzna	Limanowa	Limanowa
Jasień	Brzesko	Brzesko	Jaworzno	Chrzanów	Chrzanów
Jasień	Kalusz	Kalusz	Jazienica Polska	Kam. Strumiłowa	Kam. Strumiłowa
Jasień	Lisko	Ustrzyki Dolne	Jazienica Ruska	Kam. Strumiłowa	Kam. Strumiłowa
Jasienica	Brzozów	Jasienica	Jazłowczyk	Brody	Brody
Jasienica	Myślenice	Myślenice	Jazłowice	Buczacz	Jazłowice
Jasienica Solna	Drohobycz	Drohobycz	Jazów Nowy	Jaworów	Jaworów
Jasienica Sufczyńska	Bircza	Bircza	Jazów Stary	Jaworów	Jaworów
Jasienna	Nowy Sącz	Nowy Sącz	Jazowa	Jasło	Frysztak
Jasienów Górny	Kossów	Żabie	Jazowa	Ropczyce	Wielopole
Jasienów Polny	Horodenka	Horodenka	Jazowsko	Nowy Sącz	Łącko
Jasienowice	Dolina	Rożniatów	Jedlicze	Krosno	Dukla
Jasienówka	Dolina	Rożniatów	Jędruszków	Sanok	Nowtanice
Jasionka	Gorlice	Gorlice	Jelechowice	Złoczów	Złoczów
Jasionka	Krosno	Dukla	Jeleń	Chrzanów	Chrzanów
Jasionka	Rzeszów	Głogów	Jeleńkowate	Stryj	Skole
Jasionów	Brody	Sokołówka	Jeleśnia	Żywiec	Zabłocie
Jasionów	Brzozów	Dynów	Jelna	Nisko	Rudnik
Jasionów	Złoczów	Olesko	Jelna	Nowy Sącz	Nowy Sącz
Jasionówa	Brzozów	Brzozów	Jeriorko	Tarnobrzeg	Tarnobrzeg
Jaskowice	Wadowice	Zator	Jesionowce	Złoczów	Złoczów
Jaslany	Mielec	Mielec	Jeszczyna	Żywiec	Zabłocie
Jasliska	Sanok	Rymanów	Jezierna	Złoczów	Jezierna
Jasło	Jasło	Jasło	Jezierzanka	Borszczów	Borszczów
Jasna	Limanowa	Limanowa	Jezierzany	Borszczów	Borszczów
Jaśniska	Gródek	Janów	Jezierzany	Buczacz	Barysz
Jaśniszcze	Brody	Podkamień	Jezierzany	Rohatyń	Bursztyn
Jastew	Brzesko	Brzesko	Jezierzany	Tłumacz	Tłumacz
Jastkowice	Tarnobrzeg	Rozwadów	Jezierzenka	Złoczów	Zborów
Jastrebia	Wadowice	Kalwarya	Jeżów	Grybów	Bobowa
Jastrzałka Nowa	Tarnów	Zabno	Jeżów	Nisko	Rudnik
Jastrzębia	Grybów	Bobowa	Jezupol	Stanisławów	Jezupol
Jastrzębia	Limanowa	Limanowa	Jodłowa	Pilzno	Jodłowa
Jastrzębiec	Łańcut	Leżajsk	Jodłówka	Bochnia	Bochnia
Jastrzębiec	Stanisławów	Jezupol	Jodłówka	Jarosław	Pruchnik
Jastrzębków	Lemberg	Szczerzec	Jodłówka	Tarnów	Tarnów
Jastrzębnik	Nowy Sącz	Krynica	Jodłownik	Limanowa	Limanowa
Jaszczew	Krosno	Dukla	Jokówka	Tarnów	Tarnów
Jaszczurowa	Jasło	Frysztak	Joniny	Tarnów	Ryglice
Jaszczurowa	Ropczyce	Wielopole	Jordanów	Myślenice	Jordanów
Jaszczurowa	Wadowice	Wadowice	Jordanówka	Mościska	Hussaków
Jaszkowa	Grybów	Grybów	Jósefówka	Sokal	Sokal
Jasztrebica	Sokal	Krystynopol	Josefsberg	Drohobycz	Drohobycz
Jatwięgi	Bóbrka	Strzeliska Nowe	Josefsdorf	Mielec	Mielec
Jatwięgi	Mościska	Mościska	Józefów	Kam. Strumiłowa	Radziechów
Jatwięgi	Rudki	Rudki	Józefówka	Rawa Ruska	Uhnów
Jawcze	Rohatyń	Rohatyń	Józefówka	Tarnopol	Tarnopol
Jawczyce	Wieliczka	Klasno	Judaszówka	Nisko	Rudnik
Jawiszowice	Biała	Oświęcim	Jugowiec	Wieliczka	Podgórze
Jaworec	Lisko	Baligród	Julatycze	Żydaczów	Żurawno
Jaworki	Nowy Sącz	Szczawnica	Junaszków	Rohatyń	Bursztyn

Town	Main District	Subdistrict	Town	Main District	Subdistrict
Juraszowa	Nowy Sącz	Stary Sącz	Kanafosty	Rudki	Rudki
Jurczyce	Myślenice	Myślenice	Kańczuga	Łańcut	Kańczuga
Jureczkowa	Bircza	Rybotycze	Kańczuga Kobiernice	Biała	Kęty
Juriampol	Zaleszczyki	Korolówka	Kanina	Limanowa	Limanowa
Jurków	Brzesko	Czchów	Kaniów Dankowski	Biała	Oświęcim
Jurków	Limanowa	Limanowa	Kaniów Stary	Biała	Oświęcim
Jurowce	Sanok	Sanok	Kanna	Dąbrowa	Dąbrowa
Juseptycze	Żydaczów	Żydaczów	Kapelanka	Wieliczka	Podgórze
Juśkowice	Złoczów	Olesko	Kaplince	Brzeżany	Kozowa
Just	Nowy Sącz	Nowy Sącz	Kaptury	Trembowla	Trembowla
Justyniówka	Podhajce	Podhajce	Kapuścińce	Zaleszczyki	Tłuste
Juszczyn	Myślenice	Maków	Karaczynów	Gródek	Janów
Juszkowce	Bóbrka	Strzeliska Nowe	Karanie	Kam. Strumiłowa	Chołojów
Kabarowce	Złoczów	Zborów	Karaszyńce	Husiatyn	Chorostków
Kaczanówka	Skałat	Skałat	Karemków	Rudki	Rudki
Kaczorowy	Jasło	Jasło	Karezmiska	Tarnobrzeg	Rozwadów
Kaczyna	Wadowice	Wadowice	Karlików	Sanok	Bukowsko
Kadeza	Nowy Sącz	Łącko	Karłów	Śniatyn	Śniatyn
Kadłubiska	Brody	Sokołówka	Karlsdorf	Stryj	Skole
Kadłubiska	Złoczów	Olesko	Karniowice	Chrzanów	Chrzanów
Kadłubliska	Cieszanów	Narol	Karolówka	Zaleszczyki	Tłuste
Kadobna	Kalusz	Kalusz	Karów	Rawa Ruska	Uhnów
Kadowa	Grybów	Grybów	Karwodna	Tarnów	Tuchów
Kajmów	Tarnobrzeg	Tarnobrzeg	Kasina Mała	Limanowa	Mszana dolna
Kałahorówka	Skałat	Touste	Kasina Wielka	Limanowa	Mszana dolna
Kalembina	Jasło	Frysztak	Kasna Dolna	Grybów	Bobowa
Kalembina	Ropczyce	Wielopole	Kasna Górna	Grybów	Bobowa
Kalinów	Sambor	Sambor	Kasperowce	Zaleszczyki	Zaleszczyki
Kalinowszczyzna	Czortków	Czortków	Kaszyce	Przemyśl	Sosnica
Kalna	Biała	Lipnik	Kąt. Pozekalec	Skałat	Touste
Kalna	Dolina	Bolechów	Kątarzynice	Rudki	Komarno
Kalne	Brzeżany	Kozowa	Kąty	Brzesko	Czchów
Kalne	Stryj	Skole	Kąty	Chrzanów	Chrzanów
Kalne	Złoczów	Pomorzany	Kąty	Nisko	Ulanów
Kalnica	Lisko	Baligród	Kąty	Złoczów	Olesko
Kaltwasser	Lemberg	Zniesienie	Katyna	Bircza	Dobromil
Kalusz	Kalusz	Kalusz	Kawczykat	Stryj	Stryj
Kalwarya	Wadowice	Kalwarya	Kawec	Wieliczka	Klasno
Kalwarya	Wadowice	Kalwarya	Kawęczyn	Mielec	Radomyśl Wiel.
Kamesznica	Żywiec	Zabłocie	Kawęczyn	Pilzno	Dębica
Kamień	Kalusz	Kalusz	Kawęczyn	Ropczyce	Sędziszów
Kamień	Nisko	Rudnik	Kawęczyn	Tarnobrzeg	Rozwadów
Kamienica	Limanowa	Limanowa	Kawsko	Stryj	Stryj
Kamienna	Grybów	Grybów	Kazimirowska	Złoczów	Zborów
Kamienna	Nadwórna	Nadwórna	Kęblów	Mielec	Mielec
Kamienna Góra	Podhajce	Zawałów	Kędzierzawce	Kam. Strumiłowa	Busk
Kamienna Góra	Rawa Ruska	Magierów	Kędzierzynka	Wieliczka	Klasno
Kamienne	Sanok	Bukowsko	Keiklów	Mielec	Radomyśl Wiel.
Kamienobród	Gródek	Gródek	Kępa	Kam. Strumiłowa	Stajanów
Kamienopol	Lemberg	Zniesienie	Kępanów	Bochnia	Wiśnicz Nowy
Kamionka	Dolina	Bolechów	Kęparze Czycka	Tarnobrzeg	Rozwadów
Kamionka	Nowy Sącz	Łabowa	Kępie	Tarnobrzeg	Rozwadów
Kamionka	Ropczyce	Ropczyce	Kęty	Biała	Kęty
Kamionka	Sanok	Rymanów	Kiczna	Nowy Sącz	Łącko
Kamionka Mała	Limanowa	Limanowa	Kidałowice	Jarosław	Jarosław
Kamionka Strumiłowa	Kam. Strumiłowa	Kam. Strumiłowa	Kielanowice	Tarnów	Ryglice
Kamionka Wielka	Grybów	Grybów	Kielanówka	Rzeszów	Rzeszów
Kamionka Wołoska	Rawa Ruska	Rawa Ruska	Kielczawa Kolonice	Lisko	Baligród
Kamionki	Lisko	Baligród	Kielnacowa	Rzeszów	Tyczyn
Kamionki	Skałat	Skałat	Kierlikówka	Bochnia	Wiśnicz Nowy
Kamionki Małe	Kołomea	Kołomea	Kiernica	Gródek	Gródek
Kamionki Wielkie	Kołomea	Kołomea	Kije	Kam. Strumiłowa	Chołojów
Kamionna	Bochnia	Wiśnicz Nowy	Kijowce	Żydaczów	Rozdól
Kamionna	Bochnia	Wiśnicz Nowy	Kilichów	Śniatyn	Zabłotów
Kamyk	Bochnia	Wiśnicz Nowy	Kimirz	Przemyślany	Przemyślany

Town	Main District	Subdistrict	Town	Main District	Subdistrict
Kipiaczka	Tarnopol	Tarnopol	Kobyle	Bochnia	Wiśnicz Nowy
Kipszna	Grybów	Bobowa	Kobyle	Jasło	Frysztak
Kisielówka	Limanowa	Limanowa	Kobyle	Nowy Sącz	Nowy Sącz
Kisielówka	Tarnopol	Tarnopol	Kobylec	Bochnia	Wiśnicz Nowy
Kiskora	Tarnów	Tarnów	Kobylec	Kołomea	Gwoździec
Klapówka	Rzeszów	Głogów	Kobylnica Ruska	Cieszanów	Lubaczów
Klasno	Wieliczka	Klasno	Kobylnica Wołoska	Cieszanów	Lubaczów
Klasno	Wieliczka	Klasno	Kobylowłoki	Trembowla	Janów
Klay	Bochnia	Bochnia	Kochanówka	Jaworów	Krakówiec
Klecie	Pilzno	Brzostek	Kochany	Tarnobrzeg	Rozwadów
Klęcza Dolna	Wadowice	Wadowice	Kochawina	Żydaczów	Żydaczów
Klęcza Górna	Wadowice	Wadowice	Kocierz ad Moszczanica	Żywiec	Zabłocie
Klęcza Srednia	Wadowice	Wadowice	Kocierz ad Rychwald	Żywiec	Zabłocie
Klęczany	Gorlice	Gorlice	Kocierzyn	Mościska	Sądowa Wisznia
Klęczany	Nowy Sącz	Nowy Sącz	Kociubińce	Husiatyn	Kopyczyńce
Klęczany	Ropczyce	Sędziszów	Kociubińczyki	Husiatyn	Husiatyn
Klęczany	Wieliczka	Klasno	Kocmierzów	Tarnobrzeg	Tarnobrzeg
Kleindorf	Jaworów	Jaworów	Kocoń	Żywiec	Zabłocie
Klekotów	Brody	Brody	Kocurów	Bóbrka	Mikalajów
Kleparów	Lemberg	Zniesienie	Kojszówka	Myślenice	Maków
Kleszczowna	Przemyślany	Przemyślany	Kokoszyńce	Skałat	Touste
Klikowa	Tarnów	Tarnów	Kokotkowce	Tarnopol	Tarnopol
Klikuszowa	Nowy Targ	Nowy Targ	Kokotów	Wieliczka	Klasno
Klimkówka	Gorlice	Gorlice	Kokuszka	Nowy Sącz	Piwniczna
Klimkówka	Nowy Sącz	Nowy Sącz	Kolaczyce	Pilzno	Brzostek
Klimkówka	Sanok	Rymanów	Kolanki	Horodenka	Czernelica
Kliniec	Stryj	Skole	Kolanów	Bochnia	Bochnia
Kliszów	Mielec	Mielec	Kolbuszowa	Kolbuszowa	Kolbuszowa
Kłodne	Limanowa	Limanowa	Kolbuszowa Dolna	Kolbuszowa	Kolbuszowa
Kłodnica	Stryj	Stryj	Kolbuszowa Górna	Kolbuszowa	Kolbuszowa
Kłodno	Żólkiew	Kulików	Kołdziejów	Stanisławów	Halicz
Kłodowa	Pilzno	Jodłowa	Koledziany	Czortków	Czortków
Kłodzienko	Żólkiew	Kulików	Koleśniki	Kam. Strumiłowa	Radziechów
Kłokowice	Przemyśl	Niżankowice	Kolin	Rohatyń	Rohatyń
Kłonice	Jaworów	Wielkie Oczy	Kolińce	Tłumacz	Tłumacz
Kłonów	Tarnobrzeg	Rozwadów	Kolko	Bochnia	Bochnia
Kłubowce	Tłumacz	Tyśmienica	Kolkówka	Gorlice	Rzepienik Strzyzewski
Kluczów Mały	Kołomea	Peczeniżyn	Koło	Rohatyń	Rohatyń
Kluczów Wielki	Kołomea	Peczeniżyn	Koło	Tarnobrzeg	Baranów
Klusów	Sokal	Krystynopol	Koło Tynieckie	Wieliczka	Podgórze
Kluszkowce	Nowy Targ	Nowy Targ	Kołodrobka	Zaleszczyki	Korolówka
Kluwince	Husiatyn	Chorostków	Kołodziejówka	Skałat	Skałat
Klyżów	Nisko	Ulanów	Kołodziejówka	Stanisławów	Stanisławów
Knapy	Mielec	Mielec	Kołohury	Bóbrka	Bóbrka
Kniaźdwór	Kołomea	Peczeniżyn	Kołomea	Kołomea	Kołomea
Kniaże	Śniatyn	Śniatyn	Kołowa Wola	Tarnobrzeg	Rozwadów
Kniaże	Złoczów	Złoczów	Kołpice	Drohobycz	Drohobycz
Kniaziołuka	Dolina	Dolina	Kołtów	Złoczów	Sassów
Kniażowskie	Dolina	Rożniatów	Komańcza	Sanok	Bukowsko
Kniaźpol	Bircza	Dobromil	Komarno	Rudki	Komarno
Kniażyce	Przemyśl	Niżankowice	Komarów	Sokal	Tartaków
Kniesioło	Bóbrka	Strzeliska Nowe	Komarów	Stanisławów	Halicz
Knihinin	Stanisławów	Stanisławów	Komarów	Stryj	Stryj
Knihinin Colonie	Stanisławów	Stanisławów	Komarowice	Bircza	Nowemiasto
Knihynice	Rudki	Rudki	Komarówka	Brzeżany	Kozowa
Knihynicze	Rohatyń	Rohatyń	Komarówka	Tłumacz	Uście Zielone
Knurów	Nowy Targ	Nowy Targ	Kombornia	Krosno	Dukla
Kobacki	Kossów	Kuty	Komorniki	Wieliczka	Klasno
Kobielnik	Wieliczka	Klasno	Komorów	Kolbuszowa	Majdan
Kobienrzyn	Wieliczka	Podgórze	Komorów	Tarnów	Zabno
Kobierzyn	Tarnów	Zabno	Komorowice	Biała	Lipnik
Kobło Stare	Staremiasto	Staremiasto	Komorówka	Brody	Leszniów
Kobylanka	Gorlice	Gorlice	Konary	Tarnów	Zabno
Kobylany	Krosno	Dukla	Konary	Wieliczka	Podgórze
Kobyłczyna	Limanowa	Limanowa	Kończyce	Nisko	Rudnik

Town	Main District	Subdistrict	Town	Main District	Subdistrict
Kończyska	Brzesko	Czchów	Korniów	Horodenka	Czernelica
Kondratów	Złoczów	Gologory	Korolówka	Tłumacz	Tłumacz
Koniaczów	Jarosław	Jarosław	Korolówka	Zaleszczyki	Korolówka
Konice	Ropczyce	Wielopole	Koropiec	Buczacz	Potok
Koniczkowa	Rzeszów	Niebylec	Koropuz	Rudki	Komarno
Konieczna	Gorlice	Gorlice	Korościatyn	Buczacz	Monasterzyska
Konigsau	Drohobycz	Drohobycz	Korostów	Stryj	Skole
Konigsberg	Nisko	Rudnik	Korostowice	Rohatyń	Bursztyn
Konina	Limanowa	Mszana dolna	Korsów	Brody	Leszniów
Koniów	Sambor	Sambor	Korszów	Kołomea	Kołomea
Koniuchów	Stryj	Stryj	Korszyłów	Złoczów	Zborów
Koniuchy	Brzeżany	Kozowa	Korzelice	Przemyślany	Przemyślany
Koniusza	Przemyśl	Niżankowice	Korzelów	Żółkiew	Kulików
Koniuszki	Przemyśl	Niżankowice	Korzenica	Jarosław	Radymno
Koniuszki	Rohatyń	Rohatyń	Korzeniec	Bircza	Bircza
Koniuszki Królewskie	Rudki	Komarno	Korzenna	Grybów	Grybów
Koniuszki Nanowskie	Mościska	Hussaków	Korzowa	Podhajce	Zawałów
Koniuszki Siemianów	Rudki	Rudki	Korzuchów	Jasło	Frysztak
Koniuszki Tuligłowskie	Rudki	Komarno	Korzuchów	Ropczyce	Wielopole
Koniuszków	Brody	Brody	Kościaszyn	Sokal	Warez
Koniuszowa	Grybów	Grybów	Kościejów	Lemberg	Zniesienie
Konkolniki	Rohatyń	Bursztyn	Kościelec	Chrzanów	Chrzanów
Konkulówka	Rzeszów	Błazowa	Kościelisko	Nowy Targ	Nowy Targ
Konopkówka	Tarnopol	Mikulińce	Kościelniki	Buczacz	Potok
Konotopy	Sokal	Sokal	Kościelniki	Rudki	Rudki
Końskie	Brzozów	Brzozów	Kościelniki	Zaleszczyki	Gródek
Konstancja	Borszczów	Borszczów	Kosina	Łańcut	Przeworsk
Konstantynówka	Tarnopol	Tarnopol	Kosmacz	Borhodczany	Sołotwina
Konstantynówka	Tłumacz	Ottynia	Kosmacz	Kossów	Pistyn
Konty	Brody	Sokołówka	Kośmierzyn	Buczacz	Potok
Konty	Krosno	Żmigród	Kosowa	Wadowice	Zator
Kopacze Księże	Brzesko	Szczurowa	Kosowice	Gródek	Gródek
Kopaczyńce	Horodenka	Czernelica	Kosowy	Kolbuszowa	Kolbuszowa
Kopaliny	Bochnia	Wiśnicz Nowy	Kossocice	Wieliczka	Klasno
Kopaliny	Brzesko	Brzesko	Kossów	Czortków	Budzanów
Kopan	Przemyślany	Świrz	Kossów	Kossów	Kossów
Kopaniny	Brzesko	Szczurowa	Kossów Stary	Kossów	Kossów
Kopanka	Kalusz	Kalusz	Kostarowce	Sanok	Sanok
Kopanka	Wieliczka	Podgórze	Kostenjów	Przemyślany	Przemyślany
Kopcie	Kolbuszowa	Majdan	Kostrza	Limanowa	Limanowa
Kopcie	Rzeszów	Głogów	Kostrze	Wieliczka	Podgórze
Kopyczyńce	Husiatyn	Kopyczyńce	Koszarawa	Żywiec	Zabłocie
Kopytne	Bircza	Rybotycze	Koszary	Limanowa	Limanowa
Kopytów	Sokal	Tartaków	Kosztowa	Brzozów	Dynów
Kopytowa	Krosno	Dukla	Koszyce Małe	Tarnów	Tarnów
Kopytówka	Wadowice	Zator	Koszyce Wielkie	Tarnów	Tarnów
Korabina	Kolbuszowa	Raniżów	Koszyłowce	Czortków	Jagielnica
Korabniki	Wieliczka	Podgórze	Kotań	Krosno	Dukla
Korbielów	Żywiec	Zabłocie	Kotiatycze	Kalusz	Kalusz
Korczmin	Rawa Ruska	Uhnów	Kotoryny	Żydaczów	Żurawno
Korczów	Rawa Ruska	Uhnów	Kotów	Bircza	Bircza
Korczówka	Żydaczów	Żurawno	Kotów	Brzeżany	Brzeżany
Korczyn	Sokal	Krystynopol	Kotów	Nowy Sącz	Łabowa
Korczyn	Stryj	Skole	Kotowania	Sambor	Sambor
Korczyna	Gorlice	Gorlice	Kotówka	Husiatyn	Kopyczyńce
Korczyna	Krosno	Korczyna	Kotuzów	Podhajce	Podhajce
Kordówka	Kołomea	Kołomea	Kowalówka	Buczacz	Monasterzyska
Korków	Sokal	Warez	Kowalówka	Kołomea	Jabłonów
Kornałowice	Sambor	Sambor	Kowalowy	Jasło	Jasło
Kornatka	Wieliczka	Klasno	Kowalowy Dolne	Tarnów	Ryglice
Kornclówka	Żydaczów	Żydaczów	Kowalowy Górne	Tarnów	Ryglice
Korniaktów	Łańcut	Żolynia	Kowenice	Sambor	Sambor
Kornice	Mościska	Mościska	Kozaczówka	Borszczów	Mielnica
Kornicz	Kołomea	Kołomea	Kozaczyzna	Borszczów	Borszczów
Kornie	Rawa Ruska	Lubycza	Kozakowa Góra	Złoczów	Złoczów

Town	Main District	Subdistrict	Town	Main District	Subdistrict
Kozara	Rohatyń	Bursztyn	Kropiwinik Nowy	Drohobycz	Borysław
Koziarnia	Nisko	Rudnik	Kropiwinik Stary	Drohobycz	Borysław
Koziary	Tarnobrzeg	Rozwadów	Kropiwiszcze	Kołomea	Kołomea
Kozice	Lemberg	Zniesienie	Kropiwna	Złoczów	Gologory
Koziekie	Bircza	Rybotycze	Kropiwnik	Kalusz	Kalusz
Kozielniki	Lemberg	Winniki	Kropwinik	Bircza	Dobromil
Kozina	Stanisławów	Hałicz	Krościenko	Lisko	Ustrzyki Dolne
Kozina mit Bilka	Skałat	Touste	Krościenko	Nowy Targ	Krościenko
Koziowa	Stryj	Skole	Krościenko Niżne	Krosno	Korczyna
Kozipice	Wadowice	Wadowice	Krościenko Wyżne	Krosno	Korczyna
Kozłów	Brzeżany	Kozłów	Krosienice	Przemyśl	Przemyśl
Kozłów	Dąbrowa	Dąbrowa	Krośna	Limanowa	Limanowa
Kozłów	Kam. Strumiłowa	Busk	Krośnica	Nowy Targ	Nowy Targ
Kozłówek	Jasło	Frysztak	Krosno	Krosno	Dukla
Koźmice Małe	Wieliczka	Klasno	Krotoszyn	Lemberg	Nawarya
Koźmice Wielkie	Wieliczka	Klasno	Krowica Lasowa	Cieszanów	Lubaczów
Kozodrza	Ropczyce	Ropczyce	Krowica Sama	Cieszanów	Lubaczów
Kozowa	Brzeżany	Kozowa	Krowice	Tarnopol	Tarnopol
Kozówka	Brzeżany	Kozowa	Krowinka	Trembowla	Trembowla
Kozówka	Tarnopol	Mikulińce	Krowniki	Przemyśl	Przemyśl
Kożuszne ad Wysocz	Sanok	Bukowsko	Kruhel	Przemyśl	Przemyśl
Kozy	Biała	Lipnik	Kruhel Pawłosiowski	Jarosław	Jarosław
Krajna	Bircza	Rybotycze	Kruki	Biała	Oświęcim
Krajowice	Jasło	Jasło	Krukienice	Mościska	Mościska
Kraków	Kraków	Kraków	Krulin	Mościska	Sądowa Wisznia
Krakowice	Borhodczany	Sołotwina	Krupsko	Żydaczów	Rozdól
Krakówiec	Jaworów	Krakówiec	Kruszelnica	Stryj	Skole
Krakuszowice	Wieliczka	Klasno	Krużlowa Niżna	Grybów	Grybów
Kramarzówka	Jarosław	Pruchnik	Krużlowa Polska	Grybów	Grybów
Kranszów	Nowy Targ	Nowy Targ	Krużlowa Ruska	Grybów	Grybów
Kranzberg	Sambor	Sambor	Krużlowa Wyżna	Grybów	Grybów
Krasice	Przemyśl	Krzywcza	Krużyki	Sambor	Sambor
Krasiczyn	Przemyśl	Krzywcza	Kryczka	Borhodczany	Sołotwina
Krasiczyn	Żółkiew	Kulików	Kryg	Gorlice	Gorlice
Krasiejów	Buczacz	Monasterzyska	Kryłos	Stanisławów	Hałicz
Krasiełówka	Tłumacz	Ottynia	Krynica	Drohobycz	Drohobycz
Krasna	Brzeżany	Kozłów	Krynica	Nowy Sącz	Krynica
Krasna	Kalusz	Kalusz	Krysowice	Mościska	Mościska
Krasna	Krosno	Korczyna	Krystynopol	Sokal	Krystynopol
Krasna	Nadwórna	Nadwórna	Krywa	Gorlice	Gorlice
Krasne	Limanowa	Limanowa	Krywe	Lisko	Baligród
Krasne	Rzeszów	Rzeszów	Krywe bei Tworylne	Lisko	Lutowiska
Krasne	Skałat	Touste	Krywka	Lisko	Lutowiska
Krasne Potockie	Nowy Sącz	Nowy Sącz	Kryzywołuka	Czortków	Jagielnica
Krasno	Jarosław	Sienawa	Krzadka	Tarnobrzeg	Tarnobrzeg
Krasnoila	Kossów	Żabie	Krzęcin	Wadowice	Zator
Krasnopuszcza	Przemyślany	Dunajowce	Krzeczkowa	Przemyśl	Przemyśl
Krasnosielce	Złoczów	Pomorzany	Krzeczów	Bochnia	Bochnia
Krasnosielce	Złoczów	Złoczów	Krzeczów	Myślenice	Jordanów
Krasów	Lemberg	Szczerzec	Krzeczowice	Łańcut	Kańczuga
Krasówka	Tarnopol	Tarnopol	Krzemienica	Łańcut	Łańcut
Krawce	Tarnobrzeg	Rozwadów	Krzemienica	Mielec	Mielec
Krechów	Żółkiew	Żółkiew	Krzesławice	Wieliczka	Klasno
Krechów	Żydaczów	Żurawno	Krzeszowice	Chrzanów	Trzebina
Krechowce	Stanisławów	Stanisławów	Krzewica	Rawa Ruska	Uhnów
Krechowice	Dolina	Rożniatów	Krzezoniów	Myślenice	Myślenice
Krecilów	Skałat	Touste	Krzyszkowice	Myślenice	Myślenice
Kreców	Bircza	Bircza	Krzyszkowice	Wieliczka	Klasno
Krempna	Krosno	Dukla	Krzywa Rzeka	Wieliczka	Klasno
Kreszów	Żywiec	Zabłocie	Krzywaczka	Myślenice	Myślenice
Krogulce	Husiatyn	Kopyczyńce	Krzywcza	Przemyśl	Krzywcza
Królik Polski	Sanok	Rymanów	Krzywcze	Borszczów	Mielnica
Królik Wołoski	Sanok	Rymanów	Krzywcze Dolne	Borszczów	Mielnica
Krolówka	Bochnia	Wiśnicz Nowy	Krzywcze Górne	Borszczów	Mielnica
Kropielniki	Rudki	Rudki	Krzywczyce	Lemberg	Zniesienie

Town	Main District	Subdistrict	Town	Main District	Subdistrict
Krzywe	Bircza	Rybotycze	Kupnowice Stary	Rudki	Rudki
Krzywe	Brzeżany	Kozowa	Kurdwanówka	Buczacz	Buczacz
Krzywe	Brzozów	Brzozów	Kurmanice	Przemyśl	Niżankowice
Krzywe	Cieszanów	Cieszanów	Kurniki	Jaworów	Jaworów
Krzywe	Kam. Strumiłowa	Radziechów	Kurniki Szlacheckie	Tarnopol	Tarnopol
Krzywe	Skałat	Skałat	Kuropatniki	Brzeżany	Brzeżany
Krzywenkie	Husiatyn	Probużna	Kuropatniki	Rohatyń	Bursztyn
Krzywice	Borhodczany	Sołotwina	Kurów	Bochnia	Wiśnicz Nowy
Krzywice	Borhodczany	Sołotwina	Kurów	Nowy Sącz	Nowy Sącz
Krzywice	Przemyślany	Gliniany	Kurów	Żywiec	Zabłocie
Krzywiecka Wola	Przemyśl	Krzywcza	Kurowce	Tarnopol	Tarnopol
Krzywki	Tarnopol	Mikulińce	Kurowice	Przemyślany	Gliniany
Krzyworównia	Kossów	Żabie	Kurwanów Dolny	Wieliczka	Podgórze
Krzywotuly Nowe	Tłumacz	Ottynia	Kurwanów Górny	Wieliczka	Podgórze
Krzywotuly Stare	Tłumacz	Ottynia	Kuryłówka	Łańcut	Leżajsk
Krzywulanka	Kam. Strumiłowa	Kam. Strumiłowa	Kurypów	Stanisławów	Halicz
Krzyż	Tarnów	Tarnów	Kurzany	Brzeżany	Brzeżany
Krzyżanowice	Bochnia	Bochnia	Kurzyna Mała	Nisko	Ulanów
Krzyżowa	Żywiec	Zabłocie	Kurzyna Wielka	Nisko	Ulanów
Krzyżówka	Nowy Sącz	Łabowa	Kustyn	Brody	Szczurowice
Książnice	Bochnia	Bochnia	Kutce	Rohatyń	Rohatyń
Księczy Most	Mościska	Sądowa Wisznia	Kutenberg	Jaworów	Jaworów
Księże Kolano	Tarnobrzeg	Rozwadów	Kutkowce	Tarnopol	Tarnopol
Księżnice	Mielec	Radomyśl Wiel.	Kuty	Kossów	Kuty
Kuczwice	Lisko	Baligród	Kuty Stare	Kossów	Kuty
Kudobińce	Złoczów	Zborów	Kutyly	Nisko	Ulanów
Kudryńce Dolne	Borszczów	Mielnica	Kutyszcze	Brody	Podkamień
Kudryńce Górne	Borszczów	Mielnica	Kuywa	Ropczyce	Sędziszów
Kudynowce	Złoczów	Zborów	Kuzie	Dąbrowa	Dąbrowa
Kuhajów	Lemberg	Nawarya	Kuźmina	Bircza	Bircza
Kujdance	Kołomea	Kołomea	Kwaczała	Chrzanów	Chrzanów
Kujdanów	Buczacz	Buczacz	Kwapinka	Wieliczka	Klasno
Kukizów	Lemberg	Jaryczów	Kwaszenina	Bircza	Dobromil
Kuków	Żywiec	Zabłocie	Kwiatoń	Gorlice	Gorlice
Kułaczkowce	Kołomea	Gwoździec	Kwiatonowice	Gorlice	Gorlice
Kułaczyn	Śniatyn	Śniatyn	Kwików	Brzesko	Szczurowa
Kułakowce	Zaleszczyki	Gródek	Łabacz	Brody	Sokołówka
Kulaszne	Sanok	Bukowsko	Łabajka	Rzeszów	Głogów
Kulawa	Żółkiew	Żółkiew	Łabowa	Nowy Sącz	Łabowa
Kulczyce	Sambor	Sambor	Łabowice	Nowy Sącz	Łabowa
Kulerzów	Wieliczka	Podgórze	Lachawa	Bircza	Bircza
Kuliczków	Sokal	Bełż	Lachowce	Bohordczany	Bohordczany
Kulików	Kam. Strumiłowa	Radziechów	Lachowice	Żywiec	Zabłocie
Kulików	Żółkiew	Kulików	Lachowice Podróżne	Żydaczów	Żurawno
Kulmatycze	Mościska	Sądowa Wisznia	Lachowice Zarzeczne	Żydaczów	Żurawno
Kulparków	Lemberg	Zniesienie	Lacka Wola	Mościska	Mościska
Kulyska	Tłumacz	Niźniów	Lackie Małe	Złoczów	Złoczów
Kunaszów	Rohatyń	Bursztyn	Lackie Wielkie	Złoczów	Złoczów
Kunice	Wieliczka	Klasno	Łącko	Bircza	Dobromil
Kunicze	Rohatyń	Bursztyn	Łącko	Nowy Sącz	Łącko
Kunin	Żółkiew	Żółkiew	Łaczany	Wadowice	Zator
Kunina	Nowy Sącz	Łabowa	Łaczki	Jasło	Frysztak
Kunisowce	Horodenka	Czernelica	Łaczki	Lisko	Lisko
Kunkowa	Gorlice	Gorlice	Łaczki	Nowy Sącz	Łącko
Kunkowce	Przemyśl	Przemyśl	Łaczki	Ropczyce	Ropczyce
Kunowa	Jasło	Jasło	Ładyczyn	Tarnopol	Mikulińce
Kupcze	Kam. Strumiłowa	Busk	Ładzin	Sanok	Rymanów
Kupczynce	Tarnopol	Tarnopol	Ladzkie	Tłumacz	Tyśmienica
Kupiatycze	Przemyśl	Niżankowice	Ladzkie	Tłumacz	Uście Zielone
Kupiczwola	Żółkiew	Gross-Mosty	Laeniowa	Brzesko	Czchów
Kupienin	Dąbrowa	Dąbrowa	Łagiewniki	Wieliczka	Podgórze
Kupna	Przemyśl	Krzywcza	Łahodów	Brody	Brody
Kupno	Kolbuszowa	Kolbuszowa	Łahodów	Przemyślany	Gliniany
Kupno	Rzeszów	Głogów	Łąka	Sambor	Sambor
Kupnowice Nowy	Rudki	Rudki	Łąkta Dolna	Bochnia	Wiśnicz Nowy

Town	Main District	Subdistrict	Town	Main District	Subdistrict
Ląkta Górna	Bochnia	Wiśnicz Nowy	Łęgów	Żólkiew	Gross-Mosty
Lalin	Sanok	Sanok	Łęka	Nowy Sącz	Nowy Sącz
Lamna	Bochnia	Wiśnicz Nowy	Łęka Siedl.	Tarnów	Zabno
Lanckrona	Wadowice	Kalwarya	Łęka Szczucińka	Dąbrowa	Szczucin
Łańcut	Łańcut	Łańcut	Łęka Żabiecka	Dąbrowa	Szczucin
Łańczówka	Kam. Strumiłowa	Busk	Łękawica	Tarnów	Tarnów
Lanczyn	Nadwórna	Lanczyn	Łękawica	Wadowice	Wadowice
Landestreu	Kalusz	Kalusz	Łękawica	Żywiec	Zabłocie
Lanowce	Borszczów	Borszczów	Łękawka	Tarnów	Tuchów
Lanowice	Sambor	Sambor	Łęki	Biała	Kęty
Łany	Lemberg	Szczerzec	Łęki	Brzesko	Brzesko
Łany Niemieckie	Kam. Strumiłowa	Kam. Strumiłowa	Łęki	Jasło	Frysztak
Łany Polskie	Kam. Strumiłowa	Kam. Strumiłowa	Łęki	Krosno	Dukla
Łany Sokołówskie	Stryj	Stryj	Łęki	Nowy Sącz	Nowy Sącz
Łapajówka	Jarosław	Jarosław	Łęki Dolne	Pilzno	Pilzno
Łapajówka	Kam. Strumiłowa	Kam. Strumiłowa	Łęki Górne	Pilzno	Pilzno
Łapanów	Bochnia	Wiśnicz Nowy	Leksandrowa	Bochnia	Wiśnicz Nowy
Łapczyca	Bochnia	Bochnia	Lelechówka	Gródek	Janów
Łapiszów	Tarnobrzeg	Rozwadów	Leluchów	Nowy Sącz	Muszyna
Łapszyn	Bóbrka	Chodorów	Lemberg	Lemberg	Lemberg
Łapszyn	Brzeżany	Brzeżany	Lencze Górne	Wadowice	Kalwarya
Las	Żywiec	Zabłocie	Lenina Mała	Staremiasto	Staremiasto
Lasek	Nowy Targ	Nowy Targ	Lenina Wielka	Staremiasto	Staremiasto
Laski	Jasło	Jasło	Lepina	Żólkiew	Żólkiew
Laski	Nisko	Nisko	Lepnica	Pilzno	Dębica
Laskowa	Limanowa	Limanowa	Lesieczniki	Zaleszczyki	Zaleszczyki
Laskowa	Wadowice	Zator	Lesienice	Lemberg	Winniki
Laskowce	Czortków	Budzanów	Lesna	Żywiec	Zabłocie
Laskówka Delastowska	Dąbrowa	Szczucin	Leśnica	Nowy Targ	Nowy Targ
Lasocice	Limanowa	Limanowa	Leśnica	Wadowice	Kalwarya
Lasosina	Limanowa	Limanowa	Leśniki	Brzeżany	Brzeżany
Lastówki	Drohobycz	Borysław	Leśniowice	Gródek	Janów
Laszczyny	Łańcut	Żolynia	Leśniowice	Lemberg	Nawarya
Laszki	Jarosław	Radymno	Leśniówka	Krosno	Dukla
Laszki	Jaworów	Jaworów	Leszczańce	Buczacz	Buczacz
Laszki Dolne	Bóbrka	Brzozdowiec	Leszczatów	Sokal	Tartaków
Laszki Górne	Bóbrka	Brzozdowiec	Leszczawa Dolna	Bircza	Bircza
Laszki Gościńcowe	Mościska	Mościska	Leszczawa Górna	Bircza	Bircza
Laszki Król.	Przemyślany	Gliniany	Leszczawka	Bircza	Bircza
Laszki Murowane	Lemberg	Zniesienie	Leszcze	Ropczyce	Ropczyce
Laszki Murowane	Staremiasto	Starasól	Leszczków	Sokal	Warez
Laszki Zawiązane	Rudki	Rudki	Leszczowate	Lisko	Ustrzyki Dolne
Laszków	Brody	Szczurowice	Leszczyn	Bóbrka	Strzeliska Nowe
Latacz	Zaleszczyki	Uścieczko	Leszczyna	Bochnia	Wiśnicz Nowy
Latkowce	Borszczów	Mielnica	Leszczyny	Bircza	Rybotycze
Łatoszyn	Pilzno	Dębica	Leszczyny	Gorlice	Gorlice
Ławoczne	Stryj	Skole	Leszkowice	Bochnia	Bochnia
Ławrów	Staremiasto	Staremiasto	Leszniów	Brody	Leszniów
Ławryków	Rawa Ruska	Magierów	Letnia	Drohobycz	Drohobycz
Ławrykowce	Złoczów	Zborów	Lętowe	Limanowa	Mszana dolna
Łazany	Wieliczka	Klasno	Lętowica	Brzesko	Wojnicz
Łazarówka	Buczacz	Monasterzyska	Lętowina	Nisko	Rudnik
Łazek	Tarnobrzeg	Radomyśl	Łętownia	Myślenice	Jordanów
Łazy	Biała	Oświęcim	Łętownia	Przemyśl	Przemyśl
Łazy	Bochnia	Wiśnicz Nowy	Łętownia	Rzeszów	Strzyżów
Łazy	Jarosław	Radymno	Lewniowa	Brzesko	Brzesko
Łazy	Nowy Sącz	Łącko	Leżachów	Jarosław	Sienawa
Łazy Biegonickie	Nowy Sącz	Stary Sącz	Leżajsk	Łańcut	Leżajsk
Łazy Dębowieckie	Jasło	Jasło	Leżanówka	Skałat	Grzymałów
Łdziany	Kalusz	Kalusz	Lężany	Krosno	Dukla
Lecka	Rzeszów	Tyczyn	Lężawa	Zaleszczyki	Zaleszczyki
Lecówka	Dolina	Rożniatów	Lgota	Chrzanów	Trzebina
Lednica Górna	Wieliczka	Klasno	Lgota	Wadowice	Zator
Lednica Niemicka	Wieliczka	Klasno	Libertów	Wieliczka	Podgórze
Łęg	Nowy Sącz	Łabowa			

Town	Main District	Subdistrict	Town	Main District	Subdistrict
Libiąż Mały	Chrzanów	Chrzanów	Liwcze	Sokal	Warez
Libiąż Wielki	Chrzanów	Chrzanów	Łobozew	Lisko	Ustrzyki Dolne
Libochowa	Stryj	Skole	Łodygowice	Biała	Lipnik
Librantowa	Nowy Sącz	Nowy Sącz	Łodyna	Lisko	Ustrzyki Dolne
Libuchowa	Staremiasto	Chyrów	Łodzina	Bircza	Bircza
Libusza	Gorlice	Gorlice	Łodzinka Dolna	Bircza	Rybotycze
Lichwin	Tarnów	Tuchów	Łodzinka Górna	Bircza	Bircza
Liczkowce	Husiatyn	Husiatyn	Łojowa	Nadwórna	Delatyn
Limanowa	Limanowa	Limanowa	Lokutki	Tłumacz	Tłumacz
Lindenfeld	Lemberg	Szczerzec	Lolin	Dolina	Dolina
Lipa	Bircza	Bircza	Łomna	Bircza	Rybotycze
Lipa	Dolina	Bolechów	Łomnica	Nowy Sącz	Piwniczna
Lipiatyn	Brzeżany	Brzeżany	Łonie	Przemyślany	Gliniany
Lipica Górna	Rohatyń	Rohatyń	Łonie	Złoczów	Gologory
Lipice	Drohobycz	Drohobycz	Łoniowy	Brzesko	Brzesko
Lipie	Limanowa	Limanowa	Łopianka	Dolina	Dolina
Lipie	Nowy Sącz	Nowy Sącz	Łopienka	Lisko	Baligród
Lipie	Rzeszów	Głogów	Łopoń	Brzesko	Wojnicz
Lipinki	Gorlice	Gorlice	Łopuchowa	Ropczyce	Ropczyce
Lipiny	Dąbrowa	Dąbrowa	Łopuszanka	Bircza	Dobromil
Lipiny	Pilzno	Pilzno	Łopuszanka Chomina	Staremiasto	Staremiasto
Liplas	Wieliczka	Klasno	Łopuszany	Złoczów	Zborów
Lipna	Gorlice	Gorlice	Łopuszka Mała	Łańcut	Kańczuga
Lipnia Dolna	Bochnia	Wiśnicz Nowy	Łopuszka Wielka	Łańcut	Kańczuga
Lipnia Górna	Bochnia	Wiśnicz Nowy	Łopuszna	Nowy Targ	Nowy Targ
Lipnica	Kolbuszowa	Ranizów	Łopuszna	Rohatyń	Rohatyń
Lipnica	Rzeszów	Głogów	Łopuszna	Sambor	Sambor
Lipnica Dolna	Pilzno	Jodłowa	Łopusznica	Bircza	Dobromil
Lipnica Dolna	Rohatyń	Bursztyn	Łosiacz	Borszczów	Skała
Lipnica Górna	Jasło	Jasło	Łosie	Gorlice	Gorlice
Lipnica Murowana	Bochnia	Wiśnicz Nowy	Łosie	Nowy Sącz	Łabowa
Lipnica Wielka	Nowy Sącz	Nowy Sącz	Lososina Dolna	Nowy Sącz	Nowy Sącz
Lipnik	Biała	Lipnik	Lostówka	Limanowa	Mszana dolna
Lipnik	Wieliczka	Klasno	Loszniów	Trembowla	Trembowla
Lipniki	Mościska	Mościska	Lotatniki	Stryj	Stryj
Lipowa	Wadowice	Zator	Łowce	Jarosław	Radymno
Lipowa	Żywiec	Zabłocie	Łowcza	Cieszanów	Cieszanów
Lipowce	Limanowa	Limanowa	Łowczów	Tarnów	Tuchów
Lipowce	Przemyślany	Gliniany	Łowczowek	Tarnów	Tuchów
Lipowce	Złoczów	Gologory	Łowczyce	Rudki	Komarno
Lipowica	Krosno	Dukla	Łowczyce	Żydaczów	Żurawno
Lipowice	Cieszanów	Lubaczów	Łowisko	Nisko	Rudnik
Lipowice	Dolina	Dolina	Łozina	Gródek	Janów
Lipowice	Sanok	Rymanów	Łozowa	Tarnopol	Tarnopol
Lipowiec	Drohobycz	Drohobycz	Łozówka	Trembowla	Trembowla
Lipsko	Cieszanów	Lipsko	Luasz	Dąbrowa	Szczucin
Lisia Góra	Tarnów	Tarnów	Lubaczów	Cieszanów	Lubaczów
Lisiatycze	Stryj	Stryj	Lubanowa	Tarnów	Tuchów
Lisiejamy	Cieszanów	Lubaczów	Lubatowa	Krosno	Dukla
Liski	Kołomea	Kołomea	Lubatówka	Krosno	Dukla
Liski	Sokal	Warez	Lubcza	Pilzno	Pilzno
Lisko	Kam. Strumiłowa	Busk	Lubcza	Tarnów	Tarnów
Lisko	Lisko	Lisko	Lubella	Żólkiew	Żólkiew
Liskowate	Bircza	Dobromil	Lubenia	Rzeszów	Tyczyn
Lisów	Jasło	Jasło	Lubeszka	Bóbrka	Strzeliska Nowe
Lisowce	Zaleszczyki	Tłuste	Lubiana	Lemberg	Szczerzec
Lisowice	Dolina	Bolechów	Lubianka	Lemberg	Szczerzec
Liszna	Lisko	Baligród	Lubień	Myślenice	Jordanów
Liszna	Sanok	Sanok	Lubień Mały	Gródek	Gródek
Lisznia	Drohobycz	Drohobycz	Lubień Wielki	Gródek	Gródek
Litewska	Rudki	Komarno	Lubieńce	Stryj	Stryj
Litowisko	Brody	Podkamień	Lubienie	Jaworów	Krakówiec
Litwina	Podhajce	Podhajce	Lubinka	Tarnów	Tarnów
Litynia	Drohobycz	Drohobycz	Lubkowce	Śniatyn	Zabłotów

Town	Main District	Subdistrict	Town	Main District	Subdistrict
Lubla	Jasło	Frysztak	Lyczana	Nowy Sącz	Nowy Sącz
Lublica	Jasło	Frysztak	Lyczanka	Nowy Sącz	Nowy Sącz
Lublinec Nowy	Cieszanów	Cieszanów	Łysa	Podhajce	Podhajce
Lublinec Stary	Cieszanów	Cieszanów	Łysa Góra	Brzesko	Wojnicz
Łubne	Lisko	Baligród	Łysa Góra	Krosno	Dukla
Łubno	Brzozów	Dynów	Łysaków	Mielec	Radomyśl Wiel.
Lubomierz	Bochnia	Wiśnicz Nowy	Łysakowek	Mielec	Radomyśl Wiel.
Lubomierz	Limanowa	Mszana dolna	Łysiec	Bohordczany	Lysiec
Łubów	Sokal	Warez	Łysiec Stary	Bohordczany	Lysiec
Lubsza	Rohatyń	Rohatyń	Łysina	Żywiec	Zabłocie
Lubsza	Żydaczów	Żurawno	Łysków	Żydaczów	Żurawno
Lubycza	Rawa Ruska	Lubycza	Łysokanie	Bochnia	Bochnia
Lubycza Kniazie	Rawa Ruska	Lubycza	Łyszanka	Wieliczka	Klasno
Lubzina	Ropczyce	Ropczyce	Machlinice	Stryj	Stryj
Luczany	Bóbrka	Strzeliska Nowe	Machnów	Rawa Ruska	Uhnów
Lucze	Kołomea	Jabłonów	Machnowek	Sokal	Bełż
Łuczka	Tarnopol	Mikulińce	Machnówka	Krosno	Dukla
Łuczki	Kołomea	Jabłonów	Machów	Tarnobrzeg	Tarnobrzeg
Lucznikowice	Biała	Oświęcim	Machowa	Pilzno	Pilzno
Luczyce	Przemyśl	Przemyśl	Maciejowa	Nowy Sącz	Łabowa
Luczyńce	Rohatyń	Rohatyń	Macoszyn	Żólkiew	Żólkiew
Ludwikówka	Dolina	Dolina	Mądrzelówka	Podhajce	Podhajce
Ludwikówka	Rohatyń	Bursztyn	Madziarki	Sokal	Krystynopol
Ludwikówka	Tarnopol	Mikulińce	Magdalówka	Tarnopol	Tarnopol
Ludwinów	Wieliczka	Podgórze	Magierów	Rawa Ruska	Magierów
Ludzimierz	Nowy Targ	Nowy Targ	Majdan	Drohobycz	Borysław
Ług	Gorlice	Gorlice	Majdan	Gródek	Janów
Łuh	Lisko	Baligród	Majdan	Husiatyn	Kopyczyńce
Łuh	Nadwórna	Delatyn	Majdan	Kalusz	Kalusz
Łuhy	Dolina	Rożniatów	Majdan	Kolbuszowa	Majdan
Łuka	Horodenka	Obertyn	Majdan	Złoczów	Sassów
Łuka	Kalusz	Wojniłów	Majdan	Żólkiew	Żólkiew
Łuka	Tłumacz	Uście Zielone	Majdan Gołogórski	Złoczów	Gologory
Łuka	Złoczów	Złoczów	Majdan Górny	Nadwórna	Nadwórna
Łuka Mała	Skałat	Tarnoruda	Majdan Jarosinki	Nisko	Ulanów
Łukanowice	Brzesko	Wojnicz	Majdan Lipowiecki	Przemyślany	Gliniany
Łukawica	Cieszanów	Lipsko	Majdan Nowy	Kam. Strumiłowa	Radziechów
Łukawica	Limanowa	Limanowa	Majdan Pieniacki	Brody	Podkamień
Łukawica	Lisko	Lisko	Majdan Sienawski	Jarosław	Sienawa
Łukawica Niżna	Stryj	Stryj	Majdan Stary	Kam. Strumiłowa	Radziechów
Łukawica Wyżna	Stryj	Stryj	Majdan Zbytniowski	Tarnobrzeg	Rozwadów
Łukawice	Brody	Podkamień	Majkowice	Bochnia	Bochnia
Łukawice	Cieszanów	Lubaczów	Majnicz	Sambor	Sambor
Łukowa	Nisko	Rudnik	Majscowa	Jasło	Jasło
Łukowa	Tarnów	Zabno	Maków	Myślenice	Maków
Łukowe	Lisko	Lisko	Makowa Kolonia	Bircza	Rybotycze
Łukówka	Brzesko	Czchów	Makowa Nat.	Bircza	Rybotycze
Łupków	Lisko	Wola Michowa	Makowica	Limanowa	Limanowa
Lupuszna	Bóbrka	Bóbrka	Maksymówka	Dolina	Dolina
Lusina	Wieliczka	Podgórze	Makuniów	Mościska	Sądowa Wisznia
Lusławice	Brzesko	Czchów	Makwiska	Krosno	Dukla
Lusławiczki	Brzesko	Czchów	Makwisko	Jarosław	Jarosław
Luszowice	Chrzanów	Chrzanów	Mała Niedżwiada	Ropczyce	Ropczyce
Luszowice	Dąbrowa	Dąbrowa	Mała Wieś	Nowy Sącz	Nowy Sącz
Lutcza	Brzozów	Jasienica	Mała Wieś	Wieliczka	Klasno
Lutera	Rzeszów	Strzyżów	Małastów	Gorlice	Gorlice
Lutków	Jarosław	Radymno	Małaszowce	Tarnopol	Tarnopol
Lutków	Mościska	Hussaków	Maława	Bircza	Bircza
Lutoryż	Rzeszów	Tyczyn	Maława	Rzeszów	Rzeszów
Lutowiska	Lisko	Lutowiska	Maławka	Rzeszów	Niebylec
Lutowiska	Sambor	Sambor	Malce	Biała	Kęty
Lużek Górny	Staremiasto	Staremiasto	Malczkowice	Lemberg	Nawarya
Lużki	Dolina	Bolechów	Malczyce	Gródek	Janów
Lużna	Gorlice	Gorlice	Malechów	Lemberg	Zniesienie

Town	Main District	Subdistrict	Town	Main District	Subdistrict
Malechów	Żydaczów	Rozdół	Mazury	Kolbuszowa	Sokołów
Malejowa	Myślenice	Jordanów	Mchawa	Lisko	Baligród
Maleniska	Brody	Podkamień	Mechowiec	Kolbuszowa	Kolbuszowa
Malhowice	Przemyśl	Niżankowice	Męcina Mała	Gorlice	Gorlice
Malinie	Mielec	Mielec	Męcina Wielka	Gorlice	Gorlice
Malinówka	Brzozów	Jasienica	Męcinka	Krosno	Dukla
Malinowska	Lemberg	Nawarya	Medenice	Drohobycz	Drohobycz
Małkowice	Gródek	Gródek	Medewa	Brzeżany	Kozowa
Małkowice	Przemyśl	Przemyśl	Mędrzechów	Dąbrowa	Dąbrowa
Malonowy	Podhajce	Podhajce	Meducha	Rohatyń	Bursztyn
Maloszowice	Lemberg	Nawarya	Medwedowce	Buczacz	Buczacz
Małów	Trembowla	Trembowla	Medyka	Przemyśl	Przemyśl
Małpa	Rudki	Komarno	Medyń	Zbaraz	Zbaraz
Małyrówka	Rzeszów	Tyczyn	Medynia	Kalusz	Wojniłów
Manajów	Złoczów	Zborów	Medynia	Rzeszów	Głogów
Manaster Derczycki	Drohobycz	Drohobycz	Medynia Głogówska	Łańcut	Łańcut
Manaster Liszniański	Drohobycz	Drohobycz	Medynia Łańcucka	Łańcut	Łańcut
Manasterce	Żydaczów	Żurawno	Mełna	Rohatyń	Rohatyń
Manasterczany	Borhodczany	Sołotwina	Melsztyn	Brzesko	Czchów
Manasterek	Kam. Strumiłowa	Radziechów	Mertawa	Borszczów	Borszczów
Manasterek	Rawa Ruska	Magierów	Meszna	Biała	Lipnik
Manasterek	Zaleszczyki	Korolówka	Meszna Opacka	Tarnów	Tuchów
Manasterez	Łańcut	Kańczuga	Meszna Szlachecka	Tarnów	Tuchów
Manastersko	Kossów	Kossów	Meteniów	Złoczów	Zborów
Manasterz	Jarosław	Sienawa	Mętków Mały	Chrzanów	Chrzanów
Manasterzec	Lisko	Lisko	Mętków Wielki	Chrzanów	Chrzanów
Manasterzec	Sambor	Sambor	Mianowice	Sokal	Warez
Manasterzec	Stryj	Stryj	Michalcze	Horodenka	Horodenka
Manastyrek	Brody	Stanisławczyk	Michalczowa	Nowy Sącz	Nowy Sącz
Maniawa	Borhodczany	Sołotwina	Michalewica	Mościska	Sądowa Wisznia
Maniów	Dąbrowa	Szczucin	Michalewice	Rudki	Rudki
Maniów	Lisko	Wola Michowa	Michałków	Borszczów	Mielnica
Maniowy	Nowy Targ	Nowy Targ	Michałków	Kołomea	Kołomea
Marcinkowice	Brzesko	Radłów	Michałowice	Drohobycz	Drohobycz
Marcinkowice	Nowy Sącz	Nowy Sącz	Michałówka	Borszczów	Mielnica
Marcówka	Wadowice	Wadowice	Michałówka	Podhajce	Podhajce
Marcyporęba	Wadowice	Zator	Michałówka	Rawa Ruska	Uhnów
Marjanka	Tarnopol	Tarnopol	Michowa	Bircza	Dobromil
Marjnka	Żydaczów	Żurawno	Mickinia	Chrzanów	Trzebina
Marki	Tarnobrzeg	Baranów	Miechocin	Tarnobrzeg	Tarnobrzeg
Markopol	Brody	Podkamień	Międzybrody	Stryj	Skole
Markowa	Borhodczany	Sołotwina	Międzybrodzie	Sanok	Sanok
Markowa	Kołomea	Peczeniżyn	Międzybrodzie	Żywiec	Zabłocie
Markowa	Łańcut	Łańcut	Międzybrodzie Kob.	Biała	Kęty
Markowa	Podhajce	Zawałów	Międzybrodzie Lipnickie	Biała	Lipnik
Markowce	Sanok	Sanok	Międzyczerwone	Nowy Targ	Nowy Targ
Markowce	Tłumacz	Tyśmienica	Międzygorze	Tłumacz	Uście Zielone
Markowizna	Kolbuszowa	Sokołów	Międzyhorce	Rohatyń	Bursztyn
Markuszowa	Limanowa	Limanowa	Międzyhorce	Żydaczów	Żydaczów
Marnszyna	Nowy Targ	Nowy Targ	Międzyrzyce	Krosno	Dukla
Marszowice	Wieliczka	Klasno	Miejsce	Wadowice	Zator
Martynów Nowy	Rohatyń	Bursztyn	Miękisz Nowy	Jarosław	Radymno
Martynów Stary	Rohatyń	Bursztyn	Miękisz Stary	Jarosław	Radymno
Maruszowa	Jasło	Frysztak	Mielec	Mielec	Mielec
Maryampol	Stanisławów	Maryampol	Mielnica	Borszczów	Mielnica
Maszkienice	Brzesko	Brzesko	Mielnicz	Żydaczów	Żurawno
Maszkowice	Nowy Sącz	Łącko	Mielnów	Przemyśl	Krzywcza
Matejowce	Kołomea	Kołomea	Mielnów	Przemyśl	Przemyśl
Mateuszówka	Buczacz	Buczacz	Mierów	Kam. Strumiłowa	Chołojów
Maxymowice	Sambor	Sambor	Mierzasichle	Nowy Targ	Nowy Targ
Maziarnia	Kam. Strumiłowa	Busk	Mierzeń	Wieliczka	Klasno
Maziarnia	Nisko	Nisko	Mierzwica	Żólkiew	Żólkiew
Mazurówka	Skałat	Grzymałów	Mieszyszczów	Brzeżany	Brzeżany
Mazurówka	Żydaczów	Żurawno	Miętniów	Wieliczka	Klasno

Town	Main District	Subdistrict	Town	Main District	Subdistrict
Mikałajów	Bóbrka	Mikalajów	Mokrzany	Sambor	Sambor
Mikałajów	Brody	Szczurowice	Mokrzany Małe	Mościska	Sądowa Wisznia
Mikałajów	Żydaczów	Rozdól	Mokrzany Wielkie	Mościska	Sądowa Wisznia
Mikałajówice	Tarnów	Zabno	Mokrzec	Pilzno	Pilzno
Mikłaszów	Lemberg	Winniki	Mokrzyska	Brzesko	Brzesko
Mikłuszowice	Bochnia	Bochnia	Mokrzyszów	Tarnobrzeg	Tarnobrzeg
Mików	Sanok	Bukowsko	Molczanówka	Skałat	Skałat
Mikulice	Łańcut	Kańczuga	Mołdycz	Jarosław	Sienawa
Mikuliczyn	Nadwórna	Delatyn	Mołodylów	Nadwórna	Lanczyn
Mikulińce	Śniatyn	Śniatyn	Mołodyńcze	Bóbrka	Chodorów
Mikulińce	Tarnopol	Mikulińce	Mołoszkowice	Jaworów	Jaworów
Mikuszowice	Biała	Lipnik	Mołotków	Borhodczany	Sołotwina
Milatycze	Lemberg	Nawarya	Mołotów	Bóbrka	Chodorów
Milatyń	Gródek	Gródek	Monasterzec	Rudki	Komarno
Milatyń	Mościska	Sądowa Wisznia	Monasterzyska	Buczacz	Monasterzyska
Milatyń Nowy	Kam. Strumiłowa	Busk	Moniłowska	Złoczów	Zborów
Milatyń Stary	Kam. Strumiłowa	Busk	Monowice	Biała	Oświęcim
Milcza	Sanok	Rymanów	Moosberg	Jaworów	Jaworów
Milczyce	Mościska	Sądowa Wisznia	Morańce	Jaworów	Krakówiec
Milik	Nowy Sącz	Muszyna	Morawsko	Jarosław	Jarosław
Milków	Cieszanów	Oleszyce	Mordarka	Limanowa	Limanowa
Miłkowa	Nowy Sącz	Nowy Sącz	Morszyn	Stryj	Stryj
Milno	Brody	Zalocze	Morwczyna	Nowy Targ	Nowy Targ
Miłocin	Rzeszów	Rzeszów	Mościska	Kalusz	Kalusz
Miłowanie	Tłumacz	Tyśmienica	Mościska	Mościska	Mościska
Milowce	Zaleszczyki	Tłuste	Moskale	Tarnobrzeg	Rozwadów
Milówka	Brzesko	Wojnicz	Moskalówka	Kossów	Kossów
Milówka	Żywiec	Zabłocie	Mostki	Lemberg	Nawarya
Mirocin	Łańcut	Przeworsk	Mostki	Nisko	Ulanów
Mirów	Chrzanów	Trzebina	Mostki	Nowy Sącz	Stary Sącz
Mistkowice	Sambor	Sambor	Mosty	Rudki	Komarno
Mistyce	Mościska	Sądowa Wisznia	Mosty Małe	Rawa Ruska	Lubycza
Mizerna	Nowy Targ	Nowy Targ	Moszczanica	Cieszanów	Cieszanów
Mizuń Nowy	Dolina	Dolina	Moszczanica	Żywiec	Zabłocie
Mizuń Stary	Dolina	Dolina	Moszczaniec	Sanok	Bukowsko
Młodochów	Mielec	Mielec	Moszczenica	Bochnia	Bochnia
Młodów	Cieszanów	Lubaczów	Moszczenica	Gorlice	Gorlice
Młodów	Nowy Sącz	Piwniczna	Moszczenica niżna	Nowy Sącz	Stary Sącz
Młodowice	Przemyśl	Niżankowice	Moszczenica wyżna	Nowy Sącz	Stary Sącz
Młodzatyń	Kołomea	Peczeniżyn	Moszków	Sokal	Warez
Młoszowa	Chrzanów	Trzebina	Moszkowce	Kalusz	Wojnilów
Młyńczyska	Limanowa	Limanowa	Motycze Poduchowne	Tarnobrzeg	Rozwadów
Młyniska	Trembowla	Janów	Motycze Szlacheckie	Tarnobrzeg	Rozwadów
Młyniska	Żydaczów	Żurawno	Mraźnica	Drohobycz	Borysław
Młynne	Limanowa	Limanowa	Mrowla	Rzeszów	Rzeszów
Młynowce	Złoczów	Zborów	Mrozowice	Sambor	Sambor
Młynówka	Borszczów	Mielnica	Mrzygłód	Sanok	Sanok
Młyny	Jaworów	Krakówiec	Mszalnica	Grybów	Grybów
Mochnaczka Niżna	Grybów	Grybów	Mszana	Gródek	Janów
Mochnaczka Wyżna	Grybów	Grybów	Mszana	Krosno	Dukla
Mockowice	Przemyśl	Przemyśl	Mszana	Złoczów	Zborów
Moczary	Lisko	Ustrzyki Dolne	Mszana Dolna	Limanowa	Mszana dolna
Moczerady	Mościska	Hussaków	Mszana Górna	Limanowa	Mszana dolna
Moderówka	Krosno	Dukla	Mszanice	Husiatyn	Chorostków
Modrycz	Drohobycz	Drohobycz	Mszanice	Staremiasto	Staremiasto
Mogielnica	Trembowla	Trembowla	Mszanice	Tarnopol	Tarnopol
Mogilany	Wieliczka	Podgórze	Mszanka	Gorlice	Gorlice
Mogilno	Grybów	Grybów	Mucharz	Wadowice	Wadowice
Mohylany	Żólkiew	Kulików	Muchawka	Czortków	Jagielnica
Mokra Strona	Łańcut	Przeworsk	Muhlbach	Bóbrka	Bóbrka
Mokra Wieś	Nowy Sącz	Stary Sącz	Mukanie	Kam. Strumiłowa	Radziechów
Mokre	Sanok	Bukowsko	Mulne	Żywiec	Zabłocie
Mokrotyn	Żólkiew	Żólkiew	Munina	Jarosław	Jarosław
Mokrotyn Kolonia	Żólkiew	Żólkiew	Musikowe	Tarnobrzeg	Rozwadów

Town	Main District	Subdistrict	Town	Main District	Subdistrict
Muszkarów	Zaleszczyki	Korolówka	Nastasów	Tarnopol	Mikulińce
Muszkatówka	Borszczów	Borszczów	Nastaszczyn	Rohatyń	Bursztyn
Muszyłowice	Jaworów	Jaworów	Naszasowice	Nowy Sącz	Stary Sącz
Muszyłowice Czarnokonce	Jaworów	Jaworów	Nawarya	Lemberg	Nawarya
Muszyłowice Narodowe	Jaworów	Jaworów	Nawojówka	Nowy Sącz	Nowy Sącz
Muszyna	Nowy Sącz	Muszyna	Nawsie	Ropczyce	Wielopole
Muszynka	Nowy Sącz	Krynica	Nawsie Brzosteckie	Pilzno	Brzostek
Mutulin	Złoczów	Gologory	Nawsie Kolaczyckie	Pilzno	Brzostek
Muzylów	Podhajce	Podhajce	Nazawirów	Nadwórna	Nadwórna
Myców	Sokal	Bełż	Nazurna	Kołomea	Gwozdziec
Myczków	Lisko	Baligród	Nehrybka	Przemyśl	Przemyśl
Myczkowce	Lisko	Lisko	Nesów	Podhajce	Zawałów
Mykietyńce	Kossów	Pistyn	Nesterowce	Złoczów	Jezierna
Mykietyńce	Stanisławów	Stanisławów	Neu-Kalusz	Kalusz	Kalusz
Mymoń	Sanok	Rymanów	Neudorf	Drohobycz	Drohobycz
Myscowa	Krosno	Dukla	Neudorf	Nadwórna	Lanczyn
Myślachowice	Chrzanów	Trzebina	Neudorf	Sambor	Sambor
Myślatycze	Mościska	Mościska	Neuhof	Gródek	Gródek
Myślec	Nowy Sącz	Stary Sącz	Niagryn	Dolina	Dolina
Myślenice	Myślenice	Myślenice	Nidek	Wadowice	Andrychów
Myślów	Kalusz	Kalusz	Niebieszczany	Sanok	Bukowsko
Mysłowa	Skałat	Podwołoczyska	Niebocko	Brzozów	Brzozów
Myszków	Zaleszczyki	Korolówka	Niebylec	Rzeszów	Niebylec
Myszkowce	Husiatyn	Kopyczyńce	Niebyłów	Kalusz	Kalusz
Myszkowice	Tarnopol	Mikulińce	Niecew	Nowy Sącz	Nowy Sącz
Myszyn	Kołomea	Jabłonów	Niechobrz	Rzeszów	Rzeszów
Mytarka	Krosno	Żmigród	Nieciecza	Tarnów	Zabno
Naciszowa	Nowy Sącz	Nowy Sącz	Nieczajna	Dąbrowa	Dąbrowa
Nadbrzeże	Tarnobrzeg	Tarnobrzeg	Niedary	Bochnia	Bochnia
Nadiatycze	Żydaczów	Rozdól	Niedomice	Tarnów	Zabno
Nadolany	Sanok	Nowtanice	Niedzieliska	Chrzanów	Chrzanów
Nadole	Krosno	Dukla	Niedzielisko	Brzesko	Szczurowa
Nadorożna	Tłumacz	Tłumacz	Niedzielna	Staremiasto	Staremiasto
Nadorożniów	Brzeżany	Brzeżany	Niedźwiedź	Limanowa	Mszana dolna
Nadwórna	Nadwórna	Nadwórna	Niedźwiedza	Brzesko	Wojnicz
Nadyby	Sambor	Sambor	Niedźwiedza	Drohobycz	Drohobycz
Nadycze	Żólkiew	Kulików	Niegłowice	Jasło	Jasło
Nadziejów	Dolina	Dolina	Niegoszowice	Chrzanów	Trzebina
Nagawczyna	Pilzno	Dębica	Niegowce	Kalusz	Wojnilów
Nagnajów	Tarnobrzeg	Baranów	Niegowie	Wieliczka	Klasno
Nagórzanka	Buczacz	Buczacz	Nieledwia	Żywiec	Zabłocie
Nagórzanka	Czortków	Jagielnica	Nielepice	Chrzanów	Trzebina
Nagórzany	Lemberg	Nawarya	Nielipkowice	Jarosław	Sienawa
Nagórzany	Sanok	Nowtanice	Niemerów	Rawa Ruska	Niemerów
Nagórzany	Zaleszczyki	Uścieczko	Niemiacz	Brody	Podkamień
Nahaczów	Jaworów	Jaworów	Niemiłów	Kam. Strumiłowa	Radziechów
Nahorce	Żólkiew	Kulików	Niemstów	Cieszanów	Cieszanów
Nahorce Małe	Kam. Strumiłowa	Kam. Strumiłowa	Niemszyn	Rohatyń	Bursztyn
Nahujowice	Drohobycz	Drohobycz	Niemszyn	Stanisławów	Halicz
Nakło	Przemyśl	Sosnica	Nienadowa	Przemyśl	Dubiecko
Nakwasza	Brody	Podkamień	Nienadówka	Kolbuszowa	Sokołów
Nalepy	Nisko	Ulanów	Nienaszów	Krosno	Dukla
Nałuże	Trembowla	Strusów	Nienowice	Jarosław	Radymno
Nanczułka Mała	Staremiasto	Staremiasto	Niepla	Jasło	Jasło
Nanczułka Wielka	Staremiasto	Staremiasto	Niepołomice	Bochnia	Bochnia
Nanowa	Lisko	Ustrzyki Dolne	Nieporaz	Chrzanów	Chrzanów
Napowce	Przemyśl	Przemyśl	Niepreśnia	Bochnia	Wiśnicz Nowy
Naprawa	Myślenice	Jordanów	Niesłuchów	Kam. Strumiłowa	Busk
Naradna	Sokal	Krystynopol	Niestanice	Kam. Strumiłowa	Chołojów
Narajów	Brzeżany	Narajów	Nieszkowice	Bochnia	Wiśnicz Nowy
Narol	Cieszanów	Narol	Niewdzieliska	Przemyślany	Świr
Nart Nowy	Kolbuszowa	Ranizów	Niewiarów	Wieliczka	Klasno
Nart Stary	Kolbuszowa	Ranizów	Niewistki	Brzozów	Dynów
Nasiężna	Lisko	Lutowiska	Niewoczyn	Bohordczany	Bohordczany

Town	Main District	Subdistrict	Town	Main District	Subdistrict
Niewodna	Jasło	Frysztak	Nowosielica	Mościska	Sądowa Wisznia
Niewodna	Ropczyce	Wielopole	Nowosielica	Śniatyn	Zabłotów
Niezdów	Wieliczka	Klasno	Nowosiółka	Borszczów	Mielnica
Nieznajowa	Gorlice	Gorlice	Nowosiółka	Buczacz	Potok
Nieznanów	Kam. Strumiłowa	Chołojów	Nowosiółka	Lemberg	Szczerzec
Nieznanowice	Wieliczka	Klasno	Nowosiółka	Podhajce	Podhajce
Nieżuchów	Stryj	Stryj	Nowosiółka	Przemyślany	Dunajowce
Nieżwiska	Horodenka	Obertyn	Nowosiółka	Tłumacz	Uście Zielone
Niklowice	Mościska	Sądowa Wisznia	Nowosiółka Grzym.	Skałat	Touste
Nikonkowice	Lemberg	Szczerzec	Nowosiółka Jazłowiecka	Buczacz	Jazłowice
Nikowice	Rudki	Rudki	Nowosiółka Skalacka	Skałat	Skałat
Niniów Dolny	Dolina	Bolechów	Nowosiółki	Bircza	Rybotycze
Niniów Górny	Dolina	Bolechów	Nowosiółki	Kam. Strumiłowa	Busk
Nisko	Nisko	Nisko	Nowosiółki	Lisko	Baligród
Niskołyzy	Buczacz	Monasterzyska	Nowosiółki	Mościska	Hussaków
Niwa	Nowy Targ	Nowy Targ	Nowosiółki	Przemyśl	Przemyśl
Niwice	Kam. Strumiłowa	Radziechów	Nowosiółki	Złoczów	Gologory
Niwiska	Kolbuszowa	Kolbuszowa	Nowosiółki Gościnne	Rudki	Rudki
Niwka	Brzesko	Radłow	Nowosiółki Kostk	Zaleszczyki	Korolówka
Niwra	Borszczów	Mielnica	Nowosiółki Oparskie	Rudki	Komarno
Niżankowice	Przemyśl	Niżankowice	Nowosioło	Żydaczów	Żydaczów
Niżankowice	Przemyśl	Niżankowice	Nowostawce	Buczacz	Buczacz
Niżatycze	Łańcut	Kańczuga	Nowoszny	Rohatyń	Bursztyn
Niżbork Nowy	Husiatyn	Kopyczyńce	Nowoszyce	Sambor	Sambor
Niżbork Stary	Husiatyn	Kopyczyńce	Nowoszyn	Dolina	Dolina
Niżna Łąka	Krosno	Dukla	Nowotanice	Sanok	Nowtanice
Niżniów	Tłumacz	Niżniów	Nowsiołki Kardyn.	Rawa Ruska	Uhnów
Nizowa	Wieliczka	Klasno	Nowsiołki Przednie	Rawa Ruska	Uhnów
Nizyce	Mościska	Hussaków	Nowy Babilon	Dolina	Bolechów
Nizynice	Przemyśl	Niżankowice	Nowy Dwór	Sokal	Krystynopol
Nockowa	Ropczyce	Sędziszów	Nowy Sącz	Nowy Sącz	Nowy Sącz
Nosata	Sokal	Krystynopol	Nowy Targ	Nowy Targ	Nowy Targ
Nosowce	Tarnopol	Tarnopol	Nowy Tyczyn	Trembowla	Strusów
Nosówka	Rzeszów	Rzeszów	Nozdrzec	Brzozów	Dynów
Nowa Góra	Chrzanów	Trzebina	Nuśmice	Sokal	Warez
Nowa Grobla	Jarosław	Radymno	Nyrków	Zaleszczyki	Uścieczko
Nowa Lodyna	Kam. Strumiłowa	Kam. Strumiłowa	Obarzance	Tarnopol	Tarnopol
Nowa Wieś	Biała	Kęty	Obarzym	Brzozów	Dynów
Nowa Wieś	Bircza	Bircza	Obelnica	Rohatyń	Bursztyn
Nowa Wieś	Brzesko	Brzesko	Obersdorf	Lisko	Ustrzyki Dolne
Nowa Wieś	Kolbuszowa	Kolbuszowa	Obertyn	Horodenka	Obertyn
Nowa Wieś	Nowy Sącz	Łabowa	Obidowa	Nowy Targ	Nowy Targ
Nowa Wieś	Rudki	Komarno	Obidza	Nowy Sącz	Szczawnica
Nowa Wieś	Rzeszów	Czudec	Obladów	Kam. Strumiłowa	Radziechów
Nowa Wieś	Rzeszów	Głogów	Obłażnica	Żydaczów	Żurawno
Nowa Wieś	Wieliczka	Klasno	Obłazy	Nowy Sącz	Piwniczna
Nowe Dwory	Wadowice	Zator	Obodówka	Zbaraz	Zbaraz
Nowe Miasto	Bircza	Nowemiasto	Obojna	Tarnobrzeg	Rozwadów
Nowe Siolo	Cieszanów	Cieszanów	Obroszyn	Gródek	Gródek
Nowe Siolo	Żólkiew	Kulików	Obrotów	Kam. Strumiłowa	Witków Nowy
Nowemiasto	Bircza	Nowemiasto	Obydów	Kam. Strumiłowa	Kam. Strumiłowa
Nowica	Gorlice	Gorlice	Ochmanów	Wieliczka	Klasno
Nowica	Kalusz	Kalusz	Ochmanów	Wieliczka	Klasno
Nowiny	Cieszanów	Cieszanów	Ochodza	Wadowice	Zator
Nowiny	Tarnobrzeg	Radomyśl	Ochojno	Wieliczka	Klasno
Nowodworze	Tarnów	Tarnów	Ochotnica	Nowy Targ	Krościenko
Nowojowa Góra	Chrzanów	Chrzanów	Ocice	Tarnobrzeg	Tarnobrzeg
Nowościólki	Jaworów	Jaworów	Ocieka	Ropczyce	Ropczyce
Nowosielce	Bircza	Rybotycze	Oczków	Żywiec	Zabłocie
Nowosielce	Bóbrka	Chodorów	Odaje ad Słobódka	Tłumacz	Tyśmienica
Nowosielce	Łańcut	Przeworsk	Odment	Dąbrowa	Szczucin
Nowosielce Gniewosz	Sanok	Sanok	Odrowąż	Nowy Targ	Nowy Targ
Nowosielec	Nisko	Rudnik	Odrzechowa	Sanok	Rymanów
Nowosielica	Dolina	Dolina	Odrzykoń	Krosno	Dukla

Town	Main District	Subdistrict	Town	Main District	Subdistrict
Okleśna	Chrzanów	Trzebina	Oporzec	Stryj	Skole
Okniany	Tłumacz	Tłumacz	Oprynowce	Stanisławów	Stanisławów
Okno	Horodenka	Horodenka	Opulsko	Sokal	Sokal
Okno	Skałat	Grzymałów	Orawa	Stryj	Skole
Okocim	Brzesko	Brzesko	Orawczyk	Stryj	Skole
Okoń	Kam. Strumiłowa	Kam. Strumiłowa	Orchowice	Mościska	Sądowa Wisznia
Okonin	Ropczyce	Ropczyce	Ordów	Kam. Strumiłowa	Witków Nowy
Okopy	Borszczów	Mielnica	Orelce	Śniatyn	Śniatyn
Okopy	Rawa Ruska	Magierów	Orelec	Lisko	Lisko
Okrajnik	Żywiec	Zabłocie	Orliska	Tarnobrzeg	Rozwadów
Olchawa	Bochnia	Wiśnicz Nowy	Orów	Drohobycz	Drohobycz
Olchowa	Lisko	Lisko	Ortynice	Sambor	Sambor
Olchowa	Ropczyce	Sędziszów	Oryszkowce	Husiatyn	Kopyczyńce
Olchowa Lwibrat	Lisko	Lutowiska	Orzechów	Tarnobrzeg	Radomyśl
Olchowce	Sanok	Sanok	Orzechowce	Skałat	Skałat
Olchowczyk	Husiatyn	Husiatyn	Orzechowczyk	Brody	Podkamień
Olchowice	Bóbrka	Bóbrka	Orzechowice	Przemyśl	Przemyśl
Olchowice	Borszczów	Mielnica	Orzechówka	Brzozów	Jasienica
Olchowice	Brzeżany	Brzeżany	Oserdów	Sokal	Bełż
Olchowice	Horodenka	Czernelica	Osieczany	Myślenice	Myślenice
Olchowice	Krosno	Dukla	Osiek	Biała	Kęty
Olchówka	Dolina	Rożniatów	Osielec	Myślenice	Maków
Olejów	Złoczów	Zborów	Oskrzesińce	Kołomea	Kołomea
Olejowa Korniów	Horodenka	Czernelica	Oskrzesińce	Rohatyń	Rohatyń
Olejowa Korolówka	Horodenka	Czernelica	Osławy Biale	Nadwórna	Delatyn
Oleksice Nowe	Stryj	Stryj	Osławy Czarne	Nadwórna	Delatyn
Oleksice Stare	Stryj	Stryj	Osmolna	Złoczów	Złoczów
Oleksińce	Zaleszczyki	Tłuste	Osobnica	Jasło	Jasło
Olendry	Trembowla	Strusów	Osowce	Buczacz	Buczacz
Olesin	Brzeżany	Kozowa	Ostalce	Tarnopol	Mikulińce
Olesko	Złoczów	Olesko	Ostapie	Skałat	Grzymałów
Oleśnica	Dąbrowa	Dąbrowa	Ostapkowce	Kołomea	Gwozdźiec
Oleśno	Dąbrowa	Dąbrowa	Ostaszowce	Złoczów	Jezierna
Olesza	Buczacz	Monasterzyska	Ostobusz	Rawa Ruska	Uhnów
Olesza	Tłumacz	Tłumacz	Ostra	Buczacz	Potok
Oleszków	Śniatyn	Zabłotów	Ostre	Żywiec	Zabłocie
Oleszów	Tłumacz	Niźniów	Ostropole	Chrzanów	Chrzanów
Oleszyce	Cieszanów	Oleszyce	Ostrów	Bóbrka	Brzozdowiec
Oleszyce Stare	Cieszanów	Oleszyce	Ostrów	Jarosław	Radymno
Olpiny	Jasło	Olpiny	Ostrów	Kam. Strumiłowa	Busk
Olsawica	Sanok	Bukowsko	Ostrów	Łańcut	Kańczuga
Olszanica	Lisko	Lisko	Ostrów	Lemberg	Szczerzec
Olszanica	Tłumacz	Tyśmienica	Ostrów	Przemyśl	Przemyśl
Olszanica	Złoczów	Gologory	Ostrów	Rohatyń	Rohatyń
Olszanik	Sambor	Sambor	Ostrów	Ropczyce	Ropczyce
Olszanka	Nowy Sącz	Stary Sącz	Ostrów	Rudki	Rudki
Olszanka	Rawa Ruska	Rawa Ruska	Ostrów	Sokal	Krystynopol
Olszany	Przemyśl	Przemyśl	Ostrów	Stanisławów	Halicz
Olszowa	Brzesko	Czchów	Ostrów	Tarnopol	Tarnopol
Olszowice	Wieliczka	Klasno	Ostrów	Tarnów	Zabno
Olszówka	Limanowa	Mszana dolna	Ostrów Królewski	Bochnia	Bochnia
Olszyny	Brzesko	Wojnicz	Ostrów Pohorecki	Rudki	Komarno
Olszyny	Chrzanów	Chrzanów	Ostrów Szlachecki	Bochnia	Bochnia
Onyszkowce	Bóbrka	Strzeliska Nowe	Ostrowczyk	Trembowla	Strusów
Opacie	Jasło	Jasło	Ostrowczyk Polny	Złoczów	Białykamień
Opacionka	Pilzno	Brzostek	Ostrówek	Mielec	Radomyśl Wiel.
Opaka	Cieszanów	Lubaczów	Ostrówek	Tarnobrzeg	Tarnobrzeg
Opaka	Drohobycz	Drohobycz	Ostrowice	Cieszanów	Lubaczów
Opaki	Złoczów	Sassów	Ostrowice	Kołomea	Gwozdźiec
Opaleniska	Łańcut	Leżajsk	Ostrowsko	Nowy Targ	Nowy Targ
Oparówka	Jasło	Frysztak	Ostrowy Baranowskie	Kolbuszowa	Majdan
Opary	Drohobycz	Drohobycz	Ostrowy Ruszowskie	Kolbuszowa	Majdan
Opatkowice	Wieliczka	Podgórze	Ostrożce	Mościska	Mościska
Oplucko	Kam. Strumiłowa	Radziechów	Ostrusza	Grybów	Bobowa

Town	Main District	Subdistrict	Town	Main District	Subdistrict
Ostrynia	Tłumacz	Niźniów	Pawłokoma	Brzozów	Dynów
Ostrznica	Chrzanów	Trzebina	Pawłosiów	Jarosław	Jarosław
Oświęcim	Biała	Oświęcim	Pawłów	Dąbrowa	Dąbrowa
Oszanica	Jaworów	Jaworów	Pawłów	Kam. Strumiłowa	Chołojów
Otalez	Mielec	Radomyśl Wiel.	Paździmirz	Sokal	Krystynopol
Otfinów	Dąbrowa	Dąbrowa	Peczenia	Przemyślany	Gliniany
Ottenhausen	Gródek	Janów	Peczeniżyn	Kołomea	Peczeniżyn
Ottynia	Tłumacz	Ottynia	Peim	Myślenice	Myślenice
Ottyniowice	Bóbrka	Chodorów	Pełkinie	Jarosław	Jarosław
Owieczka	Limanowa	Limanowa	Pełnatycze	Jarosław	Jarosław
Ożanna	Łańcut	Leżajsk	Peratyń	Kam. Strumiłowa	Radziechów
Ożańsko	Jarosław	Jarosław	Perechrestne	Kossów	Żabie
Ożarowce	Złoczów	Złoczów	Perekosy	Kalusz	Wojniłów
Ożenna	Krosno	Dukla	Peremiłów	Husiatyn	Chorostków
Ozimina	Sambor	Sambor	Perenówka	Rohatyn	Rohatyn
Ożomla	Jaworów	Jaworów	Perepelniki	Złoczów	Zborów
Ożydów	Brody	Sokołówka	Pererów	Kołomea	Kołomea
Ożydów	Złoczów	Olesko	Perespa	Sokal	Tartaków
Packowice	Mościska	Hussaków	Peretoki	Sokal	Sokal
Packowice	Przemyśl	Niżankowice	Perla	Brzesko	Brzesko
Pacław	Bircza	Dobromil	Perłowce	Stanisławów	Halicz
Pacyków	Dolina	Dolina	Persenkówka	Lemberg	Zniesienie
Paczek Gorzycki	Tarnobrzeg	Tarnobrzeg	Perwiatycze	Sokal	Tartaków
Paczołtowice	Chrzanów	Trzebina	Petlikowce	Buczacz	Buczacz
Padew	Mielec	Mielec	Petlikowce Nowe	Buczacz	Buczacz
Padew Narodowa	Mielec	Mielec	Petlikowce Stare	Buczacz	Buczacz
Pagorzyna	Gorlice	Gorlice	Pętna	Gorlice	Gorlice
Pajówka	Skałat	Grzymałów	Petranka	Kalusz	Kalusz
Pakość	Mościska	Mościska	Petryków	Tarnopol	Tarnopol
Pakoszówka	Sanok	Sanok	Petryków	Tłumacz	Uście Zielone
Palcza	Wadowice	Kalwarya	Pewel	Żywiec	Zabłocie
Palen	Tarnobrzeg	Rozwadów	Pewel Mała	Żywiec	Zabłocie
Paleśnica	Brzesko	Czchów	Pewel Wielka	Żywiec	Zabłocie
Palikrowy	Brody	Podkamień	Pewlka	Żywiec	Zabłocie
Palszowice	Wadowice	Zator	Piadyki	Kołomea	Kołomea
Panasówka	Brody	Załoźce	Pianowice	Sambor	Sambor
Panasówka	Skałat	Skałat	Piaseczna	Żydaczów	Rozdól
Paniczna	Stanisławów	Stanisławów	Piaski	Brody	Leszniów
Paniowce	Borszczów	Mielnica	Piaski	Brzesko	Czchów
Paniszczów	Lisko	Lutowiska	Piaski	Lemberg	Szczerzec
Pankowce	Brody	Podkamień	Piaski	Mościska	Sądowa Wisznia
Panowice	Podhajce	Zawałów	Piaski	Rudki	Komarno
Pantalicha	Trembowla	Strusów	Piaski	Wieliczka	Podgórze
Pantalowice	Łańcut	Kańczuga	Piątkowa	Bircza	Bircza
Papiernia	Trembowla	Janów	Piątkowa	Nowy Sącz	Nowy Sącz
Papnortno	Bircza	Dobromil	Piątkowa	Rzeszów	Błazowa
Parchacz	Sokal	Krystynopol	Piątkowice	Mielec	Radomyśl Wiel.
Parkosz	Pilzno	Pilzno	Piechoty	Mielec	Mielec
Partyń	Tarnów	Zabno	Pieczarna	Zaleszczyki	Zaleszczyki
Partynia	Mielec	Radomyśl Wiel.	Pieczychwosty	Żółkiew	Kulików
Parypsy	Rawa Ruska	Niemerów	Pieczygory	Sokal	Warez
Paryszeże	Nadwórna	Nadwórna	Piekiełko	Limanowa	Limanowa
Pasicka	Dąbrowa	Dąbrowa	Pielawa	Buczacz	Buczacz
Pasicki Zubrzyckie	Lemberg	Winniki	Pielnia	Sanok	Nowtanice
Pasieczna	Nadwórna	Nadwórna	Pień	Mielec	Radomyśl Wiel.
Pasierbice	Bochnia	Wiśnicz Nowy	Pieniaki	Brody	Podkamień
Paszczyna	Ropczyce	Ropczyce	Pieniążkowice	Nowy Targ	Nowy Targ
Paszkówka	Wadowice	Zator	Pierszyce	Dąbrowa	Dąbrowa
Paszowa	Lisko	Lisko	Pierzchów	Wieliczka	Klasno
Paszyn	Nowy Sącz	Nowy Sącz	Pierzchowice	Wieliczka	Klasno
Pauszówka	Czortków	Jagielnica	Pietbuce	Bircza	Dobromil
Pawełcza	Stanisławów	Stanisławów	Pietniczany	Bóbrka	Bóbrka
Pawęzów	Tarnów	Zabno	Pietniczany	Stryj	Stryj
Pawlikowice	Wieliczka	Klasno	Pietrusza Wola	Jasło	Frysztak

Town	Main District	Subdistrict	Town	Main District	Subdistrict
Pietrycze	Złoczów	Białykamień	Pobereże	Stanisławów	Jezupol
Pietrzejowa	Ropczyce	Ropczyce	Pobidno	Sanok	Sanok
Pietrzykowice	Żywiec	Zabłocie	Pobiedz	Wadowice	Zator
Pikarówka	Rzeszów	Czudec	Pobitno	Rzeszów	Rzeszów
Pikorowice	Jarosław	Sienawa	Pobocz	Złoczów	Sassów
Pikulice	Przemyśl	Przemyśl	Pobreczyn	Limanowa	Limanowa
Pikułowice	Lemberg	Jaryczów	Pobuk	Stryj	Skole
Piła	Chrzanów	Chrzanów	Pobuzany	Kam. Strumiłowa	Busk
Piłatkowce	Borszczów	Borszczów	Pochówka	Bohordczany	Bohordczany
Pilichów	Tarnobrzeg	Rozwadów	Poczajowice	Drohobycz	Drohobycz
Pilipy	Kołomea	Kołomea	Poczapińce	Tarnopol	Tarnopol
Piły	Żółkiew	Żółkiew	Podberesec	Lemberg	Winniki
Pilznionek	Pilzno	Pilzno	Podbereż	Dolina	Bolechów
Pilzno	Pilzno	Pilzno	Podbereżce	Brody	Załoźce
Piniany	Sambor	Sambor	Podbereżec	Brody	Brody
Piotrkowice	Tarnów	Tuchów	Podborce	Lemberg	Winniki
Piotrów	Horodenka	Obertyn	Podborze	Dąbrowa	Dąbrowa
Piotrówka	Krosno	Dukla	Podborze	Mielec	Radomyśl Wiel.
Pisarowce	Sanok	Sanok	Podborze	Wieliczka	Klasno
Pisary	Chrzanów	Trzebina	Podbrzezie	Brzesko	Czchów
Pisarzowa	Limanowa	Limanowa	Podbuz	Drohobycz	Drohobycz
Pisarzowice	Biała	Kęty	Podbuże	Rohatyń	Rohatyń
Pistyn	Kossów	Pistyn	Podciemne	Lemberg	Nawarya
Piszczatynce	Borszczów	Borszczów	Podczerwone	Nowy Targ	Nowy Targ
Pitrycz	Stanisławów	Halicz	Podegrodzie	Nowy Sącz	Stary Sącz
Piwniczna	Nowy Sącz	Piwniczna	Podemszczyzna	Cieszanów	Cieszanów
Piwoda	Jarosław	Sienawa	Podfilipie	Borszczów	Skała
Piwowszczyzna	Sokal	Bełż	Podgać	Mościska	Mościska
Piżany	Żydaczów	Żydaczów	Podgórzany	Trembowla	Trembowla
Płaszów	Wieliczka	Podgórze	Podgórze	Wieliczka	Podgórze
Płaucza Mała	Brzeżany	Kozłów	Podgórze	Wieliczka	Podgórze
Płaucza Wielka	Brzeżany	Kozłów	Podgrodzie	Pilzno	Dębica
Pławie	Stryj	Skole	Podgrodzie	Rohatyń	Rohatyń
Pławna	Grybów	Bobowa	Podgrodzie	Stanisławów	Halicz
Pławo	Mielec	Radomyśl Wiel.	Podhajce	Podhajce	Podhajce
Pławy	Biała	Oświęcim	Podhajczyki	Kołomea	Gwozdźiec
Płaza	Chrzanów	Chrzanów	Podhajczyki	Przemyślany	Gliniany
Płazów	Cieszanów	Narol	Podhajczyki	Rudki	Rudki
Płazówka	Kolbuszowa	Majdan	Podhajczyki	Trembowla	Janów
Plebanówka	Trembowla	Trembowla	Podhajczyki	Złoczów	Zborów
Pleników	Przemyślany	Dunajowce	Podhorce	Bóbrka	Brzozdowiec
Pleskowce	Tarnopol	Tarnopol	Podhorce	Rudki	Komarno
Pleśna	Tarnów	Tarnów	Podhorce	Stryj	Stryj
Pleśniany	Złoczów	Zborów	Podhorce	Stryj	Stryj
Pleśniany	Złoczów	Złoczów	Podhorki	Kalusz	Kalusz
Pleśników	Złoczów	Gologory	Podhorodce	Stryj	Skole
Pleszowice	Mościska	Hussaków	Podhorodyszcze	Bóbrka	Mikalajów
Pleszowice	Przemyśl	Przemyśl	Podhybie	Wadowice	Kalwarya
Pletenice	Przemyślany	Przemyślany	Podjarków	Bóbrka	Mikalajów
Plichów	Brzeżany	Brzeżany	Podkamień	Brody	Podkamień
Płoki	Chrzanów	Chrzanów	Podkamień	Rohatyń	Rohatyń
Płonne	Sanok	Bukowsko	Podkościele	Dąbrowa	Dąbrowa
Płoskie	Staremiasto	Staremiasto	Podlankowina	Przemyśl	Dubiecko
Płotycz	Tarnopol	Tarnopol	Podlesie	Buczacz	Buczacz
Płotycza	Brzeżany	Kozowa	Podlesie	Skałat	Grzymałów
Płowe	Kam. Strumiłowa	Witków Nowy	Podlesie	Złoczów	Olesko
Płowie	Sanok	Sanok	Podlesie Dębowe	Tarnów	Żabno
Płozówka	Rzeszów	Głogów	Podleszany	Mielec	Mielec
Płuchów	Złoczów	Złoczów	Podłęże	Bochnia	Bochnia
Pluty	Mielec	Mielec	Podłęże	Tarnobrzeg	Tarnobrzeg
Pniatyn	Przemyślany	Przemyślany	Podlipce	Złoczów	Złoczów
Pnikut	Mościska	Mościska	Podlipie	Dąbrowa	Dąbrowa
Pniów	Nadwórna	Nadwórna	Podliski	Bóbrka	Chodorów
Pniów	Tarnobrzeg	Radomyśl	Podliski	Mościska	Sądowa Wisznia

Town	Main District	Subdistrict	Town	Main District	Subdistrict
Podliski Małe	Lemberg	Jaryczów	Polana	Lemberg	Szczerzec
Podliski Wielkie	Lemberg	Jaryczów	Polana	Lisko	Lutowiska
Podłopień	Limanowa	Limanowa	Polana	Staremiasto	Chyrów
Podłuby Wielki	Jaworów	Jaworów	Polańczyk	Lisko	Baligród
Podłuby Małe	Jaworów	Jaworów	Polanica	Dolina	Bolechów
Podmajerz	Nowy Sącz	Stary Sącz	Polanka	Krosno	Dukla
Podmanasterek	Sambor	Sambor	Polanka	Lemberg	Nawarya
Podmanastereż	Bóbrka	Bóbrka	Polanka	Myślenice	Myślenice
Podmichale	Kalusz	Kalusz	Polanka	Wadowice	Zator
Podmichałowce	Rohatyń	Rohatyń	Polanka Wielka	Biała	Oświęcim
Podmoszce	Przemyśl	Niżankowice	Polanki	Kossów	Żabie
Podniebyłe	Krosno	Dukla	Polanki	Lisko	Baligród
Podniestrzany	Bóbrka	Brzozdowiec	Polany	Grybów	Grybów
Podobin	Limanowa	Mszana dolna	Polany	Krosno	Dukla
Podolany	Wadowice	Kalwarya	Polany	Żólkiew	Żólkiew
Podolany	Wieliczka	Klasno	Polany Surowiczne	Sanok	Rymanów
Podolce	Rudki	Komarno	Poleśniki	Buczacz	Buczacz
Podole	Mielec	Radomyśl Wiel.	Polna	Grybów	Grybów
Podole	Nowy Sącz	Nowy Sącz	Połom Mały	Brzesko	Czchów
Podolsze	Wadowice	Zator	Połomeja	Pilzno	Pilzno
Podpieczary	Tłumacz	Tyśmienica	Połonice	Przemyślany	Gliniany
Podrudne	Kam. Strumiłowa	Dobrotwor	Połoniczna	Kam. Strumiłowa	Chołojów
Podrzyce	Nowy Sącz	Nowy Sącz	Połowce	Czortków	Jagielnica
Podsadki	Lemberg	Nawarya	Połowe	Kam. Strumiłowa	Kam. Strumiłowa
Podsmykowce	Tarnopol	Tarnopol	Połrzecki	Limanowa	Mszana dolna
Podsosnów	Bóbrka	Mikalajów	Połtew	Przemyślany	Gliniany
Podstolice	Wieliczka	Klasno	Poluchów Mały	Przemyślany	Przemyślany
Podsuchy	Dolina	Rożniatów	Poluchów Wielki	Przemyślany	Gliniany
Podszumlańce	Rohatyń	Bursztyn	Polupanówka	Skałat	Skałat
Podubce	Rawa Ruska	Uhnów	Połwieś	Wadowice	Zator
Podusilna	Przemyślany	Przemyślany	Pomianowa	Brzesko	Brzesko
Podusów	Przemyślany	Przemyślany	Pomonieta	Rohatyń	Rohatyń
Podwale	Brzesko	Radlów	Pomorce	Buczacz	Jazłowice
Podwerbce	Horodenka	Obertyn	Pomorzany	Złoczów	Pomorzany
Podwinie	Rohatyń	Rohatyń	Ponice	Myślenice	Jordanów
Podwołoczyska	Skałat	Podwołoczyska	Ponikew	Wadowice	Wadowice
Podwysoka	Śniatyn	Śniatyn	Ponikowica Mała	Brody	Brody
Podwysokie	Brzeżany	Brzeżany	Ponikwa	Brody	Brody
Podwysokie	Rudki	Komarno	Ponikwa Wielka	Złoczów	Olesko
Podzamcze	Kam. Strumiłowa	Kam. Strumiłowa	Popardowa	Nowy Sącz	Łabowa
Podzamczek	Buczacz	Buczacz	Popędzyna	Bochnia	Bochnia
Podziacz	Przemyśl	Przemyśl	Popielany	Lemberg	Szczerzec
Podzwierzynice	Łańcut	Łańcut	Popiele	Drohobycz	Drohobycz
Podzwierzynice	Rudki	Komarno	Popielniki	Śniatyn	Zabłotów
Pogórska Wola	Tarnów	Tarnów	Popławniki	Rohatyń	Bursztyn
Pogorzałka	Nisko	Nisko	Popowce	Brody	Podkamień
Pogorzany	Limanowa	Limanowa	Popowce	Zaleszczyki	Tłuste
Pogorzeliska	Rawa Ruska	Magierów	Popowice	Mościska	Hussaków
Pogorzyce	Chrzanów	Chrzanów	Popowice	Nowy Sącz	Stary Sącz
Pogwizdów	Bochnia	Wiśnicz Nowy	Popowice	Przemyśl	Przemyśl
Pogwizdów	Kolbuszowa	Ranizów	Popowice	Tarnobrzeg	Radomyśl
Pogwizdów	Łańcut	Łańcut	Poraba	Brzozów	Dynów
Pogwizdów	Rzeszów	Głogów	Porąbka	Biała	Kęty
Pohar	Stryj	Skole	Porąbka	Limanowa	Limanowa
Poherbce	Złoczów	Zborów	Porąbka Mała	Brzesko	Czchów
Pohonia	Tłumacz	Tyśmienica	Porąbka Uszewska	Brzesko	Brzesko
Pohorylec	Dolina	Rożniatów	Poraj	Krosno	Dukla
Pohorylec	Przemyślany	Gliniany	Poraż	Lisko	Lisko
Pojawce	Brzesko	Szczurowa	Porchowa	Buczacz	Barysz
Pojło	Kalusz	Kalusz	Poręba	Myślenice	Myślenice
Pokrepiwna	Brzeżany	Kozłów	Poręba Wielka	Biała	Oświęcim
Pokrowce	Żydaczów	Żydaczów	Poręba Wielka	Limanowa	Mszana dolna
Polana	Bircza	Dobromil			

Town	Main District	Subdistrict	Town	Main District	Subdistrict
Poręba Wolna	Tarnów	Tarnów	Poznanka Gniła	Skałat	Skałat
Poręba Żegoty	Chrzanów	Chrzanów	Poznanka Hetmańska	Skałat	Grzymałów
Poręby	Ropczyce	Ropczyce	Pozowice	Wadowice	Zator
Poręby	Sanok	Rymanów	Pralkowce	Przemyśl	Przemyśl
Poręby Dębskie	Tarnobrzeg	Tarnobrzeg	Prehinsko	Dolina	Rożniatów
Poręby Dymarskie	Kolbuszowa	Kolbuszowa	Prelukie	Sanok	Bukowsko
Poręby Furmanskie	Tarnobrzeg	Tarnobrzeg	Prinzenthal	Staremiasto	Chyrów
Poręby Kupińskie	Kolbuszowa	Kolbuszowa	Probabin	Horodenka	Horodenka
Poręby Kupińskie	Rzeszów	Głogów	Probużna	Husiatyn	Probużna
Poremba	Bochnia	Wiśnicz Nowy	Prochowce	Przemyśl	Przemyśl
Pornczyn	Brzeżany	Narajów	Procisne	Lisko	Lutowiska
Porohy	Borhodczany	Sołotwina	Prokocim	Wieliczka	Podgórze
Porohy	Borhodczany	Sołotwina	Prokurowa	Kossów	Pistyn
Poronin	Nowy Targ	Nowy Targ	Proniatyn	Tarnopol	Tarnopol
Porszna	Lemberg	Nawarya	Proszowa	Tarnopol	Mikulińce
Poruby	Jaworów	Jaworów	Proszowki	Bochnia	Bochnia
Porudenko	Jaworów	Jaworów	Protesy	Żydaczów	Żurawno
Porudno	Jaworów	Jaworów	Prowala	Żólkiew	Żólkiew
Porzecze Grunt	Rudki	Komarno	Pruchnik	Jarosław	Pruchnik
Porzecze Nadwórne	Rudki	Komarno	Prunka	Grybów	Grybów
Porzycze Janowskie	Gródek	Janów	Prusie	Rawa Ruska	Rawa Ruska
Porzycze Lubieńkie	Gródek	Gródek	Prusinów	Sokal	Bełż
Posada Chyrowska	Staremiasto	Chyrów	Prusy	Lemberg	Zniesienie
Posada Dolna	Sanok	Rymanów	Prusy	Sambor	Sambor
Posada Felsztyńska	Staremiasto	Felsztyn	Prybyń	Przemyślany	Świrz
Posada Górna	Sanok	Rymanów	Prysowce	Złoczów	Zborów
Posada Jacmierska	Sanok	Rymanów	Przebieczany	Wieliczka	Klasno
Posada Jasliska	Sanok	Rymanów	Przecieszyn	Biała	Oświęcim
Posada Liska	Lisko	Lisko	Przeciszów	Wadowice	Zator
Posada Nowomiejska	Bircza	Nowemiasto	Przecław	Mielec	Radomyśl Wiel.
Posada Olchowska	Sanok	Sanok	Przeczyca	Pilzno	Jodłowa
Posada Rybotycka	Bircza	Rybotycze	Przedbórz	Kolbuszowa	Kolbuszowa
Posada Sanocka	Sanok	Sanok	Przedbórze	Jaworów	Kraków iec
Posada Zarszyńska	Sanok	Rymanów	Przedmieście Strzyz.	Rzeszów	Strzyżów
Posadowa	Grybów	Grybów	Przedmieście	Buczacz	Jazłowice
Posagowa	Nowy Sącz	Nowy Sącz	Przedmieście	Łańcut	Łańcut
Posiecz	Bohordczany	Lysiec	Przedmieście	Przemyśl	Dubiecko
Postołów	Lisko	Lisko	Przedmieście	Rawa Ruska	Niemerów
Postołówka	Husiatyn	Chorostków	Przedmieście	Ropczyce	Sędziszów
Posuchów	Brzeżany	Brzeżany	Przedmieście Czudeckie	Rzeszów	Czudec
Poswierz	Rohatyń	Bursztyn	Przedmieście Dynowskie	Brzozów	Dynów
Potakówka	Jasło	Jasło	Przedrzymichy Małe	Żólkiew	Kulików
Potoczany	Przemyślany	Dunajowce	Przedrzymichy Wielkie	Żólkiew	Kulików
Potoczek	Śniatyn	Śniatyn	Przędzel	Nisko	Rudnik
Potoczyska	Horodenka	Horodenka	Przędzielnica	Bircza	Dobromil
Potok	Brzeżany	Brzeżany	Przegnojów	Przemyślany	Gliniany
Potok	Buczacz	Potok	Przegonina	Gorlice	Gorlice
Potok	Krosno	Dukla	Przekopana	Przemyśl	Przemyśl
Potok	Rawa Ruska	Lubycza	Przemiwółki	Żólkiew	Kulików
Potok	Rohatyń	Rohatyń	Przemoziec	Buczacz	Jazłowice
Potok Czarny	Nadwórna	Delatyn	Przemyśl	Przemyśl	Przemyśl
Potok Wielki	Staremiasto	Staremiasto	Przemyślany	Przemyślany	Przemyślany
Potom	Bochnia	Wiśnicz Nowy	Przemyślów	Sokal	Bełż
Potorzyca	Sokal	Sokal	Przeniczniki	Tłumacz	Tyśmienica
Pututory	Brzeżany	Brzeżany	Przenosza	Limanowa	Limanowa
Potylicz	Rawa Ruska	Rawa Ruska	Przerośl	Nadwórna	Nadwórna
Potylicze	Tłumacz	Tłumacz	Przestanie	Żólkiew	Gross-Mosty
Powerchów	Rudki	Komarno	Przewłoczna	Brody	Toporów
Powitno	Gródek	Janów	Przewodów	Sokal	Bełż
Powrożnik	Nowy Sącz	Muszyna	Przewołka	Buczacz	Buczacz
Poznachowice Dolne	Wieliczka	Klasno	Przewórsk	Łańcut	Przeworsk
Poznachowice Górne	Wieliczka	Klasno	Przewóz	Tarnobrzeg	Baranów

Town	Main District	Subdistrict	Town	Main District	Subdistrict
Przewóz	Wieliczka	Podgórze	Rabe	Lisko	Ustrzyki Dolne
Przewoziec	Kalusz	Wojniłów	Rabka	Myślenice	Jordanów
Przewrotne	Kolbuszowa	Raniżów	Rąbkowa	Nowy Sącz	Nowy Sącz
Przewrotne	Rzeszów	Głogów	Raby	Lisko	Baligród
Przyborów	Brzesko	Brzesko	Rachin	Dolina	Dolina
Przyborów	Żywiec	Zabłocie	Raciborsko	Wieliczka	Klasno
Przybówka	Jasło	Frysztak	Raciborzany	Limanowa	Limanowa
Przybrodz	Wadowice	Zator	Raciechowice	Wieliczka	Klasno
Przybyłów	Grybów	Bobowa	Racławice	Gorlice	Gorlice
Przybyłów	Tłumacz	Chocimirz	Racławice	Nisko	Nisko
Przybysławice	Brzesko	Radłów	Racławoka	Rzeszów	Rzeszów
Przybyszów	Sanok	Bukowsko	Raczyna	Jarosław	Pruchnik
Przybyszówka	Rzeszów	Rzeszów	Radajowice	Nowy Sącz	Nowy Sącz
Przychojce	Łańcut	Leżajsk	Radawa	Jarosław	Sienawa
Przycorów	Pilzno	Dębica	Radcza	Bohordczany	Lysiec
Przydonica	Nowy Sącz	Nowy Sącz	Radelicz	Drohobycz	Drohobycz
Przykop	Mielec	Mielec	Radenice	Mościska	Mościska
Przyłbice	Jaworów	Jaworów	Radlna	Tarnów	Tarnów
Przylek	Mielec	Mielec	Radłów	Brzesko	Radłów
Przyleków	Żywiec	Zabłocie	Radłówice	Sambor	Sambor
Przyłkowice	Wadowice	Kalwarya	Radochońce	Mościska	Hussaków
Przysicki	Jasło	Jasło	Radocza	Wadowice	Wadowice
Przysietnica	Brzozów	Brzozów	Radoczyna	Gorlice	Gorlice
Przysietnica	Nowy Sącz	Piwniczna	Radomyśl	Tarnobrzeg	Radomyśl
Przyslup	Gorlice	Gorlice	Radomyśl Wielkie	Mielec	Radomyśl Wiel.
Przyslup	Lisko	Baligród	Radoszcz	Dąbrowa	Dąbrowa
Przysłup	Kalusz	Kalusz	Radoszyce	Sanok	Bukowsko
Przyszów Kameralny	Nisko	Nisko	Radruz	Rawa Ruska	Niemerów
Przyszów Szlachecki	Nisko	Nisko	Radwan	Dąbrowa	Dąbrowa
Przyszów Szlachecki	Tarnobrzeg	Rozwadów	Radwańce	Sokal	Krystynopol
Przyszowa	Limanowa	Limanowa	Radwanowice	Chrzanów	Trzebina
Psary	Chrzanów	Trzebina	Radymno	Jarosław	Radymno
Psary	Rohatyń	Rohatyń	Radymno	Jarosław	Radymno
Pstrągowa	Ropczyce	Wielopole	Radzichów	Żywiec	Zabłocie
Pstrążne	Gorlice	Gorlice	Radziechów	Kam. Strumiłowa	Radziechów
Pstręgówka	Jasło	Frysztak	Radziejowa	Lisko	Baligród
Ptaszkowa	Grybów	Grybów	Radziszów	Myślenice	Myślenice
Ptaszniki	Kam. Strumiłowa	Dobrotwor	Rajsko	Biała	Oświęcim
Ptonus	Tarnobrzeg	Rozwadów	Rajsko	Brzesko	Szczurowa
Pukaczów	Kam. Strumiłowa	Radziechów	Rajsko	Lisko	Baligród
Pukarowce	Stanisławów	Hałicz	Rajsko	Wieliczka	Klasno
Pukienicze	Stryj	Stryj	Rajtarowice	Mościska	Hussaków
Puklaki	Borszczów	Skała	Rakobuty	Kam. Strumiłowa	Busk
Puków	Rohatyń	Rohatyń	Raków	Dolina	Dolina
Pułanki	Jasło	Frysztak	Rakowa	Sambor	Sambor
Puławy	Sanok	Rymanów	Rakowa	Sanok	Tyrawa woloska
Pustawola	Jasło	Jasło	Rakowężyk	Kołomea	Peczeniżyn
Pustomyty	Lemberg	Nawarya	Rakowice	Horodenka	Czernelica
Pustynia	Pilzno	Dębica	Rakowice	Lemberg	Szczerzec
Putiatycze	Gródek	Gródek	Rakowice	Podhajce	Złotniki
Putiatycze	Mościska	Sądowa Wisznia	Rakszawa	Łańcut	Żolynia
Putiatynce	Rohatyń	Rohatyń	Raniowice	Drohobycz	Drohobycz
Putków	Ropczyce	Ropczyce	Ranisów	Rzeszów	Głogów
Puźniki	Buczacz	Barysz	Raniżów	Kolbuszowa	Raniżów
Puźniki	Tłumacz	Chocimirz	Raniżów Kolonie	Rzeszów	Głogów
Pychowice	Wieliczka	Podgórze	Raniżowska Wola	Kolbuszowa	Raniżów
Pyszkowce	Buczacz	Jazłowice	Raszków	Horodenka	Horodenka
Pysznica	Nisko	Ulanów	Rasztowce	Skałat	Touste
Pyzówka	Nowy Targ	Nowy Targ	Ratawica	Sanok	Bukowsko
Raba Niżna	Limanowa	Mszana dolna	Ratnawy	Brzesko	Wojnicz
Raba Wyżna	Myślenice	Jordanów	Ratulów	Nowy Targ	Nowy Targ
Rabczyce	Drohobycz	Drohobycz	Ratyszcze	Brody	Zołożce

Town	Main District	Subdistrict	Town	Main District	Subdistrict
Rawa Ruska	Rawa Ruska	Rawa Ruska	Ropki	Gorlice	Gorlice
Ray	Brzeżany	Brzeżany	Ropki	Nisko	Rudnik
Raybrot	Bochnia	Wiśnicz Nowy	Rosechy	Staremiasto	Chyrów
Raycza	Żywiec	Zabłocie	Rosenberg	Lemberg	Szczerzec
Rażniów	Brody	Sokołówka	Rosochacz	Czortków	Ulaszkowce
Rdzawa	Bochnia	Wiśnicz Nowy	Rosochate	Lisko	Lutowiska
Rdzawka	Myślenice	Jordanów	Rosochowaciec	Podhajce	Złotniki
Rdziostów	Nowy Sącz	Nowy Sącz	Rosochowaciec	Skałat	Skałat
Rechtberg	Jaworów	Krakówiec	Rosolin	Lisko	Lutowiska
Reczpol	Przemyśl	Krzywcza	Rostoka	Bircza	Bircza
Regetów Niżny	Gorlice	Gorlice	Rostoki Dolne	Lisko	Baligród
Regetów Wyżny	Gorlice	Gorlice	Roszniów	Tłumacz	Uście Zielone
Regulice	Chrzanów	Chrzanów	Rottenhan	Gródek	Janów
Rehberg	Mościska	Mościska	Równe	Krosno	Dukla
Rehfeld	Bóbrka	Bóbrka	Równia	Kalusz	Kalusz
Reichau	Cieszanów	Lubaczów	Równia	Lisko	Ustrzyki Dolne
Reichenbach	Lemberg	Szczerzec	Rozalin	Tarnobrzeg	Tarnobrzeg
Reichsheim	Mielec	Mielec	Rozalówka	Sokal	Sokal
Rekszyn	Przemyślany	Dunajowce	Rożanka	Jasło	Frysztak
Remenów	Lemberg	Jaryczów	Rożanka	Ropczyce	Wielopole
Reniów	Brody	Zołożce	Rożanka	Żółkiew	Gross-Mosty
Repechów	Bóbrka	Strzeliska Nowe	Rożanka Niżna	Stryj	Skole
Repużyńce	Horodenka	Czernelica	Rożanka Wyżna	Stryj	Skole
Reszniate	Dolina	Rożniatów	Rożanówka	Zaleszczyki	Tłuste
Rochynie	Kołomea	Gwozdźiec	Rozbórz	Łańcut	Przeworsk
Rocmirowa	Nowy Sącz	Nowy Sącz	Rozbórz Długi	Jarosław	Pruchnik
Roczyny	Wadowice	Andrychów	Rozbórz Okrągły	Jarosław	Pruchnik
Rodatycze	Gródek	Gródek	Rozdół	Żydaczów	Rozdól
Rodze	Wadowice	Zator	Rożdżałów	Sokal	Tartaków
Rogi	Krosno	Dukla	Rozdziałowice	Rudki	Rudki
Rogi	Nowy Sącz	Stary Sącz	Rozdziele	Bochnia	Wiśnicz Nowy
Rogoźnica	Rzeszów	Głogów	Rozdziele	Gorlice	Gorlice
Rogoźnik	Nowy Targ	Nowy Targ	Rozdziele	Nowy Sącz	Nowy Sącz
Rogoźno	Łańcut	Przeworsk	Rozembark	Gorlice	Gorlice
Roguźno	Jaworów	Jaworów	Rozeń Mały	Kossów	Kuty
Roguźno	Sambor	Sambor	Rozeń Wielki	Kossów	Kuty
Roguźno	Żydaczów	Żydaczów	Rozenburg	Bircza	Dobromil
Rohaczyn	Brzeżany	Narajów	Rozhadów	Złoczów	Pomorzany
Rohatyń	Rohatyń	Rohatyń	Rozhurcze	Stryj	Stryj
Rojatyń	Sokal	Sokal	Rozkochów	Chrzanów	Chrzanów
Rojówka	Nowy Sącz	Nowy Sącz	Rozkowice	Nowy Sącz	Nowy Sącz
Rokieciny	Myślenice	Jordanów	Rożniatów	Dolina	Rożniatów
Rokietnica	Jarosław	Pruchnik	Rożniatów	Jarosław	Jarosław
Rokitno	Gródek	Janów	Rożniaty	Mielec	Mielec
Roków	Wadowice	Wadowice	Rożnów	Śniatyn	Zabłotów
Rokówkat	Husiatyn	Chorostków	Rożnowa	Wieliczka	Klasno
Rokszyce	Przemyśl	Przemyśl	Rozpucie	Bircza	Bircza
Rolikówka	Sokal	Sokal	Rozsochacz	Kołomea	Gwozdźiec
Rolów	Drohobycz	Drohobycz	Rozstajne	Krosno	Dukla
Romanów	Bóbrka	Mikalajów	Roztocki	Jasło	Jasło
Romanówka	Brody	Szczurowice	Roztoczki	Dolina	Bolechów
Romanówka	Kam. Strumiłowa	Stajanów	Roztoka	Brzesko	Wojnicz
Romanówka	Rudki	Komarno	Roztoka	Limanowa	Limanowa
Romanówka	Tarnopol	Tarnopol	Roztoka	Nowy Sącz	Nowy Sącz
Romanówka	Trembowla	Janów	Roztoka Mała	Nowy Sącz	Łabowa
Romaszówka	Czortków	Budzanów	Roztoka Wielka	Nowy Sącz	Łabowa
Ropa	Gorlice	Gorlice	Roztoka Zyterska	Nowy Sącz	Piwniczna
Ropczyce	Ropczyce	Ropczyce	Roztoki	Kossów	Kuty
Ropea Polska	Gorlice	Gorlice	Rożubowice	Przemyśl	Przemyśl
Ropianka	Krosno	Dukla	Rozulna	Borhodczany	Sołotwina
Ropica Ruska	Gorlice	Gorlice	Rozwadów	Tarnobrzeg	Rozwadów
Ropienka	Lisko	Lisko	Rozwadów	Tarnobrzeg	Rozwadów

Town	Main District	Subdistrict	Town	Main District	Subdistrict
Rozwadów	Żydaczów	Rozdól	Rusinówska Wola	Kolbuszowa	Majdan
Rozważ	Złoczów	Białykamień	Ruska Wieś	Przemyśl	Dubiecko
Rozwienica	Jarosław	Jarosław	Ruska Wieś	Rzeszów	Rzeszów
Rozworzany	Przemyślany	Gliniany	Ruskie	Lisko	Lutowiska
Rożyska	Skałat	Tarnoruda	Russów	Śniatyn	Śniatyn
Ruchniszcze	Kołomea	Gwozdźiec	Rustweczko	Mościska	Hussaków
Ruda	Bóbrka	Brzozdowiec	Ruszelczyce	Przemyśl	Krzywcza
Ruda	Brzesko	Radłów	Ruzdwiany	Rohatyń	Bursztyn
Ruda	Nisko	Rudnik	Ruzdwiany	Stanisławów	Hałicz
Ruda	Rawa Ruska	Magierów	Ruzdwiany	Trembowla	Strusów
Ruda	Rohatyń	Rohatyń	Rybaki	Wieliczka	Podgórze
Ruda	Ropczyce	Sędziszów	Rybarzowice	Biała	Lipnik
Ruda	Żydaczów	Żydaczów	Rybe Nowe	Limanowa	Limanowa
Ruda Justkowska	Tarnobrzeg	Rozwadów	Rybe Stare	Limanowa	Limanowa
Ruda Kameralna	Brzesko	Czchów	Rybień	Nowy Sącz	Łabowa
Ruda Kochanowska	Jaworów	Krakówiec	Rybitwy	Wieliczka	Podgórze
Ruda Kołtowska	Złoczów	Sassów	Rybne	Lisko	Baligród
Ruda Krakowiecka	Jaworów	Krakówiec	Rybnik	Drohobycz	Borysław
Ruda Krechowska	Żólkiew	Żólkiew	Rybniki	Brzeżany	Brzeżany
Ruda Lasowa	Rawa Ruska	Magierów	Rybno	Kossów	Kuty
Ruda Rożaniecka	Cieszanów	Narol	Rybno	Stanisławów	Stanisławów
Ruda Sielecka	Kam. Strumiłowa	Kam. Strumiłowa	Rybotycze	Bircza	Rybotycze
Ruda Zazamcze	Dąbrowa	Dąbrowa	Rybów	Złoczów	Złoczów
Rudance	Lemberg	Jaryczów	Rycerka Dolna	Żywiec	Zabłocie
Rudawa	Chrzanów	Trzebina	Rycerka Górna	Żywiec	Zabłocie
Rudawka	Bircza	Bircza	Rychcice	Drohobycz	Drohobycz
Rudawka	Lisko	Ustrzyki Dolne	Rychwald	Gorlice	Gorlice
Rudawka Jaśliska	Sanok	Rymanów	Rychwald	Tarnów	Tuchów
Rudawka Rymanowska	Sanok	Rymanów	Rychwald	Żywiec	Zabłocie
Rudec	Brody	Sokołówka	Rychwaldek	Żywiec	Zabłocie
Rudenka	Lisko	Lisko	Ryczka	Kossów	Kossów
Rudenko Lackie	Brody	Szczurowice	Ryczów	Wadowice	Zator
Rudenko Ruskie	Brody	Szczurowice	Ryczychów	Rudki	Komarno
Rudka	Brzesko	Wojnicz	Rydoduby	Czortków	Czortków
Rudka	Cieszanów	Narol	Rydzów	Mielec	Radomyśl Wiel.
Rudka	Jarosław	Pruchnik	Ryglice	Tarnów	Ryglice
Rudka	Tarnów	Zabno	Ryhów	Stryj	Skole
Rudki	Rudki	Rudki	Ryje	Limanowa	Limanowa
Rudna	Tarnów	Zabno	Rylowa	Brzesko	Szczurowa
Rudna Mała	Rzeszów	Głogów	Rymanów	Sanok	Rymanów
Rudna Wielka	Rzeszów	Głogów	Rymizowce	Złoczów	Złoczów
Rudnik	Myślenice	Myślenice	Rypianka	Kalusz	Kalusz
Rudnik	Nisko	Rudnik	Rypne	Dolina	Rożniatów
Rudnik	Wieliczka	Klasno	Ryszkowa Wola	Jarosław	Jarosław
Rudniki	Mościska	Mościska	Ryszyce	Wieliczka	Klasno
Rudniki	Podhajce	Podhajce	Rytro	Nowy Sącz	Piwniczna
Rudniki	Śniatyn	Zabłotów	Rzachowa	Brzesko	Szczurowa
Rudniki	Żydaczów	Rozdól	Rzaka	Wieliczka	Klasno
Rudno	Chrzanów	Trzebina	Rzatkowice	Mościska	Mościska
Rudno	Lemberg	Zniesienie	Rzeczyca Długa	Tarnobrzeg	Rozwadów
Rudolowice	Jarosław	Jarosław	Rzeczyca Okragla	Tarnobrzeg	Rozwadów
Rudy Rysie	Brzesko	Szczurowa	Rzędzianowice	Mielec	Mielec
Rukomysz	Buczacz	Buczacz	Rzędzin	Tarnów	Tarnów
Rumno	Rudki	Komarno	Rzędzińska Wola	Tarnów	Tarnów
Rumosz	Sokal	Sokal	Rzegocin	Ropczyce	Wielopole
Rungury	Kołomea	Peczeniżyn	Rzegocina	Bochnia	Wiśnicz Nowy
Rupniów	Limanowa	Limanowa	Rzeki	Limanowa	Limanowa
Rusianówka	Tarnopol	Tarnopol	Rzeklińce	Żólkiew	Gross-Mosty
Rusiłów	Buczacz	Potok	Rzemień	Mielec	Mielec
Rusiłów	Kam. Strumiłowa	Busk	Rzepedź	Sanok	Bukowsko
Rusin	Sokal	Warez	Rzepienik Strzyżowski	Gorlice	Rzepienik Strzyżewski
Rusinów	Kolbuszowa	Majdan	Rzepiennik Biskupi	Gorlice	Rzepienik Strzyżewski

Town	Main District	Subdistrict	Town	Main District	Subdistrict
Rzepińce	Buczacz	Jazłowice	Schodnica	Drohobycz	Borysław
Rzeplin	Jarosław	Pruchnik	Schönanger	Mielec	Radomyśl Wiel.
Rzepnik	Jasło	Frysztak	Schönthal	Gródek	Janów
Rzepnik	Krosno	Korczyna	Scianka	Złoczów	Gologory
Rzepniów	Kam. Strumiłowa	Busk	Ścianka	Buczacz	Potok
Rzęsna Polska	Lemberg	Zniesienie	Sędziszów	Ropczyce	Sędziszów
Rzęsna Ruska	Lemberg	Zniesienie	Sędziszowa	Grybów	Bobowa
Rzeszotary	Wieliczka	Klasno	Sękowa	Gorlice	Gorlice
Rzeszów	Rzeszów	Rzeszów	Sękowa Wola	Sanok	Nowtanice
Rzeszyca	Rawa Ruska	Uhnów	Semenów z Zieleńcem	Trembowla	Trembowla
Rzezawa	Bochnia	Bochnia	Semenówka	Horodenka	Czernelica
Rzochów	Mielec	Mielec	Semerówka	Jaworów	Jaworów
Rzozów	Wieliczka	Podgórze	Seneczów	Dolina	Dolina
Rzuchów	Łańcut	Leżajsk	Sępnica	Ropczyce	Ropczyce
Rzuchowa	Tarnów	Tarnów	Serafince	Horodenka	Horodenka
Rzyczki	Rawa Ruska	Rawa Ruska	Serdyca	Lemberg	Szczerzec
Rzyki	Wadowice	Andrychów	Seredce	Brody	Załóźce
Sabinówka	Kam. Strumiłowa	Stajanów	Seredne	Kalusz	Wojniłów
Sadek	Limanowa	Limanowa	Seredne	Podhajce	Zawałów
Sadki	Zaleszczyki	Uścieczko	Serednica	Lisko	Ustrzyki Dolne
Sadkowa	Jasło	Jasło	Seredni Małe	Lisko	Lutowiska
Sadkowa Góra	Mielec	Radomyśl Wiel.	Serednie Wielkie	Lisko	Lisko
Sadkowice	Mościska	Hussaków	Seredyńce	Tarnopol	Tarnopol
Sądowa Wisznia	Mościska	Sądowa Wiśnia	Serwiry	Złoczów	Jezierna
Sadzawa	Bohordczany	Bohordczany	Siarczana Góra	Wieliczka	Podgórze
Sadzawki	Skałat	Grzymałów	Siary	Gorlice	Gorlice
Sakowczyk	Lisko	Baligród	Sichów	Lemberg	Zniesienie
Salamonowa Górka	Dolina	Bolechów	Sidorów	Husiatyn	Husiatyn
Salasze	Rawa Ruska	Uhnów	Sidzina	Myślenice	Jordanów
Salmopol	Biała	Lipnik	Sidzina	Wieliczka	Podgórze
Salówka	Czortków	Jagielnica	Siebieczów	Sokal	Bełż
Sambor	Sambor	Sambor	Siechów	Stryj	Stryj
Samborek	Wieliczka	Podgórze	Siechowce	Tarnów	Tarnów
Samborówka	Tarnopol	Tarnopol	Sieciechów	Lemberg	Jaryczów
Samocice	Dąbrowa	Dąbrowa	Siedlanka	Kolbuszowa	Kolbuszowa
Samołuskowce	Husiatyn	Husiatyn	Siedlanka	Łańcut	Kańczuga
Sanka Północna	Chrzanów	Trzebina	Siedlanka	Łańcut	Leżajsk
Sanka Południowa	Chrzanów	Trzebina	Siedlce	Nowy Sącz	Nowy Sącz
Sanniki	Mościska	Sądowa Wisznia	Siedlec	Bochnia	Bochnia
Sanoczany	Przemyśl	Niżankowice	Siedlec	Chrzanów	Trzebina
Sanok	Sanok	Sanok	Siedlec	Tarnów	Zabno
Sanoka	Tarnów	Zabno	Siedliska	Bóbrka	Mikalajów
Sapahów	Stanisławów	Hałicz	Siedliska	Brzozów	Dynów
Sapieżanka	Kam. Strumiłowa	Kam. Strumiłowa	Siedliska	Grybów	Bobowa
Sapohów	Borszczów	Mielnica	Siedliska	Jasło	Jasło
Sapowa	Buczacz	Buczacz	Siedliska	Jaworów	Jaworów
Saranczuki	Brzeżany	Brzeżany	Siedliska	Krosno	Dukla
Sarnki	Bóbrka	Bóbrka	Siedliska	Lemberg	Nawarya
Sarnki Dolne	Rohatyń	Bursztyn	Siedliska	Przemyśl	Przemyśl
Sarnki Górne	Rohatyń	Bursztyn	Siedliska	Rawa Ruska	Rawa Ruska
Sarnki Średnie	Rohatyń	Bursztyn	Siedliska	Rzeszów	Tyczyn
Sarny	Jaworów	Krakówiec	Siedliska	Stanisławów	Hałicz
Sarny	Mościska	Mościska	Siedliska	Tarnów	Tuchów
Sarysz	Limanowa	Limanowa	Siedliszczany	Tarnobrzeg	Baranów
Sarzyna	Nisko	Rudnik	Siegenthal	Lisko	Ustrzyki Dolne
Sąsiadowice	Sambor	Sambor	Siekierczyce	Sambor	Sambor
Saska	Rudki	Komarno	Siekierczyn	Horodenka	Obertyn
Saska Kameralna	Drohobycz	Drohobycz	Siekierczyna	Grybów	Bobowa
Sassów	Złoczów	Sassów	Siekierzyńce	Husiatyn	Husiatyn
Sawa	Wieliczka	Klasno	Sieklerczyna	Limanowa	Limanowa
Sawaluski	Buczacz	Monasterzyska	Sieklówka Dolna	Jasło	Frysztak
Sawczyn	Sokal	Sokal	Sieklówka Górna	Jasło	Frysztak

Town	Main District	Subdistrict	Town	Main District	Subdistrict
Sielce	Stanisławów	Jezupol	Skomorochy Nowe	Rohatyń	Bursztyn
Sielec	Kam. Strumiłowa	Kam. Strumiłowa	Skomorochy Stare	Rohatyń	Bursztyn
Sielec	Przemyśl	Przemyśl	Skomorosze	Czortków	Budzanów
Sielec	Ropczyce	Sędziszów	Skopańce	Tarnobrzeg	Baranów
Sielec	Sambor	Sambor	Skopów	Przemyśl	Krzywcza
Sielec	Sokal	Krystynopol	Skopówka	Nadwórna	Lanczyn
Sielec	Tarnobrzeg	Tarnobrzeg	Skorodne	Lisko	Lutowiska
Sielnica	Przemyśl	Dubiecko	Skorodyńce	Czortków	Czortków
Siemakowce	Horodenka	Horodenka	Skotniki	Wieliczka	Podgórze
Siemakowce	Kołomea	Gwozdźiec	Skowiatyń	Zaleszczyki	Korolówka
Siemiakowce	Czortków	Czortków	Skretka	Nowy Sącz	Nowy Sącz
Siemianówka	Lemberg	Szczerzec	Skrudzina	Nowy Sącz	Stary Sącz
Siemiechów	Tarnów	Tuchów	Skrzydlna	Limanowa	Limanowa
Siemień	Żywiec	Zabłocie	Skrzynka	Dąbrowa	Szczucin
Siemiginów	Stryj	Stryj	Skrzynka	Wieliczka	Klasno
Siemikowce	Rohatyń	Bursztyn	Skrzypne	Nowy Targ	Nowy Targ
Siemuszowa	Sanok	Sanok	Skrzyszów	Ropczyce	Ropczyce
Sieniawa	Jarosław	Sienawa	Skurowa	Pilzno	Jodłowa
Sieniawa	Myślenice	Jordanów	Skwarzawa	Złoczów	Białykamień
Sieniawa	Sanok	Rymanów	Skwarzawa Nowa	Żólkiew	Żólkiew
Sieniawka	Cieszanów	Lubaczów	Skwarzawa Stara	Żólkiew	Żólkiew
Sienikowice	Podhajce	Złotniki	Skwirtne	Gorlice	Gorlice
Sieńków	Kam. Strumiłowa	Radziechów	Skyrsów	Tarnów	Tarnów
Sienna	Nowy Sącz	Nowy Sącz	Słabasz	Mościska	Sądowa Wisznia
Sienna	Żywiec	Zabłocie	Sławencin	Jasło	Jasło
Siennów	Łańcut	Kańczuga	Sławentyn	Podhajce	Zawałów
Siepietnica	Jasło	Jasło	Sławki	Gródek	Janów
Sierakosce	Przemyśl	Niżankowice	Sławna	Złoczów	Zborów
Sieraków	Wieliczka	Klasno	Sławna	Złoczów	Złoczów
Siercza	Wieliczka	Klasno	Śleszowice	Wadowice	Wadowice
Siersza	Chrzanów	Chrzanów	Ślęzaki	Tarnobrzeg	Baranów
Sietesz	Łańcut	Kańczuga	Śtiwki	Kalusz	Kalusz
Sietnica	Gorlice	Rzepienik Strzyzewski	Śliwnica	Przemyśl	Dubiecko
Signiówka	Lemberg	Zniesienie	Śliwnica	Przemyśl	Krzywcza
Sikorzyce	Dąbrowa	Dąbrowa	Śliwnica	Staremiasto	Chyrów
Sikorzynice	Wieliczka	Klasno	Słoboda	Jarosław	Pruchnik
Sińków	Zaleszczyki	Korolówka	Słoboda Bolechowska	Dolina	Bolechów
Siołko	Kalusz	Wojnilów	Słoboda Dolińska	Dolina	Dolina
Siołko	Podhajce	Podhajce	Słoboda Niebyłowska	Kalusz	Kalusz
Siołkowa	Grybów	Grybów	Słoboda Równiańska	Kalusz	Kalusz
Siwka Kałuska	Kalusz	Kalusz	Słoboda Rungurska	Kołomea	Peczeniżyn
Siwka Wojniłowska	Kalusz	Wojnilów	Słoboda Złota	Brzeżany	Kozowa
Skała	Borszczów	Skała	Słobódka	Brzeżany	Kozłów
Skałat	Skałat	Skałat	Słobódka	Kalusz	Wojnilów
Skalnik	Krosno	Dukla	Słobódka	Kossów	Kuty
Skawa	Myślenice	Jordanów	Słobódka	Stanisławów	Hałicz
Skawce	Wadowice	Wadowice	Słobódka	Zaleszczyki	Tłuste
Skawica	Myślenice	Maków	Słobódka ad Odaje	Tłumacz	Tłumacz
Skawina	Wieliczka	Podgórze	Słobódka ad Tłumacz	Tłumacz	Tłumacz
Skawinki	Wadowice	Kalwarya	Słobódka Bolszowiecka	Rohatyń	Bursztyn
Skidzin	Biała	Oświęcim	Słobódka Bukacz.	Rohatyń	Bursztyn
Skład Solny	Przemyśl	Sosnica	Słobódka Dolna	Buczacz	Monasterzyska
Składziste	Nowy Sącz	Łabowa	Słobódka Dżuryńska	Czortków	Czortków
Skole	Stryj	Skole	Słobódka Górna	Buczacz	Monasterzyska
Skolin	Jaworów	Wielkie Oczy	Słobódka Janowska	Trembowla	Janów
Skołyszyn	Jasło	Jasło	Słobódka Konkelnicka	Rohatyń	Bursztyn
Skomielna Biała	Myślenice	Jordanów	Słobódka Leśna	Kołomea	Kołomea
Skomielna Czarna	Myślenice	Jordanów	Słobódka Muszkat	Borszczów	Borszczów
Skomierzyn	Tarnobrzeg	Rozwadów	Słobódka Polna	Kołomea	Gwozdźiec
Skomorochy	Buczacz	Potok	Słobódka Strusowska	Trembowla	Strusów
Skomorochy	Sokal	Sokal	Słobódka Turylecka	Borszczów	Skała
Skomorochy	Tarnopol	Mikulińce	Słocina	Rzeszów	Tyczyn

Town	Main District	Subdistrict	Town	Main District	Subdistrict
Słomianka	Mościska	Sądowa Wisznia	Sokal	Sokal	Sokal
Słomiróg	Wieliczka	Klasno	Sokloszów	Jarosław	Radymno
Słomka	Bochnia	Bochnia	Sokół	Gorlice	Gorlice
Słomka	Limanowa	Mszana Dolna	Sokole	Kam. Strumiłowa	Kam. Strumiłowa
Słona	Brzesko	Czchów	Sokole	Lisko	Ustrzyki Dolne
Słone	Zaleszczyki	Uścieczko	Sokole	Mościska	Mościska
Słonne	Myślenice	Jordanów	Sokolki	Brzesko	Szczurowa
Słońsko	Drohobycz	Drohobycz	Sokolniki	Lemberg	Nawarya
Słopnice Królewskie	Limanowa	Limanowa	Sokolniki	Podhajce	Złotniki
Słopnice Szlacheckie	Limanowa	Limanowa	Sokolniki	Tarnobrzeg	Tarnobrzeg
Słotwina	Brzesko	Brzesko	Sokołoska Wulka	Kolbuszowa	Sokołów
Słotwina	Żywiec	Zabłocie	Sokołów	Buczacz	Potok
Słotwiny	Nowy Sącz	Krynica	Sokołów	Kam. Strumiłowa	Busk
Słowikowa	Nowy Sącz	Nowy Sącz	Sokołów	Kolbuszowa	Sokołów
Słowita	Przemyślany	Gliniany	Sokołów	Podhajce	Złotniki
Słupice	Dąbrowa	Szczucin	Sokołów	Stryj	Stryj
Słupie	Limanowa	Limanowa	Sokołówa Wola	Lisko	Ustrzyki Dolne
Słupki	Tarnopol	Tarnopol	Sokołówka	Bóbrka	Bóbrka
Smarzów	Brody	Szczurowice	Sokołówka	Brody	Sokołówka
Smarzowa	Pilzno	Dębica	Sokołówka	Kossów	Kossów
Smęgorzów	Dąbrowa	Dąbrowa	Sokulec	Buczacz	Potok
Smereczna	Staremiasto	Chyrów	Sólca	Przemyśl	Niżankowice
Smereczne	Krosno	Dukla	Solce	Drohobycz	Drohobycz
Smerek	Lisko	Baligród	Solina	Lisko	Ustrzyki Dolne
Smereków	Żólkiew	Żólkiew	Solinka	Lisko	Wola Michowa
Smerekowiec	Gorlice	Gorlice	Solinka	Lisko	Wola Michowa
Śmichów	Żydaczów	Żurawno	Solonice	Rohatyń	Rohatyń
Śmietana	Brzesko	Radłów	Solonka	Rzeszów	Tyczyn
Śmigno	Tarnów	Zabno	Solonka Mała	Lemberg	Nawarya
Smodna	Kossów	Kossów	Solonka Wielka	Lemberg	Nawarya
Smolanka	Tarnopol	Mikulińce	Sołotwina	Borhodczany	Sołotwina
Smolarzyny	Łańcut	Żolynia	Solowa	Przemyślany	Gliniany
Smolice	Wadowice	Zator	Sonina	Łańcut	Łańcut
Smolin	Rawa Ruska	Niemerów	Soposzyn	Żólkiew	Żólkiew
Smolnica	Lisko	Ustrzyki Dolne	Sopotnia Mała	Żywiec	Zabłocie
Smolnik	Lisko	Lutowiska	Sopotnia Wielka	Żywiec	Zabłocie
Smolnik	Lisko	Wola Michowa	Sopotnik	Bircza	Dobromil
Smolno	Brody	Brody	Sopów	Kołomea	Kołomea
Smolno	Drohobycz	Drohobycz	Soput	Stryj	Skole
Smorze Dolne	Stryj	Skole	Sorocko	Skałat	Skałat
Smorze Górne	Stryj	Skole	Soroka	Skałat	Touste
Smorze Kolonia	Stryj	Skole	Soroki	Buczacz	Buczacz
Smykan	Limanowa	Limanowa	Soroki	Horodenka	Horodenka
Smyków Mały	Dąbrowa	Dąbrowa	Sośnica	Przemyśl	Sosnica
Smyków Wielki	Dąbrowa	Dąbrowa	Sosnice	Ropczyce	Wielopole
Smykowce	Tarnopol	Tarnopol	Sosnów	Podhajce	Złotniki
Śniatyn	Śniatyn	Śniatyn	Sosnowice	Wadowice	Zator
Śniatynka	Drohobycz	Drohobycz	Sosolówka	Czortków	Ulaszkowce
Śnietnica	Grybów	Grybów	Sowina	Pilzno	Brzostek
Snowicz	Złoczów	Złoczów	Sowliny	Limanowa	Limanowa
Snówidów	Buczacz	Potok	Sozań	Staremiasto	Staremiasto
Sobin	Kam. Strumiłowa	Radziechów	Spas	Dolina	Rożniatów
Sobjecin	Jarosław	Jarosław	Spas	Kam. Strumiłowa	Kam. Strumiłowa
Sobniów	Jasło	Jasło	Spas	Staremiasto	Staremiasto
Sobolów	Bochnia	Wiśnicz Nowy	Spasków	Sokal	Tartaków
Sobolówka	Złoczów	Białykamień	Sporysz	Żywiec	Zabłocie
Soboniewice	Wieliczka	Klasno	Spytkowice	Myślenice	Jordanów
Sobotów	Stanisławów	Halicz	Spytkowice	Wadowice	Zator
Sobów	Tarnobrzeg	Tarnobrzeg	Średni	Kalusz	Kalusz
Sochnia	Limanowa	Limanowa	Średnia	Przemyśl	Krzywcza
Sochy	Tarnobrzeg	Rozwadów	Średnia Wieś	Lisko	Lisko
Sojkowa	Nisko	Rudnik	Środopolce	Kam. Strumiłowa	Radziechów

Town	Main District	Subdistrict	Town	Main District	Subdistrict
Srogów Dolny	Sanok	Sanok	Stawkowice	Wieliczka	Klasno
Srogów Górny	Sanok	Sanok	Stawsko	Stryj	Skole
Sroki Lwowskie	Lemberg	Zniesienie	Stebne	Kossów	Żabie
Sroki Szcz.	Lemberg	Szczerzec	Stebnik	Bohordczany	Lysiec
Srołmienice	Rudki	Rudki	Stebnik	Drohobycz	Drohobycz
Sromowce Niżne	Nowy Targ	Nowy Targ	Stebnik	Lisko	Ustrzyki Dolne
Sromowce Wyżne	Nowy Targ	Nowy Targ	Stechnikowce	Tarnopol	Tarnopol
St. Johannesberg	Limanowa	Limanowa	Stecowa	Śniatyn	Śniatyn
St. Stanisław	Stanisławów	Hałicz	Stefkowa	Lisko	Ustrzyki Dolne
Stadło	Nowy Sącz	Stary Sącz	Steinau	Nisko	Rudnik
Stadniki	Wieliczka	Klasno	Steinfeld	Lisko	Ustrzyki Dolne
Staje	Rawa Ruska	Uhnów	Steniatyn	Sokal	Sokal
Stałe	Tarnobrzeg	Tarnobrzeg	Stepina z Chytrówka	Jasło	Frysztak
Staniątki	Wieliczka	Klasno	Sterkowiec	Brzesko	Brzesko
Stanila	Drohobycz	Drohobycz	Stężnica	Lisko	Baligród
Stanimirz	Przemyślany	Gliniany	Stobierna	Pilzno	Dębica
Stanin	Kam. Strumiłowa	Radziechów	Stochynia	Staremiasto	Felsztyn
Stanisław Dolny	Wadowice	Kalwarya	Stodółki	Gródek	Gródek
Stanisław Górny	Wadowice	Kalwarya	Stojance	Mościska	Mościska
Stanisławczyk	Brody	Stanisławczyk	Stojanów	Kam. Strumiłowa	Stajanów
Stanisławczyk	Przemyśl	Przemyśl	Stoki	Bóbrka	Bóbrka
Stanisławice	Bochnia	Bochnia	Stołowa	Pilzno	Pilzno
Stanisławów	Stanisławów	Stanisławów	Stołpin	Brody	Toporów
Stanislówka	Żólkiew	Gross-Mosty	Stopczatów	Kołomea	Jabłonów
Staniszewskie	Kolbuszowa	Raniżów	Strachocina	Sanok	Sanok
Stańków	Stryj	Stryj	Straconka	Biała	Lipnik
Stańkowa	Lisko	Lisko	Stradcz	Gródek	Janów
Stańkowa	Nowy Sącz	Nowy Sącz	Stradomka	Bochnia	Wiśnicz Nowy
Stańkowa	Żydaczów	Żurawno	Straszęcin	Pilzno	Dębica
Stańkowce	Bóbrka	Brzozdowiec	Straszewice	Staremiasto	Staremiasto
Stańkowce	Dolina	Bolechów	Stratyń Wieś	Rohatyń	Rohatyń
Stany	Nisko	Nisko	Strażów	Łańcut	Łańcut
Stara Wieś	Brzozów	Brzozów	Strażydle	Rzeszów	Baligród
Stara Wieś	Drohobycz	Drohobycz	Stregocice	Pilzno	Pilzno
Stara Wieś	Grybów	Grybów	Streptów	Kam. Strumiłowa	Kam. Strumiłowa
Stara Wieś	Limanowa	Limanowa	Strojców	Dąbrowa	Dąbrowa
Stararopa	Staremiasto	Starasól	Stroniatyn	Lemberg	Jaryczów
Starasól	Staremiasto	Starasól	Stronie	Limanowa	Limanowa
Starawieś Dolna	Biała	Kęty	Stronie	Wadowice	Kalwarya
Starawieś Górna	Biała	Kęty	Stroniowice	Mościska	Hussaków
Stare Stawy	Biała	Oświęcim	Stronna	Gródek	Janów
Starebystre	Nowy Targ	Nowy Targ	Stronowice	Przemyśl	Niżankowice
Staremiasto	Łańcut	Leżajsk	Strosówka	Czortków	Czortków
Staremiasto	Podhajce	Podhajce	Stróża	Limanowa	Limanowa
Staremiasto	Staremiasto	Staremiasto	Stróża	Myślenice	Myślenice
Staresioło	Bóbrka	Bóbrka	Stróże	Brzesko	Czchów
Staresioło	Cieszanów	Oleszyce	Stróże	Nisko	Rudnik
Starogród	Sokal	Warez	Stróże Małe	Sanok	Sanok
Staromiejszczyzna	Skałat	Podwołoczyska	Stróże Niżne	Grybów	Grybów
Staromieście	Rzeszów	Rzeszów	Stróże Wielkie	Sanok	Sanok
Staroniwa	Rzeszów	Rzeszów	Stróże Wyżne	Grybów	Grybów
Starunia	Borhodczany	Sołotwina	Stróżna	Grybów	Bobowa
Stary Sącz	Nowy Sącz	Stary Sącz	Stróżówka	Gorlice	Gorlice
Stary Skałat	Skałat	Skałat	Strubowiska Kalnica	Lisko	Baligród
Starzawa	Bircza	Dobromil	Struga	Nowy Sącz	Nowy Sącz
Starzawa	Mościska	Mościska	Strumiany	Wieliczka	Klasno
Starzyska	Jaworów	Jaworów	Strupków	Nadwórna	Lanczyn
Stasiowa Wola	Rohatyń	Bursztyn	Strusów	Trembowla	Strusów
Stasiówka	Pilzno	Dębica	Strusówka	Trembowla	Strusów
Staszkówka	Gorlice	Rzepienik Strzyzewski	Strutyń	Złoczów	Złoczów
Stawczany	Gródek	Gródek	Strutyń Niżny	Dolina	Rożniatów
Stawki Kraśnieńskie	Skałat	Touste	Strutyń Wyżny	Dolina	Rożniatów

Town	Main District	Subdistrict	Town	Main District	Subdistrict
Strwiążyk	Lisko	Ustrzyki Dolne	Sulimów	Sokal	Warez
Stryhańce	Przemyślany	Dunajowce	Sulimów	Żólkiew	Kulików
Stryhańce	Stryj	Stryj	Sulistrowa	Krosno	Dukla
Stryhańce	Tłumacz	Uście Zielone	Sułków	Wieliczka	Klasno
Stryhanka	Kam. Strumiłowa	Dobrotwór	Sułkowice	Myślenice	Myślenice
Stryj	Stryj	Stryj	Sułkowice	Wadowice	Andrychów
Strymba	Nadwórna	Nadwórna	Sułkowszczyzna	Mościska	Mościska
Stryszawa	Żywiec	Zabłocie	Sułów	Wieliczka	Klasno
Stryszów	Wadowice	Kalwarya	Sułuków	Dolina	Dolina
Stryszowa	Wieliczka	Klasno	Supranówka	Skałat	Skałat
Strzałki Lany	Bóbrka	Bóbrka	Surmaczówka	Jarosław	Pruchnik
Strzałków	Stryj	Stryj	Surochów	Jarosław	Jarosław
Strzałkowce	Borszczów	Borszczów	Surowa	Mielec	Radomyśl Wiel.
Strzałkowice	Sambor	Sambor	Surowica	Sanok	Bukowsko
Strzelbice	Staremiasto	Staremiasto	Surowki	Wieliczka	Klasno
Strzelczyska	Mościska	Mościska	Susułów	Rudki	Komarno
Strzelec Małe	Brzesko	Szczurowa	Suszczyn	Tarnopol	Mikulińce
Strzelec Wielkie	Brzesko	Szczurowa	Suszno	Kam. Strumiłowa	Witków Nowy
Strzeliska Nowe	Bóbrka	Strzeliska Nowe	Suszyca Mała	Staremiasto	Chyrów
Strzeliska Stare	Bóbrka	Strzeliska Nowe	Suszyca Wielka	Staremiasto	Chyrów
Strzemien	Żólkiew	Gross-Mosty	Swaryczów	Dolina	Rożniatów
Strzemilcze	Brody	Szczurowice	Swarzów	Dąbrowa	Dąbrowa
Strzeszyce	Limanowa	Limanowa	Swerzowa Polska	Krosno	Dukla
Strzeszyn	Gorlice	Gorlice	Świątkowa Mała	Krosno	Żmigród
Strzylawka	Grybów	Grybów	Świątkowa Wielka	Krosno	Żmigród
Strzylcze	Horodenka	Horodenka	Świątniki Dolne	Wieliczka	Klasno
Strzyżów	Rzeszów	Strzyżów	Świątniki Górne	Wieliczka	Podgórze
Stubienko	Przemyśl	Sosnica	Świątoniowa	Łańcut	Przeworsk
Stubno	Przemyśl	Sosnica	Świdnica	Jaworów	Wielkie Oczy
Studenne	Lisko	Baligród	Świdnik	Limanowa	Limanowa
Studzianka	Kalusz	Kalusz	Świdnik	Nowy Sącz	Nowy Sącz
Studziany	Łańcut	Przeworsk	Świdowa	Czortków	Jagielnica
Studzienne	Nisko	Ulanów	Świdówka	Wieliczka	Klasno
Stulsko	Żydaczów	Rozdół	Świdrówka	Dąbrowa	Szczucin
Stupnica	Sambor	Sambor	Świebodna	Jarosław	Pruchnik
Stuposiany	Lisko	Lutowiska	Świebodzin	Dąbrowa	Dąbrowa
Styberówka	Brody	Podkamień	Świebodzin	Tarnów	Tarnów
Styków	Rzeszów	Głogów	Święcany	Jasło	Jasło
Stynawa Niżna	Stryj	Skole	Świerczów	Kolbuszowa	Kolbuszowa
Stynawa Wyżna	Stryj	Skole	Świerdzków	Tarnów	Tarnów
Sucha	Żywiec	Zabłocie	Świerkla	Nowy Sącz	Stary Sącz
Sucha Struga	Nowy Sącz	Piwniczna	Świerzkowce	Zaleszczyki	Uścieczko
Suchawola	Cieszanów	Oleszyce	Świerzowa	Krosno	Dukla
Suchodół	Bóbrka	Bóbrka	Święte	Przemyśl	Sosnica
Suchodół	Dolina	Dolina	Świlcza	Rzeszów	Rzeszów
Suchodół	Husiatyn	Husiatyn	Świniarsko	Nowy Sącz	Nowy Sącz
Suchodół	Krosno	Dukla	Świnna Poreba	Wadowice	Wadowice
Suchodoły	Brody	Brody	Świnna Sól	Żywiec	Zabłocie
Suchoraba	Wieliczka	Klasno	Świrż	Przemyślany	Świrż
Suchorów	Bóbrka	Chodorów	Świstelniki	Rohatyń	Bursztyn
Suchorzów	Tarnobrzeg	Baranów	Świtarzów	Sokal	Sokal
Suchostaw	Husiatyn	Kopyczyńce	Swoszowa	Jasło	Olpiny
Suchowola	Brody	Brody	Swoszowice	Wieliczka	Podgórze
Suchowola	Gródek	Janów	Sygneczów	Wieliczka	Klasno
Suchy Grunt	Dąbrowa	Szczucin	Synowódzko	Stryj	Skole
Suczyca Rykowa	Staremiasto	Staremiasto	Synowódzko Dolne	Stryj	Skole
Sudkowice	Rudki	Rudki	Synowódzko Niżne	Stryj	Skole
Sufczyn	Brzesko	Wojnicz	Synowódzko Wyżne	Stryj	Skole
Sufczyna	Bircza	Bircza	Szade	Sambor	Sambor
Sukmanie	Brzesko	Wojnicz	Szaflary	Nowy Targ	Nowy Targ
Sukowate	Lisko	Baligród	Szafranów	Mielec	Radomyśl Wiel.
Sulichów	Tarnobrzeg	Rozwadów	Szalowa	Gorlice	Gorlice

Town	Main District	Subdistrict	Town	Main District	Subdistrict
Szare	Żywiec	Zabłocie	Szutromińce	Zaleszczyki	Uścieczko
Szarów	Wieliczka	Klasno	Szwajkowce	Czortków	Czortków
Szarpance	Sokal	Tartaków	Szwedy	Tarnobrzeg	Rozwadów
Szarwark	Dąbrowa	Dąbrowa	Szwejków	Podhajce	Podhajce
Szczakowa	Chrzanów	Chrzanów	Szwiniarów	Bochnia	Bochnia
Szczawa	Limanowa	Limanowa	Szybalin	Brzeżany	Brzeżany
Szczawne	Sanok	Bukowsko	Szychtory	Sokal	Warez
Szczawnica	Nowy Sącz	Szczawnica	Szydłowce	Husiatyn	Husiatyn
Szczawnica Niżna	Nowy Sącz	Szczawnica	Szydłowiec	Mielec	Mielec
Szczawnica Wyżna	Nowy Sącz	Szczawnica	Szyk	Limanowa	Limanowa
Szczawnik	Nowy Sącz	Muszyna	Szymanowice	Nowy Sącz	Stary Sącz
Szczepańcowa	Krosno	Korczyna	Szymbark	Gorlice	Gorlice
Szczepanów	Brzesko	Brzesko	Szynwald	Tarnów	Tarnów
Szczepanów	Podhajce	Podhajce	Szyperki	Nisko	Ulanów
Szczepanowice	Tarnów	Tarnów	Szypowce	Zaleszczyki	Tłuste
Szczepiatyń	Rawa Ruska	Uhnów	Szyszkowce	Brody	Podkamień
Szczepłoty	Jaworów	Wielkie Oczy	Szyszkowce	Zaleszczyki	Korolówka
Szczerbanówka	Lisko	Wola Michowa	Tabaszowa	Nowy Sącz	Nowy Sącz
Szczereż	Nowy Sącz	Łącko	Tadanie	Kam. Strumiłowa	Kam. Strumiłowa
Szczerzec	Lemberg	Szczerzec	Tamanowice	Mościska	Hussaków
Szczerzyce	Rawa Ruska	Niemerów	Taniawa	Dolina	Bolechów
Szczucin	Dąbrowa	Szczucin	Tapin	Przemyśl	Sosnica
Szczurowa	Brzesko	Szczurowa	Targanica	Wadowice	Andrychów
Szczurowice	Brody	Szczurowice	Targoszyna	Wieliczka	Klasno
Szczutków	Cieszanów	Lubaczów	Targowica	Horodenka	Horodenka
Szczygłów	Wieliczka	Klasno	Targowica	Tłumacz	Ottynia
Szczyrk	Biała	Lipnik	Targowiska	Krosno	Dukla
Szczyrzyce	Limanowa	Limanowa	Targowisko	Bochnia	Bochnia
Szczytna	Jarosław	Jarosław	Targowisko	Tarnów	Zabno
Szczytniki	Wieliczka	Klasno	Tarnawa	Bircza	Dobromil
Szebnic	Jasło	Jasło	Tarnawa	Bochnia	Wiśnicz Nowy
Szechynie	Przemyśl	Przemyśl	Tarnawa	Żywiec	Zabłocie
Szeczygelówka	Kam. Strumiłowa	Stajanów	Tarnawa Dolna	Lisko	Lisko
Szeparowce	Kołomea	Peczeniżyn	Tarnawa Górna	Lisko	Lisko
Szeptyce	Rudki	Rudki	Tarnawce	Przemyśl	Przemyśl
Szerszeniowce	Zaleszczyki	Tłuste	Tarnawica Polna	Tłumacz	Tłumacz
Szertowce	Zaleszczyki	Gródek	Tarnawka	Bircza	Bircza
Szerzyny	Jasło	Olpiny	Tarnawka	Borszczów	Borszczów
Szeszerowice	Mościska	Sądowa Wisznia	Tarnawka	Łańcut	Kańczuga
Szeszory	Kossów	Pistyn	Tarnawka	Sanok	Rymanów
Szklary	Rzeszów	Tyczyn	Tarnawka	Staremiasto	Starasól
Szklary	Sanok	Rymanów	Tarnawka	Stryj	Skole
Szkło	Jaworów	Jaworów	Tarnawka	Żydaczów	Żurawno
Szkodna	Ropczyce	Ropczyce	Tarnobrzeg	Tarnobrzeg	Tarnobrzeg
Szlachtowa	Nowy Sącz	Szczawnica	Tarnogóra	Nisko	Rudnik
Szlacińce	Tarnopol	Tarnopol	Tarnopol	Tarnopol	Tarnopol
Szlembarg	Nowy Targ	Nowy Targ	Tarnoruda	Skałat	Tarnoruda
Szmańkowce	Czortków	Czortków	Tarnoszyn	Rawa Ruska	Uhnów
Szmańkowczyki	Czortków	Czortków	Tarnów	Tarnów	Tarnów
Szmitków	Sokal	Warez	Tarnowica Leśna	Nadwórna	Nadwórna
Sznyrów	Brody	Brody	Tarnowica Zielona	Nadwórna	Nadwórna
Szołomyja	Bóbrka	Mikalajów	Tarnowice	Jasło	Jasło
Szówsko	Jarosław	Jarosław	Tarnowice	Tarnów	Tarnów
Szpiklosy	Złoczów	Złoczów	Tarnowska Wola	Tarnobrzeg	Tarnobrzeg
Szufnarowa	Jasło	Frysztak	Tartaków	Sokal	Tartaków
Szufnarowa	Ropczyce	Wielopole	Tartaków	Sokal	Tartaków
Szulhanówka	Czortków	Jagielnica	Tartakowice	Sokal	Tartaków
Szumina	Staremiasto	Starasól	Tartarów	Nadwórna	Delatyn
Szumlan	Jaworów	Jaworów	Taszezówka	Skałat	Tarnoruda
Szumlany	Podhajce	Zawałów	Taszyce	Wieliczka	Klasno
Szumlany Małe	Brzeżany	Brzeżany	Tatarsko	Stryj	Stryj
Szuparka	Zaleszczyki	Korolówka	Tatary	Sambor	Sambor

Town	Main District	Subdistrict	Town	Main District	Subdistrict
Tatarynów	Rudki	Komarno	Towarnia	Sambor	Sambor
Tatowce	Kołomea	Gwozdźiec	Trąbki	Wieliczka	Klasno
Taurów	Brzeżany	Kozłów	Tracz	Kołomea	Kołomea
Tęczynek	Chrzanów	Chrzanów	Trawniki	Bochnia	Bochnia
Tęgoborze	Nowy Sącz	Nowy Sącz	Trawotłoki	Złoczów	Zborów
Tęhlów	Rawa Ruska	Uhnów	Trędowacz	Złoczów	Gologory
Tejsarów	Żydaczów	Żydaczów	Trembowla	Trembowla	Trembowla
Teklówka	Zaleszczyki	Uścieczko	Trepeza	Sanok	Sanok
Tekucze	Kołomea	Jabłonów	Tresna	Żywiec	Zabłocie
Telacze	Podhajce	Podhajce	Trofanówka	Kołomea	Gwozdźiec
Teleśnica Oszwar.	Lisko	Ustrzyki Dolne	Trójca	Bircza	Rybotycze
Teleśnica Sanna	Lisko	Ustrzyki Dolne	Trójca	Borszczów	Skała
Temerowce	Stanisławów	Hałicz	Trójca	Brody	Toporów
Temeszów	Brzozów	Brzozów	Trójca	Śniatyn	Zabłotów
Tenczyn	Myślenice	Jordanów	Trójczyce	Przemyśl	Sosnica
Tenetniki	Rohatyń	Bursztyn	Tropie	Nowy Sącz	Nowy Sącz
Teodorówka	Krosno	Dukla	Trościaniec	Brzeżany	Brzeżany
Teodorshof	Żólkiew	Żólkiew	Trościaniec	Dolina	Dolina
Teofipolka	Brzeżany	Kozowa	Trościaniec	Jaworów	Jaworów
Teresia	Kam. Strumiłowa	Chołojów	Trościaniec	Śniatyn	Zabłotów
Tereskuła	Kossów	Żabie	Trościaniec	Tłumacz	Uście Zielone
Teresówka	Dolina	Dolina	Trościaniec	Żydaczów	Rozdól
Terka	Lisko	Baligród	Trościaniec Mały	Złoczów	Złoczów
Terlo	Staremiasto	Chyrów	Trościaniec Wielkie	Brody	Zołożce
Terszaków	Rudki	Komarno	Trubczyn	Borszczów	Mielnica
Terszów	Staremiasto	Staremiasto	Truchanów	Stryj	Skole
Tetewczyce	Kam. Strumiłowa	Stajanów	Truskawice	Drohobycz	Drohobycz
Tetylkowce	Brody	Podkamień	Truszowice	Bircza	Dobromil
Tiapeze	Dolina	Bolechów	Trybuchowce	Bóbrka	Strzeliska Nowe
Tiutków	Trembowla	Strusów	Trybuchowce	Buczacz	Jazłowice
Tłuczan Dolna	Wadowice	Zator	Trybuchowce	Husiatyn	Husiatyn
Tłuczan Górna	Wadowice	Zator	Tryńcza	Łańcut	Przeworsk
Tłumacz	Tłumacz	Tłumacz	Trynitatis	Bochnia	Bochnia
Tłumaczyk	Kołomea	Peczeniżyn	Trzciana	Krosno	Dukla
Tłuste	Zaleszczyki	Tłuste	Trzciana	Mielec	Radomyśl Wiel.
Tłustenkie	Husiatyn	Probużna	Trzciana	Rzeszów	Rzeszów
Tobolów	Kam. Strumiłowa	Witków Nowy	Trzcianice	Bircza	Rybotycze
Tokarnia	Sanok	Bukowsko	Trzcienice	Mościska	Mościska
Toki	Krosno	Dukla	Trzcinica	Jasło	Jasło
Tołszczów	Lemberg	Nawarya	Trzebienczyce	Wadowice	Zator
Tomaszkowice	Wieliczka	Klasno	Trzebina	Chrzanów	Trzebina
Tomaszowce	Kalusz	Wojnilów	Trzebinia	Żywiec	Zabłocie
Tomice	Wadowice	Wadowice	Trzebionka	Chrzanów	Trzebina
Tonie	Dąbrowa	Dąbrowa	Trzebos	Kolbuszowa	Sokołów
Topolnica	Staremiasto	Staremiasto	Trzebownisko	Rzeszów	Głogów
Topolsko	Kalusz	Kalusz	Trzebunia	Myślenice	Myślenice
Toporów	Brody	Toporów	Trzebuska	Kolbuszowa	Sokołów
Toporów	Mielec	Mielec	Trzeiana	Bochnia	Wiśnicz Nowy
Toporówce	Horodenka	Horodenka	Trzemeśnia	Myślenice	Myślenice
Toporzysko	Myślenice	Jordanów	Trzemeśnia	Tarnów	Tarnów
Torczynowice	Sambor	Sambor	Trześń	Kolbuszowa	Kolbuszowa
Torhanowice	Sambor	Sambor	Trześń	Tarnobrzeg	Tarnobrzeg
Torhów	Złoczów	Pomorzany	Trześnia	Mielec	Mielec
Torkarnia	Myślenice	Jordanów	Trześniów	Brzozów	Brzozów
Torki	Przemyśl	Przemyśl	Trzęsówka	Kolbuszowa	Kolbuszowa
Torki	Sokal	Tartaków	Trzetrzewina	Nowy Sącz	Nowy Sącz
Toroszówka	Krosno	Dukla	Tuchla	Jarosław	Radymno
Torskie	Zaleszczyki	Uścieczko	Tuchla	Stryj	Skole
Touste	Skałat	Touste	Tucholka	Stryj	Skole
Toustogłowy	Złoczów	Zborów	Tuchów	Tarnów	Tuchów
Toustoług	Tarnopol	Tarnopol	Tuczapy	Jaworów	Jaworów
Toutobaby	Podhajce	Zawałów	Tuczapy	Śniatyn	Zabłotów

Town	Main District	Subdistrict	Town	Main District	Subdistrict
Tuczepy	Jarosław	Jarosław	Tysowjec	Stryj	Skole
Tuczna	Przemyślany	Świrż	Tyszawice	Przemyśl	Przemyśl
Tudiów	Kossów	Kuty	Tyszkowce	Horodenka	Horodenka
Tudorkowice	Sokal	Warez	Tyszkowice	Mościska	Hussaków
Tudorów	Husiatyn	Kopyczyńce	Tyszownica	Stryj	Skole
Tuława	Śniatyn	Śniatyn	Tyszyca	Sokal	Krystynopol
Tuligłowy	Jarosław	Pruchnik	Tywonia	Jarosław	Jarosław
Tuligłowy	Mościska	Sądowa Wisznia	Ubieszyn	Łańcut	Przeworsk
Tuligłowy	Rudki	Komarno	Ubinie	Kam. Strumiłowa	Busk
Tułkowice	Jasło	Frysztak	Ubrzeż	Bochnia	Wiśnicz Nowy
Tułkowice	Mościska	Hussaków	Udnów	Żółkiew	Kulików
Tułuków	Śniatyn	Zabłotów	Ugartsberg	Drohobycz	Drohobycz
Tumierz	Stanisławów	Maryampol	Ugartsthal	Kalusz	Kalusz
Turady	Żydaczów	Żydaczów	Uhełna	Stryj	Stryj
Turbia	Tarnobrzeg	Rozwadów	Uherce	Lisko	Lisko
Turka	Kam. Strumiłowa	Kam. Strumiłowa	Uherce Niezabitowskie	Gródek	Gródek
Turka	Kołomea	Gwozdźiec	Uherce Wieniawskie	Rudki	Rudki
Turka	Turka	Turka	Uherce Zapłatyńskie	Sambor	Sambor
Turkocin	Przemyślany	Gliniany	Uhersko	Stryj	Stryj
Turkowa	Tłumacz	Tyśmienica	Uhnów	Rawa Ruska	Uhnów
Turówka	Skałat	Tarnoruda	Uhorce	Złoczów	Pomorzany
Tursko	Grybów	Bobowa	Uhorniki	Tłumacz	Ottynia
Turylcze	Borszczów	Skała	Uhryń	Czortków	Czortków
Turynka	Żółkiew	Żółkiew	Uhryń Dolny	Stanisławów	Stanisławów
Turza	Gorlice	Rzepienik Strzyzewski	Uhryniów Górny	Stanisławów	Stanisławów
Turza	Kolbuszowa	Sokołów	Uhryńkowce	Zaleszczyki	Uścieczko
Turza Gnila	Dolina	Dolina	Uhrynów	Podhajce	Podhajce
Turza Wielka	Dolina	Dolina	Uhrynów	Sokal	Warez
Turzanowce	Bóbrka	Brzozdowiec	Uhrynów Średni	Kalusz	Kalusz
Turzansk	Sanok	Bukowsko	Uhrynów Stary	Kalusz	Kalusz
Turze	Brody	Toporów	Ujanowice	Limanowa	Limanowa
Turze	Staremiasto	Staremiasto	Ujazd	Bochnia	Wiśnicz Nowy
Turzepole	Brzozów	Brzozów	Ujazd	Brzesko	Czchów
Tustań	Stanisławów	Halicz	Ujazd	Pilzno	Jodłowa
Tustanowice	Drohobycz	Borysław	Ujazd	Rohatyń	Rohatyń
Tuszków	Sokal	Bełż	Ujezna	Łańcut	Przeworsk
Tuszów	Mielec	Mielec	Ujkowice	Przemyśl	Przemyśl
Tuszów Narodowy	Mielec	Mielec	Ujsol	Żywiec	Zabłocie
Tuszyma	Ropczyce	Ropczyce	Uka Wielka	Tarnopol	Mikulińce
Tutkowice	Ropczyce	Wielopole	Ulanica	Brzozów	Dynów
Tużłów	Kalusz	Kalusz	Ulanów	Nisko	Ulanów
Twierdza	Jasło	Frysztak	Ułaszkowce	Czortków	Ulaszkowce
Twierdza	Mościska	Mościska	Ulazów	Cieszanów	Cieszanów
Tworkowa	Brzesko	Czchów	Ulicko Seredkiewicz	Rawa Ruska	Magierów
Tworylne	Lisko	Baligród	Ulicko Zarębane	Rawa Ruska	Magierów
Tycha	Staremiasto	Staremiasto	Ulryn	Nowy Sącz	Łabowa
Tyczyn	Rzeszów	Tyczyn	Ulucz	Bircza	Bircza
Tylawa	Krosno	Dukla	Ulwówek	Sokal	Sokal
Tylicz	Nowy Sącz	Krynica	Ulyczno	Drohobycz	Drohobycz
Tylka	Nowy Targ	Krościenko	Umieszcz	Jasło	Jasło
Tylmanowa	Nowy Sącz	Łącko	Uniatycze	Drohobycz	Drohobycz
Tymbark	Limanowa	Limanowa	Uniów	Przemyślany	Gliniany
Tymowa Wesołów	Brzesko	Czchów	Uniszowa	Tarnów	Ryglice
Tyniatyska	Rawa Ruska	Lubycza	Uniż	Horodenka	Czernelica
Tynice	Wieliczka	Podgórze	Unterbergen	Lemberg	Winniki
Tyniowice	Jarosław	Pruchnik	Unterwalden	Przemyślany	Gliniany
Tynów	Drohobycz	Drohobycz	Urlów	Złoczów	Zborów
Tyrawa Solna	Sanok	Sanok	Urman	Brzeżany	Brzeżany
Tyrawa Wołoska	Sanok	Tyrawa woloska	Uroż	Sambor	Sambor
Tyskowa	Lisko	Baligród	Urycz	Stryj	Skole
Tyśmienica	Tłumacz	Tyśmienica	Urzejowice	Łańcut	Przeworsk
Tysowica	Staremiasto	Staremiasto	Uście	Żydaczów	Rozdól

Town	Main District	Subdistrict	Town	Main District	Subdistrict
Uście Biskupie	Borszczów	Mielnica	Weleśnica	Nadwórna	Nadwórna
Uście nad Prutem	Śniatyn	Śniatyn	Wełykie	Bircza	Dobromil
Uście Ruskie	Gorlice	Gorlice	Werbiąż Niżny	Kołomea	Kołomea
Uście Solne	Bochnia	Bochnia	Werbiąż Wyżny	Kołomea	Kołomea
Uście Zielone	Tłumacz	Uście Zielone	Werbie	Rudki	Komarno
Uścieczko	Zaleszczyki	Uścieczko	Werchrata	Rawa Ruska	Rawa Ruska
Uścierzyki	Kossów	Żabie	Weremien	Lisko	Lisko
Ustrobna	Krosno	Dukla	Wereszyce	Gródek	Janów
Ustrzyki Dolne	Lisko	Ustrzyki Dolne	Werhobuz	Złoczów	Sassów
Ustrzyki Górne	Lisko	Lutowiska	Wertelka	Brody	Zołożce
Ustyanowa	Lisko	Ustrzyki Dolne	Weryń	Żydaczów	Rozdól
Uszew	Brzesko	Brzesko	Werynia	Kolbuszowa	Kolbuszowa
Uszkowice	Przemyślany	Przemyślany	Werynia	Rzeszów	Głogów
Usznia	Złoczów	Sassów	Wesoła	Brzozów	Dynów
Uszwica	Bochnia	Wiśnicz Nowy	Wetlina	Lisko	Baligród
Uthowek	Rawa Ruska	Uhnów	Wiątowice	Wieliczka	Klasno
Utoropy	Kossów	Pistyn	Wiątrowice	Nowy Sącz	Nowy Sącz
Uwin	Brody	Szczurowice	Wiązowa	Żółkiew	Żółkiew
Uwisla	Husiatyn	Chorostków	Wiązownica	Jarosław	Pruchnik
Uwsie	Podhajce	Podhajce	Wiciów	Staremiasto	Staremiasto
Uzin	Stanisławów	Jezupol	Wicza	Sanok	Rymanów
Vorderberg	Gródek	Gródek	Widacz	Jasło	Frysztak
Wacowice	Drohobycz	Drohobycz	Widaczów	Łańcut	Przeworsk
Wadowice	Wadowice	Wadowice	Widełka	Kolbuszowa	Kolbuszowa
Wadowice Dolne	Mielec	Radomyśl Wiel.	Widełka	Rzeszów	Głogów
Wadowice Górne	Mielec	Radomyśl Wiel.	Widynów	Śniatyn	Śniatyn
Waksmund	Nowy Targ	Nowy Targ	Wieciorka	Myślenice	Myślenice
Wał Ruda	Brzesko	Radłów	Wieckowice	Brzesko	Wojnicz
Walawa	Przemyśl	Przemyśl	Wieckowice	Mościska	Hussaków
Walddorf	Gródek	Janów	Wieczerza	Myślenice	Jordanów
Walki	Tarnów	Tarnów	Wieczorki	Żółkiew	Gross-Mosty
Wałowa Góra	Limanowa	Limanowa	Wieleśniów	Buczacz	Barysz
Wałówka	Sokal	Sokal	Wielha	Jarosław	Radymno
Wampierzów	Mielec	Radomyśl Wiel.	Wieliczka	Wieliczka	Klasno
Waniów	Sokal	Bełż	Wielkawieś	Brzesko	Wojnicz
Waniowice	Sambor	Sambor	Wielkie Drogi	Wadowice	Zator
Wańkowa	Lisko	Lisko	Wielkie Oczy	Jaworów	Wielkie Oczy
Wańkowice	Rudki	Rudki	Wielkopole	Gródek	Janów
Wapienne	Gorlice	Gorlice	Wielogłowy	Nowy Sącz	Nowy Sącz
Wara	Brzozów	Dynów	Wielopole	Dąbrówa	Dąbrowa
Warez	Sokal	Warez	Wielopole	Nówy Sącz	Nówy Sącz
Warwaryńce	Trembowla	Strusów	Wielopole	Ropczyce	Wielopole
Warys	Brzesko	Brzesko	Wielopole	Sanok	Sanok
Warys	Brzesko	Radłów	Wielowieś	Tarnobrzeg	Tarnobrzeg
Wasiuczyn	Rohatyń	Rohatyń	Wielunice	Przemyśl	Niżankowice
Wasyłków	Husiatyn	Probużna	Wieniawa	Lemberg	Nawarya
Wasylkowce	Husiatyn	Husiatyn	Wienice	Bochnia	Wiśnicznówy
Wasylów Wielkie	Rawa Ruska	Uhnów	Wieprz	Wadówice	Andrychów
Waszyce	Jasło	Jasło	Wieprz ad Żywiec	Żywiec	Zabłocie
Wawrzka	Grybów	Grybów	Wieprzce	Myślenice	Maków
Wawrzkowa	Kam. Strumiłowa	Busk	Wiercany	Ropczyce	Sędziszów
Węcina	Limanowa	Limanowa	Wierchomla Mała	Nówy Sącz	Piwniczna
Węgerka	Jarosław	Pruchnik	Wierchomla Wielka	Nówy Sącz	Piwniczna
Węglarzyska	Lemberg	Nawarya	Wierczany	Stryj	Stryj
Węgliska	Łańcut	Łańcut	Wieruszyce	Bochnia	Wiśnicznówy
Węgliska	Rzeszów	Głogów	Wierzawice	Łańcut	Leżajsk
Węglówka	Krosno	Korczyna	Wierzbanówa	Wieliczka	Klasno
Węglówka	Wieliczka	Klasno	Wierzbiałyn	Buczacz	Barysz
Węgrzyce Wielkie	Wieliczka	Klasno	Wierzbiany	Jaworów	Jaworów
Weinbergen	Lemberg	Winniki	Wierzbiaz	Sokal	Bełż
Weisenberg	Gródek	Janów	Wierzbica	Bóbrka	Chodorów
Wełdzirz	Dolina	Dolina	Wierzbica	Rawa Ruska	Uhnów

Town	Main District	Subdistrict
Wierzblany	Kam. Strumiłowa	Busk
Wierzblany	Żółkiew	Kulików
Wierzbna	Jarosław	Jarosław
Wierzbolowce	Rohatyń	Rohatyń
Wierzbów	Brzeżany	Narajów
Wierzbów	Podhajce	Podhajce
Wierzbowce	Horodenka	Horodenka
Wierzbowce	Kossów	Kossów
Wierzbowczyk	Brody	Podkamień
Wierzbowiec	Czortków	Budzanów
Wierzbówka	Borszczów	Skała
Wierzchniakowce	Borszczów	Borszczów
Wierzchosławice	Tarnów	Zabno
Wierzchowce	Husiatyn	Chorostków
Wierznica	Nowy Sącz	Łącko
Wiesenberg	Żółkiew	Kulików
Wietrzno	Krosno	Dukla
Wieza	Wieliczka	Klasno
Wiktorów	Stanisławów	Hałicz
Wiktorówka	Brzeżany	Kozowa
Wilamowice	Biała	Kęty
Wilcza	Przemyśl	Przemyśl
Wilcza Góra	Jaworów	Wielkie Oczy
Wilcza Wola	Kolbuszowa	Raniżów
Wilczkowice	Biała	Oświęcim
Wilczyce	Limanowa	Limanowa
Wilczyska	Grybów	Bobowa
Wildenthal	Kolbuszowa	Raniżów
Wildenthal	Rzeszów	Głogów
Wilkonosza	Nowy Sącz	Nowy Sącz
Wilkowice	Biała	Lipnik
Wilkowisko	Limanowa	Limanowa
Wilsznia	Krosno	Dukla
Wincentówka	Kam. Strumiłowa	Chołojów
Winiary	Wieliczka	Klasno
Winiatyńce	Zaleszczyki	Korolówka
Winniczki	Lemberg	Winniki
Winniki	Lemberg	Winniki
Winniki	Sambor	Sambor
Winograd	Tłumacz	Ottynia
Winogród	Kołomea	Gwozdźiec
Wirchne	Gorlice	Gorlice
Wisłoboki	Lemberg	Jaryczów
Wisłoczek	Sanok	Rymanów
Wisłok Wielki	Sanok	Bukowsko
Wiśnicz	Bochnia	Wiśnicz Nowy
Wiśnicz Mały	Bochnia	Wiśnicz Nowy
Wiśnicz Nowy	Bochnia	Wiśnicz Nowy
Wiśnicz Stary	Bochnia	Wiśnicz Nowy
Wiśniowa	Jasło	Frysztak
Wiśniowa	Ropczyce	Sędziszów
Wiśniowa	Ropczyce	Wielopole
Wiśniowa	Wieliczka	Klasno
Wiśniowczyk	Podhajce	Złotniki
Wiśniowczyk	Przemyślany	Dunajowce
Wiśniowczyk	Złoczów	Gologory
Wistowa	Kalusz	Kalusz
Wistowice	Rudki	Rudki
Wiszenka	Jaworów	Jaworów
Wiszenka	Mościska	Sądowa Wisznia
Wiszniów	Rohatyń	Bursztyn
Witanowice	Wadowice	Wadowice
Witków	Sokal	Bełż
Witków Nowy	Kam. Strumiłowa	Witków Nowy
Witków stary	Kam. Strumiłowa	Witków Nowy
Witkowice	Biała	Kęty
Witkowice	Ropczyce	Ropczyce
Witkowice	Tarnobrzeg	Radomyśl
Witkówka	Nowy Sącz	Nowy Sącz
Witów	Limanowa	Mszana dolna
Witów	Nowy Targ	Nowy Targ
Witowice Dolne	Nowy Sącz	Nowy Sącz
Witowice Górne	Nowy Sącz	Nowy Sącz
Witryłów	Brzozów	Brzozów
Wituszyńce	Przemyśl	Przemyśl
Witwica	Dolina	Bolechów
Władypol	Mościska	Hussaków
Władypole	Sokal	Bełż
Włonowice	Nowy Sącz	Nowy Sącz
Włosań	Wieliczka	Podgórze
Włosienica	Biała	Oświęcim
Włostówka	Limanowa	Limanowa
Woczuchy	Mościska	Sądowa Wisznia
Wodna	Chrzanów	Chrzanów
Wodniki	Bóbrka	Bóbrka
Wodniki	Sokal	Warez
Wodniki	Stanisławów	Maryampol
Wodniki	Stanisławów	Stanisławów
Wojaczówka	Jasło	Frysztak
Wojakowa	Brzesko	Czchów
Wojciechowice	Przemyślany	Przemyślany
Wojcina	Dąbrowa	Szczucin
Wojków	Mielec	Mielec
Wojkowa	Nowy Sącz	Muszyna
Wojkowice	Mościska	Sądowa Wisznia
Wojkówka	Bircza	Rybotycze
Wojkówka	Jasło	Frysztak
Wojkówka	Krosno	Korczyna
Wojnarowa	Grybów	Bobowa
Wojnicz	Brzesko	Wojnicz
Wojniłów	Kalusz	Wojniłów
Wojsław	Mielec	Mielec
Wojsławice	Sokal	Sokal
Wojtkowa	Bircza	Rybotycze
Wojtostwo	Bochnia	Bochnia
Wojtowa	Gorlice	Gorlice
Wojutycze	Sambor	Sambor
Wokowice	Brzesko	Brzesko
Wola	Brzozów	Dynów
Wola	Pilzno	Dębica
Wola Antoniowska	Tarnobrzeg	Radomyśl
Wola Baraniecka	Mościska	Hussaków
Wola Batorska	Bochnia	Bochnia
Wola Blazowska	Sambor	Sambor
Wola Blizsza	Łańcut	Łańcut
Wola Brzosterka	Pilzno	Brzostek
Wola Buchowska	Jarosław	Pruchnik
Wola Chlipelska	Rudki	Rudki
Wola Chorzelowska	Mielec	Mielec
Wola Cicha	Rzeszów	Głogów
Wola Czerwona	Jarosław	Pruchnik
Wola Dalsza	Łańcut	Łańcut
Wola Dębińska	Brzesko	Brzesko
Wola Dębowiecka	Jasło	Jasło

Town	Main District	Subdistrict	Town	Main District	Subdistrict
Wola Dobrostańska	Gródek	Janów	Wolczatycze	Bóbrka	Chodorów
Wola Dolholucka	Stryj	Stryj	Wolczków	Stanisławów	Maryampol
Wola Drwińska	Bochnia	Bochnia	Wolczkowce	Śniatyn	Zabłotów
Wola Duchacka	Wieliczka	Podgórze	Wolczuchy	Gródek	Gródek
Wola Filipowska	Chrzanów	Chrzanów	Wolczyniec	Stanisławów	Stanisławów
Wola Gnojnicka	Jaworów	Krakówiec	Wolczyszczowice	Mościska	Sądowa Wisznia
Wola Gołego	Tarnobrzeg	Baranów	Woldzimierce	Żydaczów	Żurawno
Wola Gorzańska	Lisko	Baligród	Wolerbowce	Złoczów	Zborów
Wola Jakubowa	Drohobycz	Drohobycz	Wolica	Bochnia	Wiśnicz Nowy
Wola Jasienicka	Brzozów	Jasienica	Wolica	Brzeżany	Brzeżany
Wola Koblańska	Staremiasto	Staremiasto	Wolica	Jasło	Jasło
Wola Komborska	Krosno	Dukla	Wolica	Lemberg	Nawarya
Wola Korzeniecka	Bircza	Bircza	Wolica	Limanowa	Limanowa
Wola Kosnowa	Nowy Sącz	Łącko	Wolica	Lisko	Ustrzyki Dolne
Wola Kręcowska	Sanok	Tyrawa woloska	Wolica	Pilzno	Dębica
Wola Krogulecka	Nowy Sącz	Piwniczna	Wolica	Podhajce	Podhajce
Wola Kurowska	Nowy Sącz	Nowy Sącz	Wolica	Sanok	Bukowsko
Wola Lubecka	Pilzno	Pilzno	Wolica	Skałat	Touste
Wola Luźniańska	Gorlice	Gorlice	Wolica	Stryj	Stryj
Wola Mała	Żydaczów	Rozdól	Wolica	Trembowla	Trembowla
Wola Matyaszowa	Lisko	Baligród	Wolica	Żólkiew	Gross-Mosty
Wola Mazowiecka	Tarnopol	Mikulińce	Wolica Baryłowa	Kam. Strumiłowa	Radziechów
Wola Michowa	Lisko	Wola Michowa	Wolica Derewlanska	Kam. Strumiłowa	Busk
Wola Mielecka	Mielec	Mielec	Wolica Hnizdyczowska	Żydaczów	Żydaczów
Wola Mieszkowska	Bochnia	Wiśnicz Nowy	Wolica Komarowa	Sokal	Tartaków
Wola Niżnia	Sanok	Rymanów	Wolica Lugowa	Ropczyce	Sędziszów
Wola Ostregowska	Tarnów	Tarnów	Wolica Piaskowa	Ropczyce	Sędziszów
Wola Otalezka	Mielec	Radomyśl Wiel.	Wolina	Nisko	Rudnik
Wola Pelkińska	Jarosław	Jarosław	Wolka Gradzka	Dąbrowa	Dąbrowa
Wola Piotrowa	Sanok	Bukowsko	Wolkiew	Lemberg	Nawarya
Wola Piskulina	Nowy Sącz	Łącko	Wołków	Lemberg	Nawarya
Wola Pławska	Mielec	Radomyśl Wiel.	Wołków	Przemyślany	Przemyślany
Wola Podłażanska	Wieliczka	Klasno	Wołków	Przemyślany	Przemyślany
Wola Postołów	Lisko	Lisko	Wołkowce	Borszczów	Mielnica
Wola Przemykowska	Brzesko	Szczurowa	Wołkowce ad Perejmy	Borszczów	Borszczów
Wola Radłowska	Brzesko	Radłów	Wołkowce ad Borszczów	Borszczów	Borszczów
Wola Radziszowska	Myślenice	Myślenice	Wołkowyja	Lisko	Baligród
Wola Rafałowska	Rzeszów	Tyczyn	Wołochy	Brody	Brody
Wola Rajnowa	Sambor	Sambor	Wołodzia	Brzozów	Dynów
Wola Romanowa	Lisko	Ustrzyki Dolne	Wołopcza	Sambor	Sambor
Wola Rzeszycka	Tarnobrzeg	Radomyśl	Wołosate	Lisko	Lutowiska
Wola Skrzydlańska	Limanowa	Limanowa	Wołosianka	Stryj	Skole
Wola Starzyska	Jaworów	Jaworów	Wołoska Wieś	Dolina	Bolechów
Wola Stróżka	Brzesko	Czchów	Wołosów	Nadwórna	Nadwórna
Wola Szeżucińska	Dąbrowa	Szczucin	Wołosówka	Złoczów	Zborów
Wola Wadowska	Mielec	Radomyśl Wiel.	Wołostków	Mościska	Sądowa Wisznia
Wola Węgierska	Jarosław	Pruchnik	Wołoszczyzna	Podhajce	Podhajce
Wola Wielka	Cieszanów	Lipsko	Wołoszynowa	Staremiasto	Starasól
Wola Wielka	Żydaczów	Rozdól	Wołoszyny	Tarnobrzeg	Rozwadów
Wola Wieruszycka	Bochnia	Wiśnicz Nowy	Wołowa	Kołomea	Kołomea
Wola Wysocka	Żólkiew	Żólkiew	Wołowe Laszki	Bóbrka	Bóbrka
Wola Wyżnia	Sanok	Rymanów	Wołowice	Gorlice	Gorlice
Wola Zabierzowska	Bochnia	Bochnia	Wołowszczyzna	Bóbrka	Bóbrka
Wola Zaderewacka	Dolina	Bolechów	Wołśniów	Żydaczów	Rozdól
Wola Zakrzowska	Brzesko	Wojnicz	Wołświń	Sokal	Krystynopol
Wola Zaleska	Jarosław	Radymno	Wołtuszowa	Sanok	Rymanów
Wola Zarczycka	Nisko	Rudnik	Worobiówka	Tarnopol	Tarnopol
Wola Zdaków	Mielec	Mielec	Worochta	Nadwórna	Delatyn
Wola Zerekowska	Pilzno	Dębica	Worochta	Sokal	Bełż
Wola Zglobieńska	Rzeszów	Czudec	Worochta	Sokal	Bełż
Wola Zoltaniecka	Żólkiew	Kulików	Worona	Tłumacz	Ottynia
Wolanka	Drohobycz	Borystaw	Woroniaki	Złoczów	Złoczów

Town	Main District	Subdistrict	Town	Main District	Subdistrict
Woronów	Rawa Ruska	Uhnów	Wyłów	Mielec	Radomyśl Wiel.
Worwolińce	Zaleszczyki	Tłuste	Wymsłówka	Brzeżany	Kozłów
Woszczeńce	Rudki	Rudki	Wypyski	Przemyślany	Przemyślany
Wownia	Stryj	Stryj	Wyrów	Kam. Strumiłowa	Kam. Strumiłowa
Wożilów	Buczacz	Potok	Wyrzne	Rzeszów	Czudec
Wożniczna	Tarnów	Tarnów	Wyskitna	Grybów	Grybów
Wożniki	Wadowice	Zator	Wysocko	Brody	Brody
Wróblaczyn	Rawa Ruska	Niemerów	Wysocko	Jarosław	Radymno
Wróblik Królewski	Krosno	Dukla	Wysocko	Złoczów	Olesko
Wróblik Szlachecki	Sanok	Rymanów	Wysoczany	Sanok	Bukowsko
Wróblowa	Jasło	Jasło	Wysoka	Jasło	Frysztak
Wróblowice	Drohobycz	Drohobycz	Wysoka	Łańcut	Łańcut
Wróblowice	Tarnów	Tuchów	Wysoka	Myślenice	Jordanów
Wróblowice	Wieliczka	Podgórze	Wysoka	Rzeszów	Głogów
Wróblówka	Nowy Targ	Nowy Targ	Wysoka	Wadowice	Kalwarya
Wrocanka	Jasło	Jasło	Wysokie	Limanowa	Limanowa
Wrocanka	Krosno	Dukla	Wyspa	Rohatyń	Rohatyń
Wroców	Gródek	Janów	Wysuczka	Borszczów	Borszczów
Wrzasowice	Wieliczka	Podgórze	Wyszatyce	Przemyśl	Przemyśl
Wrzawy	Tarnobrzeg	Rozwadów	Wyszowa	Gorlice	Gorlice
Wrzepia	Bochnia	Bochnia	Wyszowadka	Krosno	Dukla
Wujskie	Sanok	Sanok	Wytrzyszczka	Brzesko	Czchów
Wulka	Brzeżany	Brzeżany	Wywczanka	Stanisławów	Halicz
Wulka	Lemberg	Zniesienie	Wyzków	Dolina	Dolina
Wulka	Sanok	Rymanów	Wyżłów	Sokal	Bełż
Wulka	Sokal	Sokal	Wyżłów	Stryj	Skole
Wulka beim Walde	Łańcut	Łańcut	Wyżniany	Przemyślany	Gliniany
Wulka Bielinska	Nisko	Ulanów	Wyżyce	Bochnia	Bochnia
Wulka Dulecka	Mielec	Radomyśl Wiel.	Wzary	Wieliczka	Klasno
Wulka Grodziska	Łańcut	Leżajsk	Wzdów	Brzozów	Brzozów
Wulka Horyniecka	Cieszanów	Cieszanów	Zabawa	Brzesko	Radłów
Wulka Kuninska	Żółkiew	Żółkiew	Zabawa	Kam. Strumiłowa	Witków Nowy
Wulka Laneuska	Nisko	Ulanów	Zabawa	Wieliczka	Klasno
Wulka Letowska	Nisko	Rudnik	Żabcze Murowane	Sokal	Bełż
Wulka Malkowa	Łańcut	Przeworsk	Zabełcze	Nowy Sącz	Nowy Sącz
Wulka Mazowiecka	Rawa Ruska	Rawa Ruska	Żabie	Kossów	Żabie
Wulka Mędrzechowska	Dąbrowa	Dąbrowa	Zabierzów	Bochnia	Bochnia
Wulka Niedźwiedzka	Łańcut	Leżajsk	Zabierzów	Rzeszów	Rzeszów
Wulka Ogryzkowa	Łańcut	Przeworsk	Żabińce	Husiatyn	Probużna
Wulka pod Lasem	Rzeszów	Głogów	Zabledna	Tarnów	Tuchów
Wulka Rosnowska	Jaworów	Krakówiec	Zabłocie	Wieliczka	Klasno
Wulka Suszanska	Kam. Strumiłowa	Radziechów	Zabłocie	Żywiec	Zabłocie
Wulka Turebska	Tarnobrzeg	Rozwadów	Zabłotce	Brody	Sokołówka
Wulka Zapałowska	Cieszanów	Oleszyce	Zabłotce	Jarosław	Radymno
Wulka Zmijowska	Jaworów	Wielkie Oczy	Zabłotce	Przemyśl	Niżankowice
Wybranówka	Bóbrka	Bóbrka	Zabłotce	Sanok	Sanok
Wybranówka	Trembowla	Janów	Zabłotów	Śniatyn	Zabłotów
Wybudów	Brzeżany	Kozowa	Zabłotowce	Żydaczów	Żurawno
Wychwatyńce	Skałat	Touste	Zabłotówka	Czortków	Ulaszkowce
Wyczółki	Buczacz	Monasterzyska	Żabnica	Żywiec	Zabłocie
Wydma	Brzozów	Brzozów	Żabno	Tarnobrzeg	Radomyśl
Wydra	Sokal	Krystynopol	Żabno	Tarnów	Zabno
Wydreń	Lisko	Lutowiska	Żabojki	Tarnopol	Tarnopol
Wydrze	Łańcut	Żołynia	Żabokruki	Bóbrka	Strzeliska Nowe
Wydrze	Tarnobrzeg	Rozwadów	Żabokruki	Horodenka	Obertyn
Wygiełzów	Chrzanów	Chrzanów	Zaborów	Brzesko	Szczurowa
Wyglanowice	Nowy Sącz	Nowy Sącz	Zaborów	Rzeszów	Czudec
Wygnanka	Czortków	Czortków	Zaborze	Biała	Oświęcim
Wygoda	Borszczów	Mielnica	Zaborze	Rawa Ruska	Rawa Ruska
Wykoty	Sambor	Sambor	Zabratów	Rzeszów	Tyczyn
Wylewa	Jarosław	Pruchnik	Zabrnie	Dąbrowa	Szczucin
Wyłkowyja	Rzeszów	Rzeszów	Zabrnie	Tarnobrzeg	Rozwadów

Town	Main District	Subdistrict	Town	Main District	Subdistrict
Zabrodzie	Lisko	Lisko	Zalcze	Jasło	Jasło
Zabrzez	Nowy Sącz	Łącko	Zalęna	Wadowice	Kalwarya
Zabrzydowice	Wadowice	Kalwarya	Zaleśce	Bóbrka	Brzozdowiec
Zaburze	Sokal	Sokal	Zalesiany	Wieliczka	Klasno
Zabutyń	Sanok	Sanok	Zalesie	Buczacz	Barysz
Zachwiejów	Mielec	Mielec	Zalesie	Czortków	Czortków
Zaczarnice	Tarnów	Tarnów	Zalesie	Gródek	Janów
Zaczernie	Rzeszów	Rzeszów	Zalesie	Łańcut	Żolynia
Zadąbrowie	Przemyśl	Sosnica	Zalesie	Limanowa	Limanowa
Zadarów	Buczacz	Monasterzyska	Zalesie	Nisko	Rudnik
Zaderewacz	Dolina	Bolechów	Zalesie	Rzeszów	Tyczyn
Zadubrowce	Śniatyn	Zabłotów	Zalesie	Złoczów	Złoczów
Zaduszniki	Mielec	Mielec	Zalesie Antoniowskie	Tarnobrzeg	Radomyśl
Zadwórze	Lisko	Ustrzyki Dolne	Zalesie Biskupie	Borszczów	Mielnica
Zadwórze	Przemyślany	Gliniany	Zalesie Gorzyckie	Tarnobrzeg	Tarnobrzeg
Zadziele	Żywiec	Zabłocie	Zaleszany	Tarnobrzeg	Rozwadów
Zadziszówka	Skałat	Podwołoczyska	Zaleszczyki	Zaleszczyki	Zaleszczyki
Zagoczyce	Ropczyce	Sędziszów	Zaleszczyki Małe	Buczacz	Jazłowice
Zagoreczko	Bóbrka	Chodorów	Zaleszczyki Stare	Zaleszczyki	Zaleszczyki
Zagórnik	Wadowice	Andrychów	Zalęże	Rzeszów	Rzeszów
Zagorów	Limanowa	Limanowa	Zalipie	Rohatyń	Rohatyń
Zagórz	Sanok	Sanok	Załokieć	Drohobycz	Drohobycz
Zagórzany	Gorlice	Gorlice	Załóźce	Brody	Załóźce
Zagórzany	Wieliczka	Klasno	Załubińcze	Nowy Sącz	Nowy Sącz
Zagórze	Brody	Zołożce	Załucze	Borszczów	Skała
Zagórze	Chrzanów	Chrzanów	Załucze nad Prutem	Kołomea	Kołomea
Zagórze	Kalusz	Kalusz	Załucze nad Czer.	Śniatyn	Śniatyn
Zagórze	Łańcut	Kańczuga	Załuczne	Nowy Targ	Nowy Targ
Zagórze	Lemberg	Nawarya	Załukiew	Stanisławów	Halicz
Zagórze	Nowy Sącz	Nowy Sącz	Załuż	Sanok	Sanok
Zagórze	Pilzno	Jodłowa	Załuże	Cieszanów	Lubaczów
Zagórze	Rudki	Rudki	Załuże	Dąbrowa	Szczucin
Zagórze	Wieliczka	Klasno	Załuże	Gródek	Janów
Zagórze Knihynickie	Rohatyń	Rohatyń	Załuże	Jaworów	Jaworów
Zagórze Konkolnickie	Rohatyń	Bursztyn	Załuże	Rohatyń	Rohatyń
Zagórzyn	Nowy Sącz	Łącko	Zamarstynów	Lemberg	Zniesienie
Zagrobela	Tarnopol	Tarnopol	Zameczek	Żólkiew	Żólkiew
Zagródki	Lemberg	Szczerzec	Zamek	Rawa Ruska	Magierów
Zagrody	Mościska	Sądowa Wisznia	Zamiechów	Jarosław	Radymno
Zagwóźdź	Stanisławów	Stanisławów	Zamieście	Limanowa	Limanowa
Zahajce	Podhajce	Podhajce	Zamłynowe	Lisko	Ustrzyki Dolne
Zahajpol	Kołomea	Gwozdziec	Zamojsce	Jarosław	Radymno
Zahelmno	Wadowice	Kalwarya	Zamoście	Brzesko	Wojnicz
Zahoczewie	Lisko	Baligród	Zamoście	Przemyślany	Gliniany
Zahorce	Złoczów	Olesko	Zamowa	Rzeszów	Strzyżów
Zakliczyn	Brzesko	Czchów	Zamulińce	Kołomea	Gwozdziec
Zakliczyn	Wieliczka	Klasno	Zany	Stanisławów	Maryampol
Zakomarze	Złoczów	Olesko	Zapałów	Cieszanów	Oleszyce
Zakopane	Nowy Targ	Nowy Targ	Zapole	Ropczyce	Ropczyce
Zakościele	Mościska	Mościska	Zapolednik	Tarnobrzeg	Rozwadów
Zakowice Nowe	Tarnów	Zabno	Zapytów	Lemberg	Jaryczów
Zakowice stare	Tarnów	Zabno	Zarajsko	Sambor	Sambor
Zakrzewie	Tłumacz	Ottynia	Zarawce	Rawa Ruska	Lubycza
Zakrzów	Brzesko	Wojnicz	Zarębki	Kolbuszowa	Kolbuszowa
Zakrzów	Tarnobrzeg	Tarnobrzeg	Zarki	Chrzanów	Chrzanów
Zakrzów	Wadowice	Kalwarya	Żarków	Złoczów	Olesko
Zakrzów	Wieliczka	Klasno	Żarnowiec	Krosno	Dukla
Zakrzówek	Wieliczka	Podgórze	Żarnówka	Myślenice	Maków
Zalanów	Rohatyń	Rohatyń	Żarównie	Mielec	Mielec
Zalas	Chrzanów	Chrzanów	Żarszyn	Sanok	Rymanów
Zalasowa	Tarnów	Ryglice	Zarubińce	Skałat	Grzymałów
Zalawie	Gorlice	Gorlice	Zarudec	Lemberg	Zniesienie

Town	Main District	Subdistrict	Town	Main District	Subdistrict
Zarudka	Złoczów	Zborów	Zawatka	Ropczyce	Wielopole
Zarudzie	Tarnopol	Tarnopol	Zawidcże	Brody	Szczurowice
Zarudzie	Złoczów	Zborów	Zawidowice	Gródek	Gródek
Zarwanica	Podhajce	Złotniki	Zawierzbie	Dąbrowa	Dąbrowa
Zarwanica	Złoczów	Złoczów	Zawisznia	Sokal	Sokal
Żary	Chrzanów	Trzebina	Zawodzie	Brzesko	Wojnicz
Zaryte	Myślenice	Jordanów	Zawodzie	Tarnów	Tarnów
Zarzecze	Mościska	Sądowa Wisznia	Zawoj	Kalusz	Kalusz
Zarzecze	Żywiec	Zabłocie	Zawoj	Lisko	Baligród
Zarzekowice	Tarnobrzeg	Tarnobrzeg	Zawoja	Myślenice	Maków
Zarzyce	Nisko	Ulanów	Zawoje	Sanok	Rymanów
Zarzyce	Rzeszów	Czudec	Zawośnia	Sokal	Krystynopol
Zarzyce Małe	Wadowice	Kalwarya	Zawóz	Lisko	Baligród
Zarzyce Wielkie	Wadowice	Kalwarya	Zazameże	Dąbrowa	Dąbrowa
Zarzycze	Jarosław	Jarosław	Zazdrość	Trembowla	Strusów
Zarzycze	Nadwórna	Delatyn	Zazule	Złoczów	Złoczów
Zarzycze	Nowy Sącz	Łącko	Zbadyń	Jaworów	Jaworów
Zasadne	Limanowa	Mszana Dolna	Zbaraż	Zbaraz	Zbaraz
Zasań	Wieliczka	Klasno	Zbek	Nowy Sącz	Nowy Sącz
Zaścianka	Tarnopol	Tarnopol	Żbik	Chrzanów	Trzebina
Zaścinocze	Trembowla	Trembowla	Żbikowice	Nowy Sącz	Nowy Sącz
Zaskale	Nowy Targ	Nowy Targ	Zbłudza	Limanowa	Limanowa
Zasław	Sanok	Sanok	Zboiska	Krosno	Dukla
Zastawce	Podhajce	Podhajce	Zboiska	Lemberg	Zniesienie
Zastawce	Podhajce	Zawałów	Zboiska	Sanok	Bukowsko
Zastawie	Rawa Ruska	Uhnów	Zboiska	Sokal	Tartaków
Zastawie	Tarnopol	Mikulińce	Zbora	Kalusz	Kalusz
Zasulince	Zaleszczyki	Korolówka	Zborczyce	Wieliczka	Klasno
Zaszków	Lemberg	Zniesienie	Zborów	Złoczów	Zborów
Zaszków	Złoczów	Gologory	Zborowek	Wieliczka	Klasno
Zaszkowice	Gródek	Gródek	Zborowice	Grybów	Bobowa
Zatawie	Trembowla	Janów	Zbrzyź	Borszczów	Skała
Zatoka	Bochnia	Bochnia	Zbydniów	Bochnia	Wiśnicz nowy
Zator	Wadowice	Zator	Zbydniów	Tarnobrzeg	Rozwadów
Zaturzyn	Podhajce	Zawałów	Zbydniowice	Wieliczka	Podgórze
Zatwarnica	Lisko	Lutowiska	Zbyszyce	Nowy Sącz	Nowy Sącz
Zawada	Bochnia	Wiśnicz Nowy	Zbytkowska Góra	Tarnów	Tarnów
Zawada	Limanowa	Limanowa	Zdarzec	Brzesko	Radlów
Zawada	Myślenice	Myślenice	Zdonia	Brzesko	Czchów
Zawada	Nowy Sącz	Nowy Sącz	Zdroheć	Brzesko	Radlów
Zawada	Pilzno	Dębica	Zdzianna	Staremiasto	Staremiasto
Zawada	Tarnów	Tarnów	Ździary	Nisko	Ulanów
Zawada Lanekorońska	Brzesko	Wojnicz	Ździary	Ropczyce	Ropczyce
Zawada Uszewska	Brzesko	Brzesko	Żebranówka	Śniatyn	Zabłotów
Zawadka	Kalusz	Kalusz	Żędowice	Przemyślany	Przemyślany
Zawadka	Limanowa	Limanowa	Żegartowice	Wieliczka	Klasno
Zawadka	Lisko	Lisko	Żegestów	Nowy Sącz	Muszyna
Zawadka	Myślenice	Myślenice	Żeglce	Krosno	Dukla
Zawadka	Nowy Sącz	Nowy Sącz	Żełdec	Żólkiew	Żólkiew
Zawadka	Wadowice	Wadowice	Żelechów Mały	Kam. Strumiłowa	Kam. Strumiłowa
Zawadka ad Osiek	Jasło	Frysztak	Żelechów Wielki	Kam. Strumiłowa	Kam. Strumiłowa
Zawadka ad Buk	Sanok	Bukowsko	Żeleźnikowa	Nowy Sącz	Piwniczna
Zawadka Rymanów	Sanok	Rymanów	Żembrzyce	Wadowice	Wadowice
Zawadów	Jaworów	Jaworów	Żeniów	Przemyślany	Gliniany
Zawadów	Lemberg	Zniesienie	Żeraków	Pilzno	Dębica
Zawadów	Mościska	Mościska	Żerdenka	Lisko	Baligród
Zawadów	Mościska	Sądowa Wisznia	Żerebki Krolewskie	Skałat	Skałat
Zawadów	Stryj	Stryj	Żerebki Szlacheckie	Skałat	Skałat
Zawadówka	Podhajce	Zawałów	Żerków	Brzesko	Brzesko
Zawale	Borszczów	Mielnica	Żernica Niżna	Lisko	Baligród
Zawale	Śniatyn	Śniatyn	Żernica Wyżna	Lisko	Baligród
Zawałów	Podhajce	Zawałów	Żerosławice	Wieliczka	Klasno

Zgłobice	Tarnów	Tarnów
Zgłobień	Rzeszów	Czudec
Zieleńce	Borszczów	Borszczów
Zielensko	Sanok	Bukowsko
Zielona	Borszczów	Mielnica
Zielona	Buczacz	Buczacz
Zielona	Husiatyn	Husiatyn
Zielona	Kam. Strumiłowa	Radziechów
Zielona	Skałat	Grzymałów
Zielonka	Kolbuszowa	Sokołów
Zielów	Lemberg	Zniesienie
Ziempniów	Mielec	Radomyśl Wiel.
Zimna Woda	Jasło	Jasło
Zimna Woda	Lemberg	Zniesienie
Zimno Wódka	Grybów	Bobowa
Zimno Wódka	Lemberg	Zniesienie
Ziniatyn	Sokal	Bełż
Złockie	Nowy Sącz	Muszyna
Złoczów	Złoczów	Złoczów
Złoczówka	Brzeżany	Kozowa
Złota	Brzesko	Czchów
Złotkowice	Mościska	Hussaków
Złotne	Nowy Sącz	Łabowa
Złotniki	Mielec	Mielec
Złotniki	Podhajce	Złotniki
Złucisko	Nisko	Rudnik
Zmiąca	Limanowa	Limanowa
Zmiennica	Brzozów	Brzozów
Żmigród	Krosno	Zmigród
Żmigród Nowy	Krosno	Zmigród
Żmigród Stary	Krosno	Zmigród
Żmijowiska	Jaworów	Wielkie Oczy
Zmysłówka	Łańcut	Żolynia
Zmysłówka	Sanok	Rymanów
Znamirowice	Nowy Sącz	Nowy Sącz
Zneżyce	Sokal	Tartaków
Żnibrody	Buczacz	Jazłowice
Zniesienie	Lemberg	Zniesienie
Zniesienie	Lemberg	Zniesienie
Zohatyń	Bircza	Bircza
Zolczów	Rohatyń	Rohatyń
Zolibory	Rohatyń	Bursztyn
Żólkiew	Żólkiew	Żólkiew
Żołków	Jasło	Jasło
Żołnówka	Brzeżany	Brzeżany
Żołobek	Lisko	Ustrzyki Dolne
Zołtańce	Żólkiew	Kulików
Żołynia	Łańcut	Żolynia
Żornska	Lemberg	Zniesienie
Zręcin	Krosno	Dukla
Zręczyce	Wieliczka	Klasno
Zródła	Chrzanów	Chrzanów
Zrotowice	Mościska	Hussaków
Zrotowice	Przemyśl	Niżankowice
Zrzyce	Jasło	Jasło
Zubarmosty	Żólkiew	Gross-Mosty
Zubków	Sokal	Tartaków
Zubów	Trembowla	Strusów
Zubów	Złoczów	Gologory
Zubracze	Lisko	Wola Michowa
Zubrzec	Buczacz	Barysz
Zubrzyk	Nowy Sącz	Muszyna
Zubsuche	Nowy Targ	Nowy Targ
Zuchorzyce	Lemberg	Jaryczów
Żuklin	Łańcut	Kańczuga
Żukocin	Kołomea	Kołomea
Żuków	Brzeżany	Brzeżany
Żuków	Cieszanów	Cieszanów
Żuków	Kołomea	Kołomea
Żukowce	Złoczów	Zborów
Żulice	Złoczów	Białykamień
Żulin	Stryj	Stryj
Żupanie	Stryj	Skole
Żupawa	Tarnobrzeg	Tarnobrzeg
Żuraki	Borhodczany	Sołotwina
Żuratyn	Kam. Strumiłowa	Busk
Żurawica	Przemyśl	Przemyśl
Żurawiczki	Jarosław	Jarosław
Żurawienko	Rohatyń	Bursztyn
Żurawin	Lisko	Lutowiska
Żurawińce	Buczacz	Buczacz
Żurawków	Żydaczów	Żydaczów
Żurawniki	Lemberg	Jaryczów
Żurawno	Żydaczów	Żurawno
Żurów	Rohatyń	Rohatyń
Żurowa	Jasło	Olpiny
Żuszyce	Gródek	Janów
Żużel	Sokal	Bełż
Zwertów	Żólkiew	Kulików
Zwiahel	Borszczów	Borszczów
Zwiary	Tarnów	Tarnów
Zwieczyca	Rzeszów	Rzeszów
Zwiernik	Pilzno	Pilzno
Zwierzeń	Lisko	Lisko
Zwierzyce	Ropczyce	Sędziszów
Zwiniacz	Czortków	Budzanów
Zwór	Sambor	Sambor
Zwyżeń	Brody	Podkamień
Żydaczów	Żydaczów	Żydaczów
Żydatycze	Lemberg	Zniesienie
Żydnia	Gorlice	Gorlice
Żydowskie	Krosno	Dukla
Żygodowice	Wadowice	Zator
Zyndranowa	Krosno	Dukla
Żyrawa	Bóbrka	Chodorów
Żyrawa	Żydaczów	Żurawno
Żyrawka	Lemberg	Nawarya
Żyrawka	Zaleszczyki	Zaleszczyki
Żyrnów	Rzeszów	Strzyżów
Żywaczów	Horodenka	Obertyn
Żywiec	Żywiec	Zabłocie
Żywiec Stary	Żywiec	Zabłocie
Żyznomierz	Buczacz	Buczacz

❀ Bibliography ❀

Arad, Yitzhak, Shmuel Krakowski and Shmuel Spector, eds. *The Einsatzgruppen reports: Selections from the Dispatches of the Nazi Death Squads' Campaign Against the Jews, July 1941–January 1943.* New York: Holocaust Library, 1989.

Austria, Government of. *Justiz Ministerium. Fuhrung Der Geburts-, Ehe- und Sterbematrikeln Fur Die Israeliten in Galicien.* Vienna, 1877.

Bałaban, Majer. *Dzieje Żydów w Galicji i Rzeczypospolitej Krakowskiej, 1772–1868* (History of the Jews of Galicia and Kraków Republic, 1772–1868). Lwów, 1914.

———. *Historja Żydów w Krakowie i na Kazimierzu, 1304–1868* (History of the Jews of Kraków and Kazimierz, 1304–1868), vols. 1 and 2. Lwów, 1936, (reprinted in the 1990s in Yiddish).

Bonar, Andrew A., and Robert Murray M'Cheyne. *Narrative of a Mission of Inquiry to the Jews from the Church of Scotland in 1839.* Philadelphia: Presbyterian Board of Publication, 1839.

Bronstein, Sz. *Ludność żydowska w Polsce w okresie międzywojennym* (Jewish population in Poland during the interwar period). Wrocław: Studium Statystyczne, 1963.

Brook-Shepherd, Gordon. *The Austrians: A Thousand-Year Odyssey.* New York: Carroll & Graf, 1996.

Buzek, J. *Rozsiedlenie ludnosci Galicji według wyznania i języka* (Migration of the population of Galicia by denomination and language). Lwów, 1909.

Chorzempa, Rosemary A. *Korzenie Polskie: Polish Roots.* Baltimore: Genealogical Publishing Company, 1993.

Cohen, Chester G. *Shtetl Finder.* Los Angeles: Periday Company, 1980; Bowie, Md.: Heritage Books, 1989.

Dabrowska, Danuta, Abraham Wein and Aharon Weiss, eds., *Pinkas Hakehillot: Poland—Vol. II, Eastern Galicia,* Jerusalem: Yad Vashem, 1976.

Encyclopedia Judaica, "Galicia." Jerusalem, 1972.

Frazin, Judith. *A Translation Guide to 19th Century Polish-Language Civil-Registration Documents.* Self published. 1025 Antique Lane, Northbrook, IL 60062.

Fuks, Marian, Zygmunt Hoffman, Maurycy Horn and Jerzy Tomaszewski. *Polish Jewry: History and Culture.* Warsaw: Interpress, 1982.

Gilbert, Martin. *The Boys: The Story of 732 Young Concentration Camp Survivors.* New York: Henry Holt, 1997.

Gruber, Ruth Ellen. *Upon the Doorposts of Thy House: Jewish Life in East-Central Europe, Yesterday and Today.* New York: John Wiley and Sons, 1994.

Gruinski, S. *Materialy do kwestii żydowskiej w Galicji* (Material about the Jewish question in Galicia).

Guzik, Estelle. *Genealogical Resources in the New York Metropolitan Area.* New York: Jewish Genealogical Society, 1989.

Hauser, L. *Monografia miasta Przemyśla* (Monograph of the town of Przemyśl). wyd. II. Przemyśl, 1991.

Henisch, Meir. "Galician Jews in Vienna" in *The Jews of Austria: Essays on their Life, History and Destruction,* edited by Joseph Fraenkel. London: Valentine, Mitchell & Co., 1967.

Honey, Michael. "Jewish Family Names in Tarnobrzeg Demonstrated by Propinacja and Konsygnacya Listings" *The Galitzianer,* vol. 2, Winter 1994/5.

Jewish Encyclopedia, "Galicia." New York: Funk & Wagnalls, 1925.

Kramarz, W. *Ludność Przemyśla w latach 1521–1921* (Population of Przemyśl for the years 1521–1921). Przemyśl, 1930.

Krochmal, Anna. "Izraelickie Gminy Wyznaniowe" in *Akta Wyznaniowe w Zasobie Archiwiwum Państwowego w Przemyślu*. Przemysl: 1993. Translation into English by Jerzy Gorzyca.

Kugelmass, Jack and Jonathan Boyarin, *From A Ruined Garden: The Memorial Books of Polish Jewry*. New York: Schocken Books, 1983.

Kurzweil, Arthur. *From Generation to Generation*, 2d ed. New York: Harper Collins.

Lenius, Brian J. *Genealogical Gazetteer of Galicia*. Box 18, Group 4 R.R. #1, Anola, Manitoba, Canada R0E 0A0, 1993.

Levine, Hillel. *Economic Origins of Antisemitism: Poland and Its Jews in the Early Modern Period*. New Haven: Yale University Press, 1991.

Lewin, Isaac. *The Jewish Community in Poland*.

Menczer, Arie. *Sefer Przemyśl*. Israel: Irgun Yotzei Przemyśl, 1964.

Metzler, Wilhelm. *"Die Heimat und Ihre Geschichte: Galizien, Land und Leute* (The Home and their history: Galicia, country and people)" *Galizien German Descendants* 10 April 1997 (translated by John Forkheim and Eva Rowley).

Mokotoff, Gary, and Sallyann Amdur Sack. *Where Once We Walked: A Guide to the Jewish Communities Destroyed in the Holocaust*. Teaneck, N.J.: Avotaynu, 1991.

Najnowsze dzieje Żydów w Polsce (Modern history of the Jews of Poland), pod. red. J. Tomaszewskiego, Warsaw: 1993.

Pogonowski, Iwo Cyprian. *A Historical Atlas*. New York: Hippocrene Books, 1987.

Sack, Sallyann Amdur and Israel Genealogical Society. *A Guide to Jewish Genealogical Resources in Israel*. Teaneck, N.J.: Avotaynu, 1993.

Sanders, Ronald. *Shores of Refuge: A Hundred Years of Jewish Emigration*. New York: Henry Holt, 1987.

Schevill, F. *History of Europe: From the Reformation to the Present Day*. New York: Harcourt, Brace, 1930.

Schipera, I., A. Tartakowera and A. Haftki. *Żydzi w Małopolsce* (Jews in the Małopolska). *Studia z dziejow osadnictwa i zycia spoleczna, gospodarcza, oswiatowa i kulturalna*. Warsaw b.d.w.

Schorr, M. *Żydzi w Przemyślu do Konca XVIII w.* (Jews in Przemyśl to the end of the 18th century). Reprinted in Jerusalem from the original publication, 1991.

Schwartz, Rosaline and Susan Milamed, *A Guide to YIVO's Landsmanshaftn Archive*. New York: YIVO Institute for Jewish Research, 1986.

Subtelny, Orest. *Ukraine: A History*. Toronto: Toronto University Press, 1988.

Teller, A, H. Volovici and H. Assouline. *Guide to the Sources for the History of the Jews in Poland in the Central Archives*. Jerusalem: Central Archives for the History of the Jewish People, 1988.

Yad Vashem. *Black of Localities Whose Jewish Population Was Exterminated by the Nazis*. Jerusalem: Yad Vashem, 1965.

Wein, Abraham and Aharon Weiss, eds. *Pinkas Hakehillot: Poland—Vol. III, Western Galicia & Silesia*. Jerusalem: Yad Vashem, 1984.

Weiner, Miriam. *Jewish Roots in Poland: Pages from the Past and Archival Inventories*. Secaucus, N.J.: Miriam Weiner Routes to Roots Foundation, and New York: YIVO Institute for Jewish Research, 1997.

Weinryb, Bernard Dov. *The Jews of Poland: A Social and Economic History of the Jewish Community from 1100-1800*. Philadelphia: Jewish Publication Society, 1973.

Wierzbieniec, W. *Przemyska izraelicka gmina wyznaniowa w okresie autonomii Galicji* (Jewish community in Przemyśl during the autonomy of Galcia), vols. 6 ad 7. Przemyśl: Przemyskie Zapiski Historyczne, 1990.

Wunder, Rabbi Meir. *Meorei Galicia* (Encyclopedia of Galician rabbis and scholars), Jerusalem: Institute for Commemoration of Galician Jewry, 1978–1995.

❀ Index to Towns ❀

Bogoniowice 134
Bogorodchany *see* Bohorodczany
Boguchwala 134
Bogucice 134
Bogumilowice 134
Bogusza 134
Boguszówka 134
Bohatkowce 134
Bohordczany 126, 134
Bohordczany Stare 134
Bohordyczyn 134
Bohorodczany 22, 82, 84, 126
Bohutyn 134
Bojańczyce 134
Bojanice 134
Bojanów 134
Boków 134
Bolanowice 134
Bołdury 134
Bolechów 23, 51, 54, 82, 84, 87,
    127, 134, *also see* Bolekhov
Bolechów Ruski 134
Bolechówce 135
Bolęcin 135
Bolekhov 68, 78, 100, *also see*
    Bolechów
Bolesław 135
Bolestraszyce 135
Bołochów 135
Bolomyja 135
Bołozynów 135
Bolshovtsy 70, *also see* Bolszowce
Bolszowce 27, 82, 135, *also see*
    Bolshovtsy
Bonarówka 135
Boniowice 135
Boniszyn 135
Bonów 135
Bór Łodygowski 135
Bór Witkowski 135
Boratycze 135
Boratyn 135
Borchów 135
Bordulaki 135
Boreczek 135
Borek 135
Borek Fałecki 135
Borek Mały 135
Borek Nowy 135
Borek Stary 135
Borek Szlachecki 135
Borek Wielki 135
Borislav 100, *also see* Borysław

Borkanów 135
Borki 135
Borki Dominikańskie 135
Borki Janowskie 135
Borki Małe 135
Borki Wielkie 135
Borodczyce 135
Borowa 56, 135
Borowa Gora 135
Borowe 135
Borowna 135
Borownica 101, 135
Borschov 100
Borshchev 78, *also see* Borszczów
Borszczów 22, 51, 85, 86, 126,
    135, *also see* Borshchev
Borszów 135
Borszowice 135
Bortiatyn 135
Bortniki 135
Borusowa 135
Borwałd Górny 135
Boryczówka 135
Boryków 135
Borynicze 135
Borysław 9, 23, 51, 54, 59, 66, 80,
    82, 111, 112, 115, 119, 120, 127,
    135, *also see* Borislav
Borysławka 135
Boryszkowce 135
Borzęcin 135
Borzęta 135
Boszyry 135
Bouszów 135
Boża Wola 135
Boznów 135
Braciejowa 135
Brandwica 135
Bratkowce 135
Bratkowice 135
Bratówka 135
Bratucice 135
Bratyszów 135
Brelików 135
Breń Osuchowski 135
Brigidyn 135
Brnik 135
Brodki 135
Brodła 135
Brody 9, 12, 22, 46, 51, 73, 78, 80,
    82, 87, 100, 101, 112, 113, 116,
    126, 135
Brody Stare 135

Bronica 135
Bronisławówka 135
Broniszów 135
Broszniów 54, 82, 135
Browary 135
Bruchnal 135
Bruckenthal 135
Brunndorf 135
Bruśnik 135
Brusno Nowe 135
Brusno Stare 135
Brustury 135
Brykoń 135
Brykuta Nowa 135
Brykuta Stara 135
Brylińce 135
Bryły 135
Bryńce Cerkiewne 135
Bryńce Zagóne 135
Bryszcze 135
Brząćzowice 135
Brzana Dolna 135
Brzana Górna 135
Brzaza 135
Brzczowa 135
Brzeczyczany 135
Brzegi 135
Brześciany 135
Brzesko 11, 31, 37, 46, 51, 55, 82,
    84, 118, 127, 135
Brzeszcze 135
Brzeżanka 135
Brzeżany 22, 46, 51, 84, 87, 112,
    113, 127, 135
Brzeżawa 135
Brzezhany 82
Brzezice 135
Brzezie 135
Brzezina 135
Brzezinka 135
Brzezinka ad Kopytówka 135
Brzeziny 135, 136
Brzezna 136
Brzeżnica 136
Brzeżnica Stara 82
Brzezowa 136
Brzezowice 136
Brzezówka 136
Brzodzowce 136
Brzostek 34, 82, 84, 128, 136
Brzostowa Gora 136
Brzoszkowice 136
Brzoza 136

Chochłów 137
Chochołów 137
Chochoniów 137
Chochorowice 137
Chocimierz 23
Chocimirz 29, 129, 137
Chocin 137
Chocznia 137
Chodaczków Mały 137
Chodaczków Wielki 137
Chodaczów 137
Chodenice 137
Chodnowice 137
Chodorów 22, 63, 68, 82, 126, 137,
    also see Khodorov
Chodorowa 137
Chodowice 137
Chojnik 137
Cholewiana Góra 137
Chołojów 24, 51, 82, 127, 137
Chołowice 137
Chomczyn 137
Chomiakówka 137
Chomranice 137
Chomrzyska 137
Chorągwica 137
Chorderkowce 137
Chorkówka 137
Chorobrów 137
Chorocowa 137
Choronów 137
Chorosiec 137
Chorosnica 137
Chorostkov see Chorostków
Chorostków 23, 51, 82, 88, 116,
    127, 137
Chorowiec 137
Chortkov 76, 78, also see
    Czortków and Tchortchov
Chortków 42, 88
Chorzelów 137
Chorzów 137
Chotowa 137
Chotowice 137
Chotylub 137
Chotynice 137
Chrabuzna 137
Chraplice 137
Chreniów 137
Chrewt 137
Chromohorb 137
Chronów 137
Chrość 137

Chrostowa 137
Chruślice 137
Chrusno 25
Chrusno Nowe 137
Chrusno Stare 137
Chryplin 137
Chrzanów 31, 46, 51, 55, 82, 127,
    137
Chrząstów 137
Chrząstowice 137
Chrząstówka 137
Chudykowce 137
Chudyowce 137
Chwalibog 137
Chwałowice 137
Chwatów 137
Chyrów 28, 46, 82, 129, 137
Chyrzyna Kortyniki 138
Chyszów 138
Chyżówka 138
Cichawa 138
Cichawka 138
Ciche Miętustwo 138
Ciechania 138
Ciechanów 114, 117
Cięcina 138
Cieczyna 138
Cieląż 138
Ciemierzowice 138
Ciemierzyńce 138
Ciemieżypce 138
Cieniawa 138
Cieplice 138
Cierpisz 138
Cieszanów 31, 51, 82, 101, 127,
    138
Ciezacin Mały 138
Ciezacin Wielki 138
Ciężkowice 138
Ciężów 138
Cikowice 138
Cisna 82, 101, 138
Cisów 138
Cisowa 138
Cisowiec 138
Cisowlas 138
Ciszec 138
Ciszki 138
Cmolas 138
Cracow 66, 71, also see Krakau
    and Kraków
Cucułowce 138
Cucyłów 138

Cuniów 138
Ćwików 138
Ćwitowa 138
Cygany 138
Cyranka 138
Czabalina 138
Czabarówka 138
Czaczów 138
Czahrów 138
Czajkowa 138
Czajkowice 138
Czaniec 138
Czanyż 138
Czaplaki 138
Czaple 138
Czarna 138
Czarne 138
Czarnokońce Małe 138
Czarnokońce Wielkie 138
Czarnokoniecka Wola 138
Czarnołożce 138
Czarnorzeki 138
Czarnowoda 138
Czarnuchowice 138
Czarnuszowice 138
Czarny 82
Czarny Dunajec 51, 138
Czartorya 138
Czasław 138
Cząstkowice 138
Czaszyn 138
Czatkowice 138
Czchów 31, 42, 82, 127, 138
Czechów 138
Czechowa 138
Czechówka 138
Czechy 138
Czekaj Pniowski 138
Czekaj Wrzawski 138
Czelatycze 138
Czelowice 138
Czeluśnica 138
Czepiele 138
Czerchawa 138
Czercze 138
Czerczyk 24, 138
Czeremcha 138
Czeremchów 138
Czeremosznia 138
Czerepin 138
Czerhanówka 138
Czerkasy 138
Czerkawszczyzna 138

Dobromil 30, 51, 69, 82, 84, 90, 126, 140
Dobroniów 140
Dobropole 140
Dobrostany 140
Dobrotvor *see* Dobrotwór
Dobrotwór 24, 82, 128, 140
Dobrowa 112
Dobrowlany 140
Dobrowódka 140
Dobrowody 29, 140
Dobrucowa 140
Dobrynin 140
Dobrzanica 140
Dobrzanka 140
Dobrzany 140
Dobrzechów 140
Dołega 140
Dolgoye *see* Dolhe
Dołha Wojniłowska 140
Dołhe 23, 88, 140
Dołhe Kałuskie 140
Dołhomosciska 140
Dołhopol 140
Dolina 23, 78, 82, 115, 119, 127, 140
Dolina ad Zaluz 140
Doliniany 140
Dolnawieś 140
Dołobów 140
Dołpotów 140
Dołuszyce 140
Doły 140
Dołżanka 140
Dołżka 140
Dołżyca 140
Dołżyce 140
Domacyny 140
Domalkówka Wola 140
Domaradz 82, 140
Domaszer 140
Domaszów 140
Domatków 140
Dombrowa 112
Dominikowice 140
Domosławice 140
Domostawa 140
Dora 119, 140
Dorbrosin 140
Dornbach 140
Dornfeld 140
Dorochów 140
Dorofijówka 140

Dorohin 140
Doroszów Mały 140
Doroszów Wielkie 140
Dorozów 140
Doznamorycz 140
Drabimanka 140
Draganowa 140
Draganówka 140
Drahasymów 140
Droginia 140
Drogobych 76, 78, 80, 81, 100, *also see* Drohobycz
Drohiczówka 140
Drohobycz 23, 51, 54-56, 59, 73, 82, 84, 88, 117, 127, 140, *also see* Drogobych
Drohobyczka 140
Drohojów 140
Drohomirczany 140
Drohomyśl 140
Drohowycze 140
Drohowyże 140
Drozdowice 140
Drwinia 140
Dryszczów 140
Duba 140
Dubaniowice 140
Dubas 140
Dubetsk *see* Dubiecko
Dubie 140
Dubiecko 34, 46, 51, 56, 82, 101, 128, 140
Dubienko 140
Dubkowce 140
Dubkowice 140
Dublany 27, 140
Dubowce 140
Dubowica 114, 140
Dubrawka 140
Dubryniów 140
Dubszara 140
Dubszcze 140
Dudyn 140
Dudynice 140
Dukla 8, 33, 57, 58, 82, 84, 101, 116, 128, 140
Dulcza Mała 141
Dulczówka 141
Duliby 141
Dulowa 141
Dunaiv *see* Dunajowce
Dunajów 82
Dunajowce 26, 129, 141

Duninów 141
Duńkowice 141
Duńkowiczki 141
Dupliska 141
Durdy 141
Dusanów 141
Dusowce 141
Duszatyn 141
Dwerniaczek 141
Dwernik 141
Dworce 141
Dwory 141
Dybków 141
Dyczków 141
Dydiatycze 141
Dydnia 141
Dylągówa 141
Dylągówka 141
Dyniska 141
Dynów 11, 31, 46, 51, 82, 101, 104, 112, 127, 141
Dytiatyn 141
Dzial 141
Dzianisz 141
Dzibułki 141
Dzieduszyce Małe 141
Dzieduszyce Wielkie 141
Dziedziłów 141
Dziekanowice 141
Dzierdziówka 141
Dzierzaniny 141
Dziewięcirez 141
Dziewiętniki 141
Dziewin 141
Dziezki 141
Dzików 82, 141, *also see* Stary Dzików
Dzikowice 141
Dzikowiec 141
Dziurdziów 141
Dżurków 141
Dzurów 89, 141
Dżuryn 141
Dźwiniacz 141
Dźwiniacz Dolny 141
Dźwiniaczka 141
Dzwinograd 46
Dżwinogród 141
Dzwonowa 141
Ebenau 141
Einsiedel 141
Einsingen 141
Eleonorówka 141

Gorzeń Dolny 142
Gorzeń Górny 142
Gorzków 142
Gorzów 142
Gorzyce 142
Gosprzydowa 142
Gostov 27
Gostwica 142
Gotkowice Niemieckie 142
Gotkowice Polskie 142
Grab 142
Grabanina 142
Grabicz 142
Grabie 142
Grabieuznanskie 142
Grabina 142
Grabiny 142
Grabkowce 142
Grabnia 142
Grabno 142
Graboszyce 142
Grabów 82, 142
Grabowa 142
Grabowce 142
Grabowice 142
Grabówka 142
Grabownica 142, 143
Grabowski 143
Grajów 143
Grąziowa 143
Grebalowa 38
Grebelki 143
Grebów 82, 111, 143
Grimaylov see Grzymalów
Grobla 143
Grobla Jankowiecka 143
Groble 143
Grochowce 101
Grochowie 143
Gródek 29, 46, 54, 130, 143, *also see* Horodek
Gródek Jagielloński 23, 51, 54, 127
Grodkowice 143
Grodowice 143
Grodzisk 47
Grodzisko 118, 143
Grodzisko Dolne 101, 143
Grodzisko Górne 143
Grójec 82, 143
Gromiec 143
Gromnik 143
Gromnik Grybów 82

Grondy 143
Gronków 143
Gross Mosty 30, 88, 143, *also see* Mosty Vielkie
Grudna Dolna 143
Grudna Górna 143
Grudna Kępska 143
Grudza 143
Gruszka 143
Gruszki 143
Gruszów 143
Gruszów Mały 143
Gruszów Wielki 143
Gruszowiec 143
Grybów 32, 46, 117, 127, 143
Grywałd 143
Grzęda 143
Grzekhynia 143
Grzeska 143
Grzybów 143
Grzybowice 143
Grzymałów 27, 82, 112, 116, 129, 143
Grzymałówka 143
Guminska 143
Gura 143
Gusakov see Hussaków
Gusyatin 78, 100, *also see* Husiatyn
Gusztyn 143
Gusztynek 143
Gutynka 143
Guzowa 143
Gwizdów 143
Gwoździanka 143
Gwoździec Nowy 143
Gwoździec Stary 143
Gwożdziec 24, 128, 143
Gwoźnica Dolna 143
Gwoźnica Górna 143
Habkowce 143
Hacaki 143
Haczów 143
Hadle Kańczudzkie 143
Hadle Szklarskie 143
Hadykówka 143
Hadynkowce 143
Haiworonka 143
Halbów 101, 143
Halcnów 143
Hałicz 28, 73, 82, 115, 129, 143
Hałiczanów 143
Haller 143

Halowice 143
Haluszczynce 143
Haluszowa 143
Hamulec 143
Hanaczów 143
Hanaczówka 143
Hanczarów 143
Hanczowa 143
Handzlówka 143
Haniowce 143
Hańkowce 143
Hańkowice 143
Hankówka 143
Hanmowce 143
Hanowce 143
Hanunin 143
Harasymów 143
Harbutowice 143
Harbuzów 143
Harklowa 143
Harmięże 143
Harta 143
Hartfield 143
Haszcze 143
Hatki 143
Hawlowice Dolne 143
Hawlowice Górne 143
Hawrylak 143
Hawryłówka 143
Hecznarowice 143
Heinrichsdorf 143
Helenków 143
Hemia 143
Herbutów 143
Hermanów 143
Hermanowa 143
Hermanowice 143
Hińkowce 143
Hinowiec 143
Hladki 143
Hlebówka 143
Hleszczawa 143
Hlibów 143
Hłomcza 143
Hluboczek 28
Hłuboczek Wielki 143
Hłudno 143
Hnatkowice 144
Hnidawa 144
Hnizdyesów 144
Hoczew 144
Hodów 144
Hodowice 144

Iwanikówka 145
Iwanków 145
Iwankówka 145
Iwanowce 145
Iwanowice 82
Iwanówka 27, 145
Iwkowa 145
Iwkowska 145
Iwla 145
Iwonicz 101, 145
Izabelin 145
Izbiska 145
Izby 145
Izdebki 145
Izdebnik 145
Izlickie 145
Izydorówka 145
Jabłanów 128
Jabłonica 145
Jabłonica Polska 145
Jabłonica Ruska 145
Jabłonka 51, 145
Jabłonki 145
Jabłonów 24, 145, *also see*
    Yablonov
Jabłonówka 145
Jachówka 145
Jackowce 145
Jackówka 145
Jacmanice 145
Jacmierz 57, 145
Jadachy 145
Jadamwola 145
Jadlowa 34
Jadłowa /Jodłowa 128
Jadowniki 145
Jagieła 145
Jagielnica 23, 127, 145
Jagielnica Stara 145
Jagodnik 145
Jagunia 145
Jahłusz 145
Jajkowce 145
Jakimczyce 145
Jakimów 145
Jaktorów 145
Jakubów 145
Jakubówka 145
Jala 145
Jałowe 145
Jamda 145
Jamelna 145
Jamelnica 145

Jamna 145
Jamna Dolna 145
Jamna Górna 145
Jamne 145
Jamnica 145
Jamy 145
Janczowa 145
Janczyn 145
Janikowice 145
Janiszów 93
Janiv *see* Janów
Jankowce 145
Jankowice 82, 145
Jankówka 145
Janów 23, 29, 51, 54, 82, 84, 127,
    129, 145
Janowice 145
Janówka 145
Januszkowice 146
Januszowa 146
Jarczowce 146
Jarhorów 146
Jarosin 146
Jaroslaw 32, 51, 55, 82, 84, 101,
    118, 127, 146
Jarosławice 146
Jaroszowice 146
Jaroszówka 146
Jaroszyce 146
Jaryczów 25, 82, 128, 146
Jaryczów Nowy 46, 54, 84, 146
Jaryczów Stary 146
Jarymówka 146
Jasiel 146
Jasień 146
Jasienica 31, 146
Jasienica Buczacz 127
Jasienica Rosielna 82, 101
Jasienica Solna 146
Jasienica Sufczyńska 146
Jasienna 146
Jasienów Górny 146
Jasienów Polny 146
Jasienowice 146
Jasienówka 146
Jasionka 146
Jasionów 146
Jasionówa 146
Jaskowice 146
Jaslany 146
Jasliska 82, 101, 146
Jasło 32, 42, 46, 51, 55, 57, 82,
    101, 120, 127, 146

Jasłowice 111
Jasna 146
Jaśniska 146
Jaśniszcze 146
Jastew 146
Jastkowice 146
Jastrebia 146
Jastrzałka Nowa 146
Jastrzębia 146
Jastrzębiec 146
Jastrzębków 146
Jastrzębnik 146
Jaszczew 146
Jaszczurowa 117, 146
Jaszkowa 146
Jasztrebica 146
Jatwięgi 146
Javorov 100, *also see* Jaworów
Jawcze 146
Jawczyce 146
Jawiszowice 146
Jaworec 146
Jaworki 146
Jawornik 146
Jawornik Górny 146
Jawornik Niebyłecki 146
Jawornik Polski 56, 82, 101, 104,
    146
Jawornik Ruski 146
Jawornik Szklarski 82
Jaworów 19, 24, 51, 54, 78, 82,
    127, 146, *also see* Javorov
Jaworówka 146
Jaworsko 146
Jaworze 102, 146
Jaworzna 146
Jaworzno 146
Jazienica Polska 146
Jazienica Ruska 146
Jazłowczyk 146
Jazłowice 23, 46, 82, 84, 111, 127,
    146, *also see* Pomortsy
Jazów Nowy 146
Jazów Stary 146
Jazowa 146
Jazowsko 146
Jedlicze 82, 146
Jędruszków 146
Jelechowice 146
Jeleń 146
Jeleńkowate 146
Jeleśnia 146
Jelna 146

Klebanówka 29
Klecie 148
Klęcza Dolna 148
Klęcza Górna 148
Klęcza Srednia 148
Klęczany 148
Kleindorf 148
Klekotów 148
Kleparów 148
Kleszczowna 148
Klikowa 148
Klikuszowa 148
Klimkówka 148
Kliniec 148
Kliszów 148
Kłodne 148
Kłodnica 148
Kłodno 148
Kłodowa 82, 148
Kłodzienko 148
Kłokowice 148
Kłonice 148
Kłonów 148
Kłubowce 148
Kluczów Mały 148
Kluczów Wielki 148
Klusów 148
Kluszkowce 148
Kluwince 148
Klyżów 148
Knapy 148
Kniaźdwór 148
Kniaże 148
Kniaziołuka 148
Kniażowskie 148
Kniaźpol 148
Kniażyce 148
Kniesioło 148
Knihinin 148
Knihinin Colonie 148
Knihynice 148
Knihynicze 26, 51, 148
Knurów 148
Kobacki 148
Kobielnik 148
Kobienrzyn 148
Kobierzyn 148
Kobło Stare 148
Kobuszowa 101
Kobylanka 148
Kobylany 148
Kobyłczyna 148
Kobyle 148

Kobylec 148
Kobylnica Ruska 148
Kobylnica Wołoska 148
Kobylowłoki 148
Kochanówka 148
Kochany 148
Kochawina 148
Kocierz ad Rychwald 148
Kocierz ad Moszczanica 148
Kocierzyn 148
Kociubińce 148
Kociubińczyki 148
Kocmierzów 148
Kocoń 148
Kocurów 148
Kojszówka 148
Kokoszyńce 148
Kokotkowce 148
Kokotów 148
Kokuszka 148
Kolaczyce 56, 82, 148
Kolanki 148
Kolanów 148
Kolbuszowa 32, 46, 51, 55, 59, 82,
    90, 91, 92, 114, 115, 119, 128,
    148
Kolbuszowa Dolna 148
Kolbuszowa Górna 148
Kołdziejów 148
Koledziany 148
Koleśniki 148
Kolin 148
Kolińce 148
Kolko 148
Kolkówka 148
Koło 148
Koło Tynieckie 148
Kołodrobka 148
Kołodziejówka 27, 148
Kołohury 148
Kołomea 24, 82, 113, 115, 120,
    121, 128, 148, also see
    Kolomyya
Kolomyya 42, 43, 51, 59, 100, also
    see Kolomea
Kołowa Wola 148
Kołpice 148
Kołtów 148
Komańcza 148
Komarno 27, 54, 84, 100, 129, 148
Komarów 148
Komarowice 148
Komarówka 148

Kombornia 102, 148
Komorniki 116, 148
Komorów 148
Komorowice 148
Komorówka 148
Konary 148
Kończyce 148
Kończyska 149
Kondratów 149
Koniaczów 149
Konice 149
Koniczkowa 149
Konieczna 149
Konigsau 149
Konigsberg 149
Konina 149
Koniów 149
Koniuchów 149
Koniuchy 149
Koniusza 149
Koniuszki 149
Koniuszki Królewskie 149
Koniuszki Nanowskie 149
Koniuszki Siemianów 149
Koniuszki Tuligłowskie 149
Koniuszków 149
Koniuszowa 149
Konkolniki 149
Konkulówka 149
Konopkówka 149
Konotopy 149
Końskie 149
Konstancja 149
Konstantynówka 149
Konty 149
Kopacze Księże 149
Kopaczyńce 149
Kopaliny 149
Kopan 149
Kopaniny 149
Kopanka 149
Kopcie 149
Kopychintsy see Kopyczyńce
Kopyczyńce 24, 51, 82, 127, 149
Kopytne 149
Kopytów 149
Kopytowa 149
Kopytówka 149
Korabina 149
Korabniki 149
Korbielów 149
Korczmin 149
Korczów 149

Kruki 150
Krukienice 82, 150
Krulin 150
Krupsko 150
Kruszelnica 150
Krużlowa Niżna 150
Krużlowa Polska 150
Krużlowa Ruska 150
Krużlowa Wyżna 150
Krużyki 150
Kryczka 150
Kryg 150
Kryłos 150
Krynica 34, 82, 128, 150
Krysowice 150
Krystonopil *see* Krystynopol
Krystynopol 27, 82, 117, 129, 150
Krywa 150
Krywe 150
Krywe bei Tworylne 150
Krywka 150
Kryzywołuka 150
Krzadka 150
Krzęcin 150
Krzeczkowa 150
Krzeczów 150
Krzeczowice 150
Krzemienica 150
Krzesławice 150
Krzeszowice 38, 83, 150
Krzewica 150
Krzezoniów 150
Krzyszkowice 150
Krzywa Rzeka 150
Krzywaczka 150
Krzywcza 34, 56, 83, 101, 102, 113, 128, 150
Krzywcze 22, 150
Krzywcze Dolne 150
Krzywcze Górne 150
Krzywczyce 150
Krzywe 151
Krzywenkie 151
Krzywice 151
Krzywiecka Wola 151
Krzywki 151
Krzyworównia 151
Krzywotuly Nowe 151
Krzywotuly Stare 151
Krzywulanka 151
Krzyż 151
Krzyżanowice 151
Krzyżowa 151

Krzyżówka 151
Książnice 151
Księċży Most 151
Księże Kolano 151
Księżnice 151
Kuczwice 151
Kudobińce 151
Kudryńce 22, 118
Kudryńce Dolne 151
Kudryńce Górne 151
Kudryńce. (B) 1823–91; (M) 1908–12; (D) 1851–90. I 22
Kudryńce: (B) 1853–76; Uście Biskupie: (B) 1831–76 22
Kudynowce 151
Kuhajów 151
Kujdance 151
Kujdanów 151
Kukizów 151
Kuków 151
Kułaczkowce 151
Kułaczyn 151
Kułakowce 151
Kulaszne 151
Kulawa 151
Kulczyce 151
Kulerzów 151
Kuliczków 151
Kulikov *see* Kulików
Kulików 30, 83, 130, 151
Kulmatycze 151
Kulparków 26, 151
Kulyska 151
Kunaszów 151
Kunice 151
Kunicze 151
Kunin 151
Kunina 151
Kunisowce 151
Kunkowa 151
Kunkowce 151
Kunowa 151
Kupcze 151
Kupczynce 151
Kupiatycze 151
Kupiczwola 30, 151
Kupienin 151
Kupna 151
Kupno 151
Kupnowice Nowy 151
Kupnowice Stary 151
Kurdwanówka 151
Kurmanice 151

Kurniki 24, 151
Kurniki Szlacheckie 151
Kuropatniki 151
Kurów 151
Kurowce 151
Kurowice 151
Kurwanów Dolny 151
Kurwanów Górny 151
Kuryłówka 151
Kurypów 151
Kurzany 151
Kurzyna Mała 151
Kurzyna Wielka 151
Kuskowce 28
Kustyn 151
Kutce 151
Kutenberg 151
Kutkowce 151
Kuty 24, 46, 51, 83, 100, 114, 119, 151
Kuty Stare 151
Kutyly 151
Kutyszcze 151
Kuywa 151
Kuzie 151
Kuźmina 151
Kwaczała 151
Kwapinka 151
Kwaszenina 151
Kwiatoń 151
Kwiatonowice 151
Kwików 151
Łabacz 151
Łabajka 151
Labowa 34, 83, 128, 151
Łabowice 151
Lachawa 151
Lachowce 151
Lachowice 151
Lachowice Podróżne 151
Lachowice Zarzeczne 151
Lacka Wola 26, 151
Lackie Małe 151
Lackie Wielkie 151
Lacko 34, 83, 128, 151
Łaczany 151
Łaczki 151
Ladyczyn 75, 151
Ladyzhin 48
Łаdzin 151
Ladzkie 151
Laeniowa 151
Łagiewniki 151

Lisiatycze 153
Lisiejamy 153
Liski 153
Lisko 33, 51, 128, 153, *also see* Lesko
Liskowate 153
Lisów 153
Lisowce 153
Lisowice 153
Liszki 38
Liszna 153
Lisznia 153
Litewska 153
Litowisko 153
Litwina 153
Litynia 153
Liubycha *see* Lubycza Krolewska
Liwcze 153
Łobozew 153
Łoczów 80
Łodygowice 153
Łodyna 153
Łodzina 153
Łodzinka Dolna 153
Łodzinka Górna 153
Łojowa 153
Lokutki 153
Lolin 153
Łomna 83, 153
Łomnica 153
Łonie 153
Łoniowy 153
Łopatyn 51, 80, 83
Łopianka 153
Łopienka 153
Łopoń 153
Loptin *see* Lopatyn
Łopuchowa 153
Łopuszanka 153
Łopuszanka Chomina 153
Łopuszany 153
Łopuszka Mała 153
Łopuszka Wielka 153
Łopuszna 153
Łopusznica 153
Łosiacz 153
Łosie 153
Lososina Dolna 153
Lostówka 153
Loszniów 153
Lotatniki 153
Łowce 153
Łowcza 153

Łowczów 153
Łowczowek 153
Łowczyce 153
Łowisko 153
Łozina 153
Łozowa 153
Łozówka 153
Luasz 153
Lubaczów 31, 46, 55, 57, 117, 127, 153
Lubanowa 153
Lubaszów 101
Lubatowa 153
Lubatówka 153
Lubcza 153
Lubella 153
Lubenia 153
Lubeszka 153
Lubiana 153
Lubianka 153
Lubień 153
Lubień Mały 153
Lubień Wielki 153
Lubieńce 153
Lubienie 153
Lubinka 153
Lubkowce 153
Lubla 154
Lublica 154
Lublinec Nowy 154
Lublinec Stary 154
Łubne 154
Łubno 154
Lubomierz 154
Łubów 154
Lubsza 154
Lubycza 154, *also see* Lubycza Krowlewska
Lubycza Kniazie 154
Lubycza Królewska 9, 26, 129, *also see* Lubycza
Lubzina 154
Luczany 154
Lucze 154
Łuczka 154
Łuczki 154
Lucznikowice 154
Luczyce 154
Luczyńce 154
Ludwikówka 25, 154
Ludwinów 154
Ludzimierz 154
Ług 154

Łuh 154
Łuhy 154
Łuka 154
Łuka Mała 154
Łukanowice 154
Łukawica 154
Łukawica Niżna 154
Łukawica Wyżna 154
Łukawice 154
Łukowa 154
Łukowe 154
Łukówka 154
Łupków 154
Lupuszna 154
Lusina 154
Lusławice 154
Lusławiczki 154
Luszowice 154
Lutcza 154
Lutera 154
Lutków 154
Lutoryż 154
Lutowiska 33, 43, 51, 83, 101, 102, 128, 154
Lużek Górny 154
Lużki 154
Lużna 154
Lviv 25, 40, 42, 68, 77-80, 128, *also see* Lemberg, Lvov and Lwów
Lvov 25, 51, 58, 59, 68, 100, *also see* Lemberg, Lviv and Lwów
Lwów 25, 37, 39, 43-45, 53-55, 59, 63, 64, 65, 67, 68, 128, *also see* Lemberg, Lviv and Lvov
Lyczana 154
Lyczanka 154
Łysa 154
Łysa Góra 154
Lysaków 114, 154
Łysakowek 154
Lysiec 22, 126, 154
Łysiec Stary 154
Łysina 154
Łysków 154
Łysokanie 154
Łyszanka 154
Machlinice 154
Machnów 154
Machnowek 154
Machnówka 154
Machów 154
Machowa 154

Mikulińce 28, 44, 83, 117, 118, 129, 156
Mikuszowice 156
Milatycze 25, 156
Milatyń 156
Milatyń Nowy 156
Milatyń Stary 156
Milcza 156
Milczyce 156
Milik 156
Milków 156
Miłkowa 156
Milno 156
Miłocin 156
Miloszowice 25
Miłowanie 156
Milowce 156
Milówka 156
Mirocin 156
Mirów 156
Mistkowice 156
Mistyce 156
Mizerna 156
Mizuń Nowy 156
Mizuń Stary 156
Młodochów 156
Młodów 156
Młodowice 156
Młodzatyń 156
Młoszowa 156
Młyńczyska 156
Młyniska 156
Młynne 156
Młynowce 156
Młynówka 156
Młyny 156
Mochnaczka Niżna 156
Mochnaczka Wyżna 156
Mockowice 156
Moczary 156
Moczerady 156
Moderówka 156
Modrycz 156
Mogielnica 156
Mogila 38, *also see* Kraków
Mogilany 156
Mogilno 156
Mohylany 156
Mokra Strona 156
Mokra Wieś 156
Mokre 118, 156
Mokrotyn 156
Mokrotyn Kolonia 156

Mokrzany 156
Mokrzany Małe 156
Mokrzany Wielkie 156
Mokrzec 156
Mokrzyska 156
Mokrzyszów 156
Molczanówka 156
Mołdycz 156
Mołodylów 156
Mołodyńcze 156
Mołoszkowice 156
Mołotków 156
Mołotów 156
Monasterzec 156
Monasterzyska 23, 51, 83, 111, 127, 156, *also see* Monastyriska
Monastyriska 78, 100, 117, *also see* Monasterzyska
Moniłowska 156
Monowice 156
Moosberg 156
Morańce 156
Morawsko 156
Mordarka 156
Morszyn 156
Morwczyna 156
Mościska 26, 46, 54, 83, 128, 156, *also see* Mostiska
Moskale 156
Moskalówka 156
Mostiska 78, 100, *also see* Mościska
Mostki 25, 156
Mosty 156
Mosty Małe 156
Mosty Velikieye *see* Gross Mosty
Mosty Wielki 30, 51, 130
Moszczanica 156
Moszczaniec 156
Moszczenica 156
Moszczenica niżna 156
Moszczenica wyżna 156
Moszków 156
Moszkowce 156
Motycze Poduchowne 156
Motycze Szlacheckie 156
Mrażnica 23, 156
Mrowla 156
Mrozowice 156
Mrzyglód 101, 156
Mszalnica 156
Mszana 156
Mszana Dolna 33, 83, 128, 156

Mszana Górna 156
Mszanice 156
Mszanka 156
Mucharz 156
Muchawka 156
Muhlbach 156
Mukanie 156
Mulne 156
Munina 156
Musikowe 156
Muszkarów 157
Muszkatówka 157
Muszyłowice 157
Muszyłowice Czarnokonce 157
Muszyłowice Narodowe 157
Muszyna 34, 83, 115, 128, 157
Muszynka 157
Mutulin 157
Muzylów 157
Mycków 157
Myczków 157
Myczkowce 157
Mykietyńce 157
Mykolaiv *see* Mikolajów
Mykulyntsi *see* Mikulińce
Mymoń 157
Myscowa 157
Myślachowice 157
Myślatycze 157
Myślec 157
Myślenice 34, 51, 55, 57, 83, 128, 157
Myślów 157
Mysłowa 157
Myszków 157
Myszkowce 157
Myszkowice 157
Myszyn 157
Mytarka 157
Naciszowa 157
Nadbrzeże 157
Nadiatycze 157
Nadolany 157
Nadole 57, 157
Nadorożna 157
Nadorożniów 157
Nadvorna *see* Nadworna
Nadworna 26, 51, 128, 157
Nadyby 157
Nadycze 157
Nadziejów 157
Nagawczyna 157
Nagnajów 157

Nowy Sącz 34, 42, 46, 51, 55, 57, 58, 83, 84, 118, 121, 128, 158
Nowy Targ 34, 38, 46, 52, 55, 57, 83, 128, 158
Nowy Tyczyn 158
Nowy Wiśnicz 57
Nowy Żmigród 101
Nozdrzec 158
Nuśmice 158
Nyrków 158
Obarzance 158
Obarzym 158
Obelnica 158
Obersdorf 158
Obertin *see* Obertyn
Obertyn 23, 83, 112, 115, 127, 158
Obidowa 158
Obidza 158
Obladów 158
Obłażnica 158
Obłazy 158
Obodówka 29, 158
Obojna 158
Obroszyn 158
Obrotów 158
Obydów 158
Ochmanów 158
Ochodza 158
Ochojno 158
Ochotnica 158
Ocice 158
Ocieka 158
Oczków 158
Odaje ad Słobódka 158
Odment 158
Odrowąż 158
Odrzechowa 158
Odrzykoń 158
Okleśna 159
Okniany 159
Okno 159
Okocim 159
Okoń 159
Okonin 159
Okopy 22, 159
Okrajnik 159
Olchawa 159
Olchowa 159
Olchowa Lwibrat 159
Olchowce 159
Olchowczyk 159
Olchowice 159
Olchowiec 22

Olchówka 159
Olejów 159
Olejowa Korniów 159
Olejowa Korolówka 159
Oleksice Nowe 159
Oleksice Stare 159
Oleksińce 159
Olendry 159
Olesin 159
Olesko 30, 83, 84, 130, 159
Oleśnica 159
Oleśno 159
Olesza 159
Oleszków 159
Oleszów 159
Oleszyce 31, 57, 83, 101, 127, 159
Oleszyce Stare 159
Oleyevo Korolevka *see* Korolówka
Olkusz 52, 55, 57
Olpiny 32, 83, 127, 159
Olsawica 159
Olszanica 159
Olszanik 159
Olszanka 159
Olszany 159
Olszowa 159
Olszowice 159
Olszówka 159
Olszyny 159
Onyszkowce 159
Opacie 159
Opacionka 159
Opaka 159
Opaki 159
Opaleniska 159
Oparówka 159
Opary 159
Opatkowice 159
Opatów 7, 58
Oplucko 159
Oporzec 159
Oprynowce 159
Opulsko 159
Orawa 159
Orawczyk 159
Orchowice 159
Ordów 159
Orelce 159
Orelec 159
Orliska 159
Orów 159
Ortynice 159
Oryszkowce 159

Orzechów 159
Orzechowce 159
Orzechowczyk 159
Orzechowice 56, 159
Orzechowiec 27
Orzechówka 159
Oserdów 159
Osieczany 159
Osiek 83, 159
Osielec 159
Oskrzesińce 159
Osławy Biale 159
Osławy Czarne 159
Osmolna 159
Osobnica 159
Osowce 159
Ostalce 159
Ostapie 159
Ostapkowce 159
Ostaszowce 159
Ostobusz 159
Ostra 159
Ostre 159
Ostropole 159
Ostrów 25, 159
Ostrów Królewski 159
Ostrów Pohorecki 159
Ostrów Szlachecki 159
Ostrowczyk 159
Ostrowczyk Polny 159
Ostrówek 83, 159
Ostrowice 159
Ostrowsko 159
Ostrowy Baranowskie 159
Ostrowy Ruszowskie 159
Ostrożce 159
Ostrusza 159
Ostrynia 160
Ostrznica 160
Oświęcim 30, 46, 58, 66, 83, 84, 126, 160
Oszanica 160
Otalez 160
Otfinów 160
Ottenhausen 160
Ottynia 29, 120, 129, 160, *also see* Otynya
Ottyniowice 160
Otynya 27, *also see* Ottynia
Owieczka 160
Ożanna 160
Ożańsko 160
Ożarowce 160

Ożenna 160
Ozernyany *see* Jezierna
Ozeryany 78, *also see* Jezierzany
Ozimina 160
Ożmla 24
Ożomla 160
Ożydów 160
Packowice 160
Pacław 160
Pacyków 160
Paczek Gorzycki 160
Paczołtowice 160
Padew 160
Padew Narodowa 160
Pagorzyna 160
Pajówka 160
Pakość 160
Pakoszówka 160
Palcza 160
Palen 160
Paleśnica 160
Palikrowy 160
Palszowice 160
Panasówka 160
Paniczna 160
Paniowce 160
Paniszczów 160
Pankowce 160
Panowice 160
Pantalicha 160
Pantalowice 160
Papiernia 160
Papnortno 160
Parchacz 160
Parkosz 160
Partyń 160
Partynia 160
Parypsy 160
Paryszeże 160
Pasicka 160
Pasicki Zubrzyckie 160
Pasieczna 160
Pasierbice 160
Paszczyna 160
Paszkówka 160
Paszowa 160
Paszyn 160
Pauszówka 160
Pawełcza 160
Pawęzów 160
Pawlikowice 160
Pawłokoma 160
Pawłosiów 160

Pawłów 160
Październirz 160
Pechenezhin 100, *also see*
    Peczeniżyn
Peczenia 160
Peczeniżyn 24, 83, 128, 160, *also*
    see Pechenezhin
Peim 160
Pełkinie 160
Pełnatycze 160
Peratyń 160
Perechrestne 160
Perehińsko 52
Perekosy 160
Peremilów 160
Peremyshlyany 78, 100, *also see*
    Przemyślany
Perenówka 160
Perepelniki 160
Pererów 160
Perespa 160
Peretoki 160
Perla 160
Perłowce 160
Persenkówka 160
Perwiatycze 160
Petlikowce 160
Petlikowce Nowe 160
Petlikowce Stare 160
Pętna 160
Petranka 160
Petryków 160
Pewel 160
Pewel Mała 160
Pewel Wielka 160
Pewlka 160
Piadyki 160
Pianowice 160
Piaseczna 160
Piaski 25, 160
Piątkowa 160
Piątkowice 160
Pidvolochyska *see* Podwołoczyska
Piechoty 160
Pieczarna 160
Pieczychwosty 160
Pieczygory 160
Piekiełko 160
Pielawa 160
Pielnia 160
Pień 160
Pieniaki 160
Pieniążkowice 160

Pierszyce 160
Pierzchów 160
Pierzchowice 160
Pietbuce 160
Pietniczany 160
Pietrusza Wola 160
Pietrycze 161
Pietrzejowa 161
Pietrzykowice 161
Pikarówka 161
Pikorowice 161
Pikulice 161
Pikułowice 161
Piła 161
Piłatkowce 161
Pilichów 161
Pilipy 161
Piły 161
Pilznionek 161
Pilzno 34, 83, 102, 114, 128, 161
Piniany 161
Piotrkowice 161
Piotrow 23, 161
Piotrówka 161
Pipielniki 89
Pisarowce 161
Pisary 161
Pisarzowa 161
Pisarzowice 161
Pistyn Krakow 128
Pistyn 24, 161
Piszczatynce 161
Pitrycz 161
Piwniczna 34, 83, 128, 161
Piwoda 161
Piwowszczyzna 161
Piżany 161
Płaszów 161
Płaucza Mała 161
Płaucza Wielka 161
Pławie 161
Pławna 161
Pławo 161
Pławy 161
Płaza 161
Plazów 83, 161
Płazówka 161
Plebanówka 161
Pleników 161
Pleskowce 161
Pleśna 161
Pleśniany 161
Pleśników 161

Pleszowice 161
Pletenice 161
Plichów 161
Płock 47
Płoki 161
Płonne 161
Płoskie 161
Płotycz 161
Płotycza 161
Płowe 161
Płowie 161
Płozówka 161
Płuchów 161
Pluty 161
Pniatyn 161
Pnikut 161
Pniów 161
Pobereże 161
Pobidno 161
Pobiedz 161
Pobitno 161
Pobocz 161
Pobreczyn 161
Pobuk 161
Pobuzany 161
Pochówka 161
Poczajowice 161
Poczapińce 161
Podberesec 161
Podbereż 161
Podbereżce 161
Podbereżec 161
Podborce 161
Podborze 161
Podbrzezie 161
Podbuż 83, 161
Podbuże 161
Podciemne 25, 161
Podczerwone 161
Podegrodzie 161
Podemszczyzna 161
Podfilipie 161
Podgać 161
Podgaysty 78, *also see* Podhajce
Podgórzany 161
Podgórze Wadowice 130
Podgórze 35, 38, 118, 161
Podgrodzie 161
Podhajce 26, 44, 46, 52, 83, 84, 89, 116, 119, 128, 161, *also see* Podgaytsy
Podhajczyki 161
Podhorce 161

Podhorki 161
Podhorodce 161
Podhorodyszcze 161
Podhybie 161
Podjarków 161
Podkamen 100, *also see* Podkamien
Podkamien 22, 84, 101, 126, 161, *also see* Podkamen
Podkościele 161
Podlankowina 161
Podlesie 161
Podlesie Dębowe 161
Podleszany 161
Podłęże 161
Podlipce 161
Podlipie 161
Podliski 161
Podliski Małe 162
Podliski Wielkie 162
Podłopień 162
Podluby Wielki 162
Podłuby Małe 162
Podmajerz 162
Podmanasterek 162
Podmanastereż 162
Podmichale 162
Podmichałowce 162
Podmoszce 162
Podniebyłe 162
Podniestrzany 162
Podobin 162
Podolany 162
Podolce 162
Podole 162
Podolsze 162
Podpieczary 162
Podrudne 162
Podrzyce 162
Podsadki 25, 162
Podsmykowce 162
Podsosnów 162
Podstolice 162
Podsuchy 162
Podszumlańce 162
Podubce 162
Podusilna 162
Podusów 162
Podwale 162
Podwerbce 162
Podwinie 162
Podwołoczyska 27-29, 83, 115, 129, 162

Podwysoka 162
Podwysokie 162
Podzamcze 162
Podzamczek 162
Podziacz 162
Podzwierzynice 162
Pogórska Wola 162
Pogorzałka 162
Pogorzany 162
Pogorzeliska 162
Pogorzyce 162
Pogwizdów 162
Pohar 162
Poherbce 162
Pohonia 162
Pohorylec 162
Pojawce 162
Pojło 162
Pokrepiwna 162
Pokrowce 162
Polana 162
Polańczyk 162
Polanica 162
Polanka 162
Polanka Wielka 162
Polanki 162
Polany 162
Polany Surowiczne 162
Poleśniki 162
Polna 162
Połom Mały 162
Połomeja 162
Połonice 162
Połoniczna 162
Połowce 162
Połowe 162
Połrzecki 162
Połtew 162
Poluchów Mały 162
Poluchów Wielki 162
Polupanówka 162
Połwieś 162
Pomianowa 162
Pomonieta 162
Pomorce 162
Pomortsy *see* Jasłowice
Pomoryany *see* Pomorzany
Pomorzany 30, 83, 84, 130, 162
Ponice 162
Ponikew 162
Ponikowica Mała 162
Ponikwa 162
Ponikwa Wielka 162

Przyszów Kameralny 164
Przyszów Szlachecki 164
Przyszowa 164
Psary 164
Pstrągowa 164
Pstrążne 164
Pstręgówka 164
Ptaszkowa 164
Ptaszniki 164
Ptonus 164
Pukaczów 164
Pukarowce 164
Pukienicze 164
Puklaki 164
Puków 164
Pułanki 164
Puławy 164
Pustawola 164
Pustomyty 164
Pustynia 164
Putiatycze 164
Putiatynce 164
Putków 164
Puźniki 164
Pychowice 164
Pyszkowce 164
Pysznica 164
Pyzówka 164
Raba Niżna 164
Raba Wyżna 164
Rabczyce 164
Rabe 164
Rabka 52, 83, 164
Rabka Zdrój 58
Rąbkowa 164
Raby 164
Rachin 164
Raciborsko 164
Raciborzany 164
Raciechowice 164
Racławice 164
Racławoka 164
Raczyna 164
Radajowice 164
Radawa 164
Radcza 164
Radekhov see Radziechów
Radelicz 164
Radenice 26, 164
Radgoszcz 83
Radiechów 127
Radlna 164
Radłów 31, 83, 127, 164

Radłówice 164
Radochońce 164
Radocza 164
Radoczyna 164
Radogoszcz 83
Radomyśl 35, 112, 114, 116, 118,
    120, 121, 129, 164
Radomyśl Wielki 52
Radomyśl Wielkie 33, 83, 91, 112,
    118, 128, 164
Radoszcz 164
Radoszyce 83, 164
Radruz 164
Radwan 164
Radwańce 164
Radwanowice 164
Radymno 32, 83, 101, 119, 127,
    164
Radzichów 164
Radziechów 24, 52, 83, 164
Radziejowa 164
Radziszów 164
Rajsko 164
Rajtarowice 164
Rakobuty 164
Raków 83, 117, 119, 164
Rakowa 164
Rakowężyk 164
Rakowice 164
Rakszawa 164
Raniowice 164
Ranisów 164
Raniżów 32, 101, 128, 164
Raniżów Kolonie 164
Raniżowska Wola 164
Raszków 164
Rasztowce 164
Ratawica 164
Ratnawy 164
Ratulów 164
Ratyszcze 22, 164
Rava Russkaya see Rawa Ruska
Rawa 26, 129
Rawa Ruska 52, 83, 84, 112, 115,
    120, 129, 165
Ray 165
Raybrot 165
Raycza 165
Rażniów 165
Rdzawa 165
Rdzawka 165
Rdziostów 165
Rechtberg 165

Reczpol 165
Regetów Niżny 165
Regetów Wyżny 165
Regulice 165
Rehberg 165
Rehfeld 165
Reichau 165
Reichenbach 165
Reichsheim 165
Rekszyn 165
Remenów 165
Reniów 165
Repechów 165
Repużyńce 165
Reszniate 165
Rochynie 165
Rocmirowa 165
Roczyny 165
Rodatycze 165
Rodze 165
Rogatin see Rohatyn
Rogi 165
Rogoźnica 165
Rogoźnik 165
Rogozno 24, 165
Roguźno 165
Rohaczyn 165
Rohatyń 26, 46, 52, 78, 84, 117,
    121, 129, 165
Rojatyń 165
Rojówka 165
Rokieciny 165
Rokietnica 165
Rokitno 115, 165
Roków 165
Rokówkat 165
Rokszyce 112, 165
Rolikówka 165
Rolów 165
Romanów 83, 165
Romanówka 29, 165
Romaszówka 165
Ropa 165
Ropczyce 11, 34, 46, 83, 101, 119,
    129, 165
Ropea Polska 165
Ropianka 165
Ropica Ruska 165
Ropienka 101, 165
Ropki 165
Rosechy 165
Rosenberg 165
Rosochacz 165

Rzepniów 167
Rzęsna Polska 167
Rzęsna Ruska 167
Rzeszotary 167
Rzeszów 34, 37, 40, 42, 52, 55-57,
    68, 83, 90, 92, 93, 101, 103, 113,
    116-121, 129, 167
Rzeszyca 167
Rzezawa 167
Rzochów 167
Rzozów 167
Rzuchów 167
Rzuchowa 167
Rzyczki 167
Rzyki 167
Sabinówka 167
Sadek 167
Sadki 167
Sadkowa 167
Sadkowa Góra 167
Sadkowice 167
Sadowa Wiśnia 26, 54, 128, 167,
    also see Sudovaya Vishnaya
Sadzawa 167
Sadzawki 167
Sakowczyk 167
Salamonowa Górka 167
Salasze 167
Salmopol 167
Salówka 167
Sambor 27, 42, 43, 46, 52, 59, 78,
    83, 100, 115, 129, 167, *also see*
    Stary Sambor
Samborek 167
Samborówka 167
Samocice 167
Samołuskowce 167
Sandomierz 120
Sanka Północna 167
Sanka Południowa 167
Sanniki 83, 167
Sanoczany 167
Sanok 35, 42, 46, 47, 52, 55, 56,
    58, 92, 101, 103, 112, 118, 119,
    129, 167
Sanoka 167
Sanz *see* Nowy Sącz
Sapahów 167
Sapieżanka 167
Sapohów 167
Sapowa 167
Saranczuki 167
Sarnki 167

Sarnki Dolne 167
Sarnki Górne 167
Sarnki Średnie 167
Sarny 167
Sarysz 167
Sarzyna 56, 167
Sąsiadowice 167
Saska 167
Saska Kameralna 167
Sasov 100, *also see* Sassów
Sassów 30, 52, 89, 116, 130, 167,
    also see Sasov
Sawa 167
Sawaluski 167
Sawczyn 167
Schodnica 23, 167
Schönanger 167
Schönthal 167
Scianka 167
Sędziszów 34, 59, 113, 129, 167
Sędziszów Małopolski 101, *also see*
    Sędziszów
Sędziszowa 167
Sękowa 167
Sękowa Wola 167
Semenów z Zieleńcem 167
Semenówka 167
Semerówka 167
Seneczów 167
Sępnica 167
Serafince 167
Serdyca 167
Seredce 167
Seredne 167
Serednica 167
Serednie Małe 167
Serednie Wielkie 167
Seredyńce 167
Serwiry 167
Shchurovichi *see* Szezurowice
Shchyrets *see* Szczerzec
Siarczana Góra 167
Siary 167
Sichów 167
Sidorów 167
Sidzina 167
Siebieczów 167
Siechów 167
Siechowce 167
Sieciechów 167
Siedlanka 167
Siedlce 167
Siedlec 167

Siedliska 101, 167
Siedliszczany 167
Siegenthal 167
Siekierczyce 167
Siekierczyn 167
Siekierczyna 167
Siekierzyńce 167
Sieklerczyna 167
Sieklówka Dolna 167
Sieklówka Górna 167
Sielce 114, 119, 168
Sielec 168
Sielnica 168
Siemakowce 168
Siemiakowce 168
Siemianówka 168
Siemiechów 168
Siemień 168
Siemiginów 168
Siemikowce 168
Siemuszowa 168
Sieniawa 32, 101, 103, 114, 127,
    168
Sieniawka 168
Sienikowice 168
Sienków 52, 168
Sienna 168
Siennów 168
Siepietnica 168
Sierakosce 168
Sieraków 168
Siercza 168
Siersza 168
Sietesz 168
Sietnica 168
Signiówka 168
Sikorzyce 168
Sikorzynice 168
Sińków 168
Siołko 168
Siołkowa 168
Siwka Kałuska 168
Siwka Wojniłowska 168
Skala Podolskaya 78
Skala Podolskaya *see* Skała
Skała 22, 52, 83, 126, 168
Skałat 27, 28, 52, 83, 129, 168
Skalnik 168
Skawa 168
Skawce 168
Skawica 168
Skawina 83, 168
Skawinki 168

Sorocko 169
Soroka 169
Soroki 169
Sosnica 34, 128, 169
Sosnice 169
Sosnów 169
Sosnowice 83, 169
Sosolówka 169
Sowina 169
Sowliny 169
Sozań 169
Spas 169
Spasków 169
Sporysz 169
Spytkowice 169
Średni 169
Średnia 169
Średnia Wieś 169
Środopolce 169
Srogów Dolny 170
Srogów Górny 170
Sroki Lwowskie 170
Sroki Szcz. 170
Srołmienice 170
Sromowce Niżne 170
Sromowce Wyżne 170
St. Johannesberg 170
St. Stanisław 170
Stadło 170
Stadniki 170
Staje 170
Stałe 170
Staniątki 170
Stanila 170
Stanimirz 170
Stanin 170
Stanislau see Stanislav,
   Stanisławów and Ivano-
   Frankovsk
Stanislav 27, 129, also see Ivano-
   Frankovsk and Stanislawów
Stanislavchyk see Stanisławczyk
Stanisław Dolny 170
Stanisław Górny 170
Stanisławczyk 22, 52, 83, 126, 170
Stanisławice 170
Stanisławów 27, 41-44, 52, 59, 66,
   83, 100, 111-113, 118-120, 129,
   170, also see Ivano-Frankovsk
   and Stanislav
Stanislówka 170
Stanislowów 116
Staniszewskie 170

Stańków 170
Stańkowa 170
Stańkowce 170
Stany 170
Stara Sól 28, 83, also see Starasól
Stara Wieś 170
Starachowice 83
Stararopa 170
Starasól 28, 129, 170, also see
   Stara Sól
Starawieś Dolna 170
Starawieś Górna 170
Staraya Sil see Stara Sól and
   Starasól
Stare Miasto 129
Stare Stawy 170
Starebystre 170
Staremiasto 28, 43, 170
Staresioło 170
Starogród 170
Staromiejszczyzna 170
Staromieście 170
Staroniwa 170
Starunia 170
Stary Dzików 82, 101, also see
   Dzików
Stary Sącz 34, 83, 128, 170
Stary Sambor 52, 83, also see
   Sambor
Stary Skałat 170
Starzawa 26, 170
Starzyska 24, 170
Stasiowa Wola 170
Stasiówka 170
Staszkówka 170
Stawczany 170
Stawki Kraśnieńskie 170
Stawkowice 170
Stawsko 170
Stebne 170
Stebnik 83, 170
Stechnikowce 170
Stecowa 170
Stefkowa 170
Steinau 170
Steinfeld 170
Steniatyn 27, 170
Stepina z Chytrówka 170
Sterkowiec 170
Stężnica 170
Stobierna 170
Stochynia 170
Stodółki 170

Stojance 170
Stojanów 24, 52, 83, 127, 170
Stoki 170
Stołowa 170
Stołpin 170
Stopczatów 170
Stoyaniv see Stojanów
Strachocina 170
Straconka 170
Stradcz 170
Stradomka 170
Straszęcin 170
Straszewice 170
Stratyń 83
Stratyń Wieś 170
Strażów 170
Strażydle 170
Stregocice 170
Streptów 170
Strilychi Novi see Strzeliska Nowe
Strojców 170
Stroniatyn 170
Stronie 170
Stroniowice 170
Stronna 170
Stronowice 170
Strosówka 170
Stróża 170
Stróże 170
Stróże Małe 170
Stróże Niżne 170
Stróże Wielkie 170
Stróże Wyżne 170
Stróżna 170
Stróżówka 58, 170
Strubowiska Kalnica 170
Struga 170
Strumiany 170
Strupków 170
Strusów 29, 52, 83, 129, 170
Strusówka 170
Strutyń 170
Strutyń Niżny 170
Strutyń Wyżny 170
Strwiążyk 171
Stryhańce 171
Stryhanka 171
Stryj 28, 42, 43, 52, 68, 83, 121,
   129, 171, also see Stryy
Strymba 171
Stryszawa 171
Stryszów 171
Stryszowa 171

Szklary 172
Szkło 172
Szkodna 172
Szlachtowa 172
Szlacińce 172
Szlembarg 172
Szmańkowce 172
Szmańkowczyki 172
Szmitków 172
Sznyrów 172
Szołomyja 172
Szówsko 172
Szpiklosy 172
Szufnarowa 172
Szulhanówka 172
Szumina 172
Szumlan 172
Szumlany 172
Szumlany Małe 172
Szuparka 172
Szutromińce 172
Szwajkowce 172
Szwedy 172
Szwejków 172
Szwiniarów 172
Szybalin 172
Szychtory 172
Szydłowce 172
Szydłowiec 172
Szyk 172
Szymanowice 172
Szymbark 172
Szynwald 172
Szyperki 172
Szypowce 172
Szyszkowce 172
Tabaszowa 172
Tadanie 172
Tamanowice 172
Taniawa 172
Tapin 172
Targanica 172
Targoszyna 172
Targowica 172
Targowiska 172
Targowisko 172
Tarnawa 172
Tarnawa Dolna 172
Tarnawa Górna 172
Tarnawce 172
Tarnawica Polna 172
Tarnawka 172

Tarnobrzeg 8, 13, 14, 35, 38, 46,
    52, 55, 70, 83, 92, 112, 117, 119,
    120, 129, 172, 182
Tarnogóra 172
Tarnopol 28, 42-44, 52, 66, 73, 83,
    84, 112, 115, 117, 118, 120, 129,
    172, also see Ternopol
Tarnoruda 27, 83, 129, 172
Tarnoszyn 172
Tarnów 35-37, 42, 46, 52, 55, 57,
    59, 68, 83, 84, 92, 113, 114, 119,
    129, 172
Tarnowica Leśna 172
Tarnowica Zielona 172
Tarnowice 172
Tarnowska Wola 172
Tartakiv see Tartaków
Tartaków 27, 83, 129, 172
Tartakowice 172
Tartarów 172
Taszezówka 172
Taszyce 172
Tatarsko 172
Tatary 172
Tatarynów 173
Tatowce 173
Taurów 173
Tchortchov 100, also see
    Czortków
Tęczynek 173
Tęgoborze 173
Tęhlów 173
Tejsarów 173
Teklówka 173
Tekucze 173
Telacze 173
Teleśnica Oszwar. 173
Teleśnica Sanna 173
Temerowce 173
Temeszów 173
Tenczyn 173
Tenetniki 173
Teodorówka 173
Teodorshof 173
Teofipolka 173
Terebovlya see Trembowla
Teresia 173
Tereskuła 173
Teresówka 173
Terka 173
Terlo 173
Ternopil 77

Ternopol 76, 78, 100, also see
    Tarnopol
Ternoruda see Tarnoruda
Terpilówka 29
Terszaków 173
Terszów 173
Tetewczyce 173
Tetylkowce 173
Tiapeze 173
Tiutków 173
Tłuczan Dolna 173
Tłuczan Górna 173
Tlumach see Tłumacz
Tłumacz 29, 52, 83, 129, 173
Tłumaczyk 83, 173
Tłuste 29, 52, 83, 100, 130, 173
Tłustenkie 173
Tobolów 173
Tokarnia 173
Toki 173
Tolstoye see Tłuste
Tolszczów 25, 173
Tomaszkowice 173
Tomaszowce 173
Tomice 173
Tonie 173
Topolnica 173
Topolsko 173
Toporov see Toporów
Toporów 22, 52, 126, 173
Toporówce 173
Toporzysko 173
Torczynowice 27, 173
Torhanowice 173
Torhów 173
Torkarnia 173
Torki 173
Toroszówka 173
Torski 115
Torskie 115, 173
Touste 27, 83, 129, 173
Toustogłowy 173
Toustoług 173
Toutobaby 173
Tovste see Tłuste
Towarnia 173
Trąbki 173
Tracz 173
Trawniki 173
Trawotłoki 173
Trędowacz 173
Trembowla 29, 46, 52, 83, 129,
    173

Urzejowice 174
Uście 84, 174
Uście Biskupie 22, 85, 175
Uście nad Prutem 175
Uście Ruskie 175
Uście Solne 175
Uście Zielone 29, 83, 129, 175
Uścieczko 29, 83, 130, 175, *also see* Ustechko
Uścierzyki 175
Uścieszczko 76
Uste Zelene *see* Uście Zielone
Ustechko 76, *also see* Uscieczko
Ustia Zelene *see* Uscie Zielone
Ustrobna 175
Ustrzyki Dolne 33, 52, 83, 101, 128, 175
Ustrzyki Górne 175
Ustyanowa 175
Uszew 175
Uszkowice 175
Usznia 175
Uszwica 175
Uthowek 175
Utoropy 175
Uwin 175
Uwisla 175
Uwsie 175
Uzin 175
Uzlovoye *see* Chołojów
Variazh *see* Warez
Velikiye Mosty *see* Mosty Vielkie
Verkhovina *see* Zabie
Vinniki *see* Winniki
Vorderberg 175
Voynilov *see* Wojnilów
Wacowice 175
Wadowice 36, 37, 42, 52, 55, 57, 130, 175
Wadowice Dolne 175
Wadowice Górne 175
Waksmund 175
Wał Ruda 175
Walawa 175
Walddorf 175
Walki 175
Wałowa Góra 175
Wałówka 175
Wampierzów 175
Waniów 175
Waniowice 175
Wańkowa 175
Wańkowice 175

Wapienne 175
Wara 175
Warcz 27, 129
Warez 27, 129, 175
Warowicz 102
Warwaryńce 175
Warys 175
Wasiuczyn 175
Wasyłków 175
Wasylkowce 117, 175
Wasylów Wielkie 175
Waszyce 175
Wawrzka 175
Wawrzkowa 175
Węcina 175
Węgerka 175
Węglarzyska 175
Węgliska 175
Węglówka 175
Węgrzyce Wielkie 175
Weinbergen 175
Weisenberg 175
Wełdzirz 175
Weleśnica 175
Wełykie 175
Werbiąż Niżny 175
Werbiąż Wyżny 175
Werbie 175
Werchrata 175
Weremien 175
Wereszyce 175
Werhobuz 175
Wertelka 175
Weryń 175
Werynia 175
Wesola 83, 175
Wetlina 175
Wiątowice 175
Wiątrowice 175
Wiązowa 175
Wiązownica 175
Wiciów 175
Wicza 175
Widacz 175
Widaczów 175
Widełka 175
Widinów 112
Widynów 112, 175
Wieciorka 175
Wieckowice 175
Wieczerza 175
Wieczorki 175
Wieleśniów 175

Wielha 175
Wieliczka 35, 52, 83, 118, 130, 175
Wielkawieś 175
Wielkie Drogi 175
Wielkie Oczy 24, 83, 101, 127, 175
Wielkopole 175
Wielogłowy 175
Wielopole Rudki 129
Wielopole 34, 112, 175
Wielopole Skrzyńskie 101
Wielowieś 175
Wielunice 175
Wieniawa 175
Wienice 175
Wieprz 175
Wieprz ad Żywiec 175
Wieprzce 175
Wiercany 175
Wierchomla Mała 175
Wierchomla Wielka 175
Wierczany 175
Wieruszyce 175
Wierzawice 101, 175
Wierzbanówa 175
Wierzbiałyn 175
Wierzbiani 24
Wierzbiany 175
Wierzbiaz 175
Wierzbica 175
Wierzblany 176
Wierzbna 176
Wierzbolowce 176
Wierzbów 176
Wierzbowce 176
Wierzbowczyk 176
Wierzbowiec 176
Wierzbówka 176
Wierzchniakowce 176
Wierzchosławice 176
Wierzchowce 176
Wierznica 176
Wiesenberg 176
Wietrzno 176
Wieza 176
Wiktorów 176
Wiktorówka 176
Wilamowice 176
Wilcza 176
Wilcza Góra 176
Wilcza Wola 176
Wilczkowice 176
Wilczyce 176
Wilczyska 176

Wolica Lugowa 177
Wolica Piaskowa 177
Wolina 177
Wolka Gradzka 177
Wolkiew 25, 177
Wołków 177
Wołkowce 177
Wołkowce ad Perejmy 177
Wołkowce ad Borszczów 177
Wołkowyja 177
Wołochy 177
Wołodzia 177
Wołopcza 177
Wołosate 177
Wołosianka 177
Woloska Wieś 114, 177
Wołosów 177
Wołosówka 177
Wołostków 177
Wołoszczyzna 177
Wołoszynowa 177
Wołoszyny 177
Wołowa 177
Wołowe Laszki 177
Wołowice 177
Wołowszczyzna 177
Wołśniów 177
Wołświń 177
Wolszcza 27
Wołtuszowa 177
Worobiówka 177
Worochta 177
Worona 177
Woroniaki 177
Woronów 178
Worwolińce 178
Woszczeńce 178
Wownia 178
Wożiłów 178
Wożniczna 178
Wożniki 178
Wróblaczyn 178
Wróblik 114
Wróblik Królewski 178
Wróblik Szlachecki 178
Wróblowa 178
Wróblowice 178
Wróblówka 178
Wrocanka 178
Wroców 178
Wrzasowice 178
Wrzawy 178
Wrzepia 178

Wujskie 178
Wulka 178
Wulka beim Walde 178
Wulka Bielinska 178
Wulka Dulecka 178
Wulka Grodziska 178
Wulka Horyniecka 178
Wulka Kuninska 178
Wulka Laneuska 178
Wulka Letowska 178
Wulka Malkowa 178
Wulka Mazowiecka 178
Wulka Mędrzechowska 178
Wulka Niedźwiedzka 178
Wulka Ogryzkowa 178
Wulka pod Lasem 178
Wulka Rosnowska 178
Wulka Suszanska 178
Wulka Turebska 178
Wulka Zapałowska 178
Wulka Zmijowska 178
Wybranówka 178
Wybudów 178
Wychwatyńce 178
Wyczółki 178
Wydma 178
Wydra 178
Wydreń 178
Wydrze 178
Wygiełzów 178
Wyglanowice 178
Wygnanka 178
Wygoda 178
Wykoty 27, 178
Wylewa 178
Wyłkowyja 178
Wyłów 178
Wymsłówka 178
Wypyski 178
Wyrów 178
Wyrzne 178
Wyskitna 178
Wysocko 178
Wysoczany 178
Wysoka 55, 178
Wysokie 178
Wyspa 178
Wysuczka 178
Wyszatyce 178
Wyszowa 178
Wyszowadka 178
Wytrzyszczka 178
Wywczanka 178

Wyzków 178
Wyżłów 178
Wyżniany 178
Wyżyce 178
Wzary 178
Wzdów 178
Yablonov 100, *also see* Jablonów
Yagelnitsa *see* Jagielnica
Zabawa 178
Żabcze Murowane 178
Zabełcze 178
Żabie 24, 83, 128, 178
Zabierzów 178
Żabińce 178
Zabledna 178
Zabłocie 36, 130, 178
Zabłotce 178
Zabłotów 27, 52, 83, 89, 112, 129, 178, *also see* Zabolotov
Zabłotowce 178
Zabłotówka 178
Żabnica 178
Zabno 35, 83, 129, 178
Żabojki 178
Żabokruki 178
Zabolotov 78, 89, *also see* Zablotów
Zaborów 178
Zaborze 178
Zabratów 178
Zabrnie 178
Zabrodzie 179
Zabrzez 179
Zabrzydowice 179
Zaburze 179
Zabutyń 179
Zachwiejów 179
Zaczarnice 179
Zaczernie 179
Zadąbrowie 179
Zadarów 179
Zaderewacz 179
Zadubrowce 179
Zaduszniki 179
Zadwórze 179
Zadziele 179
Zadziszówka 179
Zagoczyce 179
Zagoreczko 179
Zagórnik 179
Zagorów 179
Zagórz 52, 83, 101, 179
Zagórzany 179

Zagórze 22, 83, 113, 179
Zagórze Knihynickie 179
Zagórze Konkolnickie 179
Zagórzyn 179
Zagrobela 28, 179
Zagrodki 25, 179
Zagrody 179
Zagwóźdź 179
Zahajce 179
Zahajpol 179
Zahelmno 179
Zahoczewie 179
Zahorce 179
Zakliczyn 83, 120, 179
Zakomarze 179
Zakopane 52, 83, 179
Zakościele 179
Zakowice Nowe 179
Zakowice stare 179
Zakrzewie 179
Zakrzów 179
Zakrzówek 179
Zalanów 179
Zalas 179
Zalasowa 179
Zalawie 179
Zalcze 179
Zalęna 179
Zaleśce 179
Zaleshchiki 76, *also see*
   Zaleszczyki
Zalesiany 179
Zalesie 179
Zalesie Antoniowskie 179
Zalesie Biskupie 179
Zalesie Gorzyckie 179
Zaleszany 179
Zaleszczyki 9, 29, 83, 112, 114,
   119, 130, 179, *also see*
   Zaleshchiki
Zaleszczyki Małe 179
Zaleszczyki Stare 179
Zależe 179
Zalipie 179
Załokieć 179
Założce 22, 83, 84, 126, 179
Zalozhtsy *see* Założce
Załubińcze 179
Załucze 179
Załucze nad Prutem 179
Załucze nad Czer. 179
Załuczne 179
Załukiew 179

Załuż 179
Zaluze 24, 29, 179
Zalzitsi *see* Założce
Zamarstynów 179
Zameczek 179
Zamek 179
Zamiechów 179
Zamieście 179
Zamłynowe 179
Zamojsce 179
Zamoście 179
Zamowa 179
Zamulińce 179
Zany 179
Zapałów 179
Zapole 179
Zapolednik 179
Zapytów 179
Zarajsko 179
Zarawce 179
Zarębki 179
Zarki 179
Żarków 179
Zarnowiec 46, 83, 179
Żarnówka 179
Żarównie 179
Zarszyn 52, 57, 179
Zarubińce 179
Zarudec 179
Zarudka 180
Zarudzie 180
Zarwanica 180
Żary 180
Zaryte 180
Zarzecze 180
Zarzekowice 180
Zarzyce 180
Zarzyce Małe 180
Zarzyce Wielkie 180
Zarzycze 180
Zasadne 180
Zasań 180
Zaścianka 180
Zaścinocze 180
Zaskale 180
Zasław 180
Zastawce 180
Zastawie 180
Zasulince 180
Zaszków 180
Zaszkowice 180
Zatawie 180
Zatoka 180

Zator 36, 83, 130, 180
Zaturzyn 180
Zatwarnica 180
Zavaliv *see* Zawalów
Zawada 83, 180
Zawada Lanekorońska 180
Zawada Uszewska 180
Zawadka 180
Zawadka ad Osiek 180
Zawadka ad Buk 180
Zawadka Rymanów 180
Zawadów 180
Zawadówka 180
Zawale 180
Zawalów 26, 83, 128, 180
Zawatka 180
Zawidcze 52, 180
Zawidowice 180
Zawierzbie 180
Zawisznia 27, 180
Zawodzie 180
Zawoj 180
Zawoja 180
Zawoje 180
Zawośnia 180
Zawóz 180
Zazameże 180
Zazdrość 180
Zazule 180
Zbadyń 180
Zbaraz 29, 83, 84, 130, 180
Zbarazh *see* Zbaraż
Zbek 180
Żbik 180
Żbikowice 180
Zbłudza 180
Zboiska 180
Zbora 180
Zborczyce 180
Zboriv *see* Zborów
Zborów 30, 52, 84, 130, 180
Zborowek 180
Zborowice 180
Zbrzyz 22, 180
Zbydniów 180
Zbydniowice 180
Zbyszyce 180
Zbytkowska Góra 180
Zdarzec 180
Zdonia 180
Zdroheć 180
Zdzianna 180
Ździary 180

Żebranówka 180
Żędowice 180
Żegartowice 180
Żegestów 180
Żeglce 180
Żełdec 180
Żelechów Mały 180
Żelechów Wielki 180
Żeleźnikowa 180
Żembrzyce 180
Żeniów 180
Żeraków 180
Żerdenka 180
Żerebki Krolewskie 180
Żerebki Szlacheckie 180
Żerków 180
Żernica Niżna 180
Żernica Wyżna 180
Żerosławice 180
Zgłobice 181
Zgłobień 181
Zhovka see Zolkiew
Zhovten see Jezupol
Zhuravno see Zurawno
Zieleńce 181
Zielensko 181
Zielona 181
Zielonka 181
Zielów 181
Ziempniów 181
Zimna Voda see Zimnowoda
Zimna Woda 181
Zimno Wódka 181
Zimnowoda 26
Ziniatyn 181
Złockie 181
Zloczów 30, 42, 43, 52, 83, 84, 89,
    112, 118, 130, 181, also see
    Zolochev
Złoczówka 181
Złota 181
Złotkowice 181
Złotne 181
Zlotniki 26, 83, 128, 181
Złucisko 181
Zmiąca 181
Zmiennica 181
Żmigrod 33, 128, 181
Żmigród Nowy 83, 84, 181
Żmigród Stary 181
Żmijowiska 181
Zmysłówka 181
Znamirowice 181

Zneżyce 181
Żnibrody 181
Zniesienie 26, 128, 181
Zohatyń 181
Zolczów 181
Zolibory 181
Zolkiew 30, 42, 43, 46, 52, 54, 64,
    83, 100, 111, 130, 181
Żołków 181
Żołnówka 181
Żołobek 181
Zolochev 78, 100, also see Zloczów
Zolocze 118
Zolotnyky see Zlotniki
Zoloty Potok 118
Żołtańce 181
Żolynia 33, 56, 83, 101, 128, 181
Żornska 181
Zręcin 181
Zręczyce 181
Zródła 181
Zrotowice 181
Zrzyce 181
Zubarmosty 181
Zubków 181
Zubów 181
Zubracze 181
Zubrzec 181
Zubrzyk 181
Zubsuche 181
Zuchorzyce 181
Żuklin 181
Żukocin 181
Żuków 181
Żukowce 181
Żulice 181
Żulin 181
Żupanie 181
Żupawa 181
Żuraki 181
Żuratyn 181
Żurawica 181
Żurawiczki 181
Żurawienko 181
Żurawin 181
Żurawińce 181
Żurawków 181
Żurawniki 181
Żurawno 30, 83, 84, 116, 130, 181
Żurów 181
Żurowa 181
Żuszyce 181
Żużel 181

Zuzmir 84
Zwertów 181
Zwiahel 181
Zwiary 181
Zwieczyca 181
Zwiernik 181
Zwierzeń 181
Zwierzyce 181
Zwiniacz 181
Zwór 181
Zwyżeń 181
Zydachov see Zydaczów
Zydachów 100
Żydaczów 30, 46, 130, 181
Żydatycze 181
Żydnia 181
Żydowskie 181
Żygodowice 181
Zyndranowa 181
Żyrawa 181
Żyrawka 181
Żyrnów 181
Żywaczów 181
Żywiec 36, 55, 57, 83, 130, 181
Żywiec Stary 181
Żyznomierz 181

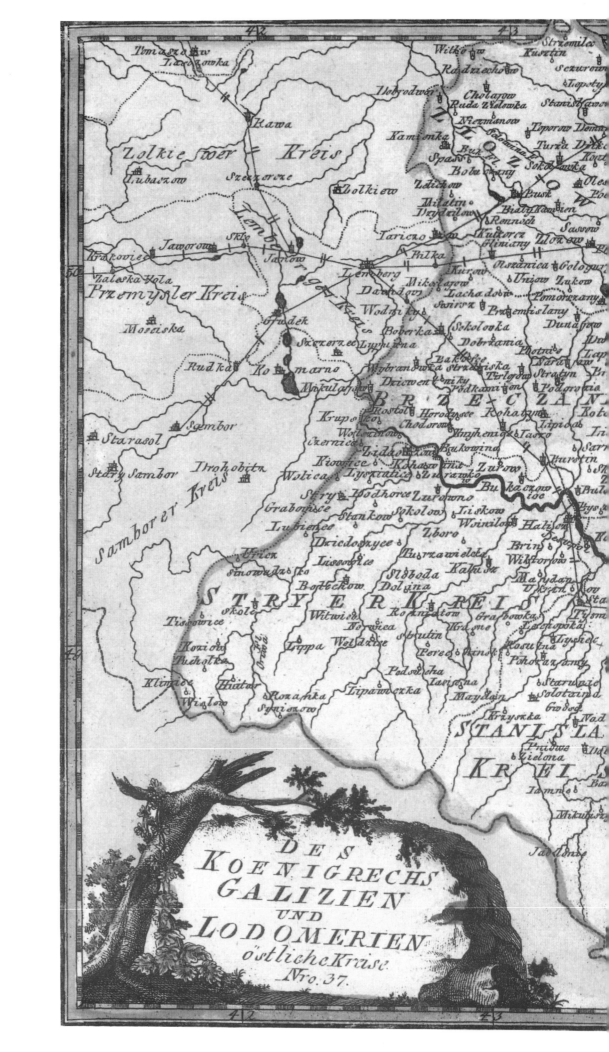

42   43

Tomaszow
Tarłowka
Wilkow
Radziechow
Strzemilec
Kurstin
Szczuroum
Hobrodwor
Chołojow
Ruda Żyłowka
Niemanow
Toporow Demn
Rapsty
Stanisławow

Zolkiewer   Kreis
Rawa
Kamionka
Spas
Boba czany
Turza Dzie
Koet
Sokołowka

Lubaczow
Szczerzec
Zolkiew
Zdichow
Mitatin
Drydułow
Ronnzch
Busk
Biały Kamien
Nes
Poe
Sassow

Jaworow
Skle
Krakowiec
Janow
Taricze
Kulborcz
Gliniany
Zborow
Uniow
Zukow
Plka
Pilka
Olszanica
Gologui

Zaleska Wola
Lemberg
Mikołajow
Dawidow
Przemysler Kreis
Kurow
Pomorzany
Dunaisw

Mosciska
Grudek
Wodniki
Swirz
Przemislany

Szczerzec
Boberka   Sokołowka
Rudka
Komarno
Lumizna
Dobrzania
Płotnis
Lap
Waris

Myculajow
Drieweniki
Bakorce strzeliska
Tirlow
Stratyn
Podkami on
Podgrozia

Starasol
Sęmbor
Krupe Teo
Rostol
Horożanee
Rohatyn
Lipicsa
Tabro
Zota
Ti

Wolszinow
Czernice
Chodorow
Wujhenig
Sarr
Kurstin

Stary Sambor
Drohobitz
Kiowice
Wolica
Zidaczow
Lysiniatie
Kohawinie
Zuranow
Zukow
Bukaczow ce
Puło

Stry
Podhorce
Zurowno
Grabowce
Stankow
Sokołow
Tiskow
Wsnilow
Halicz

Lubieniec
Dwiedosyce
Zboro
Brin
Wiktorow

Krion
Inosowice
Tura wielda
Kałusz
Maydan
Ukrain

Sinowudzko
Boitekow
Slboda
Dołgina

STRYER   KREIS

Tisowice
Skole
Witwice
Rożnatow
Grabowka
Lachopka
Tysom

Kozion
Tuchołka
Trppa
Nowica
Wełdzise
Strutin
Krume
Kosutna
Tyszec

Klimice
Huiar
Wisłow
Rożanka
Synieszow
Tipawiczka
Podsicha
Zasiczna
Peres Kinst
Pohoran smny
Starunie
Solotwina

Maydan
Krzyszka
Swodes
Nad

STANISLA

Pniuws
Zielona

KREIS
Jamnie
Ba

Mitubisz

Jabłonie

DES
KOENIGRECHS
GALIZIEN
UND
LODOMERIEN
östliche Kreise.
Nro. 37.

42   43